CRIMINAL JUSTICE, LAW ENFORCEMENT AND CORRECTIONS

A CLOSER LOOK AT CRIMINAL JUSTICE

Criminal Justice, Law Enforcement and Corrections

Additional books and e-books in this series can be found on Nova's website under the Series tab.

CRIMINAL JUSTICE, LAW ENFORCEMENT AND CORRECTIONS

A CLOSER LOOK AT CRIMINAL JUSTICE

JONATHON A. COOPER
AND
KAYLA G. JACHIMOWSKI
EDITORS

nova
science publishers
New York

Library of Congress Cataloging-in-Publication Data

ISBN: 978-1-53615-782-6
Library of Congress Control Number: 2019943194

Published by Nova Science Publishers, Inc. † New York

The authors dedicate this book to the following individuals:

Miriam

-JC

Nikki and Isabel

-KGJ

CONTENTS

ACKNOWLEDGMENTS

A special thanks to all the authors who contributed to this book: your ideas and passion have truly given shape to the book we set out to create: Shavonne Arthurs, Samantha Bennett, Ed Bowman, David Champion, Sarah Daly, Kerry Edwards, Katie Ely, Blair Hillgrass, Sarah Kuehn, Selye Lee, Liana Marmolejos, Daniel Scott, Carley Smathers, Lindsey Smathers, London Smith Andrea Weathersby. We would also like to extend our deep appreciation to each of our reviewers whose critical review of the chapters were instrumental in the preparation of this manuscript: James Bumar, Chelsea Clark, Timothy Holler, Glen Ishoy, John Lewis, Dennis Marsili, Alexandra Murphy, Philip Wagner, Kyle Ward, Richard Wentling, Mark Zebracki, and Paige Zurenski. We also wish to thank Shelby Noel, graduate student in Saint Vincent College's Department of Criminology, Law, and Society, for her assistance with the production of our book. We are deeply grateful for the opportunity and assistance in seeing this book to print provided by Nova Science Publishers, Inc., and particularly of Carra Feagaiga.

INTRODUCTION

The vision behind this volume is straightforward: we wanted to provide a venue for authors to *say something* about the state of criminal justice and criminology, both as an academic discipline and in terms of the system. This means authors were given considerable latitude in terms of what they could write about. The goal was to find fresh, even controversial, ideas about the state of the discipline and the administration of justice, and where either needs to go. To this end, we invited both established scholars and insightful graduate students who each had that *something to say* which we were seeking. We wanted to provide an outlet for authors to express informed, researched, and well-thought-out ideas about their areas of expertise with the same level of scrutiny as the peer review process, but without the typical (though by no means requisite) requirement of original research - although some of our contributors do engage in such empirical exercises in their chapter. Ultimately, we wanted to give our authors the chance to pontificate about important issues in the criminal justice discipline which could too easily be overlooked.

This book would be best suited in senior seminars, capstone, or contemporary issues courses; master's level classes on the criminal justice system; and will also be important to faculty members and doctoral students with a vested interest in the current tempo of criminal justice practice, research, education, and thought. As professors, we place a lot of emphasis on critical thinking and the formation of supported opinions. This is especially true for the criminal justice discipline as most students become key players in the system as a career. Reading this book, students should have a better idea of the current issues facing our discipline, particularly those issues that do not get as much exposure as other issues.

The chapters that follow have been grouped based on thematic concepts, starting with Part 1: Criminal Justice and Criminology in Education. In this section, chapters discuss how we teach our undergraduate students about race, the way we treat our graduate students, and inmate education. We wanted to highlight criminal justice education at the university level in the first part of the book in large part because this book is best suited in the classroom, but especially because as educators, we live and breathe the importance of education. The book progresses in Part 2, Theory and Praxis, with a discussion of applicable criminological theory and research methodology in criminal justice where the goal is to highlight the importance of using theory and research as the foundation for policy positions, support, and understanding. The remaining part of the book, Persistent Issues in Criminal Justice, provides fresh insights on "old" subjects and problems in the administration of justice, such as community policing, the aging prison population, and marijuana use in the United States of America.

We are exceedingly pleased with the quality of thought and writing produced by our contributors. We hope this book educates students, offers a unique perspective on important criminal justice and criminological topics, and, most importantly, inspires future researchers who may be sitting in a classroom reading and discussing this right now.

PART 1: CRIMINAL JUSTICE AND CRIMINOLOGY IN EDUCATION

In: A Closer Look at Criminal Justice
Editors: J. A. Cooper and K. G. Jachimowski ISBN: 978-1-53615-782-6

Chapter 1

LEGITIMACY AT STAKE: CRIMINAL JUSTICE, CRIMINOLOGY, AND LEARNING RACE

Sarah E. Daly*[*] *and London S. Smith
Saint Vincent College, Latrobe, PA, US

ABSTRACT

As cities and towns continue to struggle with police-community relations, the importance of understanding the function of race in criminal justice issues becomes even more pressing. Undergraduate and graduate criminology and criminal justice curricula often offer race-related courses, raising concerns about the content taught, the elective/required option, and the expected outcomes. This chapter offers and overview of racial disparities and inequality in the criminal justice system and highlights the challenges and importance of discussing and studying race in the classroom. By outlining the goals of learning and talking about race, the chapter encourages students and educators alike to confront the problems directly through conversation and research while acknowledging and learning from the discomfort that arises in discussions about race.

INTRODUCTION

On October 29, 2009, Dr. Barry Krisberg, the then-President of the National Council of Crime and Delinquency, testified before the House of Representatives Subcommittee on Crime, Terrorism, and Homeland Security. In this special hearing on racial disparities in the criminal justice system, he began his testimony by asserting, "I would say that the very legitimacy of the justice system is at stake. And the effectiveness of our law enforcement system is certainly at stake if we cannot make progress on this issue of

[*] Corresponding Author's Email: sarah.daly@stvincent.edu

enormous racial disparity in the system" (Racial Disparities in the Criminal Justice System, 2009, p. 14).

A year later, New York Times [Nonfiction] Best Author Michelle Alexander's book, *The New Jim Crow: Mass Incarceration in the Age of Colorblindness,* highlighted these disparities and pointed to social, political, and legal mechanisms through which mass incarceration and racial disparities continue America's long history of racial discrimination. It provides a historical examination of racial injustice and a compelling argument that "Rather than rely on race, we use our criminal justice system to label people of color 'criminals' and then engage in all the practices we supposedly left behind...We have not ended racial caste in America; we have merely redesigned it" (Alexander, 2010, p. 2).

The conversation about racial injustices and disparities in the criminal justice system comes at a time when it seems that tensions between minorities and police have reached critical levels. While mass incarceration and racial disparities in the criminal justice system are somewhat hidden from public view, highly publicized shootings thrust issues of race and deadly force into the spotlight. In 2014, the city of Ferguson, Missouri became a national stage for violence, frustration, and anger about perceived injustice. After a grand jury decided to not indict Officer Darren Wilson in the shooting death of Michael Brown, an 18-year-old unarmed Black man, protesters took to the streets. Throughout the city, community members clashed with officers, setting fires and throwing rocks, while the police responded with tear gas and rubber bullets.

Across the country, people watched the chaos unfold, and most had a strong opinion about what they saw. Some expressed confusion and anger at the protests and violence, suggesting that had Michael Brown complied or not approached the officer, he would have lived. Others pointed to the long history of deadly force and contentious police-community relationships[1]. In an interview with USA Today, Kwame Rose explained, "Black people have been having these conversations in our living rooms...But social media has invited our followers, and millions of them, into our living rooms to have this conversation with us, in a sense" (Hafner, 2016, para. 7). Perhaps one of the most notable, persistent outcomes of Ferguson conflicts was the rise of the Black Lives Matter movement. As Freelon, McIlwain, and Clark (2016) explain, "Although the #BlackLivesMatter hashtag was created in July 2013, it was rarely used through the summer of 2014 and did not come to signify a movement until the summer after the Ferguson protests" (p. 5).

As Ted Conover (2014) writes, "Unfairness in the Justice system is a major theme of our age" (para. 1). Since Dr. Krisberg's testimony in 2009 and Michael Brown's death in

---

[1] The United States Department of Justice Civil Rights Division (2015) published a 105-page report on the investigation of the Ferguson Police Department and found "Ferguson Law Enforcement practices violate the law and undermine community trust, especially among African Americans" (p. i). The full report can be found at https://www.justice.gov/sites/default/files/opa/press-releases/attachments/2015/03/04/ferguson_police_ department_report.pdf.

2014, the hashtag has reemerged and the debates have continued, particularly after the deaths of Eric Garner in New York; Laquan McDonald in Illinois; Tamir Rice in Ohio; Walter Scott in South Carolina; Freddie Gray in Maryland; Sandra Bland in Texas; Alton Sterling in Louisiana; Philando Castile in Minnesota; and Antwon Rose in Pennsylvania. In cities across the country, tensions simmer between police and minority community members who feel targeted, frustrated, and victimized by a system that is designed to incarcerate the most vulnerable. Similarly, many police officers felt vilified, misunderstood, and defensive about their profession. Attacks and ambushes on police officers in Texas, Louisiana, and other states only heightened these fears.

It is nearly impossible to discuss any aspect of the criminal justice system without considering race. Though many would like to believe that prejudice, discrimination, and bias have no effect on today's modern world, continued research and advocacy groups highlight alarming disparities in the treatment of racial minorities (ABA, 2012; Amnesty International, 2003, Equal Justice Initiative, 2017; Western, 2006; Walker, Spohn, & DeLone, 2017; Wilson, 2012). The findings are often consistent, and they are clear.

National statistics highlight substantial racial differences in incarceration rates. Nellis (2016) found "African Americans are incarcerated in state prisons at a rate that is 5.1 times the imprisonment of [W]hites," and "in eleven states, at least 1 in 20 adult [B]lack males is in prison" (p. 3). If incarceration rates were to remain the same as they were in 1991, Black men are six times more likely than White men to serve time in prison (Bonczar & Beck, 1997). Despite a continuous decrease in national crime trends since the early 1990s, incarceration rates in State and Federal facilities increased steadily until 2009 (Bureau of Justice Statistics, 2018). Discussions about equality, equity, and decarceration are happening across the country, but the issue of race is still one that is uncomfortable, sometimes contentious, and often unwelcomed.

Regardless of beliefs, ideologies, and political affiliations, college students who major in criminology or criminal justice cannot simply ignore race. Those who plan to work in the criminal justice system—to serve as agents of change and justice—must, at the very least, confront the research about racial disparities and hear (and listen to) the stories of those who are affected. All students who study juvenile delinquency, justice system processes, and community corrections and sentencing must understand the ways in people of color might experience them. For students who have personal and academic goals of protecting and serving communities, upholding justice, and "locking up the bad guys," must understand the fundamental responsibility to recognize how race and lived experiences might affect how the police do their job, and how others perceive them. If, as students, they are willing to dismiss the overwhelming body of literature that suggests racial disparities, institutional racism, and discriminatory practices, then what will they be willing to overlook as a police officer, a prosecutor, or a judge?

Criminologists, researchers, students, practitioners, and educators bear the responsibility of addressing and improving a system that has long been troubled. As Van Jones noted (2017):

> One of the few things that a growing number of liberals and conservatives agree upon today is this: "The United States locks up too many people, for too long, at too high a cost, often for unjustifiable reasons and with indefensible results. Our broken criminal justice system is a fundamental threat to our safety, our security, and our democracy". (p. 143).

Like Dr. Krisberg, Jones understands what many already know injustice is a threat to all that democracy and the justice system represent. Students of criminology and criminal justice can recognize this and begin to tackle the myriad issues that require not only large-scale, macrosystemic change, but also street-level, microsystem action. Such change will ensure that today's students will not simply perpetuate problematic, unfair, or ineffective policies.

This chapter begins by providing a brief overview of racial disparities in the modern criminal justice system. It continues by outlining ways in which perceptions of racial inequality can affect criminality, deviance, and consequences. The chapter concludes by highlighting the challenges and importance of discussing and studying race; the goals of such learning; and finally, the need for change.[2]

Racial Disparities and Inequality in the Criminal Justice System

With the election of President Barack Obama in 2008, and again in 2012, many felt that the United States had finally overcome its tumultuous, violent history with racism. If Americans could elect a Black man whose middle name is *Hussein*, then clearly, racism and discrimination were historical relics left in museums and only discussed during Black History Month. Minorities in the United States are afforded all the same rights as White citizens, and the path to racial harmony seemed clear. Scholars and pundits referred to the period as "post-racial America," but a closer look at the current statistics and research prove otherwise.

---

[2] These topics and problems are complex and often supported by a significant amount of research. Full books and volumes have been written about each issue. This chapter, however, is designed to be broad in its scope to introduce students to the issue, but due to the limited nature of the medium, it cannot address each issue in totality. As such, interested readers are encouraged to seek out additional resources and writings on the issues, including those in the references and the appendix provided at the end of the chapter.

Discrimination and Disparities

Walker, Spohn, and DeLone (2017) highlight the difference between discrimination and disparities. As they write, "A disparity involves a *difference* [italics in original], but one that does not necessarily involve discrimination…Discrimination involves a difference in outcome based on *differential treatment* of individuals or groups without reference to behavior, qualifications, or some other legal factor" (pp. 28-29). This is an important distinction, because the root causes are different for each; the difference lies in motivation, intent, and root causes. Disparities can arise from legitimate reasons such as legal factors or circumstances, while discrimination results from differential treatment of specific groups of people. Both disparities and discrimination can exist simultaneously, though. For example, one can observe racial disparities in arrests in a city that may arise from increased policing in specific areas due to increased crime rates, while there may also be a specific judge who sentences minorities more harshly than their white counterparts which would, by definition, constitute discrimination.

As Banks, Eberhardt, and Ross (2006) explain:

> "In the criminal justice context alone there are many instances where private citizens and public officials alike act in a race conscious fashion and yet are not viewed as racially biased. The crime victim who notices the race of an assailant, and the police officer who only stops people of the same race as the assailant are not viewed as having engaged in racial discrimination". (p. 1185).

While many believe that a post-racial, harmonious society would be "colorblind," realistically, this is not the case (or even the goal). There are many ways in which law enforcement officers and other agents of the criminal justice system can examine and utilize racial identity without engaging in overtly discriminatory practices, as in the example above, but this does not mean that issues and concerns about racial disparities are inconsequential or dismissible. Rather, these matters require a critical examination, an understanding of the history and research about the influence of race and the criminal justice system outcomes, and a willingness to improve upon current policies and change the nature of perceptions and disparities.

In Policing

After the death of Michael Brown and the public unrest that followed, President Barack Obama created The President's Task Force on 21st Century Policing in 2014. The goal was "identifying best practices and offering recommendations on how policing practices can promote effective crime reduction while building public trust" (Final Report of the President's Task Force on 21st Century Policing, 2015, p. 1). Concerns about race and policing can include issues of racial profiling, implicit bias, and the use of excessive and lethal force, especially given that the racial makeup of many police departments is often not as ethnically diverse as the communities they serve.

Racial profiling refers to police and other law enforcement agents using race or ethnicity when suspecting someone of a crime as opposed to some other individual criteria. As an example, New Jersey struggled with allegations of racial profiling for years, as many drivers alleged that they were stopped based only on their race (Baxter, 2014). Coupled with allegations of racism against and hazing of Black State Troopers, the state faced years of legal battles that, in 2005, ultimately resulted in "New Jersey [becoming] the first state in America to prohibit racial profiling and [requiring] every police officer…to undergo intensive instruction on profiling and the protection of citizen rights" (Collum, 2010, p. 3).

Research has repeatedly shown cases of profiling and racial disparities. Using propensity score matching in cases in Louisville, Vito, Gross, and Higgins (2017) found that "When considering race and gender of the driver…it was significant that African American male drivers would be more likely to be issued a citation" (p. 444). In 2013, The Vera Institute surveyed nearly 500 young men in New York City to examine their experiences with stop-and-frisk practices and how those experiences affected their perceptions of police. The study found that nearly half had been stopped nine times or more in their lifetime with many never being informed of the reason for the stop. As Fratello, Rengifo, and Trone (2013) wrote, "71 percent of young people surveyed report being frisked at least once, and 64 percent said they had been searched (p. 2). More than 80 percent of the respondents (who were mostly young men of color) felt that the officers did not have reason to talk to them, and more than half felt that they were treated worse because of their race or ethnicity (Fratello, Rengifo, & Trone, 2013). Some may argue that the New York Police Department (NYPD) the stop-and-frisk practices were simply designed to make the city streets safer. Others would argue that if the respondents had nothing to hide, there should be no problem with the practice. However, the consequences of stop-and-frisk in neighborhoods has had alarming effects. As the researchers found, "Nearly 9 out of 10 agreed with statement: 'People in my neighborhood don't trust the police" (Fratello, Rengifo, & Trone, 2013, p. 7).[3]

It is important to note, though, that many departments across the country have enacted policies and practices to prevent or address racial profiling and improve race relations with community members. As Mauer (2010) explained, "Evidence of racial profiling…does not suggest by any means that all agencies or all officers engage in such

---

[3] New York City Mayor Bill de Blasio ended stop-and-frisk practices in 2014 after a federal district court judge found that the practice "had become 'a policy of indirect racial profiling and that the police had searched innocent people without any objective reason to suspect them of wrongdoing" (Cullen, 2016, para. 5). A report on the history and findings of the post-stop-and-frisk crime rates can be found at https://www.brennancenter.org/blog/ending-new-yorks-stop-and-frisk-did-not-increase-crime.

behaviors. In fact, in recent years, many police agencies have initiated training and oversight measure designed to prevent and identify such practices" (p. 15).

Walker, Spohn, and DeLone (2017) argue that the effects of racially motivated traffic stops and other encounters not only lead to resentment against the police, but they can also affect feelings about American society as a whole. In neighborhoods and cities, though, perceptions of racial profiling and discrimination by the police can have devastating effects on police-community relations, particularly within communities of color. Cochran and Warren (2011) note, "[The] research has overwhelmingly shown that Blacks and Latinos hold lower levels of trust and confidence in the police than do Whites and other racial minorities" (p. 206). Similarly, Unah & Wright (2015) noted, "[Certain experiences] may contribute to African Americas, particularly those living in areas with aggressive policing [are] more inclined to resent law enforcement and associated institutions compared to [W]hites and even Hispanics" (p. 251). As with stop-and-frisk policies, though, many people believe that racial profiling is unavoidable. Some justify it or claim that it may not even exist, but other simply accept it as a practice and refuse to acknowledge its harm as a practice that is fundamentally discriminatory that contributes to racial disparities. Gau and Jordan (2015) acknowledge that "Profiling might not get a ringing endorsement, but the fundamental acceptance of it as 'what needs to be done' allows the practice to continue" (p. 13).

Distrust in law enforcement can affect perceptions of legitimacy and procedural justice which, in turn, affect law-breaking and deviance. Conversely, in examining why people obey the law, Tyler (2006) defined legitimacy as "the perceived obligation to obey the law and as support for legal authorities" (p. 45). It seems obvious that those who believe that laws and police are fair would be less likely to break the law, however, his research conclusively found that "Citizens who view legal authority as legitimate are generally more likely to comply with the law" (p. 62). Applying this notion to policing and race, it becomes increasingly important to improve race relations between police and citizens. Trust and respect could not only reduce racial profiling and tension, but it could reduce crime and deviance in communities.

The President's Task Force (2015) asserted, "Law enforcement cannot build community trust if it as seen as an occupying force coming in from outside to rule and control the community" (p. 11). Additionally, many police departments do not require officers to live in the city or town where they work, which may further alienate them from the community and highlight the differences between police and citizens they are serving and policing. By enhancing legitimacy and procedural justice and ensuring that officers do not engage in racial bias, discrimination, and profiling, departments can begin to improve perceptions of fairness and restore relationships so that police officers and citizens can feel safer.

In Sentencing

Like other research, there is evidence of racial disparities in sentences for minorities as compared to Whites who are convicted of similar crimes. Methodological issues often complicate sentencing with issues such as measurement of criminal history and offenses, but the research continuously shows "…that minorities, especially African-Americas, receive sentences that are somewhat more punitive than those imposed on similarly situated [Whites]" (Mitchell, 2018, p. 30). These disparities are even more pronounced when examining drug offenses, especially considering drug enforcement efforts in urban minority communities versus suburban areas, despite continued studies that show similar rates of use and sales among Black and White users. Rosenberg, Groves, and Blankenship (2017) found that "…equal percentages of Blacks and Whites in our study reported using drugs in the thirty days" and "Blacks reported preferring marijuana to harder drugs, and having less serious drug problems" (p. 139).

Research findings have been mixed, and some have argued that racial discrimination and disparities in sentencing have been declining, but historically, this has not always been the case. One of the most notorious examples of a racially charged policy was the differentiation in sentencing for possession of crack and cocaine. Michelle Alexander (2012) highlighted the federal laws that "punish crack offenses one hundred times more severely than offenses involving powder cocaine. A conviction for the sale of five hundred grams of powder cocaine triggers a five-year mandatory sentence, while only five grams of crack triggers the same sentence" (p. 112). At the time, many argued that crack was more dangerous or a greater threat to society and users (although this was later discredited and disproven), but others noted that the law discriminated against Black Americans because "the majority of those charged with crimes involving crack at the time were [B]lack (approximately 93 percent of convicted crack offenders were black, 5 percent were white), whereas powder cocaine users were predominantly [W]hite" (Alexander, 2012, p. 112). Many of these offenders are still incarcerated today.

Walker, Spohn, and DeLone (2017) offer five possible explanations for racial disparities in sentencing and determine if the differences are due to discrimination. They assert that there is clear evidence of racial disparities, but most of the explanations are due to institutional or economic causes rather than direct discrimination of individual actors.

They continue by explaining that many factors beyond contribute to sentencing, however many of these factors are inexorably linked to race. Factors such as employment, education levels, and quality of representation (e.g., public defenders or private attorneys) often correlate to characteristics and risk-factors for criminality and deviant behavior. The intersection of factors such as race/ethnicity, gender, age, and employment can lead to perilous outcomes in sentencing for certain groups of people, and most often, the harshest sentences are imposed against young, unemployed Black men, often known as the "punishment penalty."

In examining reasons for this, they write, "A number of scholars suggest that certain categories of offenders are regarded as more dangerous and more problematic than others and thus more in need to formal social control" (Walker, Spohn, & DeLone, 2017, p. 315). While this may be a remnant of "the superpredator" (discussed in the next section), it may also be fueled by media overrepresentations of local violent crimes, portrayals of offenders in movies and fictional crime shows, and implicit biases and beliefs in the notion that young Black men are more aggressive.

The disparities in sentencing, particularly for drug offenses, and the racially-bound explanations for these disparities highlight the ways in which race (and the intersection of race, class, and gender) still affect criminal justice outcomes and outline the need for change.

Other Issues

There are other areas of the criminal justice in which race and ethnicity can have a profound impact on criminal justice outcomes. One area is reentry and employment. Many offenders serve their time in jail or prison and struggle with the demands of reentry. Often, they must find employment as a condition of their parole or probation, but the stigma of criminality lasts long after they have served their sentence and paid their debt to society. Pager (2003) found that it was significantly more difficult for an African-American to find employment with a criminal record. While she also found that the stigma of a criminal record often impedes employment, she also found negative effects when combined with race as compared to White job seekers. Such difference can affect strains and individual stressors, thus affecting recidivism, continued law-breaking, homelessness, and more.

One might argue that the most profound, outrageous disparities in race relate to the death penalty. The most serious punishment of the criminal justice system, there is a myriad of statistical, legal, and anecdotal evidence that race plays an overwhelming role in the death penalty. Race-related factors include not only the race of the alleged offender, but the race of the victim as well; the makeup of the jury and the exclusionary tactics used by the prosecution; quality of legal representation; racially-motivated witnesses and false testimony; and the history of lynching in the state where the trial occurs.

Advocacy groups including the Death Penalty Information Center, Amnesty International, and the Equal Justice Initiative argue that the practice is unjust, unconstitutional in many cases, and ineffective in deterring crime. Additionally, as of

November 5, 2018, 164 people have been exonerated through acquittal, a dismissal of chargers, or a pardon since 1973. 84 of those were Black, and 15 were Latino.

This is a topic that needs a close examination of the resources, research, and literature available. A strong, profound starting place is Bryan Stevenson's book, *Just Mercy: A Story of Justice and Redemption.* His work shines a harsh, evaluative light on the problems in the criminal justice system, the impact of the race and poverty on outcomes, and stories of inmates who became victims of a system that seemed determined to kill them. His words should echo in the minds of all students, practitioners, and researchers:

> *Each of us is more than the worst thing we've ever done*...I've come to believe that the true measure of our commitment to justice, the character of our society, our commitment to the rule of law, fairness, and equality cannot be measured by how we treat the rich, the powerful, the privilege, and the respected among us. The true measure of our character is how we treat the poor, the disfavored, the accused, the incarcerated, and the condemned. (Stevenson, 2015, p. 18).

Conclusion

This section provided a brief, though certainly not exhaustive, overview of the ways in which race can play an important factor in the treatment of people in the criminal justice system. It is not meant to be a scathing condemnation of police officers or courts; rather, it is a review of the research as well as a presentation of the most pressing matters that students of criminology and criminal justice will face as they continue their academic careers and enter the professional world.

These issues shape how many the discussions that people have, the legitimacy of the criminal justice system, and the perceptions of the people who are tasked with upholding the law and protecting communities. The following section discusses the importance and influence of those perceptions as well as the devastating effects of mistrust, racial stereotypes, and fear.

How Perceptions of Crime Affect the Criminal Justice System

In 2014, The New York Times revisited a dark moment in the history of criminology. The article recalled,

> The superpredator 'is so impulsive, so remorseless, that he can kill, rape, maim, without giving it a second thought,' said John DiIulio Jr., the Princeton scientist who coined the term in 1995. News reports—usually featuring images of glowering black teenagers—warned of the coming wave of violence that would flood the country. (New York Times, 2014, para. 2-3).

This prediction—ultimately disproven with the nationwide decrease in crime, even among juvenile homicides—led to a nationwide panic about the coming wave of remorseless juvenile delinquents that triggered changes to many state policies regarding the transfers of juveniles to adult courts[4]. Many of these laws are still in effect today.

Policies driven by fear are not new in the United States. Fears of crime and victimization have led to support for policies like Megan's Law and Three Strikes and You're Out, enacted after highly publicized cases. In addition to drawing ire and shock, the crimes that inspired these punitive policies ultimately stemmed from public fear that similar crimes could happen to them or their loved ones. Researchers note that "fear of crime among [W]hites has been…the driving force behind harsher criminal sentences and the enormous increase in the American prison population since the mid-1970s" (Walker, Spohn, & DeLone, 2017, p. 4). "Tough on crime" politicians garner support from conservative voters who often view punishment as more effective and satisfying than rehabilitative approaches. Elected lawmakers who focus on punitive measures support and implement state and federal policies that have widespread and far-reaching consequences, often for poor minority communities.

Perceptions of crime and fear lead to the election of politicians who often attempt to apply social control through increased policing, harsher sentences, and mass incarceration. Those policies and their consequences, in turn, can affect how people view and perceive minorities, particularly Black and Hispanic men, as offenders. Thus, we now face the challenge of discourse about racial disparities and criminal system. For many, "If learning that Black men are 6 times more likely than White men triggers the stereotype that Blacks are criminals and criminals are black, then such information is no longer concerning on its face. Rather, it becomes expected or even justifiable" (Hetey & Eberhardt, 2018, p. 185).

The images of Black and minority offenders are often splashed across local news and social media. Callanan (2012) wrote, "Local television news elevated perceptions and fear of crime irrespective of race/ethnicity. Since it focuses on violent street crimes, especially among strangers, a stable and pervasive message may be of violent suspects/offenders as non-[W]hite" (p. 108). Students who attended a college in a rural area that is predominantly White visited a state prison as part of a 200-level Corrections course. In discussing the visit later, none of the students mentioned the obvious, glaring fact that most of the inmates they saw were Black or brown. The lack of awareness could be due to their own fear of addressing it, as they may have seemed racist. However, it could be due to the "widespread stereotyping of Blacks as prone to violence and

---

[4] Both John DiIulio, Jr. and James Fox later admitted they were wrong. They were among many influential criminologists who filed a 2012 amicus brief in a case arguing that mandatory life-without-parole was two 14-year-old defendants violate the Eight Amendment against cruel and unusual punishment. More information can be found at https://eji.org/news/superpredator-myth-20-years-later. The amicus brief can be found at https://eji.org/sites/default/files/miller-amicus-jeffrey-fagan.pdf, and a short documentary from the New York Times provides an overview of the superpredator: http://nyti.ms/1hjlin8.

criminality" (Pickett, Chiricios, Golden, & Gertz, 2012, p. 150). It is possible that the students' implicit notion of Black and brown men as "criminal" explains the stark disparity between the racial demographics in the prison and the area outside of it.

Distrust and negative perceptions of police can also affect how police do their jobs or interact with those they serve. Media coverage of deadly force has led to what researchers have called "the Ferguson effect." Nix and Pickett (2017) found that "…officers who believed media coverage of the police had been more hostile in recent years were significantly more likely to believe that civilians had become more distrustful, resentful, and disrespectful of police. Such officers were also more likely to report greater fear of being falsely accused of wrongdoing by civilians" (p. 30).

Students of criminal justice and criminology can and should learn the history of racial discrimination and the mechanisms through which they still persist today and contribute to racial disparities. If students are willing to discuss and confront the many ways that social influences, media, and implicit bias affect criminal justice outcomes, they may be the change that, over time, decreases bias and fear-driven policies. As future law enforcement officers, federal agents, lawyers, and researchers, today's students have the potential to disrupt harmful practices and promote equitable, fair, and just treatment for all people.

THE GOALS OF TALKING ABOUT RACE

In 1993, LaFree and Russell lamented, "While there are undoubtedly a number of reasons that race has not been examined as carefully as other variables, the unfortunate result has been that it has been virtually ignored in criminal justice education" (p. 285). In the 15 years since they wrote these words, race has become a central theme in national discussions about the criminal justice system, and, concomitantly, many programs have begun to offer courses in race and ethnic issues. Examining many of the top criminal justice program curricula, most offer undergraduate courses specifically designed to address race and ethnicity. Courses like Race, Crime, and Criminal Justice (University of Maryland—College Park and University of Cincinnati); Race, Ethnicity, and Social Control (University of California—Irvine); and Race and Crime (Rutgers University—Newark) are designed to address the relationship between race and offending, victimization, and criminal justice policies. Many specifically note racial disparities in the criminal justice system, but it does not appear that these are required core course as opposed to electives.

Students who take these courses may feel apprehensive about taking the course or fear that it might be "liberal brainwashing" (of which academics and college professors are so often accused). Yet, Rasheed (2018) encourages professors and students by noting, "It is crucial [that]…instead of being apathetic to or fearful of current societal and political oppressions, we challenged ourselves and each other to confront systems that further oppress us" (p. 235). The willingness to take the course and have the discussions is the first step toward progress, but simply talking is exhausting and often non-productive.

In the age of social media when opinions that are posted, tweeted, liked, and debated, one might argue that these are not discussions, but fights or opportunities to announce one's own views and defend them against those of other, faceless users. Similarly, on cable news, pundits talk, and viewers listen. Kay (2018) writes, "Our networks cram eight analysts into eight tiny boxes, then put them in a moderated struggle to be the most quotable. It's not a new habit—we have always appreciated a chance to bloviate about race" (p. 3). If online and news interactions are models for criminal justice students, conversations in the classroom can seem discouraging, disheartening, or daunting.

The goals of these courses, though, should include 1.) examining how race and ethnicity affect experiences with the criminal justice system; 2.) identifying ways in which the criminal justice system affect people of color and other ethnic groups; 3.) highlighting policies and practices in the criminal justice system and explain causes of racial disparities; and, perhaps most importantly, 4.) engaging in thoughtful, respectful, experientially- and empirically-informed discussions about race and criminal justice issues. Having such conversations are difficult because they require students to use and apply research and literature to inform their comments and responses. Additionally, teaching and learning how to have conversations in which participants can disagree or debate respectfully and actually listen to each other. In his sermon to White America, Michael Eric Dyson (2017) wrote:

> I offer this sermon to you, my dear [W]hite friends, my beloved comrades of faith and country…I do so in the interest of healing our nation through honest, often blunt, talk. It will make you squirm in your seat with discomfort before, hopefully pointing a way to relief…And without [W]hite American wrestling with these truths and confronting these realities, we may not survive. (p. 7).

If educators are willing to teach these skills and concepts, and students are willing to learn, the process can be profoundly fulfilling, meaningful, and ultimately, educational, but it can also be challenging.

The Challenges of Discussing and Learning Race

Student expectations for a course about race and criminal justice issues may differ even before the first class. Many may be apprehensive or worry that a heated debate may devolve into a full-blown fight. Others may feel nervous that they will say the wrong thing and be accused of racism by peers or even by the professor. And specifically, minority students may fear that they may be forced to educate White students or the professor or speak for their entire race. However, instructors, educators, and professors can address these challenges through open dialogue, and students can acknowledge their fears to move forward and learn in meaningful ways.

Discomfort and Fear

Students can be nervous, uncomfortable, or even fearful of engaging in open, honest discussions about race and experiences. In talking to groups of both college students and adults, Brookfield (2019) found that the top three reasons for reluctance about a race conversation were fear of saying the wrong things and being called a racist, the potential for an uncomfortable discussion, and lack of relevant experience. This is likely true for many students in college classrooms. However, it is important to consider the implications for the first of these reasons.

With the alarming resurgence of White supremacy as seen in Charlottesville in 2017, it seemed that overt racism is no longer a belief that people want to hide anymore. Men marched in the streets, showed their faces to national media outlets, and participated in documentaries about their beliefs. People of all races and ethnicities denounced this group, and many were horrified at the public display of anti-Semitism and racism. Few would argue that those tiki-torch wielding, "you will not replace us"-chanting men are, in fact, anything but racist. Similarly, many would agree that one of the most offensive, debilitating names to call someone in today's world is "racist."

Educators must consider why it is that students and adults alike fear being the label of racist. If someone accuses them of being racist or racist things, does he fear that they will be categorized with the Klan and suddenly be initiated with a pointy hat and a burning cross? Others might reflect on recent social media attacks on people who have been filmed engaging in discriminatory or racist behaviors and consequently lost their jobs and were subjects of public ridicule. It bears consideration that the accusation may be contrary to their own notions of the kind of people that they are. If most believe that they are good people at heart who are not racist and have no biases or prejudicial beliefs, then such a label is essentially contrary to their own views of themselves. Students in the classroom must understand key differences between lack of experiences or exposure, bias, misinformation, prejudice, and racism. In fact, courses about race should focus primarily on the institutional definition of racism, focusing on larger practices and policies that oppress specific groups and perpetuate privilege for others.

Professors and moderators must also consider when people might use the term racist for a peer and the purpose that it serves. There is an important distinction between calling someone a racist and addressing problematic perspectives and attempting to correct them. Essentially, in any conversation—both in the classroom and out—calling someone a racist ends the conversation or, at the very least, ends the potential for respectful discussion. Bonilla-Silva (2018) claims, "Hunting for 'racists' is the sport of choice of those who practice the 'clinical approach' to race relations—the careful separation of good and bad, tolerant and intolerant Americans" (pp. 14-15). Some may argue that failing to call racist language by using the term "racist" can perpetuate or condone such behavior, but with the goal of learning and educating in the classroom, all participants must work together to promote conversation and productive discourse. DiAngelo (2017) asserts that interrupting racism is not passive or complacent, but rather should be direct and clear. However, if everyone understands that the classroom and the course can provide a place where they can ask questions, respectfully criticize each other with the common purpose of learning and self-improvement, and say things that may be analyzed, they can all address this fear and discomfort directly. In the first class, professors and students can create guidelines or class norms that provide expectations for interactions and offer ways for students to disagree without resorting to name-calling. Even better, it can lead to a discussion that promotes progress rather than stalls with accusations and self-defense. Tatum (2017) encourages her students to turn the discomfort into action that disrupts racism by educating others where they once might have ignored it.

Guilt, Fragility, and Privilege

Minorities may fear the responsibility of speaking for or representing their entire racial group, but White students might fear that they will become scapegoats for centuries of wrongdoing against others and, of course, be labeled a racist by their peers. Paired with the term White, the words fragility, guilt, and privilege tend to evoke a host of feelings. In Robin DiAngelo's controversial book, *White Fragility: Why It's So Hard for White People to Talk about Racism*, she recounts her experiences as a consultant and trainer on issues of race. She explains, "…when we try to talk openly and honestly about race, [W]hite fragility quickly emerges as we are so often met with silence, defensiveness, argumentation, certitude, and other forms of pushback" (DiAngelo, 2017, p. 8). Similarly, Reni Eddo Lodge (2017) wrote in her blog, "I'm not talking to [W]hite people about race unless I absolutely have to…I'm no longer dealing with people who don't want to hear it, wish to ridicule it, and frankly, don't deserve it" (p. xii). (Ironically, she went on to write a seven-chapter book with a similar title.) How, then, can productive conversation happen in the classroom if defensiveness and frustration promote obstinate refusals to engage?

If students acknowledge that race and ethnicity affect the ways that minorities perceive and interact with the criminal justice system, they should also consider the fact that for White students, their race may also affect their perceptions, experiences, and beliefs. However, forcing students to accept White privilege as a notion is likely contrary to progress, but offering comparisons and scenarios that may highlight the idea may allow them to draw upon their own experiences and come to their own conclusions. Brookfield and colleagues (2019) also recommend that professors use three teaching strategies to discuss race and promote respectful discourse: scaffolding (building upon simple experiences or readings and increasing knowledge and level of complexity; modeling (demonstrating self-awareness, reflection, and sharing of racial biases); and community building (creating mutual trust and rapport in the classroom to encourage learning).

Academically, most do not use the notions of White fragility, guilt, and privilege to force people to apologize for their race. Rather, they are often utilized to describe ways in which conversation and progress can be stymied by those who refuse to acknowledge that discrimination, racism, and racial disparities still exist in a so-called post-racial era. In a classroom with the aforementioned goals, these notions should not be used as weapons, but as tools for understanding the intricacies of racial discussions and the ongoing work necessary to improve the criminal justice system.

In colleges and universities across the country, students in these courses hail from all states, other countries, and rural, suburban, and urban areas. They come from a variety of families, neighborhoods, and cultural backgrounds, and their experiences are unique and important. Many, however, have grown up in racially homogenous towns and had limited interactions with those of other races. Given the current literature about hypersegregation[5] and class-based segregation (which is often inexorably linked to race and ethnicity), many students lack experience in interacting with people who look different than them or have different experiences. Despite advances in communication and technology, many have simply not had the opportunity to experience racial, ethnic, and cultural diversity, and they simply cannot be held solely responsible for that, especially if they were children who lived with their parents until they went to college. Instead, courses can challenge them to learn, read, and most importantly, listen. Educators can also request that students also examine and reflect on their own unwillingness to recognize the research and data on racial disparities.

Their education should also be complemented with service learning, experiential opportunities, and study abroad prospects that expose them to racial and ethnic diversity. As Hill (2017) explains, "Our history of race has resulted in a variety of inequalities throughout society, and we can't fully understand these inequalities from a distance. We can learn about ideas like race, culture, and identity in a classroom setting, but it's far more transformational to learn through actual proximity to suffering" (p. 166).

[5] Massey and Tannen (2015) found that a number of cities across the country that were still categorized by hypersegregation as of 2010, and that "...roughly one-third of all black metropolitan residents lived in a hypersegregated area" (p. 1025). They conclude their study by noting, "Although hypersegregation may have become less common in recent years, it hasn't disappeared, but has instead become centered in a subset of metropolitan areas containing some of the nation's largest black communities" (p. 1033).

A NOTE ON #BLACKLIVESMATTER

One of the most controversial topics related to race and criminal justice issues relates to lethal force and the #BlackLivesMatter hashtag and movement. Respectful discussions can devolve quickly at even the mention of three words. However, one of the most important goals of a course on race and criminal justice should be to correct the misconceptions and ask students to examine the tenets of the movement. As a student in a course entitled The Criminology of Race wrote:

> When I first heard of the Black Lives Matter movement, it was shortly after the incidents in Ferguson, MO. The way that the hashtag was used on social media made it seem like supporters of the movement hated the police and white people and believed their own lives were more important than others. I did not like that. At all. All of the information I had gotten about the Black Lives Matter movement came from social media. However, after having discussed this topic in class I better understand why the movement is around and what it is protesting... I think for many people, they associate the hashtag with the extreme views of the supports of the movement like down with the police and white people.

This student acknowledged her misconceptions about the movement, recognized why she believed this, and ultimately recommended that more discussions like the one in her class should happen to correct these issues.

By first learning and researching the tenets of the movement (rather than simply drawing conclusion from singular social media posts), they can also learn that people do not necessarily need to choose sides in the Black vs. Blue Lives Matter movements. Students can realize that those who support Black Lives Matter do not clearly wish for the murder of police officers, and they can also recognize that Blue Lives Matter arose as a counterargument to the original movement but does not explicitly wish for the murder of Black citizens by police officers. Ideally, they will acknowledge that they are not two binary ideas, but rather a continuum, and they should be able to identify similarities between the two. While there is most certainly a complex discussion to have about the movements, starting here can lead to a larger, more reasonable discussion about social protests, police brutality and lethal force, and ways to understand perspective.

MOVING FORWARD

In today's world, when issues arise about prejudice and racial discrimination, many have the option of simply continuing through their feed or timeline, turning off the television, or ignoring conversation. However, these problems—these disparities, injustices, and wrongs—are not ones that students of criminology and criminal justice can ignore. At the very least, they demand consideration, conversation, and close examination, but they also require that students have a greater understanding of the need for change.

Undergraduate studies undoubtedly focus on the words of Martin Luther King, Jr. and Frederick Douglass. Students learn the historical context and the importance of their words, but they do not necessarily recognize that while they both called for equality and justice, they also called upon everyone—of all races—to be agents of change. Frederick Douglass (1852) gave an impassioned plea to a Society of White women and proclaimed, "The feeling of the nation must be quickened; the conscience of the nation must be rouse; the propriety of the nation must be startled; the hypocrisy of the nation must be exposed; and its crimes against God and man must be proclaimed and denounced" (para. 45). More than 100 years later, Martin Luther King (1963), in *Letters from a Birmingham Jail* wrote, "Lukewarm acceptance is much more bewildering than outright rejection" (para. 19).

Students who believe in community, civil rights, patriotism, and justice must be willing to face the discomfort of discussing race. Professors, educators, and instructors must present them with the opportunity to have this discussion, to learn the history and the research, and to read works by authors of color. They must exhibit patience and guidance and lead the discussions with respect and fairness for the students and their vulnerability. Most importantly, all of us who are passionate about equality and the fairness of the criminal justice system must be open to the idea of examining our own beliefs, perceptions, and biases while remaining committed to the notion of justice for all. Without introspection, conversation, and action, Dr. Krisberg's predictions about the legitimacy of our law enforcement system may become reality.

The future looks bright, though, when students are willing to sit in a classroom and truly listen to each other. If they can reflect on the things that they have learned and find ways to apply that knowledge to create a more just criminal justice system, we can, as Michael Eric Dyson (2017) wrote, "heal our nation through honest, often blunt, talk" (p. 7). If more students and professors are willing to partake in this discussion, then healing can begin.

Appendix – Recommended Reading

Books

Alexander, M. (2012). *The new Jim Crow: Mass incarceration in the age of colorblindness.* New York: The New Press.

Anderson, E. (1999). *Code of the Street: Decency, Violence, and the Moral Life of the Inner City.* New York: W. W. Norton & Company, Inc.

Chang, J. (2016). *We Gon' be Alright: Notes on Race and Resegregation.* New York: Picador.

Collum, J. (2010). *The Black Dragon: Racial Profiling Exposed.* Fort Lauderdale, FL: Gulf Stream Press.

DiAngelo, R. (2018). *White Fragility: Why It's So Hard for White People to Talk about Racism.* Boston: Beacon Press.

Dyson, M. E. (2017). *Tears We Cannot Stop: A Sermon to White America.* New York: St. Martin's Press.

Hill, M. L. (2016). *Nobody: Casualties of America's War on the Vulnerable from Ferguson to Flint and Beyond.* New York: Atria Books.

Jones, V. (2017). *Beyond the Messy Truth: How We Came Apart, How We Come Together.* New York: Ballantine Books.

Kozol, J. (2005). *The Shame of the Nation: The Restoration of Apartheid Schooling in America.* New York: Crown Publishers.

Stevenson, B. (2014). *Just Mercy: A story of Justice and Redemption.* New York: Spiegel & Grau.

Tyler, T. (2006). *Why People Obey the Law.* Princeton, NJ: Princeton University Press.

United States Department of Justice. (2017). *Federal Reports on Police Killings: Ferguson, Cleveland, Baltimore, and Chicago.* New York: Melville House.

Western, B. (2007). *Punishment and Inequality in America.* New York: Russell Sage Foundation.

Wilson, W. J. (2012). *The Truly Disadvantaged: The Inner City, the Underclass, and Public Policy* (2nd ed.). Chicago: The University of Chicago Press.

Publications

Amnesty International. (2003). *United States of America: Death by discrimination – The continuing role of race in capital cases.* Retrieved from: https://www.amnesty.org/download/Documents/104000/amr510462003en.pdf.

Children's Defense Fund. (2007). *America's cradle to prison pipeline.* Retrieved from: https:// www.childrensdefense.org/ wp-content/ uploads/ 2018/ 08/ cradle-prison-pipeline-report-2007-full-lowres.pdf.

Emsellem, M. & Avery, B. (2016). Racial profiling in hiring: A critique of new "Ban the Box" studies. *National Employment Law Project.* Retrieved from: https://nelp.org/wp-content/ uploads/ Policy-Brief-Racial-Profiling-in-Hiring-Critique-New-Ban-the-Box-Studies.pdf.

The Sentencing Project. (2014). *Race and punishment: Racial perceptions of crime and support for punitive policies.* Retrieved from: https://sentencingproject.org/wp-content/uploads/2015/11/Race-and-Punishment.pdf.

Organizations

American Civil Liberties Union (ACLU)
Equal Justice Initiative (@eji_org)
The Innocent Project (@innocence)
National Association for the Advancement of Colored People (@NAACP)
Pew Research Center (@pewresearch)
The Sentencing Project (@SentencingProj)
Southern Poverty Law Center (@splcenter)
Vera Institute (@verainstitute)

REFERENCES

Alexander, M. (2012). *The New Jim Crow: Mass Incarceration in the Age of Colorblindness*. New York: The New Press.

American Bar Association. (2012). *Justice for all? Challenging racial disparities in the criminal justice system.* The American Bar Association. Retrieved from: https://www.americanbar.org/publications/human_rights_magazine_home/human_rights_vol37_2010/fall2010/justice_for_all_challenging_racial_disparities_criminal_justice_system.

Amnesty International. (2003). *United States of America: Death by discrimination – The continuing role of race in capital cases*. Retrieved from: https://www.amnesty.org/en/ documents/AMR51/046/2003/en.

Banks, R. R., Eberhardt, J. L. & Ross, L. (2006). Discrimination and implicit bias in a racially unequal society. *California Law Review*, *94*, 1169-1190.

Baxter, C. (2014, January 10). Timeline of N.J. State Police struggles with racial discrimination. *NJ.com*. Retrieved from: https://www.nj.com/politics/index.ssf/2014/01/timeline_of_nj_state_police_struggles_with_racial_discrimination.html.

Bureau of Justice Statistics. (2018). *Prisoners in 2016*. Retrieved from: https://www.bjs.gov/content/pub/pdf/p16_sum.pdf.

Bonczar, T. P. & Beck, A. J. (1997). *Lifetime likelihood of going to State or Federal prison.* Bureau of Justice Statistics Special Report. Retrieved from: https://bjs.gov/content/pub/pdf/Llgsfp.pdf.

Brookfield, S. D. (2019). The dynamics of teaching race. In S. D. Brookfield (ed.), *Teaching race: How to Help Students Unmask and Challenge Racism* (1-17). San Francisco, CA: Josey-Bass.

Callanan, V. J. (2012). Media consumption, perceptions of crime risk and fear of crime: Examining race/ethnic difference. *Sociological Perspectives*, *55*(1), 93-115.

Cochran, J. C. & Warren, P. Y. (2012). Racial, ethnic, and gender difference in perceptions of the police: The salience of office race within the context of racial profiling. *Journal of Contemporary Criminal Justice*, *28*(2), 206-227.

Collum, J. (2010). *The Black Dragon: Racial profiling exposed.* Fort Lauderdale, FL: Gulf Stream Press.

Conover, T. (2014, October 17). 'Just Mercy,' by Bryan Stevenson. *The New York Times*, Retrieved from: https://www.nytimes.com/2014/10/19/books/review/just-mercy-by-bryan-stevenson.html.

Cullen, J. (2016, April 11). Ending New York's Stop-and-Frisk Did Not Increase Crime. *Brennan Center for Justice.* Retrieved from: https://www.brennancenter.org/blog/ending-new-yorks-stop-and-frisk-did-not-increase-crime.

Department of Justice Civil Rights Division. (2015). *Investigation of the Ferguson Police Department.* United States Department of Justice. Retrieved from: https://www.justice.gov/ sites/ default/ files/ opa/ press-releases/attachments/2015/03/04/ferguson_police_department_report.pdf.

DiAngelo, R. (2018). *White Fragility: Why It's so hard for White People to Talk about Racism.* Boston: Beacon Press.

Douglass, F. (1852). *Oration, delivered in Corinthian Hall, Rochester.* University of Rochester Frederick Douglass Project. Retrieved from: https://rbscp.lib.rochester.edu/2945.

Dyson, M. E. (2017). *Tears We Cannot Stop: A Sermon to White America.* New York: St. Martin's Press.

Eddo-Lodge, R. (2017). *Why I'm No longer Talking to White People about Race.* New York: Bloomsbury Circus.

Equal Justice Initiative. (2017). *Equal Justice Initiative.* Retrieved from: https://www.eji.org.

Fratello, J., Rengifo, A. F. & Trone, J. (2013). *Coming of age with stop and frisk: Experiences, self-perceptions, and public safety implications.* New York: Vera Institute of Justice. Retrieved from: https:// storage.googleapis.com/ vera-web-assets/ downloads/ Publications/ coming- of- age- with- stop- and- frisk- experiences- self-perceptions- and- public- safety- implications/ legacy_ downloads/ stop- and- frisk-summary-report-v2.pdf.

Freelon, D., McIlwain, C. D. & Clark, M. D. (2016). *Beyond the hashtag: #Ferguson, #Blacklivesmatter, and the online struggle for offline justice.* Center for Media and Social Impact. Retrieved from: http://cmsimpact.org/wp-content/uploads/2016/03/beyond_the_hashtags_2016.pdf.

Gau, J. & Jordan, K. L. (2015). Profiling Trayvon: Young Black males, suspicion, and surveillance. In D. Johnson, P.Y. Warren, & A. Farrell (Eds.), *Deadly Injustice: Trayvon Martin, Race, and the Criminal Justice System*, (7-22). New York: New York University Press.

Hafner, J. (2016, Aug. 8). How Michael Brown's death, two years ago, pushed #BlackLivesMatter into a movement. *USA Today*. Retrieved from: https://www.usatoday.com/story/news/nation-now/2016/08/08/how-michael-browns-death-two-years-ago-pushed-blacklivesmatter-into-movement/88424366/.

Hetey, R. C. & Eberhardt, J. L. (2018). The numbers don't speak for themselves: Racial disparities and the persistence of inequality in the criminal justice system. *Current Directions in Psychological Science, 27*(3), 183-187.

Hill, D. (2017). *White Awake: An Honest Look at What It Means to be White.* Downers Grove, IL: InterVarsity Press.

Jones, V. (2017). *Beyond the Messy Truth: How We Came Apart, How We Come Together.* New York: Ballantine Books.

King, M. L. (1963). *Letter from Birmingham Jail.* University of Pennsylvania African Studies Center. Retrieved from: https://www.africa.upenn.edu/ Articles_Gen/Letter_Birmingham.html.

LaFree, G. & Russell, K. K. (1993). The argument for studying race and crime. *Journal of Criminal Justice Education*, *4*(2), 273-289.

Massey, D. S. & Tannen, J. (2015). A research note on trends in Black hypersegregation. *Demography, 52*, 1025-1034.

Mauer, M. (2010). Justice for all? Challenging racial disparities in the criminal justice system. *Human Rights*, *37*(4), 14-16.

Mitchell, O. (2018). The continuing evolution of race and sentencing research and reviews of this research. *Journal of Criminal Justice*, *59*, 29-31.

Nellis, A. (2016). *The color of justice: Racial and ethnic disparities in state prisons*. The Sentencing Project. Retrieved from: https://www.sentencingproject.org/ publications/color-of-justice-racial-and-ethnic-disparity-in-state-prisons/#III.%20The%20Scale%20of%20Disparity.

New York Times. (2014, April 14). Echoes of the superpredator. *The New York Times*. Retrieved from: https:// www.nytimes.com/ 2014/ 04/ 14/ opinion/ echoes-of-the-superpredator.html.

Nix, J. & Pickett, J. (2017). Third-person perceptions, hostile media effects, and policing: Developing a theoretical framework for assessing the Ferguson effect. *Journal of Criminal Justice*, *51*, 24-33.

Pager, D. (2003). The mark of a criminal record. *American Journal of Sociology*, *108*, p. 937-975.

Pickett, J. T., Chiricos, T., Golden, K. M. & Gertz, M. (2012). Reconsidering the relationship between perceived neighborhood racial composition and whites' perceptions of victimization risk: Do racial stereotypes matter? *Criminology*, *50*(1), 145-186.

President's Task Force on 21st Century Policing. (2015). *Final Report of the President's Task Force on 21st Century Policing.* Washington, DC: Office of Community

Oriented Policing Services. Retrieved from: https://cops.usdoj.gov/pdf/taskforce/taskforce_finalreport.pdf.

Racial disparities in the criminal justice system: Hearing before the Subcommittee on Crime, Terrorism, and Homeland Security, House of Representatives, 111th Cong. 14 (2009) (Testimony of Barry Krisberg). Retrieved from: https://babel.hathitrust.org/cgi/pt?id=mdp.39015085454323;view=1up;seq=20.

Rasheed, S. (2018). From hostility to hospitality: Teaching about race and privilege in a post-election climate. *Studies in Philosophy and Education*, *37*(3), 231-245.

Rosenberg, A., Groves. A. K. & Blankenship, K. M. (2017). Comparing Black and White drug offenders: Implications for racial disparities in criminal justice and reentry policy and programming. *Journal of Drug Issues*, *47*(1), 132-142.

Stevenson, B. (2014). *Just Mercy: A Story of Justice and Redemption.* New York: Spiegel & Grau.

Tatum, B. D. (2017). *Why Are All the Black Kids Sitting Together in the cafeteria? And Other Conversations about Race.* New York: Basic Books.

Tyler, T. (2006). *Why People Obey the Law.* Princeton, NJ: Princeton University Press.

Unah, I. & Wright, V. (2015) Divided by race: Differences in the perceptions of justice. In D. Johnson, P.Y. Warren, & A. Farrell (Eds.), *Deadly Injustice: Trayvon Martin, Race, and the Criminal Justice System*, (245-274). New York: New York University Press.

Vito, A. G., Grossi, E. L. & Higgins, G. E. (2017). The issue of racial profiling in traffic stop citations. *Journal of Contemporary Criminal Justice*, *33*(4), 431-450.

Walker, S., Spohn, C. & DeLone, M. (2017). *The Color of Justice: Race, ethnicity, and crime in America* (6th ed.). Boston: Cengage Learning.

Western, B. (2007). *Punishment and inequality in America.* New York: Russell Sage Foundation.

Wilson, W. J. (2012). *The Truly Disadvantaged: The Inner City, the Underclass, and Public Policy* (2nd ed.). Chicago: The University of Chicago Press.

In: A Closer Look at Criminal Justice
Editors: J. A. Cooper and K. G. Jachimowski
ISBN: 978-1-53615-782-6

Chapter 2

DOCTORAL PROGRAMS AND THE POWER OF PRIVILEGE: WIDENING THE NET OF EDUCATIONAL OPPORTUNITY

Daniel Scott[*]
University of West Florida, Pensacola, FL, US

ABSTRACT

As a first-generation college student in the United States, advancing from an undergraduate to graduate program can be extremely challenging (Thayer, 2000; Somers, Woodhouse, & Cofer, 2004; Lundberg, Schreiner, Hovaguimaian, & Miller, 2007). Coupled with other barriers to higher education, students without racial, class, gender, and other privileges face ample disadvantages when applying to both undergraduate and graduate programs. Due to the intense funneling process used to select their applicants, doctoral programs, in particular, tend to select a strong pool of students mostly from highly prestigious programs. However, students from lesser-known schools or less privileged backgrounds tend to struggle to survive (or even exist) in these elitist, white-dominated spaces. The field frequently critiques the criminal justice system for favoring more privileged groups of people, however we, too, find it imperative for graduate education in criminology and criminal justice to reflect critically upon its own selection criteria, curricula, and biases. This chapter highlights the personal experiences of the author as a first-generation college student as they transitioned from lower tier programs to those that are considered more prestigious. From these examples, this chapter illustrates how systemic disregard for educational opportunity (or lack thereof) reproduces and often exacerbates some of the very inequalities that the discipline aims to ameliorate. This leads into the author's experience working at a mid-level graduate program, which highlights how the narrow funneling process of more prestigious graduate programs exacerbates what excellent students from lesser known programs must do in order to achieve a doctoral degree in Criminal Justice and/or Criminology. The chapter concludes with suggestions for moving the disciplines of criminal justice and

[*] Author's Email: dscott@iup.edu

criminology forward with regard to graduate training and strategies for widening the net of educational opportunity for students from a range of backgrounds.

INTRODUCTION

More and more people in the United States are attempting to achieve advanced degrees, but the likelihood of enrolling in a university and obtaining a degree will vary based on an individual's demographics. For example, when examining the likelihood of achieving a degree there are students with demographics of "disadvantage that tend to be negatively associated with degree attainment, which include low family income, and first-generation (Thayer, 2000)." The current chapter discusses the struggles associated with various demographics and degree attainment but focuses primarily on first generation struggles. Additional research has highlighted that being first generation in combination with being multi-ethnic reduces the likelihood of degree attainment (Somers, Woodhouse, & Cofer, 2004). In fact, even if a first-generation student comes from a high-income family they are at a disadvantage when it comes to staying in college. This is crucial to understand because even when taking academic ability into account students from lower SES families have a higher probability of not attending college compared to higher SES students (Akerheilm, et al., 1998).

Due to being first generation these students are unlikely to know what the college experience will be like (Willett, 1989). These students do not necessarily know how best to manage their time, they are unaware of the various costs associated with college beyond tuition, and generally do not really understand how higher education functions (Richardson & Skinner, 1992). The struggle of cultural boundaries has been found to be prominent among first generation college students (Rendon, 1996). To the point that it limits their involvement in cultural experiences. This can be an even bigger struggle for first generation minority students on a predominantly white campus (Chen & Carroll, 2005).

It's important to understand that first generation students tend to come from families where the question is whether or not to attend college (Somers, Woodhous, & Cofer, 2004). Given the students background they tend to want to avoid debt of any kind, but this could due to a lack of knowledge, or other family members may have poor experiences with student loans that influences their decision. Financial need is a major issue among first-generation low-income college students. This is such a concern that students will spend more time invested in activities off campus if it means making or saving money (Inman & Mayes, 1999; Nuñez & Cuccaro-Alamin, 1998). This also might potentially deter extending a student's stay into graduate study because in their mind that will cost more money and is more time away from the workforce. Additionally, graduate applications cost money except in unique circumstances. A primary concern is therefore finances. First generation college students may be unaware of the funding opportunities at the graduate level (also see Levine & Nidiffer, 1996), and given how much they spent on their undergraduate degree they may feel as though they shouldn't continue their education beyond a bachelors. Scholarship has also highlighted that students looking to attain advanced degrees have a lower probability of desisting for minor obstacles, but higher degree goals do not increase the likelihood of obtaining a bachelors' degree (Somers et al., 2004).

Why is this Chapter in a Criminal Justice Book?

In the fields of Criminology and Criminal Justice researchers, scholars, and teachers alike love to critique the system as it stands. Policing research has argued that racial bias exists in conjunction with police stops (Gelman, Fagan, & Kiss, 2007; Duran, 2009; Warren et al., 2006), and arrests (Beckett, Nyrop, Pfingst, 2006; Parker, Stults, & Rice, 2005). There have been high profile police incidents in which police practices have been questioned including Rodney King, and Ferguson just to name a couple. In addition, some research has also examined how law enforcement oppress the poor (Websdale 2001), and how the system itself is developed in a way to keep the poor down, and rich up (Reiman & Leighton 2015). Courts research and scholarship has argued that there are disparities in sentencing related to race (Mustard, 2001; Johnson, 2003), and class (Freeman, 2006; Levy-Pounds, 2007; Myers, 1987). Furthermore, work has also proposed that there are disparities across gender (Doerner & Demuth, 2010; Starr, 2014) and age (Doerner & Demuth, 2014; Steffensmeier, Kramer, & Ulmer, 1995). Furthermore, research has established issues with inequalities related to mass incarceration (Pettit & Western, 2004), issues in effective treatment (Farabee et al., 1999; Cullen & Johnson, 2011), recidivism (Gendreau, Little, & Goggin, 1996; Green & Winik, 2010), and its negative impact on released offenders and their communities (Clear, 2009; Wheelock, 2005).

The academic fields of Criminology and Criminal Justice are at the perfect position to make a difference within the Criminal Justice System, practitioner positions, and the discipline(s). This is an academic discipline that constantly critiques aspects of the system, and argues for significant changes in policing, courts, corrections, and everything in between. These changes frequently relate to addressing inequalities in the system related to race, income, sex/gender, etc. Given that the field is young and relatively prominent at public teaching universities and emerging at other institutions this is the perfect time for them to adjust the graduate student selection process from recruitment all the way to PhD.

As it stands though the academic discipline continues to conform to the traditional standards set by the more established disciplines before them. Given the founders of this discipline came from these other more established fields it makes sense, but this doesn't have to be the case. Graduate programs have made some progress in this area, selecting certain applicants from lesser known institutions or areas. But so much more could be done to provide individuals from lesser privileged backgrounds not just an opportunity to get into a well-funded graduate program, but to help them succeed in such a program.

By taking the lead on providing education to more underprivileged groups the discipline will evolve and grow with a more refreshing and versatile perspective that is arguably needed in academia in general. This will bring new ideas, and new approaches to teaching and research, and show other disciplines that just because a student comes from an IV league school with a good GPA does not mean they are a better applicant.

Privileged Ignorance

Coming from a low-income family and performing well in high school it was expected that I would go to college. But when you are a first-generation college student it is difficult to know what the best path is. For me, I took one look at the cost of a private liberal arts school and decided on an affordable public teaching school less than an hour from home. It wasn't about what excellent programs they had, or about the prestige of the university. It literally came down to affordability and feasibility from the perspective of a first-generation high school student.

This story isn't unique. I hear it time and time again from the students I teach. I heard it from my peers when I was a college student. It is something I have discussed many times with my spouse who grew up in a family of Ph.Ds. From the outset first generation, low income college students are at a disadvantage even if they perform well in high school. This isn't to say they are less likely to get into college, but they are not necessarily aware of all their options such as scholarship or financial aid opportunities, and that they could potentially afford to move far from home for a university that's right for them.

The only reason I was able to attend graduate school and obtain my PhD from a well ranked Criminology program was by random chance. Due to my lack of knowledge in academia at the time I assumed I would have to pay for graduate school. Given how much my undergraduate degree was costing me, I assumed I would go into the work force and attend graduate school later if I wanted. By chance, I had an interaction with an individual that directed the McNair Scholar's program on campus. This program revealed to me the options for achieving funding for both a master's and doctorate, and showed me that applying directly to a doctoral program was not uncommon. In order to conduct my own research, I cold-contacted professors at other universities. I was overjoyed to receive a positive response from a professor in a well ranked Criminology program. At the time I did not realize how big of a deal this was, but given my lower GRE score, I know the individual's letter of recommendation had a huge impact on my admission to graduate school.

Upon entering graduate school, I slowly learned how far I had "jumped" in terms of academic prestige. Every single one of the people in my cohort either had a degree from a large R1 university, or a small private liberal arts school. It appeared that I was an outlier. When I talked with many of my peers they said where they went to school previously, and immediately assumed I would be familiar with the institution. It almost felt embarrassing to say what university I attended (even though I should have felt proud, I was currently enrolled at the same institution as they were). There was an assumption of prestige that occurred not only among my peers but also with faculty members. One clear example from my first year as a graduate student was a professor from a different department that taught one of my classes asking what school I came from. Upon hearing the name, he gave me an extremely confused and almost surprised look that said, "What are you doing here?" I need to be clear here, most of my peers and faculty in my department were extremely supportive and did not react differently upon hearing where I came from. In fact, I really loved my program, and my years spent there were some of the best years of my life. These were isolated incidents that just stuck with me throughout my graduate career and beyond.

A clear example that highlights an assumption of privilege was during my first year of graduate study. I was out at a site with a research team conducting interviews. The place was far enough away that we had to fly there and stay the night. As a first-year graduate student I was unaware of how funding for travel worked. For the flight I learned that it was a reimbursement process, so I spent most of the money in my name and off I went. Not realizing the hotel would also be a reimbursement process resulted in a surprised reaction from me that confused most of the research team. One student seemed to understand my struggle, and my unease with revealing that I was unable to afford the room. He offered to share his room, and to put it all on his credit card. As this would save the research team money overall there was no complaint. Looking back on it, I know any of them would have helped pay for my room without question. But at the time I had just met them and was still learning what was expected of me as a graduate student. Furthermore, there was an assumption that I would just be able to afford it. This assumption of privilege happened another time when my out of state driver's license expired during my first year at graduate school, and new license had not yet come in the mail. I was planning on flying the next day, and I did not have an official form of identification. An older peer of mine suggested that I use my passport and was surprised to hear that I did not have a passport at the time.

The assumption of privilege is potent at these institutions. After arriving at my graduate program, I was so happy to have made into a program that was going to fund my education and pay me for it. Many of my peers would complain constantly about how little we got paid, and rightfully so. We were getting paid below the poverty line but given my background I was just so grateful that I was getting paid to go to school at all. In fact, I was able to go from having no savings to some savings by the time I was done with graduate school without adding any more debt to my record. This is important to point out, because many students at other graduate programs whether it is a masters or doctoral program are paying thousands of dollars every year and working additional jobs just to achieve their degree. This is not necessarily because they do not qualify for the graduate programs that provide full funding. These students have a severe lack of knowledge on what their options are beyond undergrad, and what they should be doing while obtaining their bachelor's degree to improve their options.

Upon finishing my PhD, I started a job as an assistant professor at a school with a PhD program that is generally considered to be of a lower ranking. It is an excellent program that does not necessarily have the name recognition of some other programs and is also very limited in the amount of funding it can offer. The program offers a terminal master's and PhD with partial and full assistantships. These assistantships if they are full time cover everything but fees and provide a small stipend that is extremely difficult to live on. Once the student begins teaching courses though they receive twice the amount of pay, but their tuition is no longer covered. The financial struggle is so extreme that many of these students will work a second job just to make enough to survive. This wasn't something I ever considered as a graduate student because even though I wasn't making a lot, I was making enough to survive. The result of this are graduate students that are overstressed and overworked not due to just the academic rigor of the program, but because students are worried about paying tuition, going further in debt, and working additional jobs just to get by. This produces students that are working extremely hard to succeed, similar to those students in programs that provide more funding, but they are forced to split their time between their school and other jobs that provide additional income. In addition to being from a lower ranked program this places them at an additional disadvantage when it comes to being a competitive applicant in academia. They are not able to devote as much time to various academic goals such as improving their writing, familiarizing themselves with the literature, learning various techniques for analyzing data, seeking external funding, and publishing work while in school

Students in programs with better funding opportunities are able to focus completely on succeeding academically. This allows them to devote most of their time on becoming an expert in their area of expertise without having to divide their time with a job that is not at all related to their future career goals. Many times, these students with less funding don't even know there are other opportunities out there to get paid more for completing their PhD. The argument usually is they should have done their research, but the reality is many of these students thought they did. I only knew about the different opportunities for graduate study because of the McNair Scholars program. The other argument out there is that the faculty need to be pursuing more external funding then. This is true to an extent, but graduate students in many other programs are getting paid noticeably more for teaching assistantships and have summer teaching opportunities.

Another issue that comes up is how late in the term these students even know if they are receiving funding for the next term. Frequently, the students do not find out until a few weeks before the semester even starts. It is also not a guarantee that they will receive funding. This forces many of them to search elsewhere for teaching positions while completing their dissertation. Many of these students are then forced to commute an hour or two to teach classes at a different university, they are rarely ever on the campus where they are enrolled and are struggling to complete their dissertation on time. Frequently these students are also local and believe they will be able to find a job in the state. Many do not understand or realize that obtaining a career in academia usually means moving out of state, and usually out of the region. Given these struggles it is important to develop strategies and provide resources to aide these students that are struggling to jump cultural divides in order to succeed.

THE FUTURE OF CRIMINOLOGY AND CRIMINAL JUSTICE

Scholarship has suggested that since the selection of graduate program tends to be influenced by various demographic characteristics, in order to diversify graduate enrollment, it might be necessary to include faculty in recruitment, and provide more accommodating program requirements due to the increasingly stressful and complicated lives of students (Lei, Simon, & Chuang (2010). Providing additional visits to campus and including resources to assist students with specific needs such as international students could also be beneficial.

Literature has proposed addressing the common obstacles that first generation and low-income college students tend to have including limited financial resources, limited knowledge of the university environment including expectations and operations, as well inadequate preparation and minimal familial support (Somers et al., 2004). Universities can assist with these obstacles by aiding with the transition to college, assisting with the issues of cultural conflict that may occur between home and college, and being as supportive as possible (Thayer, 2000).

Rendon (1994) argues that non-traditional students have a higher probability of university participation when they are invited. One avenue would be to take this argument to the next level. Universities should make it a priority to inform their non-traditional students of their options for continuing their education including their financial aid opportunities in the form of assistantships and fellowships. In addition, universities should also assist these students early on with what they should be doing to be competitive beyond just performing well academically. This is similar to Lundberg et al. (2007) who proposed the "need for institutional agents to create opportunities in a way that validates the experience of first-generation students and students of color and embraces the cultural values they bring to the college experience."

It is possible that participation in college experiences is more beneficial for first-generation students compared to continuing-generation students (Pascarella, Piersen, Wolniak, & Terenzini, 2004). Thus, by increasing participation in the college experience among first generation students, this will allow them to noticeably increase their social capital and help to succeed in a higher education setting. Establishing university programming for students of all levels to increase interaction among students that are different than themselves could benefit campuses in general (Lundberg et al., 2007). Creating this environment in which students realize they are not alone in their differences is arguably essential to the success of those students with less privileged backgrounds at all levels of education.

Park (1950) proposes a cultural dichotomy where first-generation students do not want to sever their past, and never completely transition into this new culture where they desire to be due to preconceptions. The obstacles and transitions that occur in the movement from high school to college related to "family, interpersonal, academic, and organizational pulls and pushes that shape student learning and persistence" (Terenzini, 1994) arguably continue when the student continues into graduate study. Certain obstacles become more familiar such as the school environment, but family struggles may persist, and the student may struggle with feeling like they do not belong.

One way to understand this limited information could be looked at as cultural capital, or how "comfortable and familiar with the norms and culture of the institution" (Lundberg et al., 2007). Specifically, how a student navigates college life. Furthermore, first generation students may experience outsider syndrome. It is with these first-generation students that initiative taken by faculty and staff is crucial for retention. These individuals can support these students through providing information and helping guide them through the college environment. This helps supplement these students in their areas in which they are lacking knowledge, experience, and/or confidence.

Conversely, faculty perceptions reveal that graduate student success is primarily determined by student motivation, learning experiences, and the possession of necessary information and techniques (Gilmore, Wofford, & Maher, 2016). The focus is primarily on the graduate student, identifying that if they fail it is their own fault, and not the department or university. Students enrolled in graduate study could be proactive in developing academic relationships, and in pursuing involvement in research and scholarship. Faculty advisors can also play an essential role in the persistence of their students throughout the program, especially at the graduate level. I can attest to this from personal experience with a supportive departmental staff, faculty advisor/chair, and dissertation committee.

Excellent students come from a variety of programs, but many times the students from lower tiered programs do not understand or are even aware of the opportunities that are available to them. Sanders & Landrum (2012) surveyed psychology majors to determine what undergraduates perceived as important for an application to a graduate program. Students placed experience with research, reference letters, and academic performance of the highest importance.

Based on my experience as a student and professor many of these students will apply to programs based on what ones they believe they will get into. They don't seem to realize how competitive their application can be, so they believe that they should only apply to programs that they perceive are more at their "level." Even if a student has research experience, excellent letters of reference, and performs well academically they may still feel inadequate based on where they come from, and where they are currently.

Top programs could advertise and work more with other programs. Providing information to universities with terminal bachelors and terminal master's degrees about what opportunities there are for students interested in pursuing a degree in Criminology and/or Criminal Justice. Regional and National conferences are an excellent opportunity for representatives from doctoral programs to discuss the opportunities available to students that are accepted. Furthermore, encouraging active attendance and providing funding opportunities for undergraduates and masters' students that present at conferences. This will provide essential networking opportunities and could result in a funding offer to a doctoral program. This strategy is going to take effort from all types of universities to succeed.

Changing the nature of academia is no easy task, but if one field were to start such as Criminology and Criminal Justice maybe others will follow. As mentioned at the beginning of the chapter frequently scholarship argues for significant changes within the Criminal Justice System, so it would make sense for the field to pioneer the needed changes to not only make advanced degrees more accessible for all college students, but also develop and implement strategies to increase their probability for success. For example, not placing as much emphasis on the GRE or school name. There is an assumption in the field that if the professors are good researchers then they are good teachers that are producing good undergraduate students. When, undergraduate students at research institutions rarely interact with professors, and primarily work with graduate students. This is not to say that these professors are not potentially good teachers, but it is not something that should be assumed. Furthermore, extensive weight on the GRE is a major issue. Even though it can highlight many students that are likely to be successful, it removes many students from consideration who may be just as likely or more likely to succeed. These students may not test well, or maybe they just do not do well with the specific GRE testing format. Certain programs will attempt to put less weight on the GRE score, or at least claim to, but when it comes to the students that are accepted old practices still tend to die hard with few exceptions.

Programs with a terminal master's degree could also train their students to succeed in doctoral programs in addition to coursework. For example, funding should be set aside for a required conference presentation and attendance. This would allow students to talk to academics and professionals in the region/country and provide the students with essential academic experience to improve their application. Additionally, a thesis in which research is conducted should be required for any student that is planning to attend a doctoral program. This will also assist in enhancing their application, including a well thought out and well written sample of their work.

As an official academic field Criminology and Criminal Justice is young compared to most others. The field should set an example for increasing equality within all graduate programs. It's crucial to get past this mindset that focuses on prestige and name recognition. It's not to say these aren't factors to consider, but they shouldn't necessarily be given as much importance as they seem to be given. It is ironic to be in a field that frequently critiques the inequalities of the system but does little when it comes to changing the inequalities within their own academic discipline. This isn't to say things aren't being done. Various individuals from lower tiered institutions make it into excellent programs that are fully funded, but there could be so much more. Furthermore, these prestigious programs need to be aware of the struggles their students might experience beyond the classroom. Different resources therefore need to be in place to assist these students, as well as inform the more privileged students and faculty. Especially if they truly want these students to succeed.

REFERENCES

Akerhielm, K., Berger, J., Hooker, M. & Wise, D. (1998). *Factors related to college enrollment: Final report* (Mathematica Publication No. 3360-028). Washington, DC: U.S. Department of Education.

Beckett, K., Nyrop, K. & Pfingst, L. (2006). Race, drugs, and policing: Understanding disparities in drug delivery arrests. *Criminology*, *44*(1), 105-137.

Chen, X. & Carroll, C. D. (2005). *First-generation students in postsecondary education: A look at their college transcripts* (NCES 2005–171). U.S. Department of Education, National Center for Education Statistics. Washington, DC: U.S. Government Printing Office.

Clear, T. R. (2009). *Imprisoning communities: How mass incarceration makes disadvantaged neighborhoods worse*. Oxford University Press.

Doerner, J. K. & Demuth, S. (2010). The independent and joint effects of race/ethnicity, gender, and age on sentencing outcomes in US federal courts. *Justice Quarterly*, *27*(1), 1-27.

Doerner, J. K. & Demuth, S. (2014). Gender and sentencing in the federal courts: Are women treated more leniently? *Criminal Justice Policy Review*, *25*(2), 242-269.

Durán, R. J. (2009). Legitimated oppression: Inner-city Mexican American experiences with police gang enforcement. *Journal of Contemporary Ethnography*, *38*(2), 143-168.

Farabee, D., Prendergast, M., Cartier, J., Wexler, H., Knight, K. & Anglin, M. D. (1999). Barriers to implementing effective correctional drug treatment programs. *The Prison Journal*, *79*(2), 150-162.

Freeman, N. J. (2006). Socioeconomic Status and Belief in a Just World: Sentencing of Criminal Defendants 1. *Journal of Applied Social Psychology*, *36*(10), 2379-2394.

Gelman, A., Fagan, J. & Kiss, A. (2007). An analysis of the New York City police department's "stop-and-frisk" policy in the context of claims of racial bias. *Journal of the American Statistical Association*, *102*(479), 813-823.

Gilmore, J. A., Wofford, A. M. & Maher, M. A. (2016). The flip side of the attrition coin: faculty perceptions of factors supporting graduate student success. *International Journal of Doctoral Studies*, *11*(unknown), 419-439.

Green, D. P. & Winik, D. (2010). Using random judge assignments to estimate the effects of incarceration and probation on recidivism among drug offenders. *Criminology*, *48*(2), 357-387.

Gendreau, P., Little, T. & Goggin, C. (1996). A meta-analysis of the predictors of adult offender recidivism: What works! *Criminology*, *34*(4), 575-608.

Inman, W. E. & Mayes, L. (1999). The importance of being first: Unique characteristics of first generation community college students. *Community College Review*, *26*(4), 3-22.

Johnson, B. D. (2003). Racial and ethnic disparities in sentencing departures across modes of conviction. *Criminology*, *41*(2), 449-490.

Lei, S. A. & Chuang, N. K. (2010). Demographic Factors Influencing Selection of an Ideal Graduate Institution: A Literature Review with Recommendations for Implementation. *College Student Journal*, *44*(1).

Levine, A. & Nidiffer, J. (1996). *Beating the Odds: How the Poor Get to College. The Jossey Bass Higher and Adult Education Series*. Jossey-Bass, Inc., 350 Sansome St., San Francisco, CA 94104.

Levy-Pounds, N. (2007). From the frying pan into the fire: how poor women of color and children are affected by sentencing guidelines and mandatory minimums. *Santa Clara L. Rev.*, *47*, 285.

Lundberg, C. A., Schreiner, L. A., Hovaguimian, K. & Slavin Miller, S. (2007). First-generation status and student race/ethnicity as distinct predictors of student involvement and learning. *NASPA Journal*, *44*(1), 57-83.

Mustard, D. B. (2001). Racial, ethnic, and gender disparities in sentencing: Evidence from the US federal courts. *The Journal of Law and Economics*, *44*(1), 285-314.

Myers, M. A. (1987). Economic inequality and discrimination in sentencing. *Social Forces*, *65*(3), 746-766.

Nunez, A. M. & Cuccaro-Alamin, S. (1998). *First-Generation Students: Undergraduates Whose Parents Never Enrolled in Postsecondary Education. Statistical Analysis Report. Postsecondary Education Descriptive Analysis Reports.*

Park, R. E. (1950). *Race and culture*. New York, NY: Free Press.

Pascarella, E. T., Pierson, C. T., Wolniak, G. C. & Terenzini, P. T. (2004). First-generation college students: Additional evidence on college experiences and outcomes. *The Journal of Higher Education*, *75*(3), 249-284.

Pettit, B. & Western, B. (2004). Mass imprisonment and the life course: Race and class inequality in US incarceration. *American Sociological Review*, *69*(2), 151-169.

Reiman, J. & Leighton, P. (2015). *Rich Get Richer and the Poor Get Prison, The (Subscription): Ideology, Class, and Criminal Justice*. Routledge.

Rendón, L. I. (1996). Life on the border. *About Campus*, *1*(5), 14-20

Sanders, C. E. & Landrum, R. E. (2012). The graduate school application process: What our students report they know. *Teaching of Psychology*, *39*(2), 128-132.

Somers, P., Woodhouse, S. R. & Cofer, Sr. J. E. (2004). Pushing the boulder uphill: The persistence of first-generation college students. *Naspa Journal*, *41*(3), 418-435.

Starr, S. B. (2014). Estimating gender disparities in federal criminal cases. *American Law and Economics Review*, *17*(1), 127-159.

Steffensmeier, D., Kramer, J. & Ulmer, J. (1995). Age differences in sentencing. *Justice Quarterly*, *12*(3), 583-602.

Terenzini, P. T. (1994). Good news and bad news: The implications of Strange's propositions for research. *Journal of College Student Development*.

Thayer, P. B. (2000). *Retention of students from first generation and low income backgrounds.* Department of Education, Washington, DC; National TRIO Clearinghouse, Washington, DC.

Warren, P., Tomaskovic-Devey, D., Smith, W., Zingraff, M. & Mason, M. (2006). Driving while black: Bias processes and racial disparity in police stops. *Criminology*, *44*(3), 709-738.

Websdale, N. (2001). *Policing the Poor: From Slave Plantation to Public Housing*. Upne.

Wheelock, D. (2005). Collateral consequences and racial inequality: Felon status restrictions as a system of disadvantage. *Journal of Contemporary Criminal Justice*, *21*(1), 82-90.

Willet, L. (1989). Are two-year college students first generation students? *Community College Review*, *17*, 2, Fall.

In: A Closer Look at Criminal Justice
Editors: J. A. Cooper and K. G. Jachimowski
ISBN: 978-1-53615-782-6

Chapter 3

EDUCATING THE INCARCERATED: AN EXAMINATION OF THE BENEFITS AND MAJOR BARRIERS IN PRISON EDUCATION

Blair Hillegass*
Indiana University of Pennsylvania, Indiana, PA, US

ABSTRACT

Correctional education has moved in and out of public support. Political agendas have cut federal funded Pell Grants for postsecondary education in prisons and resulted in a large decline in the inmate population that is enrolled in educational programs. Along with funding, there are many other factors that create barriers to inmates participating in programs or completing programs. Prisons also face difficulties in providing quality education programs that meet the needs of inmates who may suffer from learning disabilities or low literacy and quantitative abilities. Research in the field suggests that education, especially postsecondary education, improves inmate behavior and self-esteem as well as reduces recidivism rates through increased employment opportunities. This chapter intends to examine the major barriers to educational attainment for inmates and propose strategies of overcoming some of these issues. This chapter concludes with a discussion of Pell Grant funding for inmates.

INTRODUCTION

Many people do not think about inmates as a population of people that will be entering back into their communities. Currently, 1 in 115 adults are in jail or prison (Gelb & Stevenson, 2017). This accounts for a large amount of the population, and when these

* Author's Email: cwns@iup.edu

people complete their sentences and enter back into society, they need to be prepared to live as law abiding citizens. According to a study conducted by Alpher, Durose, and Markman at the Bureau of Justice Statics (BJS), "An estimated 68% of released prisoners were arrested within 3 years, 79% within 6 years, and 83% within 9 years" (2018). These inmates are returning to their communities, continuing to commit crimes, and ultimately return to the criminal justice system.

Upon release, previous inmates have a multitude of factors working against them; Coley and Barton (2006) describe three main factors. The first is that ex-prisoners have a rather difficult time securing a job and earning a wage decent enough to live on as well as support their families. The second factor working against ex-prisoners is that since they have been incarcerated, they lack recent work experience or continuity of work history. The third factor then is that many employers are reluctant to hire anyone with a criminal record (Coley & Barton, 2006). Rehabilitation needs to be a major focal point in the system to help inmates return to their communities as law abiding citizens and overcome the factors working against them.

Large amounts of research have been dedicated to reducing recidivism rates, and correctional education has proven to have links to lower recidivism rates. For this reason, it is imperative to investigate the major barriers to education that are faced by individual inmates and to prisons in providing education for inmates. This chapter will give an overview of the history of inmate education and examine the different types of inmate education programs as well as their prevalence. Then, it will inspect the benefits correctional education provides for inmates as well as communities. Followed by a discussion of the barriers to inmate success in educational programs as well as the barriers that prisons face in providing inmate education programs. Finally, this chapter concludes with a discussion of Pell Grant funding for inmates, with rebuttals for three main arguments to providing Pell Grants to inmates.

SUMMARY OF THE LITERATURE

History

Education has always existed in American prisons, but the forms, purposes, and levels of institutional support for prisoner education have changed. Beginning with the Quakers and the first American prison, the Walnut Street Jail in Philadelphia, inmates were taught reading, writing, and arithmetic (Coley & Barton, 2006). Originally, education for confined persons consisted of religious studies, or simply learning to read the Bible to enhance their morals (Messemer, 2011, Kim & Clark, 2013, Coley & Barton, 2006). Gehring (1995) refers to the period of 1789 – 1875 as the period of Sabbath schools, where prisoners' only education was by a minister who volunteered to distribute bibles through the cells and instruct inmates on the alphabet to eventually read the Bible. With the rise of the industrial revolution in the United States, brought a rise in vocational training in prisons to prepare prisoners to contribute to the workforce upon release (Messemer, 2011). It was not until the 1960s that academic education became the primary focus, and secondary and postsecondary programs were offered in prisons (Tewksbury & Vannostrand, 1996, p. 275).

In 1965 the Higher Education Act provided federal funding for low income citizens trying to obtain a postsecondary education. In 1972 the Pell Grant program was established for this purpose and included funding to inmates as well (Mercer, 2009, p. 159). Although there had been prisoners in the United State taking college courses since the 1920s, a large increase in participation was brought about with Pell Grant funding for prisoners (McCarty, 2006). McCarty (2006) explains, "In 1976, there were 237 prisons that offered degree programs, compared to 12 in 1965, and by 1990, there were 772 college programs being offered around the United States" (p. 88). Beginning in the 1980s, the United States began a "tough on crime" agenda, and many people were questioning the value and benefits of education in corrections, particularly postsecondary education (McCarty, 2006). Ultimately, in 1994, the Violent Crime Control and Law Enforcement Act denied Pell Grants to inmates, which resulted in a significant drop in inmate participation in postsecondary programs (McCarty, 2006).

Escobar, Jordan, & Lohrasbi (2015) explain that most inmates will be eligible again for Pell Grants after their release. However, in 1998 an amendment was made to the 1965 Higher Education Act that barred anyone with a drug conviction from receiving Pell Grants. This amendment still exists; however, the amendment now only applies to those that received a drug conviction while they were also receiving a Pell Grant. This is the only conviction that warrants elimination of federal financial aid. Individuals can gain this funding back after completing certain requirements. Escobar, Jordan, & Lohrasbi (2015) go on to explain, "Many continue to question the role that race and class play in which communities are targeted by police for drug crime surveillance (Alexander, 2012; JFA Institute, 2007; Mauer & King, 2007). Therefore, it is believed that those who are most likely to be impacted by the AEP are the poor and people of color" (p. 36). In 2016, President Obama and the U.S. Department of Education announced the Second Chance Pell Pilot Program. The program serves as an experiment that will allow some incarcerated individuals to receive Pell Grants and participate in a postsecondary education program (U.S. Department of Education, 2016). This program is part of a larger effort in improving correctional education (U.S. Department of Education, 2016).

Education Programs

Inmate educational programs vary from prison to prison and state to state. The purposes of these programs may also vary based on the type of program. The main prison educational programs include, "…literacy, General Equivalency Degree (GED), adult basic education (ABE), vocational training, apprenticeships, and college classes" (Pompoco, Wooldredge, Lugo, Sullivan, & Latessa, 2017, p. 518). Not every program is offered in every prison. In fact, some prisons may not even have an education program. Stephan (2008) indicates 85% of federal or state prisons offer some type of educational program. However, the availability of the different types of programs differs greatly. According to the Federal Bureau of Prisons, all federal prisons offer literacy classes and require inmates that do not hold a high school diploma or an equivalent certificate to participate in a GED program for 240 hours or until they obtain their GED. Many state prisons have similar requirements. For example, Ohio prisoners that do not have a high school diploma or GED must participate in educational programming for six months (Pompoco et al., 2017, p. 520). However, there is no completion requirement, so if after six months an inmate has not obtained their GED or diploma, they may drop out. Stephan (2008) reported 77% of federal or state prisons offered GED programs. Although this number seems great, this still means that about a quarter of prisons do not have programs to help inmates get a high school degree equivalent. Few prisons offer any type of postsecondary education. According to the Stephan (2008), only 35% of federal or state prisons offer postsecondary education. Inmates that wish to take college courses, usually must pay for coursework themselves (Federal Bureau of Prisons). Vocational classes in federal prisons vary based on the needs of the inmates, prison, and labor market conditions (Federal Bureau of Prisons). Only about half of all state and federal prisons offer vocational classes, literacy and adult basic education classes are offered at a rate of about 67%, and special education classes are only offered in 37% of prisons (Stephan, 2008).

Benefits of Inmate Education Programs

Increased Employment and Wages

Increasing former inmates' employment prospects is a significant factor in lowering recidivism rates. Affording inmates with the opportunity to increase their education may increase the employment prospects, thus, assisting in avoiding new prison sentences (Pompoco et al., 2017). Lockwood, Nally, and Ho (2016) concluded that in their study, post-release employment was the most significant factor in predicting recidivism rates. Inmates who obtain a degree during their incarceration increase their employment prospects and are likely to have a higher income (Duwe & Clark, 2014, Lockwood,

Nally, and Ho, 2016). Duwe and Clark (2014) found earning a secondary degree during incarceration significantly increased the chances of gaining employment after release but did not increase wages or hours worked after release. However, earning a postsecondary degree did lead to an increase in hours worked, and therefore overall wages earned, but did not lead to a significant increase in post-release employment. Inmates with a postsecondary degree worked 176 more hours and earned $2,649 more during the two-year follow up period, than those without a postsecondary degree (p. 471). Duwe and Clark (2014) suggest some possible explanations for these findings. They propose that these results are due to differences in the types of jobs available based on the degree one holds. Someone with a postsecondary degree may be more likely to find a more permanent job with higher skill requirements than someone with a secondary degree.

Higher Self-Esteem

Participating in educational programs has a positive impact on inmates' general attitudes about themselves, and participants experienced feelings of higher self-esteem (Winterfield, Coggeshall, Burke-Storer, Correa, & Tidd, 2009, Meyer et al., 2010, Baranger, Rousseau, Mastrorilli, & Matesanz, 2018). In a study conducted by Meyer et al. (2010), they found that inmates participating in educational programs reported feeling more independent and respected (p. 163-164). Often, inmates feel a sense of purpose when they are involved in education programs (Haulard, 2001, p. 158). Winterfield et al. (2009) found that inmates reported they felt a sense of pride in completing college courses and they were often the first in their family to do so. Many inmates were surprised at how intelligent they felt as well. Some inmates in a women's prison said their self-perception changed and their self-confidence grew in aspects of their lives even outside of school (Baranger et al., 2018).

Recidivism

Perhaps the most important impact of correctional education is the impact on recidivism rates. Inmates that receive an education have lower rates of recidivism (Duwe and Clark, 2014, Pompoco et al., 2017, Winterfield et al., 2009, Batiuk, Lahm, McKeever, Wilcox, and Wilcox, 2005, Kim & Clark, 2013, Nally, Lockwood, Knutson, & Ho, 2012). Providing inmates with an education increases their human capital by equipping them with marketable skills and an increased knowledge. Increased human capital can lead to upward social mobility by making these people more marketable and increasing their chances of gaining legitimate employment (Ubah, 2004, p. 74-75). As we have discussed, the results of correctional education (increased employment, hourly wages, wages earned, and self-esteem) all contribute to inmate success post release. By providing inmates with an education, and increasing these outcomes, recidivism is ultimately decreased. Therefore, through an indirect means, education has significant impacts on lowering recidivism rates by allowing inmates to gain and maintain employment after release.

Nally, Lockwood, Knutson, & Ho, 2012 found that those who did not participate in correctional education programs while incarcerated were 3.7 times more likely to recidivate. Duwe and Clark (2014) indicated that obtaining a postsecondary degree resulted in significantly lower rates of rearrest, reconviction, and new offense reincarceration. Obtaining a postsecondary degree lowered rearrest rates by 14%, reconviction rates by 16% and reincarceration rates by 24%. Pompoco et al. (2017) found reductions in return to prison rates for inmates that completed GED programs, vocational training, apprenticeship programs, and college courses, with GED programs yielding the best results (p. 541). They also found that inmates who only started a program, but did not complete it, did not produce significant decreases in recidivism rates. These results are in part due to higher employment prospects that holding a degree affords upon entering back into the community (Meyer, Fredericks, Borden, & Richardson, 2010, p. 151). In a study conducted by Winterfield et al., (2009), two out of the three prisons studied showed correctional education participation had a statistically significant impact on re-arrest rates within one year of release. In New Mexico, 44.92% of inmates that did not participate in the postsecondary education program were re-arrested, compared to only 39.38% of inmates that did participate in the program. In Massachusetts, 29.73% of inmates that did not participate were rearrested, compared to only 15.79% of inmates that did participate in the program. The third prison in Indiana, showed a marginally significant impact on reincarceration rates within one year of release (p. 11). In a study conducted by Batiuk et al., (2005), it was found that in comparison to GED, vocational, and high school education, participants of the postsecondary education programs had substantially lower recidivism rates (p. 65). Kim and Clark (2013), explored the results of college education on inmates, controlling for self-selection bias, and concluded that obtaining a college education does significantly lower recidivism rates.

Improved Behavior

Some correctional education programs seem to have a positive impact on inmate behavior (Pompoco et al., 2017, Winterfield et al., 2009). Pompoco et al., (2017) found that inmates that participated in college classes or GED programs displayed less violent behavior than inmates that did not participate in any type of educational program (p. 534). This disparity in violent behavior was also present between inmates that completed an educational program and those that only started a program but did not complete the program. Differences in drug offenses existed as well. Pompoco et al. (2017) found that there was a modest difference in drug offenses between those that started a college program and those that did not complete any program (p.535-536). Winterfield et al. (2009) found that inmates reported avoiding prison conflict to remain in their educational program (p. 6). Baranger et al. (2018) studied women who participated in educational courses during their incarceration. Some women in the study said they felt that participating in educational courses was a meaningful and valuable way to spend their time behind bars and they enjoyed the structure of going to classes. They also reported changing their behaviors to stay in the programs so that they would not lose their opportunity to participate. A variety of factors influence an inmate's decision to participate in educational programs while in prison. Winterfield et al., (2009) found that many inmates wanted to participate to broaden their career opportunities, increase their education level and skills, and to use their time during imprisonment to do something positive. They also state that stakeholders reported many inmates were interested in participating in classes to reduce their sentences, however many inmates became genuinely interested in the coursework once beginning the program (p.6).

Based on these findings, implementing educational courses in prisons has the potential to create a safer environment for both inmates and staff (Pompoco et al., 2017). Pryor and Thompkins (2012) reported mixed findings about prisoner's perceptions on correctional education. They found that some prisoners reported only improving their behavior or participating in educational programs solely for the purpose of being released early, and this perception resulted in negative attitudes from both inmates and staff on correctional education. Prisoners felt that staff were using the educational classes as a way to control them, stating that staff would pick and choose who was allowed to participate and who was not. Inmates felt that staff used participation in educational classes as a way to punish them for any small infraction, such as being caught with tobacco. Pryor and Thompkins (2012) reported the negative feelings of staff toward correctional education as well:

> Allowing them to leave their cells to go to their work assignment or to school in exchange for "good behavior," gives us an additional means by which we can control the population. Whether or not educating prisoners has an effect on them being able to get a job when they are released is actually of less concern than our maintaining institutional security. (p. 462)

However, when educational classes were implemented properly many prisoners seemed to perceive these programs as more valuable. Pryor and Thompson (2012) reported one prisoner saying:

> I felt good about myself, man. I felt good. To learn stuff, to know stuff... My walk was different -I had books in my hand... I talked to administration a whole lot different. That's when they started respectin' me cause they knew I was for real, and that's when my level [security level] started droppin' because I wasn't gettin' in trouble no more, you know...It felt good man, felt good as hell. And when they took me away from that place I was sick. I wanted to leave, anybody wants to get from behind them walls, man, especially when it's been an amount of time, you know... but I missed the education. (p. 466)

Educational programs need to be properly implemented for both prisoners and staff to feel that they are valuable.

Major Barriers

Using data from a survey conducted by Rampey, Keiper, Mohadjer, Krenzke, Li, Thornton, and Hogan, (2016), 70% of prisoners surveyed indicated that they wanted to participate in a class or educational program, however, 58% did not participate in any formal educational program while incarcerated. During incarceration, 21% of inmates surveyed obtained a high school diploma or GED, only 2% achieved an associate degree, and 0% earned a bachelor's degree. Educational programs are not accessible or successful in all facilities for a variety of reasons, and inmates that do have access to some type of educational program face numerous challenges to successful completion. Often these challenges are not realized by the public, or sometimes even educators. Some of these barriers to success include lack of physical space, lack of supplies, and a high turnover of inmates due to transfers, paroles, or disciplinary action (Meyer et al., (2010), p. 158.). Other barriers may include the availability of classes or the number of classes an inmate is able to take in a semester, both of which slow the process of attaining a degree (Winterfield et al., 2009, p. 5).

One of the biggest challenges that inmates face is overcoming their own disabilities or shortcomings in education. Students may not have access to a tutor or be able to contact their teachers or academic advisors for help when they need to, which would make things difficult for any student, and more so for students with disabilities or low baseline education levels (Winterfield et al., 2009). To complicate things even more, a lack of qualified teachers makes it difficult to provide programming and guidance for the students. Finally, finding sources of funding can prohibit inmates from participating in a program or prohibit prisons from being able to offer certain programs. These factors when combined, seriously complicate inmate success in correctional education programs. This chapter focuses on five specific barriers: low educational attainment levels, high rates of disabilities, lack of qualified teachers, transfers, and funding for inmate education. Specifically, this chapter will discuss Pell Grant funding in detail and respond to arguments that the general public may have against Pell Grant funding for inmates.

Low Educational Attainment

Inmates typically have a lower level of educational background than the rest of the population. According to a report from the BJS, in 1997, inmates were more likely to only have a high school degree compared to the general population, 41%, compared to 18.4% respectively. When looking at high school diplomas, 22.6% of inmates achieved this compared to 33.2% of the general population. Only12.7% of inmates had a postsecondary education compared to 48.4% of the general population (Harlow, 2003, p. 1). Harlow (2003) also found minority inmates were more likely to have lower levels of education than whites; 23% of whites, 21% of blacks and 15% of Hispanics had only a high school diploma. College level education was low among all three groups; 4% white, 2% black, and 2% of Hispanics had a college degree. Although these statistics are dated, they do reflect the typical trend of inmate education levels today. The National Center for Education Statistics reported, "The U.S. incarcerated population had lower average literacy and numeracy scores than the U.S. household population" (Rampey et al., 2016, p. 34).

Again, the trend here is the incarcerated population typically has a lower education level compared with the rest of the population. This can be challenging when inmates are attempting to get an education behind bars. It is difficult for any student to be successful if they do not have the previous knowledge necessary to navigate a course. Teachers will have to keep in mind that these students are typically at a lower education level than their general student.

Learning Disabilities

Many of the incarcerated population suffers from mental, emotional or learning disabilities, which makes completing an education program difficult. Tolbert (2002), reported that 30% - 50% of inmates had a learning disability, compared to estimates ranging from 3%-15% of the general population (p. 11). In 2010, the National Center for Learning Disabilities found, "1.7% of the U.S. population reports having a learning disability" (p. 26). Of the population of those with learning disabilities, "55% of young adults with learning disabilities reported having some type of involvement with the criminal justice system within eight years of leaving high school" and 32% were arrested (p. 27). Individuals with learning disabilities are likely to make some kind of contact with the criminal justice system at some point in their life. Furthermore, almost half of inmates in U.S. prisons have a learning disability, yet less than half of our prison have special education programming (Stephan, 2008).

Students with learning disabilities, or other types of disabilities, do not process information as other students do, and will require specialized instruction. Typically, an inmate entering prison comes in with an eighth-grade equivalent education or less (Haulard, 2001, p. 158). If the teacher is not properly trained in special education, then the delivery of information will not be effective for these students. Often these students will fall behind in the class or become discouraged from continuing their education. Providing inmates with the proper education, that supports students with disabilities will be the most effective strategy in setting these students up for success in the classroom.

Availability of Teachers

Prisons providing education programs often have issues with staffing teachers. A lack of funding exists for providing certified general education teachers in the classroom (Hall, 2008, p. 316). With a lack of general education teachers, also comes a lack of specialized and special education teachers. Therefore, many of the students may not be getting the proper support that they need. An evaluation of state education programs in California indicated that 98% of programs were not staffed with a special education teacher and the student-to-teacher ratios in the classrooms were not low enough to accommodate those with learning disabilities (Koo, 2016, p. 241). Koo (2016) also discusses the state of special education programs in Illinois; classes lack general education teachers and juvenile correction facilities are struggling to meet the appropriate ratio for special education teachers (p. 241). A lack of special education teachers cannot be addressed until there are enough general education teachers to serve the inmate population. Providing both special education and general education teachers has proven difficult.

Transfers

If an inmate is transferred to a prison that does not offer the program they are currently enrolled in, then there is no possible way for them to continue their education in that program. Their education comes to a halt simply because of things they cannot control. In a qualitative study conducted by Pryor (2013), an inmate revealed his complications in financial aid due to being transferred. This inmate was transferred to another prison and was unable to complete his program. Pryor (2013) explains further,

> Once he was released from prison and attempted to get financial aid so that he could continue his education, school officials informed him that he was ineligible for financial aid because he had not completed the obligation associated with receiving financial aid, mainly by failing to complete the courses he was enrolled in. (p. 468)

Transfers of all types can disrupt the education of a prisoner. By providing prisons with different educational programs, more continuity can be achieved to help keep these students in their programs.

Funding

With a large prison population, there is not enough funding to offer sufficient education for inmates. Although there has been a lot of funding allocated towards corrections, most of that has been used to maintain the large populations and has not been helpful in establishing inmate education programs (Koo, 2016, p. 241). One of the more well-known programs, the federally funded Pell Grants, are no longer offered to inmates. Inmates that could not afford to further their education were able to get assistance in obtaining postsecondary degrees through this program. This program was cut in 1994 due to the "tough on crime" agenda in the United States and the passing of the Violent Crime Control and Law Enforcement Act. Mercer (2009) explains, "The passage of this Act was a pivotal change in the ability of inmates to access higher education opportunities and left states and prison systems with the responsibility for funding the majority of higher education costs in correctional education" (p. 159). Funding for inmate education varies by state and prison system. Some states provide more funds than others. In other states, if an inmate is interested in participating in an education program, the inmate must pay for the program out of pocket (Mercer, 2009, p. 156-159).

Despite the restored efforts to improving correctional education and reentry through the Second Chance Pell Pilot Program, there are many people who still argue Pell Grants should not be provided to inmates. However, the research shows there are many benefits to providing inmates with an education. If prisoners are simply being released with a criminal history, no recent work experience and no education, then they are being set up for failure as it will be difficult for them to gain employment and create meaningful ties to their communities. Pell Grants should be provided to inmates who wish to pursue a postsecondary education in order to further their employment opportunities. The remainder of this chapter refutes arguments that inmates do not deserve an education since they are to be punished during their incarceration, taxpayers should not spend their hard-earned money on providing an education for criminals, and that Pell Grants should not be received by those who committed crimes since there are many law-abiding citizens that deserve them. The main arguments of this chapter are that providing inmates with postsecondary education will have an impact on recidivism rates, is cost effective, will not take away from others, and that inmates are deserving of Pell Grants, especially since they typically have a lower socio-economic status.

Inmates Deserve to Be Punished, Not Rewarded

A widely argued statement is that inmates do not deserve to be rewarded in prison by receiving an education; prison should only serve as a punishment to people that have committed crimes. Mercer (2009) finds, "Federal and state governments appear to support the idea that the purpose of prison is to protect the public, confine dangerous individuals in a humane fashion, and provide rehabilitative opportunities for prison inmates (Federal Bureau of Prisons, 2009; United States Department of Education, 2009)" (n.p.). Those that see incarceration simply as a means of punishment, are not clearly seeing the purposes of incarceration. Rehabilitation is a main goal of incarceration, meaning that the criminal justice system seeks to successfully re-integrate former inmates into society and lower recidivism rates. Reducing recidivism rates was one of the five goals of the criminal justice system in a review by the United States Department of Justice (2013). A great deal of research that has been conducted in the field of correctional education has sought to examine recidivism outcomes. Much of this research supports the statement that correctional education programs are related to lower recidivism rates. However, as we have discussed, this relationship cannot be said to be direct; there are many positive outcomes of correctional education programs that lead to lower recidivism rates.

By providing inmates with a postsecondary education, their job possibilities are broadened due to the degree they now hold. Participating in a postsecondary education program was found to significantly increase inmates' total wages earned, likely due to the type of job they were able to get (Lockwood, Nally, & Ho, 2016). These are crucial factors in inmate reentry. In a qualitative study conducted by Baranger et al., (2018) on inmates' perceptions of correctional education, many inmates reported that after release they faced challenges in gaining employment because of their criminal backgrounds. The researchers noted that earning a degree while incarcerated would be a valuable asset upon release that employers may view favorably and balance out the negative aspect of having a criminal history (p. 508). If prisons do not focus on rehabilitation of inmates, and rather focus to solely punish them, then the cycle of crime will continue. Prisoners will be released with no assets to help them reintegrate back into society and create little ties to their communities, and in turn, continue to commit crime and return to prison. By increasing the chances of gaining employment, recidivism rates are decreased, and crime is ultimately reduced, increasing public safety.

Many people may believe that inmates can wait until after they are released from prison to pursue an education if they want to, but it is not that easy. Upon release inmates face a multitude of issues to figure out that may deal with housing, social relationships, employment, transportation. How can society expect them to be able to focus on furthering their education when their basic needs may not be met? Furthermore, education needs to happen before they leave prison to give them the tools to be successful upon release. Education needs to be part of the rehabilitation process to have the effects that have been discussed.

Why Should Law Abiding Citizens Pay for Criminals' Education with their Tax Dollars?

Many people resent the thought of criminals receiving a federally funded grant, which is ultimately funded by taxpayer money. However, the department of corrections itself is funded by taxpayer money as well. The cost of incarceration versus the cost of education must be weighed to refute this argument. When considering the cost of incarceration, one must take into consideration all the pieces that go into making a prison run. Prison is a 24/7 facility, which means people are working around the clock to maintain the facility, supervise inmates, service the population and provide food, provide mental care and health care, and provide security for the prison (Mai & Subramanian, 2017, p. 7). These costs can increase or decrease depending on the prison population, and the lengths of the sentences. Although the United States prison population has been declining in the past few years, it is still very high and in 2014 was about the same as it was in 2005; over 2 million people were in prison (World Prison Brief, 2014). In 2015, the average annual cost per inmate to run and maintain prisons was $33,274 (Mai & Subramanian, 2017, p. 7). Many will cry that if the Criminal Justice System would not spend so much to provide inmates with such a generous lifestyle, then the cost of incarceration would be lower. However, Mai and Subramanian (2017) found, "One major finding in Vera's analysis is that personnel costs — including salaries, overtime, and benefits —comprised the lion's share of state prison expenditures, making up more than two-thirds (68 percent) of total spending in 2015" (p. 9).

Examining and comparing the costs of educating an inmate while they are in prison to the cost of warehousing an inmate for a year, leads to a cost-savings effect. In a meta-analysis conducted by Davis, Bozick, Steele, Saunders, and Miles (2013) for The RAND Corporation, the average annual cost of correctional education was found to be between $1,400 and $1,744 per inmate, and the average annual cost of incarceration per inmate was between $28,323 and $31,286 (p. 37). In this paper, it has been established that providing an inmate with an education will reduce their chances of recidivism. This means that the inmate will be less likely to return to prison and costing taxpayers about $30,000 per year. To reduce this cost, taxpayers should be investing in correctional education, which is a much lower price to pay. Instead of sending prisoners out into the communities, unprepared to live a law-abiding life, continuing to commit crimes and get locked up again, why not invest in their education and potentially keep them out of prison? Offenders that are able to achieve legitimate employment after release, are not only less likely to recidivate, saving taxpayers money in the long run, but they would also be contributing to taxes.

What about the Law-Abiding Citizens that Deserve Pell Grants?

According to Erisman and Contardo (2005), when Pell Grants were discontinued for prisoners in 1994, the public was largely under the impression that providing Pell Grant funding to inmates would significantly take away funding for law-abiding citizens. The public was under false assumptions about the amount of Pell Grant funding that was allocated to prisoners and non-prisoners (p. x). McCarty (2006) explains, "Legislators framed the debate over federal funding for prisoner higher education in terms of "free" education for prisoners while middle-class and working-class Americans struggled to pay for college" (p. 88). However, this idea is just untrue, and every citizen that needs Pell Grant funding, will receive it.

According to the Institute for Higher Education Policy (1994), the number of prisoners receiving Pell Grants in 1993-1994 was 27,000 (p. 2). The College Board (2014) indicates that in total, there were 3.8 million recipients of Pell Grants. Inmates accounted for less than 0.5% of the population that received Pell Grants. The amount of Pell Grant money received by inmates in 1993-1994 was $35 million, which is less than 1% of the total $6 billion allocated for Pell Grants for all students (Institute for Higher Education Policy, 1994, p. 2). As for the idea that providing inmates with Pell Grants would take away opportunities for eligible law-abiding citizens, the Institute for Higher Education Policy (1994) states:

> The number of prisoners qualifying to receive Pell Grants does not affect how many non-incarcerated students qualify for grants. The Pell program is a “quasi-entitlement” program, meaning that Congress projects how many students it will need to provide with Pell money each year and appropriates that amount. If the number of students qualifying for grants surpasses that approximation, all qualifying students will still receive grants, but at a reduced average amount. (p. 2)

Baum (2015), explains that Pell Grants are allocated based on income, assets, family size and the amount of people in the family that will be attending college, as well as information about the amount that the student and their family may be able to contribute to college expenses (p. 26). When considering the incarcerated population, a clear majority come from low socio-economic backgrounds. There are large differences in income between the general population and the incarcerated population. Using data from the Bureau of Justice Statistics, Rabuy and Kopf (2015) found that prior to incarceration, men had a median annual income of $19,650 and women had a median annual income of $13,890. Compared to the general population of men and women who had median incomes of $41,250 and $23, 745 respectively. Inmates, being economically disadvantaged even prior to incarceration, should be receiving Pell Grant money based on this fact alone. The purpose of Pell Grants is to provide assistance to students in financial need and who come from low income families. Inmates, before, during and for a time after prison, fit this description more so than the general population.

CONCLUSION

An important assumption that has not been addressed throughout this chapter is that the inmates in prison are guilty. It remains unknown exactly how many innocent people spend a chunk of their life behind bars. On top of revoking many of their freedoms and taking off years of their lives, denying them of an education while wrongly incarcerated is an enormous injustice. Correctional education yields benefits not only for the inmates, but for society as a whole. The benefits include higher employment rates and potential wage earnings, feelings of higher self-esteem, lower recidivism rates, and lower inmate misconduct. With these benefits in mind, it is vital to find ways to address the barriers to education among the incarcerated. This chapter has only touched on a few of the barriers to successful completion of educational programs. Inmates typically have lower educational level backgrounds, which can make it difficult to be successful in an educational program. Aside from low education levels, many inmates have not been successful in their past studies because of mental, emotional, or learning disabilities, which U.S. prisons are not equipped to address. Overcoming these obstacles is even more difficult in the prison setting due to lack of resources. Many prisons and jails find it difficult to provide educational programs due to funding and a lack of certified available teachers. On top of all this, inmates may even lose their progress due to transfers.

Recommendations

Ultimately, Pell Grants should be provided to inmates who wish to further their education by obtaining a postsecondary degree. Upon release, having a college degree helps inmates gain employment and increases their potential wages. Education will offset the difficulty of obtaining employment due to a criminal background. By providing inmates with this opportunity, recidivism rates are reduced. If recidivism rates are reduced, then taxpayers are saving money. The cost of warehousing an inmate far exceeds the costs of educating an inmate. Not only will taxpayers be saving money by helping inmates successfully reintegrate back into their communities, but these prior offenders will contribute to taxes by holding a legitimate job. Not only will providing Pell Grants lead to benefits for the inmates and society as whole, but inmates typically make up the most deserving population of people that are deserving of Pell Grants; the economically disadvantaged. The whole concept of Pell Grant funding is to help people that cannot afford college. The prison population holds a lower socio-economic status than does the general population. To critics that say they will be taking money and opportunities away from law-abiding citizen, this statement is just wildly untrue as noted by the Institute for Higher Education Policy. Thanks to the Second Chance Pell Grant Pilot Program, researchers will be able to assess the impacts that a college education has on all the aspects that were discussed in this chapter. Furthermore, by providing Pell Grant funding for postsecondary education in prisons, a portion of the state or other budget can be shifted to support other educational programs or areas of need. This shift in budget could possibly provide additional funding for proper teacher training, or to support lower ratios of general education and special education teachers in the classroom. Clear data needs to be kept on all prisoners that can be transferred from one prison system to another, especially for educational purposes. Inmates need to be assessed before entering an educational program and progress tracked, just like any other student in the public school system. There are many aspects of correctional education that need to be improved upon, and by doing so, the benefits can only increase.

References

Alpher, M., Durose M. R., & Markman J. (2018). *2018 update on prisoner recidivism: A 9-year follow-up period (2005-2014).* Bureau of Justice Statistics Special Report, NCJ 250975. Retrieved from: http://www.bjs.gov/index.cfm?ty=pbdetail&iid=6266

Baranger, J., Rousseau, D., Mastrorilli, M. E., & Matesanz, J. (2018). Doing time wisely: The social and personal benefits of higher education in prison. *The Prison Journal, 98*(4), 490-513.

Batiuk, M. E., Lahm, K. F., Mckeever, M., Wilcox, N., & Wilcox, P. (2005). Disentangling the effects of correctional education: Are current policies misguided? An event history analysis. *Criminal Justice: International Journal of Policy & Practice, 5*(1), 55–74.

Baum, S. (2015). The federal Pell Grant program and reauthorization of the higher education act. *Journal of Student Financial Aid, 45*(3), 23–34.

Carson, E. A., & Sabol, W. J. (2016). *Aging of the state prison population, 1993-2013.* Bureau of Justice Statistics Special Report, NCJ 248766. Retrieved from: http://www.bjs.gov/index.cfm?ty=pbdetail&iid=5602

Coley, R. J., Barton, P. E., & Educational Testing Service, P. N. P. I. C. (2006). *Locked Up and Locked Out: An Educational Perspective on the U.S. Prison Population. Policy Information Report. Educational Testing Service.* Educational Testing Service. Retrieved from http://proxy-iup.klnpa.org/login?url=http://search.ebscohost.com/login.aspx?direct=true&db=eric&AN=ED496101&site=ehost-live

College Board. (2014). *Trends in student aid 2014.* Retrieved from http://trends.collegeboard.org.

Davis, L. M., Bozick, R., Steele, J. L., Saunders, J., & Miles, J. N. V. (2013). *Evaluating the effectiveness of correctional education: A meta-analysis of programs that provide education to incarcerated adults.* Santa Monica, CA: The RAND Corporation.

Duwe, G., & Clark, V. (2014). The effects of prison-based educational programming on recidivism and employment. *The Prison Journal, 94*(4), 454-478.

Erisman, W., & Contardo, J. B. (2005). *Learning to reduce recidivism: A 50-state analysis of postsecondary correctional education policy.* Washington D.C.: The Institute for Higher Education Policy.

Escobar, E. K., Jordan, T. R., & Lohrasbi, E. A. (2015). Redefining lives: Post-secondary education for currently and formerly incarcerated individuals. *The Vermont Connection, 34*(5), 32-41.

Federal Bureau of Prisons. *Education Programs.* Retrieved from: https://www.bop.gov/inmates/custody_and_care/education.jsp.

Gehring, T. (1995). Characteristics of correctional instruction, 1789-1875. *Journal of Correctional Education, 46*(2), 52-59.

Gelb, A. & Stevenson, P. (2017). *U.S. adult incarceration rate declines 13% in 8 years: Share of population behind bars falls back to 1998 level.* The Pew Charitable Trusts. Retrieved from: https://www.pewtrusts.org/en/research-and-analysis/articles/2017/01/12/us-adult-incarceration-rate-declines-13-percent-in-8-years.

Harlow, C. W. (2003). *Education and correctional populations (Bureau of Justice Statistics Special Report, NCJ 195670).* Retrieved from: http://www.bjs.gov/index.cfm?ty=pbdetail&iid=814.

Haulard, E. R. (2001). Adult education: A must for our incarcerated population. *Journal of Correctional Education, 52*(4), 157-159.

Institute for Higher Education Policy. (1994). Pell Grants: Are prisoners the program's biggest problem? *Policy Steps* 1(1): 1-8.

Kim, & Clark. (2013). The effect of prison-based college education programs on recidivism: Propensity score matching approach. *Journal of Criminal Justice, 41*(3), 196-204.

Koo, A. (2016). Comments: Correctional education can make a greater impact on recidivism by supporting adult inmates with learning disabilities. *The Journal of Criminal Law and Criminology 105*(1), 233-269.

Lockwood, S. K., Nally, J. M., & Taiping Ho. (2016). Race, education, employment, and recidivism among offenders in the United States: An exploration of complex issues in the Indianapolis metropolitan area. *International Journal of Criminal Justice Sciences, 11*(1), 57–74.

Mai, C., & Subramanian, R. (2017). *The price of prisons 2015: Examining state spending trends, 2010-2015.* New York, NY: Vera Institute of Justice.

Mercer, K. R. (2009). The importance of funding postsecondary correctional educational programs. *Community College Review, 37*(2), 153-164.

Messemer, J. E. (2011). The historical practice of correctional education in the United States: A review of the literature. *International Journal of Humanities and Social Science, 1*(17).

Meyer, S. J., Fredericks, L., Borden, C. M., & Richardson, P. L. (2010). Implementing postsecondary academic programs in state prisons: Challenges and opportunities. *Journal of Correctional Education, 61*(2), 148-184.

McCarty, H. J. (2006). Educating Felons: Reflections on Higher Education in Prison. *Radical History Review*, (96), 87–94.

Nally, Lockwood, Knutson, & Ho. (2012). An evaluation of the effect of correctional education programs on post-release recidivism and employment: An empirical study in Indiana. *The Journal of Correctional Education, 63*(1), 69-89.

Cortiella, C. & Horowitz, S. H. (2014). *The State of Learning Disabilities: Facts, Trends and Emerging Issues* (3rd ed.). New York: National Center for Learning Disabilities.

Pompoco, A., Wooldredge, J., Lugo, M., Sullivan, C., & Latessa, E. J. (2017). Reducing inmate misconduct and prison returns with facility education programs. *Criminology and Public Policy, 16*(2), 515-547.

Pryor, M., & Thompkins, D. E. (2012). The disconnect between education and social opportunity for the formerly incarcerated. *American Journal of Criminal Justice, 38*(3), 457–479.

Rabuy, B. & Kopf, D. (2015). *Prisons of poverty: Uncovering the pre-incarceration of the imprisoned.* North Hampton, MA: Prison Policy Initiative. Retrieved from https://www.prisonpolicy.org/reports/income.html.

Rampey, B.D., Keiper, S., Mohadjer, L., Krenzke, T., Li, J., Thornton, N., & Hogan, J. (2016). *Highlights from the U.S. PIAAC survey of incarcerated adults: Their skills, work experience, education, and training: Program for the international assessment of adult competencies: 2014* (NCES 2016-040). U.S. Department of Education. Washington, DC: National Center for Education Statistics. Retrieved from http://nces.ed.gov/pubsearch.

Stephan, J. J. (2008). *Census of state and federal correctional facilities, 2005* (Bureau of Justice Statistics National Prisoner Statistics Program, NCJ 222182). Retrieved from: http://www.bjs.gov/index.cfm?ty=pbdetail&iid=530.

Tewksbury, R., & Vannostrand, L.-M. (1996). Environmental and interactional barriers to job satisfaction for postsecondary correctional educators. *The Prison Journal, 76*(3), 275-292.

Tolbert, M. (2002). *State Correctional Education Programs: State Policy Update.* National Institute for Literacy.

Ubah, C. B. A. (2004). Abolition of Pell Grants for higher education of prisoners: Examining antecedents and consequences. *Journal of Offender Rehabilitation, 39*(2), 73-85.

U.S. department of education second chance Pell piece. (2016). *Journal of Correctional Education, 67*(2), 3-4.

U. S. Department of Justice. (2013). *Smart on crime: Reforming the criminal justice system for the 21st century.* Retrieved from: https:// www.justice.gov/ sites/ default/ files/ag/legacy/2013/08/12/smart-on-crime.pdf

Winterfield, L., Coggeshall, M., Burke-Storer, M., Correa, V., & Tidd, S. (2009). *The Effects of Postsecondary Correctional Education: Final Report.* Washington D.C.: Urban Institute (NJ1).

World Prison Brief, Institute for Criminal Policy Research. (2014). *United States of America.* Retrieved from: http://www.prisonstudies.org/country/united-states-america.

PART 2: THEORY AND PRAXIS

In: A Closer Look at Criminal Justice
Editors: J. A. Cooper and K. G. Jachimowski
ISBN: 978-1-53615-782-6

Chapter 4

INTEGRAL CRIMINOLOGY: QUADRANTS, LEVELS AND LINES OF CRIMINALITY

David R. Champion*
Department of Criminology and Criminal Justice
Slippery Rock University, Slippery Rock, PA, US

ABSTRACT

Criminology is a rich and eclectic field, but its enormous span of disparate subfields and specialties (from concrete practice to philosophical notions of morality and justice) threaten its cohesion. Ken Wilber's Integral Theory (IT) is a meta-theoretical model that spans psychology, counseling, social work, ecology and more. Extant applications to criminology remain limited, but the nature of IT's wide-ranging scope is such that it may effectively function as a tool for criminal justice scholars, practitioners and students. This chapter briefly highlights selected principles of the Integral perspective and examines how they serve to understand theory, practice and educational of the discipline. Despite recent critiques of the IT, the perspective's basic organizing structure and elements (including quadrants, lines and levels of human development and potential) effectively inform criminological teaching and research.

Keywords: Integral Theory and criminology, Integral Theory and criminal justice

INTEGRAL CRIMINOLOGY: A META-THEORETICAL APPROACH TO THE DISCIPLINE

The study of criminology seems at first blush, deceptively simple: Why do people inflict harm on each other, and how does the state and society react to that harm? The

* Author's Email: david.champion@sru.edu.

nature of the harm unfolds further, and its span is prodigious: everything from murder and rape to robbery and theft; from insider trading to fraud to environmental crimes, and from terrorism to voter fraud, not to mention scores of other mala prohibita and mala in se acts. Further, criminality includes the mere *potential* for harm, such as driving under the influence and other assorted acts of negligence and irresponsibility. Any discussion of criminal justice, whether academic or social, brushes up against different aspects of personal knowledge, attitudes and experiences. Criminological theories that encompass this personal/cultural/subjective dimension include social learning (Bandura, 1998, 1999), cultural criminology (Ferrell & Sanders, 1995), and rational choice theory (Becker, 1968). Further, those theories that inhabit the nexus of criminology and philosophy such as morality and the law, ethics, and the fundamental notions of good and evil all link operate primarily within the subjective internal domains as opposed to external observations.

Contemporary theorist Ken Wilber constructed a comprehensive, overarching model that spans human knowledge and potential across the realms of matter, mind and spirit. The Integral Theory (IT) model is also known as AQAL (All Quadrants All Levels, Lines, States and Types). The terms will be used interchangeably in this work. Although one critic has labeled it as "absurdly ambitious" (Meyerhoff, 2010, para. 2) in that Wilber claims it to be a "theory of everything" (Wilber, 2001), it has demonstrated value in providing generalizing orientations across communities of researchers. Wilber's position of inclusiveness is of particular value, in that all valid claims to truth (among those scholars within a particular enclave of research) receive their due respect (Edwards, 2006). The model connects the various branches from differing fields into a four-quadrant model with the objective, subjective, individual and collective domains as its basis (Table 1). Within that framework exists the knowledge, events and development of humankind and the physical world, including the ideas and activities associated with crime, law, morality and justice.

This map, as Wilber (2003) refers to it, orients the ongoing development of knowledge and potential across the sciences, arts, culture, morality, spirituality and philosophy. Despite its grand aims, the AQAL/IT model is a useful heuristic in engaging any field of knowledge. It is an overarching superstructure that orients the observer to the subject under study. As a template, it functions well in considering some of the fundamental questions of human harm, criminality, victimization, morality and justice. Wilber consistently uses the term *Kosmos* (1998; 2000; 2003) to capture all known phenomena, including not only the material world but also the subjective realms such as emotion, cognitions, morals and spirituality.

Integral Theory has been applied a variety of fields, including medicine, psychology, business, psychotherapy, ecology, and more (Wilber, 2007). Criminology is, of course, a wide-ranging and expansive field that spans both the objective and the subjective; the culture and the systems. The AQAL/IT matrix is therefore a useful and fitting approach to the investigation and discussion of criminology.

Because of the wide-range and complexity of AQAL/IT (as well as criminology), there are countless ways that the model may be used in both the study and the teaching of criminal justice. The current work serves only to highlight a few examples of how a few of the AQAL tools might be used to approach the topics associated with criminology. The current work focuses on issues of crime, society and morality, but the AQAL/IT vision is applicable to any area of interest in the field.

Table 1. Four quadrants of reality, as applied to criminology

Upper Left (UL) Interior-Individual (Intentional) *An individual's internal, subjective cognitions; affect and emotional states; awareness; individual moral stage development; internal spiritual experiences; individual criminal intentions and thinking patterns.*	Upper Right (UR) Exterior-Individual (Behavioral) *An individual's externally observable, measurable, empirical behaviors and physiological processes. Observable criminal behavior.*
Lower Left (LL) Interior-Collective (Cultural) *The collective internal experience; shared worldview; societal culture. Collective influences on criminal behaviors.*	Lower Right (LR) Exterior-Collective (Social) *Social systems: criminal justice system and processes; macro-structural factors in criminality.*

Champion, 2011, adapted from Wilber model (1998; 2000; 2007).

GOOD AND EVIL: THE INTEGRAL VISION

As stated above, Wilber's Integral model is an ambitious one that seeks to provide an overarching structure for all physical and metaphysical events, knowledge, and realities: life, matter, and spirit. Adapting the IT for understanding human potential for good and evil requires examination of several aspects of the theory. The current discussion will focus on how elements of the IT align with the fundamental questions of morality, crime, and justice. With its ambitious scope and scale, the AQAL/IT vision is perhaps the only model suited to approach these elemental components of our field. Its organizational power alone makes it a valuable tool for criminal justice students and scholars, as they strive to grasp the connections between the multiple lines of research and theories that all somehow relate back to the field. Some unifying model is necessary to assemble the many sub-disciplines and sub-sub-disciplines of the field into a meaningful whole. Considering that the field claims all aspects of harm inflicted by humans (and the reaction of state authority to that harm), the resulting scholarship is rich and vast, spanning everything from terrorism to intimate partner violence to policing technology to sentencing practices and beyond.

Discussing the nature of good, evil, morality and justice and other weighty concepts is an important aspect of the discipline, whether those discussions occur in print or in the classroom. Optimum engagement of these issues requires two vantage points: (1) Study and synthesis of the original material that includes varied perspectives and a comprehensive literature review, and (2) An orientation of how the material fits into, aligns with, a

The layout of the AQAL/IT matrix includes the traditional notion of the "Big Three", or Art, Morals and Science (Wilber, 2007) as the sum of human nature, knowledge and development. The matrix also reflects both individual and collective manifestations of these realms, resulting in a basic structure of four quadrants (see Table 1).

Within the quadrants lie the lines, levels, states and types that make up the rest of the model (not depicted). These are essential elements and only further reading of Wilber's works can fairly present the full potential of the model as a scholarly tool for criminological research and education. The current work focuses only on the quadrants and lines of development as examples of the application of the AQAL/IT model.

THE QUADRANTS OF CRIME

Table 1 represents a simplified version of Wilber's AQAL model. The AQAL image is Wilber's visual categorization of the breakdown of existence, phenomena and experiences. As such, it encompasses vast expanses of reality (everything, in essence) and needs to be broken down when tapping it for application to any particular field of knowledge. For simplicity's sake, this image does not depict the ascending stages of progressive development nor the more narrowly defined *lines* of development within each quadrant that part of Wilber's original mapping (1998, p. 64-65). Each quadrant below also contains this author's notations of potentially applicable dimensions of criminality associated with each quadrant.

THE SUBJECTIVE AND INTERSUBJECTIVE: THE LEFT QUADRANT TERRAIN OF CRIMINOLOGY

The empirical essence of criminology is essential. It organizes and lends validity to theories of criminogenesis and sets up a reliable framework for addressing the issue through a disciplined method of inquiry. However, criminology cannot sustain its resonance without dipping into personalized or intuited morals or decisions about Right and wrong. The field would not exist without internally derived conclusions about good and evil, whether those conclusions exist at the individual or the collective sphere of thinking. As such, criminology depends upon a persistent recognition of the decency or perniciousness of human activity for it to maintain a systemic core. As much as the discipline (at times) demands devotion to strictly objective observation of phenomena to maintain an acceptably rigorous status as a field of study, it also depends upon a common understanding of Right and wrong, judgments that cannot be made by structural equation modeling or regression tables. Studies of the effectiveness of day treatment centers for county DUI offenders or personality correlates of rapists rely on an assumption of sustained collective belief that people should not put others at risk through driving while intoxicated or sexually violate others. The empirical body of knowledge in criminology ultimately hinges on the subjective belief that harming others (however it is qualified or quantified) is *wrong*, and this is a judgment that can only be relegated to a different sphere of knowing than the reporting of observable, calculable and objectively reported phenomena.

If people did not delve into other quadrants of thinking (Wilber, 1998), such as internal cognitions, moral checkpoints, or emotions, then there would be no discomfort with criminal activity. A discipline that studies the most heinous and brutal acts of human capacity should recognize the very real outrage, pain, hatred and damage associated with the acts. Furthermore, the systemized study of these phenomena may be captured to an extent (either qualitatively or quantitatively) through interview or through survey. Without that affective component, the study of crime is akin to Even the most sterile review of criminological empiricism depends upon some internal judgment of Right or wrong, and once that is recognized, then the discipline needs to recognize that the necessity of a multi-spheric approach to the field (Champion, 2011; Gibbs, Giever, & Pober, 2000; Martin, 2006).

Crime as "Trends": The Role of the Intersubjective

The Lower Left quadrant intersubjective realm continues to evolve in the current culture. The mainstream culture has long ignored ongoing brutalities such as human trafficking, intimate partner violence, sexual harassment and subjugation of women, to name a few. While the problem of intoxicated drivers has been prominently championed by public service announcements and extensive campaigns by the Mothers Against Drunk Driving (MADD) organization since the 1980s, other crimes have only recently begun to filter into mainstream cultural concern. It seems that the current popular culture does not assign importance to criminal acts until a video or hashtag movement spurs the collective into some form of reaction (mixed though it may be). Intimate partner violence briefly became an issue of national conversation after the release of then-NFL player Ray Rice assaulting his fiancée (TMZ Sports, 2014). The sexual harassment and violence against women and children in the entertainment industry (and beyond) caused little widespread social disturbance until the 2017 Hollywood #metoo movement (Codreo-Rado, 2017). Human trafficking has only recently emerged as a topic of widespread concern, despite it being estimated as the third-largest criminal activity on the globe (FBI, n.d.)

As discussed elsewhere (Champion, 2011), the field of criminology relies heavily on the Left-side/subjective quadrants. The impact of crime on its victims, its prominence in culture, the desire to understand the cognitions and thinking patterns of offenders, all of these are artifacts of the interior realms. Although the impact of criminality is readily measured and quantified from the exterior/objective side, the origins of harmful acts are best understood from the subjective/inter-subjective domains. All quadrants reflect some version of reality. All should be considered in the study of crime, providing that they are not confused with one another (i.e., confusing the objective with the subjective. One's emotional reaction to hearing about crimes on the news is not the same as an external measurement of crime statistics). The latter is a *category error* (Wilber, 1998) and confounds the orderly examination and discussion of ideas.

Pre Trans Fallacy and the Romantic Elevation of Bad Acts

As detailed elsewhere (Champion, 2003, 2011), one intriguing aspect of crime is that the actual act, no matter how harmful or violent, perpetrated under some brand of justification by the offender (Bandura, 1998, 1999; Sykes & Matza, 1957). The offender engages in a brand of self-mythologization as a figure of heroic defiance, fighting a Righteous battle against oppressive, hostile others. The attraction of fostering a sympathetic identity constructing a rationalization for the most malevolent of acts, is a persistent principle of criminal cognition (Yochelson & Samenow, 1977). The construction of this narrative reflects a romanticization (or fallacious elevation) of the selfish, base, callousness of pre-conventional thinking to the high-level Righteousness of post-conventionalism.

What is striking is that this phenomenon seems to operate not only at the individual level among offenders, but also among the Lower Left cultural quadrant of social witnesses. Examples abound of cultural elevation of criminals to folk hero status. The tendency to romanticize mean, selfish, criminal actions to heroic transcendence is one of the more interesting aspects of cultural criminology. As Ferrell and Sanders point out, "Americans have historically made folk heroes of criminals," (1995, p. 97). Examples of cultural romanticism abound. Outlaw motorcycle gangs (who deal in drugs, weapons and violence) are elevated to freedom-loving rugged individualists; Italian-American Mafioso become men of respect, tradition and "honor," violent street criminals are righteously reacting against oppressive political and economic institutions.

This romantic, fallacious elevation of base, low-level consciousness to transpersonal grandeur represents (at least) two elements of the AQAL vision at work: lines and quadrants. The former as a line of moral progression, the latter as the subjective/interior realms (both individual and collective). Wilber (1998) characterizes the original Romantic Movement as one of undue sentimentality towards pre-conventional/pre-rational levels. This error results in confusion between these Lower, baser, less-developed stages with authentic trans-rational realms in a "spiraling, regressive yearning" (1998, p. 97) for some euphemistic primitivism. As an intellectual movement, Wilber considered the Romantics as holding a "descended" (2001, Section 8385, para. 2) worldview; a regressive collapse of authentically heightened consciousness to a narrow interpretation that is based entirely on sensory nature (Wilber, 2001).

This misperception relates another fallacy of thinking, and an essential AQAL/IT construct for those interested in crime and morality: the Pre-Trans Fallacy (PTF). Working from an observation of the pre-conventional/conventional/post-conventional lines of spiritual awareness, Wilber (2000) remarks "…many people confuse the warmth and heart-expanse of post-conventional awareness with the merely subjective feelings of the sensory body" (p. 120). In another work he states, "Since both pre-rational states and trans-rational states are, in their own ways, nonrational, they appear similar" (p. 211). Thus, to an untutored observer, authentically high states of spiritual awareness may appear as infantile, pre-conventional primitivism, a PTF Wilber calls reductionism. Conversely, a pre-rational narcissistic New-Ager might consider his or her own pre-conventional self-absorbed ruminations as transpersonal mysticism (known as *elevationism*).

In the above sections, Wilber was discussing arcs of spiritual consciousness. However, my own conception of the PTF is somewhat broader in that it is reasonably applied to lines of moral stage development. It is a useful descriptive model to explain not only the cognitive justification patterns of individual criminals, but also the persistent cultural tendency to elevate criminality to folk-heroism. Both may be considered a form of fallacious elevationism, or a particular brand of morality-based PTF.

This is an area where existing scholarship on criminality lend support to this overall general orientation. Bandura's (1998, 1999) work on moral disengagement as rationalization mechanism employed by perpetrators of religion-based terrorists and other atrocities, Sykes and Matza's (1957) concept of neutralization, and Yochelson & Samenow's (1976) cognitive profiles of the criminal personality all point to a propensity to escalate the criminal behaviors to Righteous grandiosity. Yochelson and Samenow (1976) identify ostensibly positive characteristics that are common in criminal thinking patterns, such as pride, religiosity, perfectionism, optimism, and fearlessness.

Thus, in an example based on the Spiral Dynamic model listed above, fundamentalist religious terrorists are primarily operating at the pathological purple stage. However, they may falsely consider themselves to be at the second tier, transpersonal stages of global-centric consciousness.

The PTF, applied to moral development, thus provides a descriptive general orientation for what has been established by criminology/social psychology researchers. The AQAL model's inclusion of developmental lines is of interest to criminologists, particularly the lines of moral development. Based heavily on Gardner's (2006) multiple intelligence theory, Wilber's incorporation adds a pathway of moral ascension not found in Gardner's work. The moral line of development is a culmination of various stage-based models, including Kohlberg (1984), Gilligan (1977) and Clare Graves' work on Spiral Dynamics (Beck & Cowan, 1996). Reflecting a common theme for Integral Theory, Wilber draws from the accumulation of diverse scholarship and identifies an overarching consensus viewpoint among them. This consensus then constitutes an established truism of sorts that then becomes part of the AQAL model. In the case of moral stage development, Wilber identifies a key characteristic of moral progression that operates at both individual as well as collective/societal levels: Moral development is marked by an increasing awareness and concern for others, beginning at the basest egocentric self-involvement and expanding towards inclusion and care of others at a global (or even universal) scale.

Wilber describes this principle of development in different ways: egocentric to ethnocentric to world-centric; pre-conventional, conventional, post-conventional (drawing from Kohlberg/Gilligan); pre-rational, rational, post-rational. This unfolding of consciousness, from self to immediate social milieu to expanding waves of care, is a basic truth of moral ascension that serves as a common link among stage-based theories of moral development.

This simple observation holds power. It is one example of the useful heuristics embodied in the AQAL/IT vision. It is of great use to criminologists, especially those with a research and teaching interest in criminal justice ethics. The model is useful for considering individual criminal offenders as well as the overall state of a particular culture. This combination of individual/collective spheres and the principle of expanding consciousness beyond one's own needs to those of others provides a working framework for myriad "territory" level inquiries. In delving into the darkest aspects of human malice (as well as the most elevated examples of human kindness), it is of great help to have an overall orientation.

Lines of Development: The Spiral Dynamic Model

Wilber draws from several stage-based models of moral development, including the work of Kohlberg (1958), Gilligan (1977) and Beck and Cowan's Spiral Dynamics (1996) (based on the work of Graves) (See Table 1). In application of the PTF to moral developmental stages as a descriptor of criminality. Importantly, each stratum (or *meme*) may manifest itself in either a healthy or pathological manner. This is an essential characteristic of the memes, from a criminological standpoint. The PTF reflects the erroneous elevation of a Lower level to a world-centric one, but there is also another fallacy of mistaking pathological manifestations of the meme for healthy ones. For example, a "Green" may hold a positive self-image of being an environmentally conscious egalitarian, but a toxic version of this meme may include rationalizations to commit acts of eco-terrorism or violence against those who do not hold the same views. (Note that the Green meme is not necessarily related to environmentalism as the popular use of "green" is currently used. It is a broader concept).

Table 2. Spiral Dynamics as applied to possible criminological types

Meme	Beck & Cowan (1996) description	Associated criminal activities
Beige	Survival/Sense-Instinctive: physiological needs;	Substance abuse; disorganized assaults/murders; sex crimes
Purple	Tribal bonds; mystical/magical thinking; clans	Gangs; terrorism
Red	"War gods"; use of violence to achieve ends	Gangs; interpersonal violence; street crimes; terrorism
Blue	Social cohesion; conformity; law and order	Corrupt/abusive police/corrections
Orange	Entrepreneurship; scientific and financial achievement	White collar criminals
Green	Egalitarianism; relativism; emotions/feelings valued over logic	Eco-terror; rationalization of crimes due to perceived victimhood of the actors.

Source: adapted from Beck & Cowan (1996).

As another example: One may make a surface presumption that the Red "War Gods" meme has no redeeming value, but the Red meme is an important survival mechanism for self-defense and survival against predators (be they animal or human). Without the Red meme to draw from, all people would be at the mercy of pathological Reds who would impose violence against them for their own gain. The Red meme is a dominating, aggressive egocentric value system that can repel life-threatening violence.

According to Wilber (1998) and Beck and Cowan (1996), all of the memes have value, and all have attending destructive aspects. In progression through the stages, each ascending level includes the previous stage. A Blue would have incorporated (and may at times regress to) the Beige, Purple and Red stages. This premise of progressive developmental strata depending on the successful completion of the previous one before further growth aligns with other stage-based theories of development, from Freud to Erikson to Kohlberg to Gilligan.

Those familiar with IT/SD memes need no extensive recapitulation of the memes, but for ease of illustrating the attending potential criminality associated with each, the first-tier waves are listed in Table 2 (adapted from Beck & Cowan, 1996). It should be noted that Spiral Dynamics involves higher memes than are listed here. For purposes of the limited scope of this chapter, only the First Tier (pre-transpersonal) strata are presented.

IT'S THE MAP, NOT THE TERRITORY

Wilber (2007) emphasizes that the Integral/AQAL vision is a roadmap, not the territory itself. In this analogy, Wilber points out that a map that is too close to the ground, depicting every blade of grass and sidewalk crack, loses its value as it becomes indistinguishable from the terrain.

Conversely, a map that is positioned from stratospheric heights, depicting the entire western hemisphere, would be unhelpful in locating the student union on campus. Therefore, a good map is general enough to avoid becoming embedded in the territory, but specific enough to identify the key components within its scope.

The "territory" here consists of the direct research, observations, and insights formulated by communities of scholars within given fields, be they medicine, geology, philosophy, art, mathematics or any other branch of knowledge. It is the on-the-ground, day-to-day work of researches who build and test theories. The territory is where law plays out in the courtroom and in the streets, and where the results are collected, discussed, and analyzed. The territory is real life playing out in real time. It is where the events and experiences of criminals, victims, police, corrections professionals, and all of the actors in the criminal justice world operate at the four quadrants.

CRITICISM OF INTEGRAL THEORY

The IT's ambitious (or audacious, depending one's viewpoint) goal is an ordering of all phenomena, embracing the sum of humankind's development and potential, to include spiritual ascension (Wilber, 1998; 2000; 2007). This rather grand objective opens the IT up to criticism from all flanks. This is not surprising, given the scope of the meta-theory and its claims to include the totality of human epistemology, morality, aesthetics, matter and spirit.

These critiques are often aimed at the overall assumptions on which Wilber has constructed his Integral map. Groothius (2010), for example, disputes Wilber's interpretations of Christian theology and criticizes his (Wilber's) reliance on describing concepts of spirit as defying verbal description. Petersen and Jaruzell II (2019) assert that many of Wilber's claims have not undergone the empirical testing necessary to support some his generalized claims.

Meyerhoff (2010) objects to the IT's expansive aims and claims that it does not truly represent an integrated framework. He disputes Wilber's premise that the IT model draws from established consensus of multiple disciplines. Meyerhoff claims that Wilber either misrepresents scholarly consensus from various disciplines, or (in other instances) that no such consensus exists. Moreover, Meyerhoff claims that the IT is not sustainable once it approaches ground level details and that, in general, Wilber's attempts at building generalizing orientations as an overall framework is not possible (2010).

Edwards (2006) shared Meyerhoff's concerns about the specific methodological processes of Integral Theory construction, and believes that the IT would benefit from a more detailed accounting of how an Integral research method might actually look, let alone be conducted. However, Edwards also counters several points of Meyerhoff's criticism, including demonstration that generalizing orientations have effectively been constructed in other pursuits, such as general systems theory and multiparadigm theory building (Edwards, 2006). In general, much of the criticism is aimed at the legitimacy of the linkages between on-the-ground observations in the field and the relatively loftiness of the overarching Integral framework.

As valid as some of these criticisms might be, it is argued here that the IT model has generated thought and discussion (entire websites exist solely to criticize his work), and that it has utility in both research and teaching. Wilber's AQAL model may best be regarded as an initial checkpoint before descending into the essential kernels of a particular field. The realms of internal/external/objective/subjective, as well as the rest of the domains, lines and levels of the map bring structure to the examination of multifaceted disciplines such as criminology. It may be Left to those who are on the ground in the direct research and practice of the field to determine the legitimacy of the Integral connections.

DISCUSSION

The current work is a brief overview that discusses only a few components of the AQAL/IT model. The current work introduces three elements of IT (quadrants, lines, and levels) and sketched out brief outlines of how they might apply to aspects of crime and justice. The AQAL/IT model is a multi-level lens that provides an orientation of existing knowledge in the field.

This work is limited by its scope, and the proposals for its application here represent only a sliver of its potential as an interrogatory tool. Further development and discussion of Wilber's Integral vision and what it may offer criminology is necessary. Expanding the breadth and depth of the contemplative span in the field holds promise for both teaching and research.

Teaching Implications

The Academy of Criminal Justice Sciences (ACJS) recommends criminal justice programs require curricular devotion to ethical decision-making, multi-cultural/diversity awareness, communication, cyber/technology competence, as well as an offering of electives and cognates that may presumably span everything from victimology to geospatial crime-mapping to criminal investigations to human trafficking. Add to this the typical core courses on policing, corrections, courts, theory and research/statistics, and it is clear that criminology is a field that spans all four quadrants. Peacemaking, Restorative Justice, and Victimology have established themselves as legitimate criminological sub-fields.

The Integral approach provides an overall framework for each of these sub-disciplines. The All-Quadrant model includes these specialized developments and brings a purposeful, unifying context to teaching at the classroom, class and curriculum level. The IT perspective establishes an overarching meta-view of how each branch operates from I/We/It domain(s) and thus clarifies the limitations, strengths, and fundamental perspective of each. Evaluating how a sub-field or theory fits into the AQAL overlay automatically sets up a methodology for comprehension and analysis for students and faculty alike. Furthermore, it allows students a working unified platform for their criminal justice/criminology curriculum. Students face unrelated and conflicting theories, principles of criminal laws, and lesson plans ranging from tactics for police dynamic entries to underlying concepts of offender re-entry. How can the cultural/inter-subjective Lower Left study of the post-modernist Gender, Race and Crime course fit in with Lower Right/empirical systems focus of Law Enforcement Tactics and Operations? What does the Ethics and Criminal Justice class have to do with the multiple regression analyses learned in the Statistics course? Even topics that reside within the same course often require a four-quadrant approach. The AQAL lens can encompass the merits of both Skinner's behaviorism and Ferrell and Sanders' (1995) Cultural Criminology.

Interpreting the Lower Left: Culture and Society

Much of the field's impact (although certainly not all of it) originates from the Lower Left inter-subjective quadrant. Also, its moral/cultural manifestations are not simply cultural clashes over Internet addiction, shopping habits, or shifting political consensus, but actual harm being perpetrated against real victims by real offenders. Furthermore, these crimes occur within the environment of a powerful state that equips its agents with coercive authority to use force to apprehend and punish offenders, which may spin off into cases of outrageous injustice. To establish these traumatic, chaotic and at-times devastating activities as an objective field of academic inquiry, the Right-side quadrants and their empirical observation/reporting are implemented as the method and language.

This perspective is necessary but insufficient. The emotional trauma of the rape victim, the fundamental injustice and greater social impact of police brutality, and the hopelessness of released offenders attempting to reintegrate into their communities (as just three examples) cannot be flattened, quantified, and externally observed as if they were as Right-sided as quarks, rocks, or solar systems. These Left-side issues are already part of teaching in the field. The IT simply provides a template that allows for a full-quadrant grasp of crime.

In the film *Dead Poet's Society* (Haft, Witt, Thomas & Weir, 1989) Professor Keating instructs the students of his 1950s prep school poetry class to read from the course textbook on how one might properly gauge the greatness of a poem. As one student recites aloud from the text, relating its formula for "calculating" the poem's worth, Keating scribbles on the board, noting the prescribed x and y axis ("Importance" and "Perfection"). Furthermore, the calculated area of the importance/perfection x and y axes results in a quantification of the poems' greatness (as illustrated by the formula P x I=G).

Keating proceeds to excoriate this idea, even encouraging his stunned students to rip the offending pages from their textbooks. In this dramatic manner, Keating effectively crushes an attack of the Right quadrants against the Left. Although this classroom method is not recommended here, the lesson is valuable: The proper lens must be employed in evaluation in learning.

Criminology's connection to the Lower Left quadrant as the domain of collective morality and is an especially salient one compared to other social sciences. Crime is inherently a disruption of collective peace and civility. Whether that violation is one perpetrated by a lone offender, a criminal gang, a corporation, or even an overreach of state powers, it exists as an assault on the social fabric. It is the subjective nature of crime that drives its resonance. Only in criminology is there an innate condition of a deliberately enacted social wrong that is to be recognized, explored and understood.

It is therefore essential to use an intellectual framework that encompasses these ideas. The Integral map is such a framework. The IT/AQAL vision can be applied in lectures as well as the class-planning and overall curriculum levels. Informing students of some of the basic concepts of AQAL can assist them in "placing" the disparate educational experiences within an integrated whole, in which all quadrants have value and meaning.

REFERENCES

Academy of Criminal Justice Sciences (2018). *Program standards.* Retrieved from https://www.acjs.org/page/ProgramStandards.

Bandura, A. (1998). Mechanism of moral disengagement. In W. Reich (Ed.). *Origins of Terrorism: Psychologies, Ideologies, Theologies, States of Mind.* (pp. 161-191). Washington, DC: Woodrow Wilson Center Press.

Bandura, A. (1999). Moral disengagement in the perpetration of inhumanities. *Personality and Social Psychology Review, 3,* 193-209. doi: 10.1207/s15327957pspr0303_3.

Beck, D.E. & Cowan, C.C. (1996). *Spiral Dynamics: Mastering Values, Leadership, and Change.* Malden, MA: Blackwell Publishing.

Becker, G. (1968). Crime and punishment: An economic approach. *The Journal of Political Economy*, 76, 169-217. doi:10.1086/259394.

Champion, D.R. (2011). An Integral model of criminality: Aspects of criminal behavior. *Insights to a Changing World Journal, 2011* (4), 23-39.

Coreo-Rado, A. (2017, October 6). #MeToo floods social media with stories of harassment and assault. *The New York Times.* Retrieved from https://www.nytimes.com/2017/10/16/technology/metoo-twitter-facebook.html.

Edwards, M. (2006, March). *Meyerhoff, Wilber and the Post-Formal Stages.* Retrieved from http://www.integralworld.net/edwards25.html.

Federal Bureau of Investigation (n.d.). *Human trafficking/involuntary servitude.* Retrieved from https://www.fbi.gov/investigate/civil-Rights/human-trafficking.

Gardner, H. (2006). *Multiple Intelligences: New Horizons.* New York, NY: Perseus Books.

Groothius, D. (2010, March 03). *A critique of Ken Wilber*. Retrieved from https://theconstructivecurmudgeon.blogspot.com/2010/03/critique-of-ken-wilber.html.

Gibbs, J.J., Giever, D. & Pober, K.A. (2000). Criminology and the Eye of the Spirit: An introduction and application of the thoughts of Ken Wilber. *Journal of Contemporary Criminal Justice, 16*(1), 99-127. Retrieved from http://ccj.sagepub.com/

Gilligan, C. (1977). In a different voice: Women's conceptions of self and of morality. *Harvard Educational Review*, 47(4), 481-517.

Haft, S., Witt, P.J., Thomas, T. (Producers) & Weir, P. (Director). (1989). *Dead Poets Society* [Motion picture]. USA: Buena Vista Pictures Distribution.

Kohlberg, L. (1984). *The Psychology of Moral Development: The Nature and Validity of Moral* (Essays on Moral Development, Volume 2). New York, NY: Harper & Row.

Meyerhoff, J. (2010). *Bald ambition: A critique of Ken Wilber's theory of everything.* Retrieved from http://www.integralworld.net/meyerhoff4.html.

Petersen, E.J. & Jaruzel II, M.E. (2019, January). *Argumentum ad Wilberiam: How truthiness and overgeneralization threaten to turn integral theory into a new scholasticism.* Retrieved from http://www.integralworld.net/petersen-jaruzel1.html.

Sykes, G.M. & Matza, D. (1957). Techniques of neutralization: A theory of delinquency. *American Sociological Review, 22,* 664-670.

Wilber, K. (1998). *The Marriage of Sense and Soul: Integrating Science and Religion.* Boston, MA: Shambhala.

Wilber, K. (2001). *A Theory of Everything.* Boston, MA: Shambhala.

Wilber, K. (2003). *Interview by T. Simon* [Sound recording]. Kosmic Consciousness, Sounds True. Boulder, CO.

Wilber, K. (2007). *The Integral Vision: A Very Short Introduction to the Revolutionary Integral Approach to Life, God, the Universe, and Everything*. Boston, MA: Shambhala.

Yochelson, S. & Samenow, S. (1977). *The Criminal Personality (vol III).* Lanham, MD: Rowan & Littlefield.

In: A Closer Look at Criminal Justice
Editors: J. A. Cooper and K. G. Jachimowski ISBN: 978-1-53615-782-6

Chapter 5

A CASE FOR THE POLICE: AN INVESTIGATION INTO LAW ENFORCEMENT AND THE COMMUNITIES THEY SERVE

Eric Kocian*
Saint Vincent College, Latrobe, PA, US

ABSTRACT

Police and the law enforcement community are more educated, diverse, trained, and professional than any other time in American history and yet, there is a growing disdain for police officers and more resistance to their authority in police encounters. Over the past several decades, the percentage of children born out of wedlock has been steadily increasing throughout the United States. In African American households, for example, out of wedlock childbirths are close to a staggering 80%. In considering Gottfredson and Hirschi's A General Theory of Crime (1990), it stands to reason that a lack of Self Control early in life (as determined by level of Parental Management) leads to problems later in life. Contact with authority-type figures, to include police officers, may result in confrontations due to an individual possessing a lower level of Self Control and having to comply with commands and procedures not fond of or liked. This chapter will examine the link between Gottfredson and Hirschi's theory, trends in policing practices, and confrontations with members of society in order to better understand the challenges facing law enforcement and the pursuit of justice.

THE ERIC CARTMAN QUESTION

In an episode of the famed animated series South Park, Eric Cartman assumes the role of a police officer and utters the infamous phrase, "You will respect my authority" in

* Author's Email: eric.kocian@stvincent.edu

countless interactions he has with the residents he confronts in the town of South Park who have violated some law or ordinance (South Park Studios, n.d.). Those who resist, fail to comply with Officer Cartman's directives, or disrespect him in any way receive some form of physical battery from Officer Cartman and are arrested. The cartoon series assumes a more satirical approach to real-life events and issues, but on occasion, provides the opportunity for deeper contemplation into a specific topic.

When reflecting on the aforementioned episode, a pressing question comes to mind. The question itself is simple and straightforward, but to answer it, one must rely on rational thinking, honest assessments, and an understanding of the law and of personal responsibility. Eric Cartman might ask the question in a way that sounds something like, "Why doesn't anyone respect my authority?" with a sense of frustration or exhaustion in his distinct voice. When taking a more academic approach to the field of Criminology and Criminal Justice, the question becomes, "Why is there so much anti-police sentimentality throughout the country?" and the question should be accompanied with a sense of concern and desire for the truth.

It would appear as though there is a growing discord for police officers in this country with the media coverage of high-profile confrontations between citizens and the law enforcement community. Accusations of racial discrimination and police brutality are immediately levied at police officers any time an African American is killed by an officer (irrespective of race), regardless of the circumstances surrounding the use of force. Following the immediate claims of racism and excessive force, rioting and protesting may take effect in the area where the alleged abuse of power transpired, and a plethora of social justice warriors, celebrities, athletes, and the uninformed or misinformed public make spectacles of themselves in person or through social media outlets in efforts to eradicate such injustices. Disturbing to some is the hypocrisy in the masses of people who fervently and passionately demonstrate and destroy private and public property under the guise they act in such outrageous fashion, so justice prevails for the victim who, in their estimation, was not guaranteed his due process rights outlined in the United States Constitution. Interestingly enough, for the majority of these mobs, allowing the system to work as intended and guaranteeing the accused *their* due process, the inalienable Constitutional rights of the accused remains the very least of their concerns. The duplicitous double-standards are rarely considered by those who feel their moral outrage trumps law, standards, rights, and equal protection for all. Those citizens who are inconvenienced, harmed, or victimized as a result of the multitudes of outraged unable to control their wrath are, at best, deemed collateral damage for the cause.

In moments where facts surface that dispel fictional narratives about precisely what transpired before, during, and after the use of force, be it in grand jury proceedings, released body camera footage, or witness accounts, the time for some people in society has passed. Instead of allowing evidence and reality to shape the narrative, certain segments of the population turn a deaf ear to any particular that challenges their narrative that officers are racist, bigoted, foolish, brutal, and out of control. Regardless of the actualities, a determination of guilt and corresponding punishment has already been levied against the officer, law enforcement, and perhaps, the community. In the aftermath of the barrage of critiques and criticisms of the law enforcement community, fervent calls for more training, greater diversity, and a better educated officer top the list of demands, all the while leaving some to wonder if those demanding justice are aiming their wrath and fury and calls for action at the proper target.

The purpose of this chapter is to examine the relationship between law enforcement and the communities they serve. In doing so, historical facts and trends will dispel myths about the law enforcement profession and the assumption of blame for the state of affairs between the police and the community; an alternative explanation will be offered with an accompaniment of appropriate theoretical and empirical support for such proclamations; and policy recommendations stemming from the theoretical model selected will be provided.

Bad Cop, Good Cop, and the Blue Wall

Rigorous studies, factual reporting, and general population polls attempting to investigate and eradicate police corruption in the United Sates is almost as old as the profession is itself. Beginning in 1894 with the Lexow Commission's focus on political corruption and police malfeasance, misfeasance, and nonfeasance and continuing through present day with Gallup polls, police misconduct remains an important focal point for law enforcement and citizens alike (Cox, McCamey, & Scaramella, 2014; Jones, 2015).

The 1932 Wickersham Commission found widespread use of police brutality, bribery, evidence tampering, intimidation, and coercion nationwide in police departments (Cox, McCamey, & Scaramella, 2014). The Knapp Commission received incredible attention, thanks in part to Al Pacino's lead role in the movie *Serpico*, when their 1973 report was published and indicated as many as half of all New York City Police Department (NYPD) officers were corrupt (McCafferty & McCafferty, 1998). As per the report, corruption contaminated all ranks within the department (Cox, McCamey, & Scaramella, 2014). The Christopher Commission in 1991, which focused exclusively on Los Angeles Police Department (LAPD) corruption, indicated that a small group of officers (44) were responsible for a significant portion of the police malfeasance while the Molen Commission of 1994 uncovered corruption linked to drug markets and other forms of police corruption that were stifled due to little or no commitment on the part of officers or supervisors to bring these allegations to light (Cox, McCamey, & Scaramella, 2014).

Couple these studies with perceptions stated in a recent Gallup poll that found confidence in police is at a 22 year low in the United States (Jones, 2015) and it would appear that departments are suffering from moral bankruptcy and that not much has changed in policing practices over the course of history. In revisiting the Eric Cartman question posed at the beginning of this chapter, "Why doesn't anyone respect my authority?" perhaps the best answer is one that begs the question, "What have the police done to earn respect for their authority?"

Over the course of the past 20 to 30 years, interest in professional ethics has grown tremendously. Higher education programs in criminology and criminal justice may have been slower to respond to the demands for a systematic approach to ethics (Braswell, McCarthy, & McCarthy, 2008), but today, any reputable college curriculum contains at least one ethics course for a criminology/criminal justice major. Discussing topics like the use of deception in an interview, physical coercion, Brady violations, and the like afford students the opportunity to consider these important issues before they are confronted with real-life situations in the field. Efforts to increase the ability to identify ethical issues for those who will someday be entering the field with badges and guns were matched by chiefs in the field hoping to provide a moral compass of sorts to assist current police officers in navigating through murky waters.

In an effort to better professionalize the law enforcement occupation as a whole, The International Association of Police Chiefs (IACP) developed a code of ethics to govern its members and their professional conduct (Grant, 2002). The code of ethics, which was originally written and established in 1957, read as follows:

> *As a law enforcement officer, my fundamental duty is to serve the community; to safeguard lives and property; to protect the innocent against deception, the weak against oppression or intimidation and the peaceful against violence or disorder; and to respect the constitutional rights of all to liberty, equality, and justice.*
>
> *I will keep my private life unsullied as an example to all and will behave in a manner that does not bring discredit to me or to my agency. I will maintain courageous calm in the face of danger, scorn or ridicule; develop self-restraint; and be constantly mindful of the welfare of others. Honest in thought and deed both in my personal and official life, I will be exemplary in obeying the law and the regulations of my department. Whatever I see or hear of a confidential nature or that is confided to me in my official capacity will be kept ever secret unless revelation is necessary in the performance of my duty.*
>
> *I will never act officiously or permit personal feelings, prejudices, political beliefs, aspirations, animosities or friendships to influence my decisions. With no compromise for crime and with relentless prosecution of criminals, I will enforce the law courteously and appropriately without fear or favor, malice or ill will, never employing unnecessary force or violence and never accepting gratuities.*
>
> *I recognize the badge of my office as a symbol of public faith, and I accept it as a public trust to be held so long as I am true to the ethics of police service. I will never engage in acts of corruption or bribery, nor will I condone such acts by other police officers. I will cooperate with all legally authorized agencies and their representatives in the pursuit of justice.*
>
> *I know that I alone am responsible for my own standard of professional performance and will take every reasonable opportunity to enhance and improve my level of knowledge and competence.*

> *I will constantly strive to achieve these objectives and ideals, dedicating myself before God to my chosen profession...law enforcement. (The International Association of Police Chiefs (IACP), n.d., n.p.)*

The original code of ethics was revised in 1989 by the International Association of Chiefs at their conference in Louisville, Kentucky and unanimously adopted in October of 1991 (Grant, 2002). Various departments and agencies have since developed and expanded upon the code of ethics devised by the International Association of Chiefs, but the rules of conduct and the understood necessity of such a code remains paramount for all.

It goes without saying that possessing a code of ethics in a profession by no means ensures all members will abide by said code, but it does dictate and promote appropriate and acceptable forms of behavior within an organization. The Federal Bureau of Investigation, for example, in their Ethics and Integrity Program Policy Directive and Policy Guide, clearly states that, "'Public service is a public trust.' This principle underlies virtually all of the rules for ethics for government employees. Each FBI employee has a responsibility to, both to the United States government (USG) and to its citizens, to place loyalty to the Constitution, observance of the United States (U.S.) laws, and public service above private gain" (Federal Bureau of Investigation Office of Integrity and Compliance, 2018, p. ii). The goal of FBI employees is "to observe the highest standards of ethical conduct in our personal and professional lives" (Federal Bureau of Investigation Office of Integrity and Compliance, 2018, p. ii).

With the advent of the aforementioned codes of conduct and a renewed interest in ethical behaviors and practices, one might wonder if the blue wall of silence is what it once was. A U.S. News and World Report article cited numerous examples of how the blue wall of silence may not have been the mighty barrier made out to be. Officers Eric Turetzky and Mark Schofield, for example, came forward and gave evidence against fellow officer Justin Volpe, who was later convicted of brutalizing Abner Louima (Lardner, 1997).

Researchers at Florida State University and the University of Michigan found that police officers do not shield fellow officers or turn a blind eye when dealing with accusations of domestic violence. Their study uncovered that police officers ranked helping the victim as their number one priority and were more oriented to the facts of the case than to their own personal traits. Additionally, police supervisors showed more support for victims than front-line officers in their departments (USA Today Magazine, 2016).

Perhaps there is a greater willingness in coming forward against a fellow officer because of a change in police procedures and rules for reporting police misconduct. Failure to report misconduct is a form of misconduct. Bringing allegations of suspicions remains an affirmative duty of any officer (Brandl, 2018).

Again, this is not to assume every law enforcement officer will respond precisely how he or she should in the course of their occupation, but it does illustrate progress in the right direction and initiatives promoting a more ethical form of public service and consequences for those who engage in a variety of forms of police misconduct and/or turn a blind eye towards others who do. Critics of police who claim officers are not held to standards of conduct, are part of a corrupt organization, and operate above the law fail to recognize the overwhelming body of evidence that speaks to the contrary. The self-serving actions and misconduct of some officers in the past should not be forgotten to ensure greater awareness of present temptations today, but to make the argument communities do not trust police today because of a lack of professional ethics and oversight is unfounded and foolish.

Police Officer 2.0 Reporting for Duty

Paralleling police departments from the 1960's and 1970's to departments in the 21st century is as mismatched as drawing comparisons between the intellectual and physical dexterity of Deputy Sheriff Barney Fife to that of Special Agent Fox Mulder. Since the 1970's police departments have undergone drastic changes in the style of policing employed, composition of departments, formal education achievements for officers, attitudes on crime prevention practices, and use of technology (Brandl, 2018). This next section will help illustrate how policing today is more diversified, educated, trained, and connected than ever before in American history. In doing so, it will partially discredit the proclamations about what is wrong with law enforcement in today's world.

Once upon a Time vs the Great White Hype of Today

During the reform era of policing (1930 to 1980), departments across the nation made a concerted effort to have greater minority representation within the ranks of policing. While minority officers far outnumbered female officers during this time (only 2% of police officers were women), the fact remains that minority officer percentages in police departments were drastically different than minority representation in the population. Washington D.C. touted a 63% minority population, but only 21% of their officers were minorities; Baltimore had a minority rate within the city of 41% while only 7% of Baltimore officers were minorities; New Orleans was even more dramatic with a 41% rate for the population and a 4% rate on the department. Overall, less than 10% of police officers were ethnic or racial minorities in 1970. In 1987, 15% of police officers were minorities. Today, females represent approximately 13% of police officers and ethnic or racial minorities represent 27% of officers across the nation, compared to 38% of the population (Brandl, 2018). The numbers today are not perfectly symmetrical, but most certainly suggest that departments are becoming more diversified and represented by female officers and ethnic or racial minority officers serving in the ranks.

In examining why there continues to be a difference between minority representation in society and minority representation in the ranks of the police, one possible explanation revolves around the idea that minorities are not applying for police jobs. Another explanation resides in the argument that barriers exist including, but are not limited to the initial application, written examination, and background investigation. Solutions to rectifying these obstacles involve adjusting the selection criteria, such as not requiring college education requirements in order to hire more racial minorities and relaxing strength and physical fitness requirements in order to attract more female recruits (Brandl, 2018). These proposed solutions have the potential to jeopardize and undermine research findings concerning formal educational achievements by police officers, which will be discussed further in this section.

Regardless of how departments are enticing females and racial or ethnic minorities to apply for positions within their communities, the fact remains that the law enforcement profession, as a whole and by department, is more diversified than at any other time in American history. This increased diversity remains an important point to consider when explaining the "perceived problems with law enforcement" and dispels the myth that all officers are white males.

Education: The Most Powerful Weapon

College education and police performance initially began in the 1960's but has gained a renewed interest due to studies like the one conducted by Paoline, Terrill, and Rossler (2014) that found college-educated police officers are less likely to use force when dealing with citizens. Their study analyzed over 2,000 police officers in mid-sized and larger departments throughout the country and found that approximately half of the officers had degrees in criminal justice, while the others ranged from psychology to business degrees. Regardless of degree, college-educated officers were less likely to use force (Paoline, Terrill, & Rossler, 2014).

This builds off work done in 2007 where Paoline and Terrill concluded that police encounters where the officer possessed any college education resulted in significantly less verbal force compared to encounters where the officer possessed only a high school education. Similarly, they also reported that encounters involving officers with a four-year degree resulted in significantly less physical force (Paoline & Terrill, 2007).

Hayeslip (1989) discussed the benefits of a college education to the police officer in terms of motivation, innovative techniques, better understanding of the profession, and clearer thinking patterns. Overall, his conclusions were that college education and police performance are consistently related. Studies have found more education on the part of police officers is associated with better communication, superior problem-solving abilities, fewer citizen complaints regarding physical and verbal abuse, less frequent disciplinary actions received, and an attitude that is less supportive of abuse of authority (Cox, McCamey, & Scaramella, 2014; Cox & Moore, 1992).

Other studies also found a correlation between college education and disciplinary issues in policing where higher education levels equated to lower levels of disciplinary issues. Research suggests higher education in law enforcement is advantageous because it provides a deeper perspective for decision making, it allows for additional time for experiences and maturity before becoming an officer, it fosters personal responsibility through college requirements, and it affords a person to learn more about the democratic processes of the United States (Cox, McCamey, & Scaramella, 2014; Cunningham, 2006; Stevens, 1999).

It stands to reason that an older and more thoroughly educated person who experienced greater reading, writing, and presentation requirements, and had the benefit of socializing with diverse people throughout his or her college experience would meet with greater success in the field of law enforcement. Perhaps this is the reason more and more departments are requiring some college experience before an applicant can be considered for employment. Very few departments require a four year degree (1% nationwide), but some states require at least 60 credits or an associate degree for consideration (Brandl, 2018).

Training Day

On average, approximately 45,000 people enter law enforcement training academies in the United States every year. By most accounts, 86% of those who start an academy complete it, meaning they successfully pass all written, physical, and institutional requirements to become a sworn law enforcement officer. Training in most of the academies includes sessions about domestic violence, mental illness, sexual assault, crimes against children, terrorism, gangs, victim response, hate crimes, sexual harassment, elder abuse, human trafficking, drug labs, and cybercrimes. Additionally, recruits receive ongoing instruction in weapons handling, use of force, legal education, self-defense, self-improvement and basic law enforcement procedures. Across the country, each recruit spends an average of 840 hours (or 21 weeks) completing basic training to become a police officer (Brandl, 2018; Reaves, 2016).

Once in the field, officers can expect to begin field training where they work alongside a field training officer who provides regular feedback and guidance during the new officer's probationary period. Upon completion of field training, which varies in the number of weeks and the number of field training officers assigned, depending on the department regulations, the officer is assigned to his or her official post. In service trainings continue for officers as long as their career entails and usually average approximately 40 hours a year, ranging from any and all topics that relate to critical police officer tasks and legal updates (Brandl, 2018).

Having noted as much, it can be argued that police officers receive more rigorous training than most other occupations throughout the country and understandably so. It remains impossible to train for every possible encounter or scenario an officer may experience during the course of the work day but suggesting police officers are not properly trained in the academy and/or fail to maintain a rigorous training regime appears to be misguided.

Centering in on talking points from the 1960's concerning demographics, education, and training in an effort to draw attention to the need for police reform in the present is nonsensical and imprudent. At the very least, it demonstrates a lack of knowledge about the subject matter. At its worst, it perpetuates false premises that are circulated by larger and larger audiences, resulting in grander, and some cases violent, demonstrations that shake the foundation of democracy and liberty and circumvent the rule of law. In contemplating this further, the question that begs asking is, "Why? Why in the face of so many advancements, achievements, and institutional changes for the better are police still viewed as if they are unethical, uneducated, unfair, and untrained white guys?"

"Just the Facts, Ma'am"

Detective Sergeant Joe Friday of the Los Angeles Police Department was a fictional character on the 1950s television show Dragnet who has been remembered throughout the years for his catch phrase when speaking to a witness or victim (The Free Dictionary by Farlex, n.d.). When people ventured away from details about the case he was working to irrelevant dribble, Detective Joe Friday would redirect them in a monotone voice saying, "Just the facts, Ma'am". With a plethora of 24-hour news channels spanning the spectrum of cable, radio, and social media platforms, one might argue there is not enough interesting news to keep people tuned in around the clock. In an age where ratings dominate the landscape and producers are more concerned with being first, as opposed to being right, the truth may be one of the first things sacrificed in order to ensure viewership. This next section will address the impact of media coverage and the ways in which racial tensions and hysteria may be fueled by the manner of coverage and where "just the facts" are not enough to keep people tuned in day and night.

Before delving into media coverage and reporting, it should be noted that people claim they want more positive news stories, but in reality, they are more interested in negative stories and coverage, as discovered in a recent study conducted by Trussler and Soroka (2014). The researchers refer to this as "negativity bias" and it helps explain peoples' collective desire to hear and remember "bad news", despite claiming they prefer more "good news" reporting (Trussler and Soroka, 2014). Natural disasters, mass shootings, terror attacks, and the like grip the nation like nothing else and compel people to stay tuned.

Perhaps "tuning in" for longer periods of time and following bad news, heartache, destruction, devastation, loss, and threat is nothing new. In 1987, baby Jessica McClure fell down a well in Midland, Texas when her mother stepped away for just a moment to answer the phone. As over 100 rescue workers worked for over 58 hours attempting to rescue her, 3.1 million people watched live on CNN which, at that time, was the largest audience ever to watch a cable news show (Thomas & Annin, 1997). Some argue that the constant coverage and miraculous recue helped make CNN what it is today.

The events of September 11, 2001 (9/11) kept people glued to their television sets, as they watched professional and amateur video footage of commercial airplanes crashing and exploding throughout the country during the deadliest terrorist attack on American soil. 9/11 ranks as the most memorable moment shared by television viewers in over 50 years, followed by coverage about Hurricane Katrina (2005), the O.J. Simpson murder verdict decision (1995), the Challenger explosion (1986), the death of Osama bin Laden (2011), the O.J. Simpson police chase (1994), the tsunami in Japan (2001) and the Columbine school shooting (1999) (CBSNews.com, 2012). The deadliest terror attack in American history and the capture and death of the mastermind responsible for the attacks, two natural disasters, a space shuttle tragedy, the O.J. drama, and the first mass school shooting captivated television audiences for hours, days, weeks, and even months following.

In previous years, the aim of journalism focused on reporting the news as it happened, without the sensationalism and controversy (Serani, 2008). Along the way, however, something changed. "It is no longer a race to break the story first or get the facts right, instead, to acquire good ratings to draw advertisers so that profits soar" (Serani, 2008, p.241). Serani cites Glassner when stating, "The success of fear-based news relies on presenting dramatic anecdotes in place of scientific evidence, promoting isolated events as trends, depicting categories of people as dangerous, and replacing optimism with fatalistic thinking" (Serani, 2008, p.241).

News programming does all of this under the hierarchical model of "if it bleeds, it leads", meaning it will dominate the time, attention, and the crucial spots in the news lineup. Media outlets continue to do this because there is merit in such an approach: it is productive and the counter-method pales in comparison. For example, in 1994, several news programs in Minneapolis, Minnesota, in response to copious focus groups' dissatisfaction with high levels of violence stories shown on local news channels, moved towards a more "family sensitive" approach in an attempt to limit violent images and graphic content relating to crime. Eight of the ten stations that adopted said practices and efforts experienced a drop-in ratings compared to the previous year (Young, 2003).

With countless national news channels and just as many media outlets where people can glean their information, one might wonder what channels and programmers can do to maintain their viewership if all media outlets assume more of a "doom and gloom" approach to broadcasting. How does a media conglomerate keep the people tuned in when there are so many other choices out there? Or, better stated, is the media making the news juicier and more controversial in order to secure and hold viewers' attention?

If It Bleeds Black and Shot by Blue, It Leads (Facts Need not Apply)

When discussing police misconduct and abuse of force in present day times, critics typically point to two or three recent cases to build their argument that police use excessive force, behave out of control, and should not be trusted. In July 2014, Eric Garner died at the hands of New York City police officers. During the struggle between the unarmed Garner and officers, Garner said, “I can’t breathe”. This became the rallying cry of demonstrators following his death (Okada, Maguire, & Sardina, 2019).

In August of 2014, Officer Daren Wilson shot unarmed 18-year old Michael Brown, Jr., which led to countless demonstrations and civil unrest (Okada, Maguire, & Sardina, 2019). The phrase “hands up, don’t shoot” functioned as the clever, attention-grabbing catch-phrase uttered by thousands, despite the fact it never happened.

In both cases, officers killed unarmed African American males, a point made by countless demonstrators and critics of law enforcement practices throughout the country. The facts of each story, however, tell a very different story worth discussing than that which circulated the country through media reports, politicians hoping to rouse support from their base, and social media campaigns.

Beto O’Rourke, in a 2018 talk at Good Street Baptist Church in Dallas, Texas said, “How can we continue to lose the lives of unarmed black men in the United States of America at the hands of white police officers? That is not justice” (Lott, Jr., 2018). O’Rourke is correct when he says it is not justice. Unfortunately for him, it is also not the whole truth. To hear O’Rourke speak, one might have the illusion that police officers, all of whom are white, hunt unarmed black men throughout the nation as if it were part of a competition. One might question, specifically, what example or examples O’Rourke would use to justify his position.

If history is any indicator of the support O’Rourke, or others who subscribe to his same ideological perspective, will utilize, they can point to names like Eric Garner and Michael Brown as examples of police brutality. They persist in their efforts by blanketing calls for justice and referendums for police reform by invoking the names of African American males who lost their lives at the hands of police, despite remaining unarmed at the time of their death. While the fact remains that each African American man they refer to in their litany of injustice was, in fact, unarmed at the time of his death, it is not the whole truth of what transpired in each scenario.

Robert McCulloch, the St. Louis County prosecutor, when discussing the difficulties of the Michael Brown investigation, for example, said, “The most significant challenge encountered in this investigation has been the 24-hour news cycle and its insatiable appetite for something, for anything, to talk about. Following closely behind were the nonstop rumors on social media” (North, 2014, p. 1). Lost in all the peaceful and violent protests, countless hashtags, candlelight vigils, calls for justice, and demands for action were the facts, which will be delineated now.

Race Aside: The Untold Eric Garner Story

The facts of the Eric Garner death lost or ignored by most commentators and social justice warriors include the following: Eric Garner resisted arrest and repeatedly flailed his arms at officers attempting to take him into custody. Before his infamous, "I can't breathe" comment were countless orders directed at police demanding, "Don't touch me" before barking, "This ends here", all of which accompanied him swatting at officers intending to arrest him. Eric Garner had more than 30 arrests throughout his life, including false impersonation, illegally selling cigarettes, which was why police were called to respond on July 17, 2014, and drug possession. Eric Garner weighed 350 pounds and was 6'3" tall. Garner did not die on the sidewalk following the takedown by police, but instead en route to the hospital as a result of cardiac arrest (McManus, 2014; Meyers, 2014). Those facts paint a very different picture than the smear campaign that shaded over the important, factual details of his arrest. Regardless of how many times race captured the attention of those reporting and demonstrating, one cannot mistake a very different rendering of exactly what happened when portraying facts and truth.

Eric Garner broke the law, plain and simple. He did not deserve to die for the minor infraction he had partaken in prior to police responding, but his choices and reactions dictated the escalation of force. Once on the scene, police attempted to take him into custody. Garner resisted. The arrest record, physical build, and temperament of Eric Garner do not suggest he deserved to die for those reasons exclusively, but illustrate the difficulties police officers faced when attempting to enforce the law and do their job. His race only mattered in the media frenzy that followed; it mattered not to police. For had Eric Garner been white and acted in the same threatening and uncontrollable manner, ignoring police directives and resisting arrest, he would have been dealt with in precisely the same manner. The only difference, the media would not have sensationalized it in order to perpetuate a frenzy that would attract the attention it did without the racial overtones.

Race Aside: The Untold Michael Brown, Jr. Story

The facts surrounding the Michael Brown, Jr. shooting death provide a more disgusting misrepresentation of reality and a more dangerous example of focusing attention elsewhere than to the facts of a specific incident. The following is a narrative of events that took place in the town of Ferguson, Missouri on Saturday Aug. 9, 2014, the day Michael Brown was shot and killed by Officer Darren Wilson: From 11:48 a.m. until noon, Officer Darren Wilson was responding to a call of a sick child. At 11:51 a.m., a call came in about a robbery at a convenience store and the dispatcher gave a description of the robber and said the suspect was walking toward the Quick Trip convenience store. Somewhere between 12:00 to 12:01, Officer Wilson encountered Michael Brown. Officer Wilson was unaware Michael Brown was a suspect in the robbery of the convenience store. Wilson stopped Brown and another male because the two were walking down the middle of the street and causing a disruption in traffic. Between 12:01 and 12:04, Michael Brown was shot 8 times and killed by Officer Wilson. At 12:04 p.m., a second officer arrived on the scene and a supervisor arrived one minute later. An ambulance drove by and responded to assess Brown (Brown, 2014).

Thirteen minutes from the time the 9-1-1 call came in to the time a robbery suspect was shot dead in the street. Thirteen minutes that, not only changed the course of the Brown family, the Wilson family, and the community, but thirteen minutes that propelled the justified and legitimate use of deadly force into a media frenzy where false narratives and misinformation fueled riots, looting, and racial tensions to levels unprecedented in the last 50 years.

While some opt to focus on the demographics of Wilson and Brown (immediately pointing out Brown was black and Wilson was white), the reality is such that the race of each actor involved in the story should remain irrelevant in examining the outcome of what transpired. The actions of Michael Brown necessitate a deeper introspection of the events that led to his death.

Michael Brown attacked Officer Wilson when Wilson confronted him for walking in the middle of the street obstructing traffic; an attack that occurred following Michael Brown attacking a convenient store owner and stealing Cigarillos (James, Heath, & Eisler, 2014). In his St. Louis grand jury statement, Officer Wilson stated, "I've never seen that much aggression so quickly from a simple request to just walk on the sidewalk." (James, Heath, & Eisler, 2014, p. 1)

The attack took place after Brown delivered several profanity-laced questions and responses at Wilson as Wilson attempted to ascertain the reasons why Brown was in the middle of the road. Brown slammed the officer's car door shut when he attempted to open it and then ducked down and began punching into the police cruiser, striking Wilson in the face repeatedly. When Officer Wilson attempted to un-holster his firearm to defend himself, Brown grabbed the gun and said, "You are too much of a ***** to shoot me." Brown grabbed Wilson's firearm attempting to turn it on the officer. At one point during the struggle, Brown squeezed the trigger and fired a bullet through the door panel. As the milieu ensued, Brown struck Wilson several more times before he disengaged and ran away from the car. Officer Wilson exited the vehicle and ordered Brown on the ground. Brown turned, made a grunting-like sound, balled up his one fist, reached his other fist into his waistband, and began to charge Wilson, who fired multiple shots to stop the assailant. Brown continued to run towards Officer Wilson, who fired a second series of shots as he backed up before delivering a fatal shot to the head of Brown who, as he approached Wilson, assumed more of a tackling posture (James, Heath, & Eisler, 2014).

Michael Brown weighed 289 pounds and dwarfed Officer Wilson and his 210 pound frame (Eisler, 2014). Again, this in no way suggests that simply because a suspect outweighs or poses a physical challenge for an officer that deadly force needs to be employed, but it provides a more complete picture of each actor than by simply commenting on the race of the men involved. It also illustrates the real fear Officer Wilson had for losing his life.

Michael Brown, Jr. broke the law, plain and simple. His choices and his actions dictated the escalation of force, resulting in deadly force. The physical build and temperament of Michael Brown, Jr. do not suggest he deserved to die for those reasons exclusively, but illustrate the difficulties Officer Wilson faced when attempting to enforce the law, do his job, and save his own life. Michael Brown's race only mattered in the media frenzy that followed; it mattered not to Officer Wilson. For had Michael Brown, Jr. been white and acted in the same threatening and uncontrollable manner, ignoring police directives, and attacking an officer attempting to disarm him, he would have been dealt with in precisely the same manner. The only difference, the media would not have sensationalized it in order to perpetuate a frenzy that would attract the attention it did without the racial overtones.

Unarmed and Dangerous

Quite frankly, when officers shoot unarmed suspects who attempt to disarm the officer, the suspects should not be considered unarmed. The moment anyone makes an effort to overpower an officer for his or her gun, that person should be considered armed and dangerous because that remains the reality of the situation. Federal agents and police officers alike learn during academy life about the dire and deadly consequences of having one's firearm taken during a confrontation.

The wisdom of not resisting an arrest follows along those same lines. Perhaps Eric Garner and Michael Brown Jr. would still be alive today, had they not resisted arrest and/or attacked police officers. It remains as simple and concise as that. When hearing claims of police brutality or unnecessary force, it seems like the first thing the media seeks to uncover and report upon deals with the race of the suspect. A more telling and meaningful question would be, "Was the person resisting arrest?" If an affirmative answer follows that question, the onus of responsibility for what transpires resides exclusively with the suspect himself or herself. Once the resistance stops and the individual complies with directives and commands from the officer, the use of force should desist as well. As long as an individual remains committed to the fight and chooses not to surrender, police retain the power to control the situation and ensure their individual and collective safety.

The primary functions of police are enforcing the law, maintaining order, and community service and they remain a salvation in protecting life, liberty, and property (Vago, 2009). The best way to avoid confrontation with police when one finds himself in the midst of a police matter, is to do precisely what one is told, when one is told, to the best of one's ability, without disrespecting the officers and escalating a situation for failure to comply with directives. So many issues could be averted by simple compliance with commands. Instead, it seems as though the media and those crying for justice through police prosecution ignore all the elements that entered into the escalation of force and why the officer had to respond in the manner he or she did.

FAKE NEWS, REAL CONCERNS

Despite the advancements in department diversity, the educational advancements of officers, and the additional training requirements for police officers mentioned at the beginning of this chapter, civilian confidence in law enforcement has fallen to an all-time low. In 2015, 25% of Americans polled indicate they have a great deal of confidence in the police, 27% a lot, 30% had some confidence, 16% had very little, and 2% had no confidence in police. The combined 18% of respondents who indicated they had very little or no confidence in police is the highest for the Gallup poll, since polling began on this issue. Conversely, the 52% combined totals for those who reported a great deal, or a lot of confidence marks a low point for those two categories not seen in 22 years (Jones, 2015).

When examining confidence levels by political affiliation, Democrat confidence in police plummeted 13 percentage points in 2014-2015, when compared with 2012-2013, indicating the largest change of any subgroup listed. Over that same time period, Republicans and Independent confidence levels remained unchanged. With those changes, Democrats (42%) report less confidence in police than their Republican counterparts (69%) and Independents (51%) (Jones, 2015).

In 2016, 56% of Americans polled reported they had a great deal or a lot of confidence in police (25% and 31% respectively) and 14 % indicated little or no confidence (down from 18%), as previously mentioned. In both the 2015 and 2016 polls, whites purport higher levels of confidences than nonwhites (Newport, 2016).

One cannot help to wonder if the slight increase in confidence levels recently is not related to changes in the White House. President Barack Obama, on several occasions, injected himself into the debate regarding law enforcement practices in the country, most notably after the shooting death of Michael Brown. President Obama provided these comments, "Of course, it's important to remember how this started. We lost a young man, Michael Brown, in heartbreaking and tragic circumstances. He was eighteen years old. His family will never hold Michael in their arms again. And when something like this happens, the local authorities, including the police, have a responsibility to be open and transparent about how they are investigating the death, and how they are protecting the people in their communities" (Christie, 2015).

This was not the first time the President voiced his concerns or opinion on matters of police protocol and procedure. On July 16, 2009, six months after President Obama took office, Professor Henry Louis Gates was arrested by Cambridge, MA Police for disorderly conduct after exhibiting loud and tumultuous behavior directed at Sergeant

James Crowley. Crowley responded to a call of a suspected burglary after Lucia Whalen, one of Gates' neighbors, observed two men with backpacks attempting to break into Gates' residence. Whalen described one of the men wedging his shoulder into the door in an attempt to gain entry. Sergeant Crowley approached Gates' residence and saw a black man standing in the foyer of the residence. When asked to step outside, Gates refused and inquired as to the officer's identity. Sergeant Crowley provided his name and rank and told Gates about the report of a break-in in progress. When Sergeant Crowley questioned Gates about anyone else being inside, Gates lashed out at the officer, calling him a racist. As the exchange continued, Sergeant Crowley asked Gates for identification to verify his identity. After initially refusing, Gates showed the officer his Harvard University identification card before continuing to accuse the officer of being a racist. As the officer was walking down the front steps of Gates' residence, the professor continued to hurl insults towards Officer Crowley, despite repeated attempts and warnings to calm down. Professor Gates was arrested after refusing to desist from making a scene, insulting the officer, and disturbing the neighborhood (Cambridge Police Department, 2009 as found in The Smoking Gun, 2015). In addressing the actions of the officer and the entire sequence of events, President Obama said,

> I don't know, not having been there and not seeing all the facts, what role race played in that [Gates case]. But I think it's fair to say, number one, any of us would be pretty angry; number two, that the Cambridge police acted stupidly in arresting somebody when there was already proof that they were in their own home; and, number three, what I think we know separate and apart from this incident is that there's a long history in this country of African-Americans and Latinos being stopped by law enforcement disproportionately. That's just a fact. (McPhee & Just, 2009, n.p.)

Perhaps the President would have been better served in learning what the specifics of the incident were before assuming race played any role in the arrest of Professor Gates. Interesting how his follow up comment, despite acknowledging his uncertainty of facts, ridiculed the actions of the officer. With all due respect for the position he held at the time, President Obama most certainly misspoke.

In any situation involving an alleged break in, immediately upon arriving at the scene and ensuring their own safety, police will ascertain the identity of occupants inside to confirm the person or persons actually live at that residence and are not causing harm or detaining the rightful occupants inside. In the Gates case, however, the Harvard professor initially refused to show proper documentation and accused the officer of being racist for even asking him to verify his identity, escalating the situation by his own disrespectful and inappropriate actions (contempt of cop). The President can cite disproportionate statistics and beliefs all he wants, but in this case, the police conducted themselves in a manner that served the public well-being. Professor Gates demonstrated misplaced righteous indignation and, despite repeated warnings, failed to control his behavior before the officer arrested him. The proper place for blame on this matter dwells exclusively with Professor Gates. Had the officer confronted a white suspect upon arriving on scene, or any other suspect for that matter, his actions would have followed suit. If political leaders, mainstream media commentators, and social justice warriors wish to illustrate examples of blatant racism and discrimination, perhaps they should cite substantiated cases instead of relying on ones that require vivid imagination and irrelevant rhetoric.

You Wanna Talk Race, Let's Talk Race, Shall We?

Despite the noted changes in police diversity, training and education, the introduction of a formalized code of ethics, and increased efforts to improve the professionalism of the entire discipline, perpetual falsehoods continue to resonate throughout the United States. According to some, the poor relationship and dismal state of affairs between the police and the community resides exclusively on the law enforcement profession for their racist and bigoted behaviors, targeting minorities, and using unnecessary force for no reason at all. Having noted as much, perhaps examining the topic of race in greater detail and under a different frame of reference will provide a unique perspective and open the door for potential ways to decrease confrontations between law enforcement officers and the general public.

Single Parents, the Singular Problem: Examining the Impact of Out of Wedlock Births

In 2013, CNN's Don Lemon noted that 72% of African American births are out of wedlock. The Centers for Disease Control and Prevention's published report of 2012 observed the number at 73%, based on their 2010 data (Jacobson, 2013). The most recent statistics indicate the number of out of wedlock births at 77% for African American births compared to 30% for whites (Bedard, 2017). Regardless of which rubric or year utilized, the fact remains that approximately 2/3 of African American children are born out of wedlock, a number that should appall anyone concerned with the well-being of people. It also demands consideration from anyone who contends "black lives matter" immediately following a police-involved shooting of a black suspect, since concern for the welfare of African Americans only after their death appears suspect and opportunistic. Genuine care encompasses the entire spectrum of life and the circumstances and conditions enveloping it. In other words, illegitimacy rates matter.

African American illegitimacy rates have been steadily increasing for the past 80 years in America, despite the lack of attention given to it. In 1940, only 14% of African American children were born out of wedlock. That number rose to 25% by the mid-1960s. As the 1970s gave way to the 1980s, the number stood at 56% (Williams, 2015). Today, the number has literally exploded out of control and yet, no one seems to give it the due attention it deserves. The perceived and actual impact of single parents and child development, discipline, and life course outcomes demands further analysis and consideration. From a criminological standpoint, few theoretical perspectives (classical, psychological, social control, social learning, strain, etc.) fail to recognize the importance of positive parenting, which may be best highlighted in Gottfredson and Hirschi's General Theory of Crime.

A General Theory of Crime

In 1990, Gottfredson and Hirschi published a General Theory of Crime to explain criminal behavior and deviance (Akers & Sellers, 2009; Vold, Bernard, & Snipes, 1998). In it, they purport that people with higher levels of self-control will be "substantially less likely at all periods of life to engage in criminal acts" (Gottfredson & Hirschi, 1990, p. 89). People with low levels of self-control, conversely, demonstrate greater propensity to engage in criminal and delinquent behaviors throughout the life course (Akers & Sellers, 2009). In short, self-control directly determines the amount of criminal and delinquent behaviors an individual will engage in throughout his or her life.

Self-control, according to Gottfredson and Hirschi, establishes itself at the age of eight or ten and remains relatively consistent within the individual moving forward. Additionally, the differences between one person and another remain relatively stable over time; meaning, a person's level of self-control at age 10 compared to someone else's level of self-control at age 10 will remain consistent over time. Those with high levels of self-control and those with low levels of self-control may experience minor changes within the individual over time, but the differences in self-control values when comparing people to each other over time remain the same (Vazsonyi & Huang, 2010).

Gottfredson and Hirschi describe the behavioral tendencies and characteristics of those with low levels of self-control as being risk-takers, short-sighted, impulsive, insensitive, physical as opposed to mental, careless, restless, and nonverbal (Gottfredson & Hirschi, 1990; Nakhaie, Silverman, & LaGrange, 2000; Vold, Bernard, & Snipes, 1998). These penchants cause the individual to partake in more criminal and delinquent behaviors, in addition to actions that provide more immediate gratification, such as smoking and drinking heavily (Vold, Bernard, & Snipes, 1998).

The authors of the theory argue that ineffective or incomplete socialization directly determines an individual's level of self-control. Social institutions and schools can impact self-control, but the major source, and most important, derives from parental management (Akers & Sellers, 2009). Proper parental management takes place when parents monitor their child, identify bad behavior in the child, and take proper steps to discipline the child in order to help extinguish bad behavior (Vold, Bernard, & Snipes, 1998). Poor parental management occurs when parents fail to monitor their children, do not recognize inappropriate behavior, and neglect to correct it (Nakhaie, Silverman, & LaGrange,

2000). Parents who consistently adhere to the three elements of proper parental management will instill higher levels of self-control in their son or daughter while parents who ignore, neglect, or improperly administer these three aspects of parental management will instill lower levels of self-control in their child (Vold, Bernard, & Snipes, 1998; Nakhaie, Silverman, & LaGrange, 2000).

Studies examining the relationship between self-control and school performance offer strong support for the General Theory of Crime in both high school and college settings (Gibbs & Giever, 1995; Nakhaie, Silverman, & LaGrange, 2000). In a survey of junior high and senior high-school students, males and older students reported lower levels of self-control than their female and younger counterparts. Those with lower levels of self-control exhibited greater resistance to school, as indicated by the authors. They state,

> Researchers who have explained gender, ethnic and class differences in resistance usually have focused on structural forces and have ignored potential mediating factors such as personality characteristics of individuals. Gottfredson and Hirschi explain the personality differences among these social categories are shaped, structured and reproduced early in life with enduring effects. Accordingly, they predicted that early in the life course, males, certain minorities, and lower-class children are more likely to internalize risk taking, impulsivity and preference for physical and simple tasks, while acquiring quick tempers and rejecting deferred gratification. These personality characteristics then become the catalyst for delinquent behavior. They also argued that self-control has an effect independent of these social groups. (Nakhaie, Silverman, & LaGrange, 2000, p. 455-456)

Gibbs and Giever (1995) found similar outcomes when assessing the impact of self-control on behaviors that can be considered crime equivalents, such as cutting class and alcohol use, at the college level. They report that self-control possessed the greatest impact on the aforementioned dependent variables, prioritizing higher than gender and Greek membership (Gibbs & Giever, 1995).

In analyzing antisocial and delinquency later in life, low self-control continues to remain a strong predictor (Boisvert, Wright, Knopik, & Vaske, 2012). "There is very good reason for suspecting that single parenthood plays a role in high crime rates generally, and high levels of violent crime in particular" (Barber, 2006, p. 442). Barber continues by acknowledging that, when compared to children living with both biological parents, children living in single-parent homes experience less emotional support, involvement, and supervision, all of which serve as predictive factors for antisocial and violent tendencies (Barber, 2006).

This section, in no way, shape, or form means to disparage single parents attempting to raise their children properly. In the majority of cases, the mother assumes responsibility for the child while the father remains absent from the picture. This section, however, does most certainly suggest that in single-parent homes, parental management operates at a 50% deficiency compared to most two-parent homes. This trend consistently fails to receive the attention it deserves, as delineated by the supporting research, but it may help explain some of the issues between the general public and law enforcement.

Little People, Little Problems… Big People, Big Problems

As evidenced by the previous paragraphs discussing the effects of self-control on behavior, from school settings to adulthood, people with low levels of self-control exhibit a greater propensity for resistance and violence later in life. One can safely assume that similar tendencies manifest themselves when people of low self-control are confronted by law enforcement. In keeping with the theory and research support for it, people of low self-control will be short-sighted, impulsive, insensitive, careless, restless, more physical as opposed to mental, and nonverbal. For children in a school setting, such behaviors can be disruptive. For adults in a police encounter, such behaviors can be deadly.

In situations where claims of police brutality rear their ugly head, from Michael Brown to Eric Garner and countless examples in between, suspects often exhibit a blatant disregard for authority, an inability or obstinate defiance to follow police commands, and/or a failure to realize they must comply with the officer(s), regardless of whether or not they want to or like it. Failure to comply and resisting arrest always end badly for the suspect… always. A situation never arises where someone resists an officer or fails to comply with commands and directives and the officer (or officers) decide it is in the best interest of society and the law enforcement profession to allow the person to go free without taking him or her into custody. That misguided fantasy never happens in reality and most people realize that. Those who flee, fight, attempt to disarm, and resist police officers must realize they have to do what they are told when they are told. They will surely get their day in court, especially if officers are engaging in discriminatory or corrupt practices, but to seek street justice at the moment of an apprehension or police stop will forever end badly for them. If Eric Garner's and Michael Brown's parent(s) perfected such teaching in their children, chances are both men would still be alive today.

The Andy Sipowicz in Me

Perhaps the most iconic police personality of this generation is Detective Andy Sipowicz, a character from the Emmy-award winning television series NYPD Blue, which aired for twelve seasons from 1993 to 2005 (IMDb, n.d.). Sipowicz's character's claim to fame, in addition to his fiery temperament, and a knack for voicing inappropriate comments when angered, and his wardrobe consisting of short-sleeve dress shirts with checkered print and high-waisted trousers, was his uncanny ability to speak boldly and bluntly on matters of policing, justice, and life. He is undoubtedly my favorite character of this genre.

I introduce Andy Sipowicz because in revisiting the television series and the 261 episodes he appeared in, political correctness, popularity, and style points mattered not to the middle-aged detective from the 15th Detective Squad. No, Sipowicz cared only about one thing: getting it right, regardless of who it offended, triggered, agitated, or infuriated. He wanted to find the truth, solve the case, and see to it that justice was served. His commentary at times could be labeled as racist, homophobic, nationalistic, and most certainly argumentative, but it bothered him not. Detective Andy Sipowicz knew who he was and those he interacted with knew him, respected him, and/or revered him as one of the "good guys" who did not discriminate when it came to policing.

In conjuring up my Andy Sipowicz, several points of interest bounce around in my head and leave me asking some very tough questions. Questions, I imagine, Detective Sipowicz would seek clarification on if he were conducting an investigation into these matters. Surely those who disagree with me even inquiring into said matters would resort to claims of racism, but those unsubstantiated claims only suggest I may be on to something.

The Sipowicz in Me on Media, Politics, and Social Justice Warriors

I find it hard to fathom community leaders, preachers, civil rights activists, social justice warriors, and politicians ignore the out of wedlock birth rate for African Americans and/or never make the connection to possible explanations for criminal propensity and problems with law enforcement. I suppose it would be a good time to point out the obvious, ridiculous odds of achieving success in terms of financial security, professional achievement, and upward mobility for single-parents as well (all facts one would think sociologists, economists, guidance counselors, educators, and political leaders would agree upon, but that can wait for a different chapter).

Why is it teaching and promoting good life choices, like avoiding out of wedlock pregnancies, never reaches the heights of attention that a false narrative like, "hands up, don't shoot" achieves in the black communities? Is it taboo to bring up the obvious? Is it not fascinating or glamorous enough for the media to cover? Conceivably, African American women can borrow the Me Too movement's hashtag when discussing how they are raising their children alone without a father figure and the many struggles they endure doing so. Almost 80% of African American new moms would be able to legitimately post "#metoo". How can people ignore this fact and not see the impact it has throughout life for children? Where is the social outcry over this incredible epidemic?

Speaking of outcries, where is all the coverage when a black officer engages in police misconduct or unnecessary use of force and why is that story not circulating the media frenzy for days and weeks? What about white victims of police excessive force, like the two white teenagers shot, one fatally, by Gardena police officers in July of 2015 (Winton, 2015)? (My guess is most people never heard of that incident or saw the footage of that shooting, despite it being captured on dashboard cameras.) Do they not count? Why was that video not played on a running loop on CNN? Am I to believe only black lives matter (if they were shot by a white cop, that is)? I venture to say if the victims were black in the Gardena shooting, those people would be household names. Instead, people resisting arrest and attempting to disarm officers, like Eric Garner and Michael Brown, gain the attention of those in the media and general public because they were black. Their noncompliant and threatening actions that warranted the use of force, unfortunately, never got the attention deserved. Instead, people simply focus on their skin color, not their actions, which become a moot point if the officer has to use deadly force to control the situation. All the while, the media stirs up commentary and discussion about the police being racist, when in fact, the exact same thing would have happened had a white person done the same thing. That, to me, is the very definition of fake news (and maybe even racism).

The Sipowicz in Me on "The Talk", Diversity in Departments, and Bad Cops

Regardless of how many parents reside in the home, perhaps "the talk" people have with their children about police should begin with instructions and imperatives to listen and comply with law enforcement, as opposed to demonizing the profession and blaming them for doing their job to enforce the law. Police remain undefeated when it comes to people resisting arrest. Granted, an individual may elude officers and escape momentarily, but it never fails that individual will eventually be apprehended and face additional charges and grief for not obeying orders. Doing what one is told, when one is told, remains the wiser option than combative resistance and blatant disrespect. One would think that when dealing with an armed individual possessing the powers of arrest, behavior resplendent with respect and compliance would be the first course of action taken from any citizen. I am guessing in households with absent, deadbeat fathers, those conversations rarely happen. Then people wonder why officers must rely on force to handle situations where people ignore police commands. Is that really a police brutality problem or is that more of a citizen compliance problem?

Does it come as a shock to anyone that African Americans choose jobs and careers other than law enforcement with such a negative portrait of the profession painted by so many in their communities and homes? Where, exactly, do people think local departments recruit from? Criticizing agencies and departments for incompatible minority rates while slamming the entire profession when speaking to children and then wondering why African Americans do not want to enlist in the ranks of uniformed officers would be comical, if the sad reality of it were not true. Noting differences in population compositions between departments and the communities they serve do not mean those departments are racist. How many nonwhite, qualified applicants apply? How many make it through the long hiring and training process? Do we really want to relax standards in order to attract more females and nonwhite applicants and would that marginalize the accomplishments of those who have achieved the established standards?

The system of law enforcement assumes more of a reactive nature; meaning, police respond to calls after an alleged crime is in progress or has taken place. If certain demographics experience higher crime tendencies, is that really a problem with policing? Perhaps a problem in the community persists.

In considering the ranks of those enlisted, allow me to point out that no one ever wants to work with a dirty cop, a selfish cop, a racist cop, or a cop who endangers others by his or her actions. The job is difficult enough and dangerous enough without having to worry if the officers in the ranks are engaging in unethical or unscrupulous behaviors. Making it a mandate to report suspicious activity involving a fellow officer ushered out the practice of turning one's head or pretending like something never happened. Officers who do not report violations face serious consequences, which could include loss of job and wages, as well it should, to help make the profession more integrity-driven. Suggesting cops do not report other cops is an outdated and ill-supported proclamation.

The Sipowicz in Me on What Have Communities Done?

It never fails that anytime the topic of police-community relations surfaces, people immediately focus their attention to what the police need to do in order to strengthen and foster this relationship. For the past fifty years or more, styles of policing, rules of engagement, legislative measures, and advancements in technology have attempted to build a better bond and connection between police and the communities they serve. Many of these changes have put officers' lives in greater jeopardy.

The use of tasers and pepper spray, for example, remain an option on the use of force continuum for police trying to control a resisting suspect without having to resort to deadly force. While I most certainly recognize the potential benefit of such tools, I cannot ignore the fact that utilizing these methods has resulted in police officers getting injured or shot when the suspect is not hindered by them or when the devise fails to work as intended. The most recent example to personify this statement involves two Pennsylvania State Troopers in Northampton County who were shot. Dashboard footage shows the driver miserably failing a field sobriety test, resisting arrest, fighting through both officers using their tasers and punches to subdue him. The driver broke free, retrieved a gun from his vehicle, and shot both troopers (New York Post, 2018). The intense footage demonstrates how quickly a traffic stop can escalate to deadly levels, but it brings other issues to attention as well.

The troopers would have been better served using their firearms to prevent the suspect from reaching into his vehicle. Granted, the coverage of the shooting and the headlines would have read something along the lines of, "Two white officers shoot unarmed black man" had they pulled their firearms when they should have. The most relevant fact that he attempted to gain access to his firearm would have found its way to the cutting room floor if this version became reality.

I realize that risk, danger, and peril will forever be associated with the job of law enforcement, as will the need for better community relations. Sixty years ago, people in all neighborhoods had reason to distrust law enforcement. Times have changed and advancements have been made ranging from community-oriented policing strategies to dashboard and body cameras for oversight and prosecution for corrupt and abusive officers. The law enforcement profession has become more diverse, focused on ethical treatment of civilians, and required more training and education to better serve all people, including those in predominantly minority neighborhoods. Yet, relations remain more distant and hostile than ever, which begs the question, "What have the minority communities done to better relationships with law enforcement?" Is this a one-way street where the law enforcement profession does what it can to salvage a relationship while the communities they serve do nothing different? How successful has that been for those communities? What has changed in 60 years within black communities regarding attitudes and behaviors towards police officers? The answer I continue to come up with is: nothing, nothing has changed.

Closing Thoughts

Until something changes in neighborhoods and communities regarding personal responsibility and the treatment of police officers, the divide between law enforcement and those populations will continue to grow and increase in resentment and hostility. By definition alone, law enforcement and crime cannot harmoniously coexist. The divide in this country spreads daily, perpetuated in part by myths and false narratives, leaving people to have to choose a side for or against law enforcement, but never fully understanding how things have become so contentious.

If this trend continues, the most vulnerable will experience increased victimization amid the aftermath of broken homes and depressed communities while police officers will continue to best serve the communities they are sworn to protect. Groups promoting strife and discourse while elevating thugs and criminals to lofty heights will continue to do so while demonizing police in order to get votes, ratings, or social media "likes". Others more committed to law and justice, will attempt to expose their nefarious ways begging the question, "How can law and order attempt to fix what generations of people have screwed up?"

Martin Luther King, Jr. shared his dream of living in a world where people would not be judged by the color of their skin, but instead on the content of their character (Martin Luther King, Jr., 1963). Perhaps those in media, politics, and in society should revisit those words and allow the content of one's character to help determine, along with facts and truth, where the responsibility should fall when a proclamation about excessive force surfaces. Instead of rising up on social media soapboxes, obsessing over Nielson ratings, and pushing political agendas, everyone needs to examine the facts instead of assuming guilt or innocence based on skin color. That is the truth, the whole truth, and nothing but the truth.

REFERENCES

Akers, R. L. & Sellers, C. S. (2009). *Criminological theories: Introduction, evaluation, and application*. New York: Oxford University Press.

Barber, N. (2006). Why is violent crime so common in the Americas? *Aggressive Behavior, vol. 32*, pp. 442-450.

Bedard, P. (2017). *77% black births to single moms, 49% for Hispanic immigrants.* The Washington Examiner. Retrieved from: https://www.washingtonexaminer.com/77-black- births-to-single-moms-49-for-hispanic-immigrants.

Boisvert, D., Wright, J. P., Knopik, V., & Vaske, J. (2012). Genctic and environmental overlap between low self-control and delinquency. *J Quant Criminol, 28*, 477-507.

Brandl, S. G. (2018). *Police in America*. Los Angeles, CA: Sage.

Braswell, M. C., McCarthy, B. R., & McCarthy, B. J. (2008). *Justice, crime, and ethics* (6th ed.). Newark, NJ: Lexis Nexis.

Brown, E. (2014). *Timeline: Michael Brown shooting Ferguson,* MO. USA Today. Retrieved from: https://www.usatoday.com/story/news/nation/2014/08/14/michael-brown-ferguson- missouri-timeline/14051827/.

CBS/AP. (2012). *TV's most memorable moments: 9/11 tops the list*. Retrieved from: https://www.cbsnews.com/news/tvs-most-memorable-moments-9-11-tops-the-list/.

Cox, S. M., McCamey, W. P., & Scaramella, G. L. (2014). *Introduction to policing* (2nd ed.). Los Angeles, CA: Sage.

Christie, R. (2015). *How the media and Obama made Ferguson even worse.* Retrieved from: https:// www.thedailybeast.com/ how-the-media-and-obama-made-ferguson-even-worse.

Eisler, P. (2014). Ferguson case: By the numbers. *USA Today.* Retrieved from: https://www.usatoday.com/story/news/nation/2014/11/25/ferguson-case-by-the-numbers/70110614/.

Federal Bureau of Investigation Office of Integrity and Compliance. (2018). *FBI Ethics and Integrity Program Policy Directive and Policy Guide 0754DPG*. Published Date: February 2, 2015; Review Date: February 2, 2018.

Gibbs, J. J. & Giever, D. (1995). Self-control and its manifestations among university students: an empirical test of Gottfredson and Hirschi's general theory. *Justice Quarterly*, 12, 2, 231-255.

Grant, K. J. (2002). Ethics and law enforcement. *FBI Law Enforcement Bulletin,* 71, 12, pp. 11-14.

The Free Dictionary by Farlex. (n.d.). *Just the facts ma'am.* Retrieved from: https://idioms.thefreedictionary.com/Just+the+facts%2c+Ma%27am.

IMBd. (n.d.). *NYPD Blue.* Retrieved from: https://www.imdb.com/title/tt0106079/.

International Association of Chiefs of Police (IACP), (n.d.). Retrieved from: https://www.theiacp.org/resources/law-enforcement-code-of-ethics.

Jacobson, L. (2013). CNN's Dom Lemon says more than 72 percent of African-Americans births are out of wedlock. *Politifact.* Retrieved from: https://www.politifact.com/truth-o-meter/statements/2013/jul/29/don-lemon/cnns-don-lemon-says-more-72-percent-african- americ/.

James, M., Heath, B., & Eisler, P. (2014). Wilson: Struggle with Brown was like fighting 'Hulk Hogan'. *USA Today.* Retrieved from: https://www.usatoday.com/story/news/nation/2014/11/25/brown-wilson-ferguson-killing-grand-jury/70076886/.

Jones, J. M. (2015). In U.S., confidence in police lowest in 22 years. *Gallup. Politics.* Retrieved from: https://news.gallup.com/poll/183704/confidence-police-lowest-years.aspx.

King, M. L., Jr. (1963). *Letter from Birmingham Jail.*

Lardner, J. (1997). A mythical blue wall of silence: in real life, cops have been willing to blow the whistle on misconduct. *U.S. News and World Report,* (8), 34.

Lott, Jr. J. R. (2018). *Why O'Rourke's rhetoric on police shootings is wrong – and dangerous.* Retrieved from: https://townhall.com/columnists/johnrlottjr/2018/10/15/politice- shooting-blacks-n2528561.

McCafferty, F. L. & McCafferty, M. A. (1998). Corruption in law enforcement: A paradigm of occupational stress and deviancy. *J Am Acad Psychiatry Law,* vol. 26, no. 1, pp. 57-65. Retrieved from: http://jaapl.org/content/jaapl/26/1/57.full.pdf.

McManus, B. (2014). *Blame only the man who tragically decided to resist. New York Post.* Retrieved from: https://nypost.com/2014/12/04/eric-garner-was-a-victim-of-himself-for- deciding-to-resist/.

McPhee, M. & Just, S. (2009). Obama: Police acted 'stupidly' in Gates case. *ABC News.* Retrieved from: https://abcnews.go.com/US/story?id=8148986&page=1.

Myers, J. (2014). 11 facts about the Eric Garner case the media won't tell you. *Newsmax.* Retrieved from: https://www.newsmax.com/Newsfront/eric-garner-chokehold-grand-jury-police/2014/12/04/id/611058/.

Newport, F. (2016). U.S. confidence in police recovers from last year's low. *Gallup. Politics.* Retrieved from: https://news.gallup.com/poll/192701/confidence-police-recovers-last- year-low.aspx.

New York Post. (2018). *Heart-stopping moment officer is shot by man pulled over for speeding.* Retrieved from: https://nypost.com/video/heart-stopping-moment-officer-is-shot-by-man- pulled-over-for-speeding/.

Nakhaie, M. R., Silverman, R. A., & LaGrange, T. C. (2000). Self-control and resistance to school. *Canadian Review of Sociology & Anthropology,* vol. 37, issue 4, pp. 443-460.

North, A. (2014). What Ferguson says about the fear of social media. *The New York Times. Opinion*. Retrieved from: https://op-talk.blogs.nytimes.com/ 2014/11/25/what-ferguson-says-about-the-fear-of-social-media/.

Okada, D., Maguire, M, & Sardina, A. (2019). *Critical issues in crime and justice: thought, policy, and practice* (3rd ed.). Los Angeles, CA: Sage.

Paoline, E. A., III & Terrill, W. (2007). Police education, experiment, and the use of force. *Criminal Justice and Behavior, 34, issue 2*, pp. 179-197.

Paoline, E.A., Terrill, W., & Rossler, M.T. (2014). Higher education, college degree major, and police occupational attitudes. *Journal of Criminal Justice Education,* 256 (1), 49-73.

Reaves, B. A. (2016). State and local law enforcement training academies, 2013. *U.S. Department of Justice, Bureau of Justice Statistics*, NCJ: 249784, pp. 1-13.

Serani, D. (2008). If it bleeds, it leads. The clinical implications of fear-based programming in news media. *Psychotherapy and Psychoanalysis*, 24(4), 240-250.

South Park Studios. (n.d.). Retrieved from: http://southpark.cc.com/clips/150368/you-will- respect-my-authoritah.

Cambridge Police Department (2009) as Found in the Smoking Gun. (2015). Retrieved from: http://www.thesmokinggun.com/documents/crime/henry-louis-gates-jr-police-report.

Thomas, E. & Annin, P. (1997). Baby Jessica grows up. *Newsweek,* 130 (17), 34. Retrieved from: https://www.newsweek.com/baby-jessica-grows-174130.

Trussler, M. & Soroka, S. (2014). Consumer demand for cynical and negative news frames. *The International Journal for Press/Politics,* vol. 19, issue 3, pp. 360-379.

USA Today Magazine. (2016). Police Officers Do Not Shield Fellow Officers. *USA Today Magazine,* (145), December issue.

Vago, S. (2009). *Law and Society* (9th ed.). Upper Saddle River, NJ: Pearson Education, Inc.

Williams, W. E. (2015). *The true black tragedy: Illegitimacy rate of nearly 75%.* The Burning Platform. Retrieved from: https://www.theburningplatform.com/2016/ 05/29/the-true- black-tragedy-illegitimacy-rate-of-nearly-75/.

Young, J. R. (2003). The role of fear in agenda setting by television stations. *American Behavioral Scientist,* vol. 46, no. 12, pp. 1673-1695.

Vazsonyi, A. T. & Huang, L. (2010). Where self-control comes from: On the development of self-control and its relationship to deviance over time. *Developmental Psychology, vol. 46, (1)*, pp. 245-257.

Vold, G. B., Bernard, T. J., & Snipes, J. B. (1998). *Theoretical Criminology* (4th ed.). New York: Oxford University Press.

Winton, R. (2015). Gardena police shooting video: Justified or 'cold blooded' killing? *L.A. Times.* Retrieved from: https://www.latimes.com/local/lanow/la-me-ln-gardena-police- shooting-video-justified-or-cold-blooded-killing-20150714-story.html.

In: A Closer Look at Criminal Justice
Editors: J. A. Cooper and K. G. Jachimowski

ISBN: 978-1-53615-782-6

Chapter 6

COMMUNITY-BASED RESEARCH IN A RURAL COMMUNITY

Katie Ely*[*] *and Ed Bowman
Lock Haven University of Pennsylvania, Lock Haven, PA, US

ABSTRACT

According to some authors, the popularity of community-based research is increasing dramatically. In the criminal justice system, participatory or community-based research involving community stake-holders can result in significant changes in local criminal justice practices and policies. This chapter examines the organization, advocacy, and implementation of community-based research in a rural community. Beginning in 2012, faculty from Lock Haven University's Criminal Justice Department began meeting with local stakeholders to diagnose, prescribe, and evaluate local criminal justice policies and practices through different community-based research designs. Community-based research designs were used to examine offender re-entry, parole recidivism, and police satisfaction. Combining elements of data collection, analysis, and implications, we were able to collaborate with our community partners on strategic planning and justice reinvestment initiatives that had a direct impact on local practice. This chapter examines how community-based research projects are translated into action and provides suggestions to universities and practitioners to successfully work together.

By its nature, all knowledge is selective: it focuses on some items and neglects others. Facts, after all, only have meaning when they are placed in some broader framework of thought and belief.

Martin Rein
Social Science and Public Policy

[*] Corresponding Author's Email: kje341@lockhaven.edu

INTRODUCTION

For years, criminologists have engaged in community-based research to examine issues related to domestic violence, patterns of policing, correctional treatment, and offender recidivism (just to name a few). Despite those efforts, the paradigm or model for community-based research does not appear to be broadly recognized or applied to criminal justice research. The lack of ascribed "community-based" research in criminal justice however, should not distract from the fact that criminal justice researchers have made considerable contributions to criminal justice planning, policies, and programs. In fact, evidence of applied research in criminal justice is found in the literature on evidence-based practices. Throughout the 1980's and into the 1990's, criminal justice researchers in collaboration with federal, state, and local criminal justice planners examined the effectiveness of interventions to identify programs impacting recidivism; research having applied consequences to criminal justice outcomes (Orchowsky, 2014). Importantly, the criminal justice field recognized the use of collaborative scientific inquiry to inform implementation of programs and interventions designed to prevent and reduce crime and victimization (i.e., they were evidence based). As such, we would argue that criminologist have been conducting community-based research for some time even if not recognized as such.

Perhaps the failure to see criminal justice research in the context of a community-based research paradigm is both practical and ideological. Practically, community-based research is not a research methodology and therefore the types of research questions and methods vary. Second, authors use different terms when describing community-based research and the terms include important constructs in the conceptualization of a community-based research project or model. For example, researchers may not be familiar (or comfortable) with the discourse used in a community-based research model; for example, "research participant" replaces the idea of research subject and "engaging the community" replaces targeting the community (see Wallerstein & Duran, 2010). Changes in discourse are not just symbolic but reflect an emergent dialogue of inclusiveness with the community (2010). Importantly, the goal of community-based research is to create successful research partnerships, formulate research questions and to test, evaluate and refine actions designed to result in a desired community change (Kusago & Miyamoto, 2014; Mandell, 2010). In disciplines such as psychology, education, sociology, and organizational theory (perhaps due to their disciplinary longevity), community-based research has long been recognized as a process to improve the well-being of community life (Kusago & Miyamoto, 2014). However, for marginalized, disempowered or stigmatized groups, community-based research is discouraged (see Kidd & Kral, 2005, p. 187). Perhaps then, bias in ascribing community-based research to the field of criminal justice is related to the subject matter (i.e., the groups under consideration) and the action to be taken.

WHAT IS COMMUNITY-BASED RESEARCH?

Let's start with the basics. Community-based research is also referred to as: participatory research, community-based participatory research, community-based action research, and participatory action research. According to Stoecker, over time, community-based researchers "have melded together participatory research and action research" with most people intending to include both "participatory inputs" and "action outcomes" as critical components to a community-based research paradigm (2009, p. 387). Seem confusing? The principles of a community-based research paradigm include participation and action. Arguably, "community" is the lynch-pin of both participation and action. The "community" (however defined) is enlisted, engaged, and recruited as co-researchers; critically involved in generating dialogue and mutual discovery of the research questions. The "community" is also responsible for action resulting from the research project. For example, outputs from conventional research methods typically involve research articles, a research report, or policy recommendations (Mandell, 2010). Outputs from a community-based research project might include workshops, practical reports or executive summaries, and meetings with community stakeholders. Despite the definitional complexity or nuances of community-based research, the method of inquiry in a community-based research paradigm provides knowledge and action directly useful to the community (Kid & Kral, 2005). Comparing a conventional research model with a community-based model can help emphasize the differences.

Table 1. Conventional and Community-Based Research Models

Research Model	Characteristics	Methodology	Outcomes
Conventional Research	Research questions are generated by experts and privilege is given to academic knowledge.	Detailed research plan developed in advance using established methodologies.	Research articles, research reports, conference presentations, or policy recommendations.
Community-Based Research (CBR)	The emphasis is on conducting research "for and with" community partners. Community partners are not passive but help to inform the research agenda and questions.	Fact finding occurs before a detail research plan is created. Methodology should be flexible and based on discovery and the needs of the community.	Community meetings, presentations, and workshops where the findings from a research project are shared with the community and action plans are developed.

Community-based research (CBR) is a process in which researchers and participants develop goals and methods, participate in gathering and analyzing data, and implement the results in a way that will promote change benefiting community life. Community-based research is not a method but a general approach to knowledge exploration and development occurring within a community context and in collaboration among researchers and community stakeholders. The outcome of a community-based research project is to improve the overall quality of life for people (or groups) in the community; for example, improving the overall quality of human services including services and outcomes related to crime and victimization.

A word of caution. The fluidity in definitions of community-based research and the under-utilization of CBR in criminal justice could be the result of issues in defining community. For example, Kusago and Miyamoto offer a broad definition of community in their examination of action research for area studies. They define "community" as "a place where people live a life" adding that definitions and size of community differ from community to community (2014, p. 276). Other definitions of community focus on common experiences linked to a geographic location. For example, a common method of defining community emphasizes people with diverse characteristics linked by social ties and common perspectives based on their geographical location (see MacQueen et al., 2001). Importantly, community-based researchers in criminal justice will need to navigate and define "community" in the context where the research is taking place.

Developing a Community-Based Research Project

It is critical to view a community-based research project as an iterative, dynamic, and reflexive process. The first step is to develop trust with the community (i.e., community partners or co-researchers). Trust evolves over time and should not simply be interpreted as good-will between the researcher and community, rather trust is foundational to democratizing the research process. Trust is critical because knowledge, in a community-based research paradigm is not objective but situated or embedded in the setting and practitioners or "people in the field" are seen as valuable contributors to the initial research questions. Trust provides the context in which researchers and community partners can engage in an honest and respectful exchange of ideas, discussion of values and beliefs, and reflections about crime and criminal justice drivers. Mandell addresses the importance of building trust over time and offers some examples for building community partnerships based on trust.

> Like trust, time is an essential ingredient in building close working partnerships. Time is needed for the parties to get to know each other and to figure out how to work effectively. By working together, both sides become comfortable in questioning, confronting and challenging each other. Action researchers are advised to allow enough time to elapse that a project can naturally emerge. To test the waters, of a potential partnership, it is wise to take on alternative roles – volunteer to help the organization in some capacity, participate and observe the actions of the group, or invite individual members to talk about their experiences with the group and its work. These "getting to

know each other" experiences allow both sides to see if it makes sense to collaborate on a more formal action research project. (Mandell, 2010, p. 152)

Building Community Partnerships (It's All about Trust)

Practitioners in the criminal justice system and researchers have an inherently conflictual relationship and their goals are quite disparate. Practitioners are focused on client management and supervision while researchers are directed by goals related to knowledge discovery and acquisition. The first hurdle in building productive partnerships is overcoming different and often conflicting goals and purposes related to a research project or program. It's not simply about overcoming difference, rather researchers should listen carefully for information about community values, beliefs, and perceptions while practitioners can learn about the technical aspects of data collection and analysis. Martin Rein in his seminal book on social science and public policy provides a critique of the positivist paradigm in policy studies (i.e., the objective search for scientific discovery) in favor of methods that account for the research (or policy) setting, context, values, and beliefs (1976). Ultimately, values and beliefs are always present in a research agenda and building trust often requires understanding other values, beliefs, and perceptions.

We began our experience initiating community-based research projects by building trust with local criminal justice practitioners and planners. Notably, our initial relationships were an effort to communicate value commitments and social aspirations (i.e., our interest in helping the local community improve criminal justice outcomes) and did not involve a research agenda or plan or philosophical discussions about the root causes of crime. We began attending meetings with constituent groups interested in criminal justice planning, mental health outcomes, offender re-entry and strategic planning. Over time, our relationships with local judges, prosecutors, police officers, probation officers, jail staff, mental health, and substance abuse professionals (just to name a few) grew exponentially. Developing local relationships required multiple meetings, informal and formal conversations, and community and university support. There is no recipe for building trust with your community, but there is guidance.

To begin, find out what is going on in your community, regarding criminal justice planning, data collection, offender demographics, and sentencing practices. We wonder how often researchers participate in a community meeting without understanding criminal justice drivers and context. Building confidence, integrity, and trust, all of which are considered valuable qualities for a community-based researcher, necessarily involve knowledge of the context in which crime occurs, how offenders are punished, and how offenders are released or supported during re-entry. Background knowledge of current criminal justice policies and programs will give you credibility and perspective with your audience. Be prepared to listen to community concerns, biases, perceptions, and beliefs about offenders, some of which are informed by fact and other opinions the result of personal experience, victimization, or media influence. Remain open minded and realize that it takes time to develop trusting relationships. More importantly, remain friendly and ingratiating. One of the advantages for researchers in criminal justice is readily available data. We've had multiple conversations with community partners who have data but do not know what to do with it. In time, some of that data routinely collected by public agencies could be very useful in a community-based research project and your initial good will can pay future dividends.

It is also important to consider some potential limitations or difficulties with building community partnerships. While many of us in higher education are familiar with the silo effect that can occur between academic disciplines, the same can occur between criminal justice agencies in the community and "outsiders". Local criminal justice agencies, particularly in rural communities, may be fearful or concerned that researchers are intent on uncovering individual or agency short-comings. Another barrier to CBR project includes local criminal justice agencies who do not work well together or have conflicting organizational goals. Another limitation can be the difficulty in obtaining sensitive information from agencies, especially in smaller rural communities. As noted above, it is important to realize that it often takes quite a bit of time to develop relationships with community agencies where they feel comfortable sharing information about their clients and practices. However, there is always the chance that despite time, effort, and patience on your part, some agencies will continue to resist participation in a CBR project.

Initiating a Research Project

Often, research questions present themselves in conversations and at other times, the warden, chief probation officer, or police chief might have questions about criminal justice outcomes in the community. We tend to stress outcomes as perhaps the standard for assessing criminal justice practices or programs. For public officials, outcomes are typically evaluated based on cost and public safety. We caution readers however, to assume that cost is the only factor influencing action. In rural communities, acquaintance density is high[6]; everyone knows everyone by a small degree of separation. When discussing offenders (in any setting) remember that a member of your audience might know or be related to a justice involved individual. Another barrier to initiating a community-based research project is the focus on a marginal population and the corresponding perception that you might be soft on crime. Our university is located in a rural location in central Pennsylvania. The context (i.e., rural Pennsylvania) is important

---

[6] According to Wodahl, rural communities provide less privacy and higher levels of acquaintance density defined as the "average proportion of the people in a community known by the community's inhabitants" (2006. p. 34).

when introducing ideas about criminal justice research, outcomes and action. There is evidence that in Pennsylvania's rural communities' offenders who commit felony property and drug offenses are more likely to receive incarceration compared with their urban counter-parts (who committed similar offenses) and less likely to receive a probation diversion (The Council of State Governments, 2016, p. 26). Often, initiating a discussion about research questions or a research project ends up as a debate over differences about the root cause of crime (which we might leave for the criminologists) and how to effectively punish offenders. Instead, we try to focus on criminal justice outcomes; mindful that outcomes reflect and involve communities, families, and individual offenders. Improving outcomes is a safe, smart, and efficient method of crime reduction and even in rural locations we find success by NOT debating assumptions about the root causes of crime and the efficacy of punish but instead by focusing on outcomes.

Again, there are no rules just heuristics. Be aware of data sources, data gaps, and potential sources of data prior to initiating a community-based research project. While initiating the project, be prepared to be the principal investigator and administrator of the project (hopefully you have a good co-researcher). Public agencies are typically the source of data and have neither the time nor the resources to help with data collection. Limited local resources should not be an obstacle but a challenge. We responded by selecting undergraduate students to participate in community-based research projects with us. Students helped with data collection and we provided much needed exposure to high impact educational experiences (i.e., experiential learning and participation in faculty sponsored research). In fact, we would not have been able to complete any of our community-based research projects without the assistance of our students.

While conversations serve as the starting point for initiating a community-based research project, we strongly recommend following up conversations with a research prospectus, research plan or timeline. Such a document will confirm your commitment to the community-based research project.

Data Collection and Analysis

Data collection obviously depends on the research questions and type of study. Our community-based research projects included quantitative, qualitative, and mixed methods research designs leading to different types of study design. Absent from the literature on community-based research is a signature research design or methodology, which is quite understandable. We used information routinely collected by public agencies (i.e., the local jail, probation office) as a source of data and conducted citizen surveys as a data source. Likewise, we interviewed, recorded, and transcribed interviews with offenders and community planners and used those interviews as data sources. We have also combined data sources (quantitative and qualitative) to get a more accurate and detailed picture and understanding of the local justice involved population(s).

Data collection and analysis is the principle responsibility of the researcher; realizing that community partners may lack the expertise and infrastructure to collect and analyze data. That does not mean however, that community partners are not involved in data collection and analysis.

We might conceptualize data collection and analysis as three separate but interrelated processes involving different forms of intelligence.

Technical/Analytical Intelligence[7]

Technical/analytical expertise or intelligence involves an understanding of the categories, definitions, and terms forming the building blocks of a community-based research project. For example, most of us are familiar with recidivism as a term common to criminal justice research however, recidivism means different things to different researchers and is measured (i.e., operationalized) differently depending on context and research questions. Democratizing the research process offers opportunities to familiarize community partners with the technical language researcher's use and helps build consensus and confirm factual agreement regarding variable names, definitions, and conventions used in the community-based research project. Technical intelligence also refers to methodological skills related to research design and skill using statistical software or data analysis programs. During this phase of the research project, researchers working with community partners will determine; the research design (experimental, quasi-experimental, survey, secondary data), sampling designs (simple random, stratified, purposive), measurement, and qualitative research methods (if needed).

Issues Intelligence

The strength of a community-based research design is contribution from the community on issues of pressing importance. In our community, we found it helpful to generate community-based research designs that focused on criminal justice intercepts (arrest, booking, detention, trial, and sentencing) as discrete opportunities to conduct systematic observations and collect data. Often, the community was already collecting data at some of the intercepts but did not know how to analyze the data. By helping our

[7] We are borrowing conventions used by Terenzini (1993), in his chapter on the conceptualization and nature of knowledge in institutional research studies. According to Terenzini, the conception of institutional research implies forms of personal competence (i.e., technical/analytical intelligence), issues, and contextual intelligence. Terenzini's conventions apply to community-based research project due to the shared roles of researchers and community partners.

community partners focus on criminal justice intercepts, we were able to get them to consider how local issues (i.e., programs or policies) impacted criminal justice processing at each of the intercepts. Ultimately, local criminal justice planners began to think about improving outcomes at each of the intercepts while also considering how a community-based research project could provide valuable data for justice re-investment. Importantly, justice re-investment necessary implicates the need for community-based research in criminal justice as the starting point for examining data related to criminal justice cost drivers and outcomes. In our experience, we were effective introducing justice re-investment initiatives when we could link programs to data and ultimately cost savings. As such, issues intelligence becomes critical to local governance structures and ultimately funding decisions. According to Terenzini, issue intelligence is a form of generalized intelligence "reflected in one's knowledge of the importance and role of political persuasion, of compromise, of prior consultation with important opinion makers and organizational and governance entities, and of personal and professional courtesy. It is a knowledge of how to work successfully with other people to accomplish some goal." (1993, p. 5) Issues intelligence is recognition of the context, values, beliefs, politics, and local influences impacting design of a community-based research project. Perhaps more importantly, awareness of issues intelligence creates a link to the next step which is action.

Contextual Intelligence

Contextual intelligence is the most important form of intelligence in terms of reciprocal trust and respect. It is a type of intelligence learned through experience, exposure to organizational culture, decision-making processes, and customs. It also entails knowledge of local government structures and processes within which the criminal justice system must function including both opportunities and constraints for action. Researchers who possess contextual intelligence are able to apply the results of community-based research projects on a local level addressing locally meaningful outcomes. Importantly, contextual intelligence captures both technical/analytical and issues intelligence "tailored to a specific… setting where real people are preparing to make real decisions" (Terenzini, 1993). Emphasis on "participation" and "action" in community-based research designs means that it is simply not enough to know about the nature of a problem or issue (i.e., knowledge as an end) instead partners working on a community-based research project should aspire to collectively developed action (Kidd & Kral, 2005). As such, the success for a community-based research project needs to go beyond "fact gathering" (2005) and develop action (i.e., practices, programs, or policies) that becomes part of the local culture.

Action Plans and Community Change

The purpose of initiating a community-based research project is action. Unfortunately, academics and community members often encounter difficulty conceptualizing and implementing action components of a community-based research project. (Stoecker, 2009). It might be a good idea then to re-visit the purpose of the project through a formal discussion or presentation with the community. Often, a community presentation can be accompanied by an executive summary to include descriptive data analysis, policy recommendations and/or action steps. Researchers can provide recommendations for improving criminal justice outcomes but should refrain from providing prescriptive solutions. Ultimately, community-based research projects enhance adoption and sustainability of action plans by vesting the community with decision making. According to Wallerstein and Duran (2010), community-based research projects enhance the effectiveness of interventions or programs including system change outcomes such as policy changes, practice, and program changes by contextualizing those changes based on the specific setting and community needs.

Case Studies on Community-Based Research

Up to this point we have been discussing the basics of community-based research projects in criminal justice. Now, we draw from our experiences with community-based research projects by discussing several case studies. Remember, community-based research requires building relationships, planning and negotiating with community co-researchers, analyzing and presenting data, and finally (and perhaps most importantly) action. We present these case studies, some of which have come to fruition in terms of action and others that continue to evolve as examples only. Case studies are necessarily idiosyncratic and local but can reveal general processes for initiating a community-based research project. We encourage readers to consider the themes and processes that are common to each case study and to community-based research projects in general.

As mentioned, the most critical component of a community-based research project is building relationships with affected stakeholders (i.e., the community). These relationships are built over time through different means including formal and informal meetings and conversations, service to the community, and support from the university. As faculty researchers, we had some idea of topics we were interested in studying but remained open minded, flexible, and responsive to community concerns and input. Initially, we were interested in issues related to offender re-entry and recidivism, specifically in rural communities. Recently, we started researching (with the help of community partners) predictors of police-community citizen satisfaction in rural communities and the prevalence of mental illness in a rural jail population. All of our community-based research projects were generated out of mutual interest, trust, and reciprocity on behalf of and in collaboration with our community partners including; the local jail, adult probation services, regional and local police, local housing authorities, and mental health and intellectual disabilities. In terms of context, our university is in a rural county in central Pennsylvania. Our location offers several advantages initiating a community-based research project. First, rural communities do not have the resources or expertise to systematically design research studies and analyze data. As such, we could help with the technical aspects of systematically studying a criminal justice issue that exceeded the counties expertise or infrastructure[8]. Second, the state of Pennsylvania, like many other locations, was reviewing criminal justice spending and urging localities to examine opportunities for justice re-investment. Justice re-investment, as some may be aware, is a data-driven approach used to examine criminal justice cost drivers and to re-invest in programs having demonstrate cost effectiveness while also producing improved offender outcomes. Combined, these factors allowed us to start conversations about criminal justice outcomes and potential research questions with our community partners. We were careful not to impose a "research agenda" on the community but instead focused our initial efforts on building relationships and understanding more about the local nature of criminal justice policy and planning.

We began to assist the community with some basic data collection activities; namely data collection process and standardizing data reporting. There was an initial need to quantify the data so criminal justice outcomes could be assessed. Over time, discussions about offender outcomes lead the community to examine and consider issues most relevant, pressing and urgent in terms of criminal justice planning and (of course) offender outcomes. As we became more involved with the local community, specifically criminal justice planners, we gradually developed several community-based research projects involving: offender re-entry, parole recidivism, and police satisfaction. While these projects did lead to conventional outcomes (two published articles and a third under revision), "action" resulting from data analysis and discussion became critical pieces of the counties criminal justice strategic plan. In reviewing these cases, we highlighted how we came to be involved in community-based research projects and how our collaboration with community agencies, stakeholders, planners, and policy makers was instrumental in justice re-investment in our community.

Parole Re-Entry Research

Our research into parole re-entry occurred in two counties: the county where our university is located as well as a neighboring county. Both counties are considered rural

---

[8] In terms of infrastructure, we are generally referring to software specifically related to quantitative and qualitative research design and analysis (i.e., SPSS, Atlas.ti, Qualtrics etc…)

as defined by the Center for Rural Pennsylvania. At the time, the local jail held a monthly meeting of individuals involved in jail re-entry, also known as the Re-entry Assessment Team or R.A.T. The R.A.T. would review and recommend local offenders for parole release and develop re-entry plans. We began to attend the monthly R.A.T. meetings regularly as our schedule permitted, more so out of interest and curiosity. At the time, we were not thinking about research; rather, we were focused on learning and building relationships with R.A.T. members and learning more about local re-entry. After about a year or so attending these meetings, we had established relationships with those running and attending the meeting and decided to initiate a research project. In coordination with the warden and other R.A.T. members, we created a study prospectus outlining a systematic evaluation of parole decision making using a mixed method design or a combination of quantitative and qualitative research methods. Essentially, we wanted to help assess the work of the re-entry team and offer recommendations for improving assessment of offender's needs prior to release. Through collaboration with the primary stakeholders (warden, jail staff, re-entry team members), we created a form for data collection that would capture information from inmate files to provide a detailed picture of local incarcerated offenders, including an examination of static and dynamic risk factors that were predictive of parole release. Once the data collection form was complete (and approved), we secured IRB approval for the study and identified student researchers from the university to begin collecting data.

Over the next three years and with the help of more than ten students, we collected data on parole releases for more than 400 cases (i.e., local offenders who were considered for release by the R.A.T.). The student researchers received academic credit for their help by using this project as an Independent Study. We carefully screened students and asked those who we felt would work hard and be consistent to represent our department and university on the research project. Eventually, we had students asking us how they could be involved in our project. Also, having students actively help with data collection is considered a high impact educational practice and we would be remiss for failing to mention the impact community-based research has on undergraduate student success. Our student researchers would spend at least 8 hours a week at the jail sorting through boxes of inmate files as well as talking to jail staff in order to fill in gaps in the data not apparent in the inmate's file. In addition to collecting data, students were able to observe staff at the jail and see some of the behind the scenes work at a correctional facility.

After data collection was complete, we took some time to analyze the data. Prior to submitting an article for publication though, we communicated our findings first to the re-entry team, and then to the county Criminal Justice Advisory Board (CJAB). Based on the results of our study, the re-entry team-initiated changes to their assessment processes resulting in a more effective and hopefully successful re-entry experience for local offenders. For example, action steps included adding an actuarial assessment during re-entry planning, soliciting input from the offenders themselves, and enhanced offender programming, including programs that helped offenders maintain contact with sources of support in the community prior to their release.

Our second community-based research project also related to offender re-entry and occurred in a neighboring county. About a year into our re-entry study at the local jail, we were contacted by a State Parole Agent (previously the manager of the Pennsylvania Board of Probation and Parole District Office) about assisting a neighboring county with an assessment of their newly developed supportive housing program. Excited about the opportunity, we arranged to meet the Executive Director of the Housing Authority and listen to what he had to say. The meeting was fascinating for several reasons. First, we knew nothing about housing authority policies or programs or why the housing authority would be involved in offender re-entry. Second, the housing authority has some general ideas about program evaluation and were interested in the impact supportive housing had on individual offenders (compared with a program evaluation of cost effectiveness). After several more meetings, we developed a qualitative research design and prospectus. Our proposal involved interviewing offenders who were re-entering the community through the newly developed supportive housing program and examining those interviews for common themes and experiences. After obtaining IRB approval, we interviewed all 17 initial participants in this supportive housing program. While we did not have student researchers conducting the interviews, we did have a student who was very interested in helping us and being involved. We responded by allowing him to transcribe several the interviews. When the data analysis was complete, the housing authority used data from the interviews and other sources to create a community "tool-kit" for localities considering design and implementation of a supportive housing program.

Parole Recidivism

Our community-based research with parole recidivism occurred due to our re-entry research as well. Shortly after becoming involved in the re-entry team, we began to attend more county meetings, including the regularly quarterly meeting of the Criminal Justice Advisory Board. Over time, we were asked to join some of the CJAB subcommittees and to attend those meetings. Through some of these meetings, we were contacted by the Chief Probation Officer from Adult Probation Services. He wanted to know about recidivism in the local offender population and with his input, we developed a research prospectus to study parole recidivism.

Thus, begin a third community-based research project and over the course of the next three years and with the help of more students, we collected data on parole releases from files maintain by county probation services. Just as before, student researchers received academic credit for their help by enrolling in Independent Study. Our student researchers would spend at least 8 hours a week at the probation office looking for information (i.e., data) using both an automated case management system and paper files. In addition to collecting data, students were able to observe staff at the probation office and see the interactions between the clients and probation officers.

After the data collection was complete, we took some time to analyze the data. Before beginning to write up our research findings for publication, we communicated our findings to the Chief Probation officer, and then to the county Criminal Justice Advisory Board (CJAB). The action steps resulting from this community-based research project are considerable and continue to emerge. While it was hardly unexpected, our data provided evidence of consistently poor outcomes for offenders supervised on parole or probation supervision. The issues contributing to failure were systemic and included the offender's initial experience at booking, opportunities for pre-trial diversion, and the effectiveness of community programs for justice involved individuals. The county responded by developing a number of different programs operating at several of the criminal justice intercepts (i.e., booking, pre-trial, sentencing, and re-entry). It is anticipated that we will replicate our community-based research project on recidivism in an effort to confirm improved criminal justice outcomes (aggregate outcomes) since inception of the county's justice re-investment efforts.

Police Satisfaction

Our start to studying community perceptions of police satisfaction was slightly different than our other community-based projects. The start of this project began through connections to a neighboring community where one of the authors of this chapter resides. Through meeting individuals informally in the community, one of the faculty members was approached to write a letter to join the town's Police Commission. The Commission had an opening for an At-Large member from one of the department's service areas. After being selected as a member of the Commission, the faculty member attended the monthly meetings of the group on a regular basis.

It was not until a year serving in this capacity when an opportunity presented itself to initiate a research study. Simply by chance, faculty from a neighboring university was conducting a study of the community's perceptions of a small rural regionalized police department. At the time, the study was publicized in the local newspaper as well as on the local news. Members of the regional police commission learned about the study being conducted in a neighboring locality and brought it to the attention of police commission members. That initiated a conversation with the faculty researcher from the neighboring university and he was more than happy to assist us in replicating the study locally. He provided us with a background of his study, access to the survey instrument, and methods for conducting the study. At that point, we presented the police commission with a prospectus for replicating the police-community citizen satisfaction survey in their jurisdiction.

Data collection for this study also involved students. We selected four students who were interested in helping with the study. Three of the students were from the local community where we were collecting the data and were therefore familiar with the area. In order to select the sample (rather than having students visit the over 2,000 residences in the service area), we needed to randomly select a number of households. This required two additional partnerships. First, we needed to get parcel data for the residences in the regional police service area from the county planning office. Once the parcel data was obtained, we reached out to a colleague and faculty member at our university (another partnership) in the Geology department who could assist us GIS mapping and the random selection of address in the regional police service area. After working together for a few weeks, we had created a random sample of approximately 400 residences. In order to increase participation (i.e., responses), we mailed postcards to the households who were selected for the survey.

When it came time for the data collection, we gave our student researchers two weeks after the end of the spring semester to visit the 400 randomly selected households who were chosen to participate in the study. The student researchers worked in teams of two; going door to door to solicit responses. This allowed the student researchers to visit a number of homes, store survey responses on an iPad, and upload survey data when they got to an area with Wi-Fi. The student researchers made over 500 visits (sometimes making repeat visits) to residences selected to participate in the survey. After two weeks, we ended up with 98 completed surveys; a 24% response rate.

We presented the findings of the citizen satisfaction survey and general policy recommendation at a recent meeting of the regional police commission. For that meeting, we also produced an executive summary that included descriptive data analysis and response mapping (we created maps indicting issues related to perceived crime and police performance). As of this time, no specific action has been taken by the regional police department however we urged the police commission to review the executive summary for purposes of action steps. Interestingly, this community-based research project lead to another opportunity to examine police-community satisfaction in another (neighboring) locality. Working with the city manager and chief of police in the city where our university is located promises additional opportunities to replicate the study and to consider patterns of policing and community-police satisfaction in rural municipal or regional police departments. Just as the community can learn from researchers, we are also learning from our community partners about the challenges of policing in rural locations. Importantly, we are learning, through the process of collaborative community-based research, that police satisfaction is one of the most critical drivers of overall community satisfaction.

ASSESSING COMMUNITY-BASED RESEARCH PROJECTS

Advantages

Reflecting on each of these community-based research projects suggests that there are a number of specific advantages conducting a community-based research project. It should be noted that other individuals pursuing community-based research may not have the same experiences. However, we wanted to document the advantages as we experienced them over the course of our involvement with the local community on community-based research projects.

First and foremost, community-based research involves numerous constituency groups that directly benefit for a collaborative approach to systematically examining local issues related to criminal justice planning, practice, programs and outcomes. One important constituent group is undergraduate students who were critical to data collection and without whom none of the projects we discussed in this chapter would have been possible. Likewise, emphasis in higher education on student engagement highlights the use of experiential learning faculty sponsored undergraduate research, and deep learning as methods of enhancing student engagement, retention and success. Ultimately, we are educators and we strongly believe that scholarly growth should occur in the context of teaching and learning, community advocacy, empowerment and change. The current generation of students is similarly motivated by projects, including community-based research projects, contributing to community well-being and social equity. As such, community-based research projects meet the growing needs of the current generation of students who are also the next generation of criminal justice planners. Another benefit to student researchers, particularly in rural communities, is the opportunity to network with local criminal justice agencies while working on a community-based research project. Networking and experience help to prepare students for a professional career in criminal justice and many of our students are hired locally.

Another advantage was developing lasting and impressionable relationships with our community agencies. To be honest, we are not exactly developing a relationship with an agency rather we are developing relationship with people who work in the criminal justice system and are therefore sources for systematic (although incremental) change. Their willingness and openness to us, as faculty researchers, continues to be reinforced through additional community-based research projects, internship opportunities for students, or service on our criminal justice advisory board. Beware, once you establish a relationship, you should be prepared to maintain the relationship which requires a bit of give and take. Each of these agencies (agency personnel) was very open to our initial involvement in their meetings and our suggestions for community-based research projects. At no point did they try to prevent us from conducting our studies, nor did they meddle in the process. We realize that this is not going to be the case for every experience, so we do discuss issues with disagreement and control as a challenge in the next section.

A third advantage involves benefits to our university. While there are a few other universities in the surrounding area, we are a smaller university in a rural community. This made it easier for us to get involved with some of these agencies, especially when we had previous relationship with the agency resulting from a student intern or agency hiring an alumnus of our program. Again, this may be a challenge for some universities depending on their size and location. The advantage of community-based research to a university is however a two-way street. The university must be supportive of community-based research projects in two ways. First, supportive administrations provides the infrastructure for conducting CBR. Specifically, research related funding, travel, software, and faculty time must be supported by university administration and the failure to support CBR can doom a project before it even gets started. Second, supportive administrations recognize CBR projects as scholarship. Specifically, we encourage university administrators to reward community-based researchers during the tenure and promotion process but considering CBR as legitimate activity related to faculty scholarship and mastery of the subject matter. Our university is generally supportive of faculty involvement in community-based research. Finally, CBR provides universities with promotional opportunities. For example, partnerships created through CBR projects can be used to highlight student success and high impact educational practices that enhance the undergraduate student experience.

A fourth advantage of our research was building partnerships with other faculty, both inside and outside of the university. While most other faculty at our university did not help with the research, they were often helpful in identifying students to help with the projects or forwarding to us any information they thought would help with the research. However, for our project on police-community satisfaction, we needed to partner with faculty in geology who had expertise with GIS mapping. While we had not interacted with him much prior to the project, once we contacted him, he was more than willing to be part of the research. We would not have been able to do much of what we did without his help. We also began a partnership with a faculty member outside of our university when we embarked on the police-community satisfaction research. When we reached out to him for assistance, he was more than willing to help. As discussed earlier, he provided the survey language and offered help when we were just getting started with our study. Part of the agreement was that we would share data, and eventually work together on a project that combined all of our survey data.

Challenges

One of the significant (and consistent) challenges to a community-based research project is funding. We had support from the university in terms of a research infrastructure, but we still needed additional funding for equipment, proprietary software, travel, and student and faculty stipends. In some cases, we were able to use resources already available to us, such as paper, printing, and postage. For the data collection forms for our re-entry and recidivism studies, we were able to print those either from our department printer, or from duplicating services on campus for minimal cost. However, we often needed additional items, such as digital recorders, qualitative data analysis software, online survey software, and iPads. Additionally, we needed reimbursement for travel, especially for our re-entry project in a neighboring county (close to 100 miles round trip). We also wanted to provide, when possible, stipends to the student researchers when they were working outside of the academic year. The majority of our funding came from small campus grants at our university. However, these were very minimal, and often did not provide enough for what we actually needed. These grants were also competitive across the university, so we often would start a project not knowing if we were going to get any funding assistance. A potential way to address this issue would be when developing partnerships with criminal justice agencies to frame the services of a research team as potential way to obtain funding (for both the researchers and the agencies).

A second challenge in conducting community-based research is dependence on community agencies for access to and maintenance of information that would eventually become the source of data. For example, when students were helping collect data from the correctional facility and probation office, the students had to be there weekdays between 8am and 4pm. They also needed space and a computer (to access online case management activity) which was not always available. In addition, at both the correctional facility and probation office, filing systems can often be in disarray and archived documents difficult to access. A related challenge, although one we did not experience, would be difficulty or tension resulting from student researchers working with the community records. It is possible that some community agencies are not open to this type of research, or if they are, they may want to control the process, including access to necessary records and data. As such, it is critical to communicate that any information contained in agency records will be treated confidentially and under no circumstance will student researchers record personal identifiers or discuss individual cases.

A final challenge we experienced was helping the community agencies to understand the data analysis and research findings. Writing up information about a research study and the data analysis for a peer reviewed journal article is very different from presenting data to a constituency group or community. In some of our initial reporting of the results, we included correlations and regression analyses. Despite doing our best to present and explain the results, there were a few instances of misunderstanding by some agency personnel. On one occasion, we discovered a significant variable related to an offender's referral to treatment and parole failure in a logistic regression model, which led some individuals in the county agencies to believe that participation in a counseling program was directly causing parolees to engage in behavior that caused their parole to be revoked. Due to this misunderstanding, we had to set up an additional meeting to reassure the staff at the counseling program that it was not the case.

It is important to note another potential challenge involving working with other faculty both inside and outside of the university. In academia, faculty can get stuck in their own knowledge silo and are hesitant to partner with other faculty. The struggle to publish and get promoted is commonly viewed as an individual task however, we strongly advocate for a research team when considering a community-based research project. In order for community-based research to work well, faculty researchers need to be able to work alongside each other and share information and ideas including expertise that may not be shared by all the members of a particular discipline. In many instances, this may be a significant challenge, and one that might prevent a project from happening.

THE BENEFITS OF COMMUNITY-BASED RESEARCH

Benefits to the University

Engaging in community-based research results in a number of benefits to the university. Essentially these benefits can impact faculty, students, and the university as whole. They are also often interrelated and connected to community benefits.

One benefit is faculty professional development and increase in scholarly growth. Most, if not all, universities emphasize faculty professional development in the tenure and promotion process. Our community-based research projects broadened our knowledge of specific local criminal justice issues, which translated not only into peer reviewed publications, but also content related to teaching. For example, we regularly use data and results from the studies we conducted to supplement course content and for data analysis activities. In addition, neither of us have a strong background in policing, so our research involving law enforcement helped us to learn more about community-police satisfaction. Not only does this research make us better educators, but it also translates into additional knowledge for students and we hope, makes us better teachers. Since a majority of our students enroll from adjacent counties, we are able to contextual issues related to the criminal justice system that is embedded in the local setting. In other words, our students are exposed to local criminal justice issues with real meaning for the lives of folks living in their community.

Another benefit is related and has to do with the student involvement in our community-based research projects. As noted previously, we would not have been able to complete these studies without the help of our student researchers. Through helping with these projects, our students are not only getting direct experiential learning that they would not get in the classroom, but they are able to learn more about conducting research and working in and with these agencies; they get an opportunity to enhance their interpersonal and professional skills. The students also learn valuable skills including verbal and written communication, data entry and analysis, systematic observation and recording of data, and working in collaboration with other. Essentially, exposing students to the working relationships between the university and various criminal justice agencies, we are increasing the likelihood of future partnerships when these students become practitioners in the field.

When faculty engage in community-based research, it also brings more recognition to the university. Most notable might be publishing in a peer reviewed journal however, community-based research can also include non-peer reviewed publications and press releases reflecting favorably on the university, community services, and faculty accomplishments. More informally, the agencies have increased knowledge of what the university offers. Engaging in community-based research also increases the strength of relationships between the university and these community agencies.

Benefits to the Community

The community also benefits directly from the research. Overall, action resulting from community-based research projects is intended to provide benefits to the community. In criminal justice, this often means practices, programs, and policies that prevent and decrease crime and victimization, improve criminal justice outcomes for convicted offenders, and enhancing community safety as well as the perceived threat of crime. Practically, community-based research projects can save taxpayer's money through re-investment in diversions or community-based programs that address offender's criminogenic needs (i.e., addiction and recovery).

The results of community-based research also directly benefits the organizations who have participated in the research project. Each study resulted in a change or action. Often, actions do not need to be titanic, rather incremental changes can have a long-term and sustainable effect over time. Also, data obtained from community-based research can be use or adopted to support additional requests for grant funding. This happened in more than one instance from our projects.

Finally, relationships developed between university faculty and community partners also supply future needs for both the university and our community agencies. For example, we have been approached by each of the agencies that we conducted research with when they have a position opening or have other research or evaluation questions that require systematic evaluation.

The Importance of Partnerships

Community-based research is made possible by partnerships between universities and community agencies. These partnerships are mutually beneficial relationships. As discussed in the previous section, there are advantages to both the university and the community when these connections are made, continued, and sustained.

An important consideration is that in reality, these relationships may take quite some time (often years) before real work can be done. Each of the examples of our community-based research illustrate the time it took between developing initial relationships, proposing a community-based research project, project inception, and project completion. Even if we mentioned at a first meeting that we would help with research, or that we wanted to conduct a study, it is unlikely to work out that way. These relationships take time to build and trust needs to be established for a collaborative research project to succeed. If community agencies perceive faculty as data pirates then it is unlikely that a research partnership will form. But if community agencies see faculty dedication and commitment to understanding local issues in context or embedded in the setting, and are willing to gain perspective through listening and discourse, and committed to community change though intention and action, then a community-based research project has a much better chance of success.

Conclusion

Community-based research projects provide an alternative to traditional research by enlisting the community as research partners and developing a research project having direct benefits to the community and its people. In rural communities, the importance of CBR cannot be understated as these communities grapple with issues related to criminal justice spending and outcomes. In our experience, community-based research provided opportunities to partner with local criminal justice agency personnel on projects that would benefit the community, university, faculty, and students. We strongly believe that criminal justice researchers consider the importance of CBR and the timely impact CBR projects can have on criminal justice programming and planning in your community. We also believe that CBR projects promote university goals and should be accepted by university administration as legitimate scholarship. We encourage the development of CBR projects that involve undergraduate students in high impact educational practices including exposure to social science research methods and deep learning experiences. Ultimately, we hope that more criminal justice researchers will consider community-based research projects as the beginning (and not end) of addressing issues of crime and justice at the local level, improving criminal justice outcomes, and preparing the next generation of criminal justice practitioners, planners, and policy makers.

References

Kidd, S. A. & Kral, M. J. (2005). Practicing participatory action research. *Journal of Counseling Psychology*, 52(2), 187 – 195. doi: 10.1037/0022-0167.52.2.187.

Kusago, T. & Miyamoto, T. (2014). The potential for community-based action research for area studies: A process evaluation method for the improvement of community life. *Psychologia*, 57, 275 – 294.

MacQueen, K. M., McLellan, E., Metzger, D. S., Kegeles, S., Strauss, R. P., Scotti, R., Blanchard, L., &, Trotter, R. T. (2001). What is community? An evidence-based definition for participatory public health. *American Journal of Public Health*, 91(12), 1929 – 1938.

Mandell, J. (2010). Advice to action research activists: Negotiating successful action research- community based social change partnerships. *Humanity & Society*, 34, 141 – 156.

Orchowsky, S. (2014). *An introduction to evidence-based practices*. Retrieved from http://www.jrsa.org/pubs/reports/ebp_briefing_paper_april2014.pdf.

Rein, M. (1976). *Social science and public policy*. New York, NY: Penguin Books.

Stoecker, R. (2009). Are we talking the walk of community-based research? *Action Research*, 7(4), 385 – 404. doi: 10.1177/1476750309340944.

The Council of State Governments (2016). *Justice reinvestment in Pennsylvania.* Retrieved from the Council of State Governments Justice Center: http://www.pccd.pa.gov/Documents/Justice%20Reinvestment/PA%20Presentation%202%20Final.pdf.

Wallerstein, N. & Duran, B. (2010). Community-based participatory research contributions to intervention research. The intersection of science and practice to improve health equity. *American Journal of Public Health*, 100(1), 40 – 46.

Wodahl, E. (2006). The challenges of prisoner re-entry from a rural perspective. *Western Criminology Review*, 7(2), 32 – 47.

PART 3: PERSISTENT ISSUES IN CRIMINAL JUSTICE

In: A Closer Look at Criminal Justice
Editors: J. A. Cooper and K. G. Jachimowski
ISBN: 978-1-53615-782-6

Chapter 7

COMMUNITY POLICING AS A PROGRESSIVE MODEL: THE ROLE OF RACE AND IMPLICATIONS FOR TRAINING

Andrea Weathersby*
Licensed Psychologist, Consultant, Charlotte, NC, US

ABSTRACT

This chapter reviews current trends in policing. Community policing is explored and posited as a *progressive* model. Community policing is operationally defined in this context. Empirically informed findings frame the evaluation of community policing programs. Central to community policing is a collaboration between community members and police in a collective effort to maintain law and order. Given the emphasis on community/police relations, aligning with marginalized groups is a key step in progressive policing. As such, this chapter examines the role of race and historically disenfranchised communities in law enforcement. Lastly, recommendations for training, such as implicit bias training, are submitted.

INTRODUCTION

This chapter explores current trends in policing, often described in headlines and triggered by public outrage or, at least, curiosity. The resulting controversy has led to increasing government resources that motivate scholarly research. Leaders and stakeholders seek to identify community and societal imperatives. A framework for analysis is needed to respond to competing approaches to the issue. Some advocate for

* (Andrea Cochran/Weathersby) Author's Email: dr.acochran@gmail.com

militarized policing, but others focus on community policing. The intent of this chapter is to present information that supports the position that community policing is a preferred model.

Reform Movement

Law enforcement has come under considerable attack within the past 20 years. It has been described as a 'public relations jungle' entangled by a myriad of divisive, polarizing, and complex issues (Culbertson, 2000). Accountability, communication, transparency, mitigating social harm (Fan, 2012), and violations to civil liberties are some of the core principles encapsulated in the need for police reform (den Heyer, 2011). The media has widely publicized recent failures within police agencies (Simmons, 2008). Given the cumulative effects of these factors, few would argue against the need for law enforcement and criminal justice reform (Schoenle, 2017). This need for reform drives a call to action for progressive policing.

The US Congress enacted legislation in 1994 that recognized the need for systematic reform of law enforcement agencies across the nation (Simmons, 2008). The US Department of Justice responded by allocating funds for the express purpose of developing and piloting police programs and innovations (Scheider et al., 2009). Over 18,000 police departments across the United States responded to this call for progressive law enforcement (Schoenle, 2017).

The criminal justice system wrestles with multiple demands and pressures, including ways to downshift crime rates in the United States (Schoenle, 2017). Crime management is complex and riddled with conflicting priorities and demands (Tilley & Laycock, 2018). In terms of the best approach, one size does not fit all. A good metaphor for the climate in law enforcement includes 'eddies and whirlpools' symbolizing community engagement and accountability coinciding with 'riptides and upwellings' of public concerns, crime, police malpractice, and the political quagmire (Fyfe, 2013).

Progressive Policing

There has been much debate about what constitutes "progressive" policing. Borrowing from the Merriam-Webster dictionary (www.merriamwebster.com), the term "progressive" means:

- of, relating to or characterized by progress;
- making use of or interested in new ideas, findings, or opportunities;
- change and social improvement by action;

- to develop a higher, better, or more advanced stage;
- a gradual betterment;
- to move forward; to proceed;
- a forward or onward movement, as to an objective or a goal;

This general definition offers a template for formulating a prototype for progressive policing.

To fulfill this definition, a progressive policing paradigm must make use of new ideas findings or opportunities. New ideas are generated from historical information. What ideas worked or did not work in the past? In cases when something did not work, it is still useful to determine what went wrong and how can it be improved upon.

While often daunting or overwhelming, change requires a great deal of energy, even to achieve minor and sometimes unnoticeable impact. By design, law enforcement and the justice system are firmly established and resistant to change. Change in this context will often 'upset the apple cart' and disturb the status quo. Yet, according to the definition above, it can be inferred that incremental change by action leads to the types of social improvement that remain the goal of progressive policing.

Again, referencing the definition of progressive, to progress is to move forward toward a better, more advanced stage. There are many great minds joining forces to develop and reform the practice of policing and law enforcement. The collective effort is bound to make meaningful changes, even if subtle. This definition reminds us that gradual change is still change. Gradual movement is still movement. It only takes the needle to move one degree to alter the trajectory.

The final point in building a template from this definition of progressive is that the reform movement requires forward, onward movement toward an objective or goal. Goals of progressive policing will be outlined throughout this chapter. Once goals have been clarified, the next step is to 'proceed onward' with action, advancing toward new levels.

Implementing progressive policing will require a shared vision, unified goals, widespread participation, and collective cooperation. A strategic framework addresses immediate needs and incorporates democratic and cooperative values (den Heyer, 2011). A collaborative approach posited by Simmons (2008) involves participation in reform efforts by stakeholders, such as community-based groups and police officers.

Community Policing

Law enforcement these days is saturated with ideas for innovation (DeGarmo, 2012). The concept of innovation in policing has presented a dizzying smorgasbord of ideas and models; each hoping to gain the attention of policy makers, public officials, and stakeholders (Scheider et al., 2009). It is worthwhile to examine a sampling of the models that are being implemented by departments and to weigh their impact on advancing the police reform movement.

The need for reform produced a philosophy chiefly focused on reducing crime and improving relationships with the community (Lawrence & McCarthy, n.d.). A parallel goal was to form direct partnerships between citizens and police to restore trust. These trends converged into what is now known as 'community policing' (Lawrence & McCarthy, n.d.)

There is mounting evidence that bureaucratic, conventional police practices have failed. They have been ineffective (Liou & Savage, 1996). The movement towards community policing is being lauded as a 'new and improved' policing paradigm (Lawrence & McCarthy, n.d.). Within the vast marketplace of ideas, community policing is therefore arguably an ideal model for transforming organizations, engaging partnerships, and collaborative problem solving (Scheider et al., 2009).

Community policing has been the front runner in modern policing (Lumb, 1995) and is growing in popularity around the world. At present, community policing is the dominant philosophy in local law enforcement (Lawrence & McCarthy, n.d.). Roughly eighty-one percent of police departments in the U.S. subscribe to a community policing model, with that number growing steadily (Lawrence & McCarthy, n.d.). Thus far, billions of dollars in grant funding have been invested in Community Oriented Policing Services (COPS; Scheider et al., 2009) through formula grants and competitive grants (Worrall & Zhao, 2003).

It is a challenge to define community policing, leading to considerable scholarly debate. The philosophy has been plagued with ambiguity and abstraction (Scheider et al., 2009). The concept of community policing is becoming lost in interpretation of its central principles, thereby diluting its potential effectivity (Scheider et al., 2009).

"Community policing" has been broadly used to describe a number of policing strategies. Terms such as neighborhood policing, community-oriented policing, and Community Oriented Policing Services (COPS) have all been cited throughout the literature and in the law enforcement field. The general term 'community policing' will be used liberally throughout this chapter. It is framed as a philosophy or paradigm whose mission is to provide transformative policing that aims to improve the quality of life in communities. Comprehensive policing strategies must be employed. These strategies must be holistic in nature, reflecting a commitment to systemic change. Core functions must be organized around community building and crime reduction; evidence-based practices must be implemented to the degree that is feasible. Ongoing engagement with the community will be accomplished through coordinated efforts with a multidisciplinary bend. As further defined in this chapter, community policing takes a humanistic approach that values its citizens as well as the officers serving in the community.

In attempts to define and operationalize progressive community policing, scholars, researchers, agencies and practitioners tend to agree on general principles and tenets. Community policing is more aptly an overarching philosophy that directs law enforcement activities. As its name implies, efforts are centered around the community (Gill et al., 2014), placing the community at the fulcrum of strategic planning. The model is flexible in its ability to adapt to social and cultural expectations and imperatives (Wetzel, 2012). The tenets of progressive community policing cluster around:

(a) community involvement
(b) organizational decentralization
(c) innovative problem solving (Chappell, 2008).

The scope of community policing is broad enough to incorporate complementary ideologies. Other interventions dovetail with this paradigm because it encompasses strategies of more traditional models that emphasize crime control, proactive responses, patrolling, investigations, and related police business (Scheider et al., 2009). The philosophy of community policing encourages forward movement, providing a structure for governance in the complex social and legal landscapes (Harmon, 2012).

This model provides at least a preliminary aid to analysis and in the end is probably even a preferred model to pursue. Indeed, community policing is synonymous to "progressive" policing. Community policing should enhance existing models by integrating proven methods and concepts, creating an integrated approach that complements rather than competes with existing models (Scheider et al., 2009)

Scheider and colleagues (2009) postulated the following definition of community policing:

> Community policing is a philosophy that promotes organizational strategies which support the systemic use of partnerships and problem-solving techniques to proactively address the immediate conditions that give rise to public safety issues, such as crime, social disorder, and fear of crime.

Oliver (1998, in Somerville, 2009) adds to the definition [paraphrased]:

> ...a systematic approach of instilling and fostering a sense of community. Community operationalized as within a defined and specified geographical area. Community policing seeks to improve the quality of life of its citizens. Community policing calls for a redistribution of police resources and decentralization. Through indigenous, proactive programs, police and community members interact to reduce crime and the fear of crime. Focusing on root causes of problems is paramount for sustained changes, and not just putting "Band-Aids" on symptoms.

A stringent definition of community policing - such as the ones above - is not meant to be applied monolithically; rather the overarching philosophy, at its core, encourages strategic adaptations by various departments to meet the unique needs of their constituents (Scheider et al., 2009). Scheider and colleagues (2009) recommend broadening the parameters so that local entities can tailor community policing activities while still adhering to the general core vision.

Community policing is a progressive and proactive approach to the business of policing, and that demands a systematic approach. Operational and strategic changes begin at the leadership and departmental levels. Only then can practices become integrated on the unit level and inform a set of tactics utilized by officers on the streets. (Gill et al., 2014).

Although a top-down approach to implementing policing strategies is recommended, the goal of community policing model is actually to de-centralize agencies. The model challenges hierarchical and bureaucratic systems by 'flattening' the hierarchical structure (Gill et al., 2014) so that officers assume more autonomous yet collaborative roles. In addition to de-centralization, management is streamlined so that officers - even at the street level - are given higher level responsibility and autonomy (Gill et al., 2014). Successful implementation of this model hinges on training, recruitment, and retention of quality talent.

Community-oriented policing maps pathways to achieve unified goals (Worrall & Zhao, 2003). The philosophy embraces the premise that police activities should not be limited to traditional crime fighting (Gill et al., 2014). The police, while not abandoning their posts in the fight against crime, would also respond to social and physical disorder by reducing fear and mistrust (Gill et al., 2014).

Direct officer involvement with local communities and citizens is a prominent feature in community policing. This concept can be mutually beneficial. By connecting police to communities, not only does the community benefit, but connection to the community diminishes officer isolation (Scheider et al., 2009), which can be an unanticipated consequence of front-line policing.

Community Policing Depends on Collaboration

Three interrelated goals of community policing are organized around: a) reducing crime, b) collaborative solution-focused initiatives, and c) improving public trust (Scheider et al., 2009). The paradigm aspires to cultivate cooperation while at the same time maintaining integrity and discipline. Mutual respect and trust are essential elements to this end (Wetzel, 2012).

Community members and law enforcement agents are 'co-producers' in solving problems, resolving conflict, and ensuring public safety. (Gill et al., 2014). Co-production, as described by Somerville (2009), prompts police and citizens to work together in the wider spectrum of problem solving and decision making. Citizens are involvement is also essential, with expectations they will report concerns, articulate perceptions, and provide regular communication and feedback.

Applying proactive approaches to community policing involves officers and community members to creatively work together (Chappell, 2008). Scholars and researchers cite police/resident partnerships as having the potential to enhance social control and reduce crime and delinquency (Renauer, 2007). Community policing identifies root causes of neighborhood crime by engaging the larger community in developing and implementing strategies to address issues (Lawrence & McCarthy, n.d.)

Law abiding citizens and community policing officers must have a voice in creating the agenda, in setting goals and in prioritizing community problems (Chappell, 2008). Notably, LePere-Schloop and Lumpkin (2016) advocate for extending invitations to 'unsavory' individuals into the collaborative efforts to achieve nuanced intel for the greater goal of crime reduction. Doing so, they argue, is an unconventional method of establishing greater trust and alignment within historically disenfranchised groups.

There are many roles that community members can play (Somerville, 2009). Each role, and any form of active prosocial participation, is integral to advancing the mission of community policing and improving quality of life. Although not limited to these suggestions, community members can participate in the following ways:

(a) enlisting participation of other members
(b) advising police about the trends or stated needs in local communities
(c) promoting education efforts
(d) offering input regarding grievance and resolution processes
(e) involvement in research by informally gathering of data and surveying effectiveness/success of interventions

Involving community members, in many respects, may be more of an idealized and lofty goal, one that will be challenging to actualize. This challenge is fraught with difficulties and circuitous stalemates. Critics shed light on the incongruence between theory and what is happening in real time in locales. Somerville (2009) extracted data to document these very real problems. For starters, community groups tend to be homogeneous in nature as a consequence of selection bias. The make-up of community forums and advisory boards rarely reflects the local demographics. Police naturally rely on self-appointed representatives, which also presents a selection bias. Additionally, community members are (indirectly) excluded from deliberations and the final stages of decision making. As a result, decisions tend to support law enforcement priorities, usually re-affirming the views of middle-class citizens. Lastly, members may feel obliged to act on behalf of law enforcement interests.

Somerville (2009) identified points to consider throughout the development of procedures that involve the community:

1. Representation – intentional diversification in representation at community forums or action boards
2. Resolution - in the event that decisions are inconclusive, or agreement has not been met, a process needs to be in place for mediating and working toward resolve
3. Accountability - establishing mechanisms for accountability with checks and balances
4. Authority - allocating appropriate levels of authority to ensure implementation of decisions

Attending to these matters goes well beyond the scope of traditional law enforcement (Somerville, 2009). The success of the community model is dependent on the police officers who are fully supported by their departments to carry out the tenets outlined. In this model, police officers act as professionals, 'beyond the scope' of their traditional roles, using foresight and planning. To bridge the gap between theory and practice, adequate support and training is absolutely essential.

Shared responsibility must identify long-term and comprehensive solutions to problems (Scheider et al., 2009). Secondary agencies who share responsibility with law enforcement will aid in crime control, prevention, and reduction (Somerville, 2009). Collaboration among law enforcement and social workers and mental health professionals is highly recommended (Sylvester and Teboh, 2016). Social service and mental health professionals have already influenced innovative approaches and policies, providing nuanced training and education, as well as partnering to build stronger community relationships (Sylvester & Teboh, 2016).

By utilizing a community-centered systems approach, industrial/organizational psychologists will play a key role in providing solutions that are centered around rebuilding relationships, establishing mutual trust, and affecting social change by building resilient communities (Hardin, 2016). Their affiliations with social workers will help officers become more attuned to the needs of the community and identify ways to address those needs (Sylvester & Teboh, 2016). Diving even deeper into the far-reaching benefits of such professional partnerships, Hardin (2006) enlists the expertise of psychologists to address citizen bias toward police ("police bias") and racial bias, specifically in cities where there are known racial tensions between police and citizens.

Community Oriented Policing: Program Review and Evaluation

It is not the intention of this chapter to thoroughly explicate and examine the myriad of programs that fall under the umbrella of community policing. Rather, the purpose here is to briefly review a sampling of programs that have been implemented in various police departments. Empirical and critical analyses of these selected programs provide data to assist in pointing the way forward.

A comprehensive program sponsored by The US Department of Justice encourages organizational transformation, problem solving, and community partnerships (https://cops.usdoj.gov/aboutcops). Community Oriented Policing Services (COPS) was established in 1994 and housed within the US DOJ. State, local, territorial, and tribal law enforcement agencies have received support and over $14 billion in funding to advance the practice of community policing. The mission of COPS is to build mutual respect and trust between communities and police. As indicated above under the description of community policing, COPS unites stakeholders, communities, and law enforcement in addressing public safety and crime. Grants have been awarded to agencies to fund professionals, develop innovative strategies, test and evaluate efficacy, and to provide technical support.

Evaluation of Community Oriented Policing

Metaphorically, this convergence of ideas provides a drawbridge that is lowering to connect researchers, scholars, practitioners, and law enforcement agencies. With innovation occurring throughout the fields of law enforcement and criminal justice, there are more opportunities for sustainable collaborative partnerships (Fyfe, 2013). Around the world, multidisciplinary 'think tanks' and innovation hubs are breeding fertile learning communities of shared knowledge. Researchers and scholars can now partake of the wisdom that results, learning from mistakes and apparent failures as well as successes. These collaborations allow for widespread communication about what works and how to implement or customize strategies in various jurisdictions.

Evidence Based Policing has been introduced as a standard in determining efficacy and establishing best practices. Evidence-based policing borrows from the tradition of evidence-based medicine as its frame of reference (Mitchell & Lewis, 2017). Evidence-based policing advances programs and practices that then undergo systematic reviews to assess quality, generalizability, and internal validity (Mitchell & Lewis, 2017). Evidence-based policing springs from fulfillment of the ethical and fiduciary responsibility of governmental agencies to ensure prudent spending of public funds, insuring honest scrutiny of interventions (Mitchell & Lewis, 2017).

Mitchell and Lewis (2017) made a case for evidence-based policing, and offered it as a roadmap to identify the best practices and interventions. They argue that the most rigorous evidence supporting an intervention follows these protocols:

(a) multiple evaluations;

(b) demonstrates consistency of effect; and,
(c) research design utilizes high standards in its analysis, such as randomized controlled trials, when possible.

The following have been included as 'evidence-based policing' interventions:

1. Hot spots geographic policing targets
2. CeaseFire - a program evidenced in Boston to reduce gang shootings by 31% during a 5 year span
3. Scanning, Analysis, Response, Assessment (SARA).

In contrast, Mitchell and Lewis (2017) provide examples of programs with weak a priori designs producing inadvertently adverse outcomes. The first on their list was the Drug Abuse Resistance Education program, better known as D.A.R.E. The D.A.R.E. program was found to be produce only negligible effects on substance abuse. Another program cited on the list of ineffective programs was Scared Straight. Review and evaluation of the Scared Straight program revealed unintentional harm to participants. Findings also uncovered an increased risk of exhibiting antisocial behaviors in participants after taking part in Scared Straight. Despite contrary evidence, both programs continue to be promoted across the United States.

Mitchell and Lewis (2017) recommend taking a more scientific and pragmatic approach to learning from apparent mistakes or failures. They recommend collecting follow-up data, making necessary adjustments, and conducting a risk/benefit analysis to provide direction for the future. Simply acknowledging mistakes or shortcomings would be a simple remedy. Acknowledging uncertainty about the outcomes of trial interventions is not admitting defeat as much as being transparent, which is a step toward accountability and legitimacy (Mitchell & Lewis, 2017).

Mitchell and Lewis (2017) offered ethical guidance to establish and implement innovative programming into law enforcement agencies. As a rule, police leadership and policy actors must introduce empirically grounded solutions wherever possible. In cases of unintentional or reported harm, those interventions need to be discontinued. Police departments can then offer options to mitigate damage or harm. Lastly, when new options and interventions surface, they should be evaluated rigorously utilizing pilot studies or trial periods.

The "What Works" initiative is a shining example of empirical innovation by design. What Works Center for Crime Reduction, or "What Works," was established by the British government in 2013. What Works entails a systematic review that distills findings from robust empirical research. The goal, simply stated, is to identify "what works." What Works has engineered a knowledge and resource hub for operational decision-making for researchers and practitioners (whatworks.college.police.uk/Pages/).

Tilley and Laycock (2018) provide an astutely articulated review of recent law enforcement efforts in England. Notably, lessons learned by the 'Brits' have ramifications for evidence-based policing. One of the most poignant lessons learned was that what may seem like a good idea in theory does not always manifest as such in reality. The British government earmarked roughly four-hundred million Euro in public money to promote evidence-based practices. Historically, this was one of the largest efforts of its kind using public funds yet failed to produce expected outcomes. It was not possible to assess pertinent needs, evaluate, refine, then agree to proposed programming within the allotted timeframe. Additionally, staffing the program was a monumental effort, as was the process of conducting systematic evaluations. Researchers and practitioners had to coordinate efforts to run the programs, re-evaluate, write-up findings, and then fully implement the program. Each step took time and resources; and the totality of completing all of the steps required for a project to be deemed a robust, evidence-based practice was often not feasible given time and budget constraints.

What's more, priorities changed and political campaigns shifted the focus, making it that much more difficult to stay ahead of trends. Figuratively, like building a sandcastle at high tide, by the time a program went through the rigorous process of being tested and approved, a more pressing crisis swelled, thereby 'washing away' the efforts.

All is not wasted with the British policing campaign because the illustrious College of Policing was conceived during the process. Inaugurated by the British Government in 2012, the College of Policing was established as a professional body and resource for officer support and professional development. The College of Policing's brainchild, What Works Commissional Partnership Programme, is a consortium that catalogues evidence-based crime reduction interventions. What Works organized a comprehensive toolkit that is being used as a source of reference worldwide. The toolkit has netted millions of online views (Tilley & Laycock, 2018).

Empirical Evaluation: Community Oriented Policing

Does community policing represent a paradigm shift or is it merely a change in operational activities that are posing as innovation, while priorities remain unchanged? Zhao, He, and Lovrich (2003) asked this quintessential question. Scholars and researchers have been waiting for a conclusive answer. In their attempt to answer this question, Zhao et al. designed a study using robust statistical analysis. He collected longitudinal data, combining that with information from the Uniform Crime Report database.

Results were mixed. When there was a spike in crime rates, agencies that focused on fighting that crime then became less attentive to providing service and preventing crime. Conversely, the community policing approach provided a comprehensive framework that worked both ends of the dilemma. It enhanced police/community relations while still providing valuable services to citizens and simultaneously reducing social disorder and controlling crime.

Helms and Gutierrez (2007) designed a robust study to assess the effects of federal funding on progressive efforts reflected by Community Oriented Policing Services. One hundred seventy-seven agencies with at least 100 full-time officers were studied. Organizations that received support in the form of federal innovation and 'manpower' grants succeeded in contributing to progressive reform. Findings of this study support claims that law enforcement agencies that adopt changes that are consistent with community-oriented policing are effecting meaningful change in the police reform movement.

A study conducted by Maguire and Katz (2002) provided a sample size of more than 1,600 departments and produced a 71% response rate of usable data. The study analyzed the validity of the claims made by community policing agencies. The general claims made by these agencies were in fact supported. Statistical coefficients linked organizational and officer activities to effectively influencing community policing.

COMPSTAT is short for COMPare STATistics, which is a computer file name for the comprehensive computer program it uses. It is a tool for organizing and synthesizing data and management processes. COMPSTAT materialized as one of the promising innovations that combines intricate, cutting-edge crime analysis, geographic systems, and management directives to systematically reduce crime (Willis et al., 2007). Crime analysts are integral to the COMPSTAT model, as they collect, analyze, and map crime data (Willis et al., 2007). COMPSTAT uses a four-pronged approach in its management of crime:

1. information dissemination, allowing information to be available at all levels
2. problem solving matrices
3. deployment of resources
4. assessment/evaluation and follow-up

Willis and colleagues (2007) evaluated three police departments that supported community policing: Lowell, Massachusetts, Minneapolis, Minnesota, and Newark, New Jersey. These three departments were chosen because COMPSTAT was well established in each. Intensive site investigations were performed in each department. Field research techniques included observation and interviews. The departments were assessed to determine the effectiveness of COMPSTAT in police operations. Both quantitative and qualitative analyses was done.

The findings of this research raised some important issues that may be of particular interest to departmental leaders. The COMPSTAT model holds managers more accountable, but the researchers observed instances when managers sent conflicting messages creating confusion in the department. When COMPSTAT was coupled with other core operations, competing demands were identified. Officers experienced incongruence when they were unable to fulfill a request to help a citizen because they were assigned to COMPSTAT specific duties, such as monitoring the behavior of citizens.

Overall, the results as reported by Willis (et al., 2007) indicate that the COMPSTAT model, which boasts promises of highly impactful and meaningful reform, did not live up to its promise. COMPSTAT was not flexible enough to accommodate changes in priority. In the discussion of the results, the researchers inferred that:

(a) overall accountability suffered as a result of limitations in internal accountability;
(b) problems that arose were unpredictable and resources were insufficient to rapidly respond to every problem, as recommended by the COMPSTAT model;
(c) COMPSTAT was overly rigid and failed to allow for adjustments. As such, agencies struggled in their ability to respond to non-routine demands;
(d) 'impressive' crime data presentations were not found to be as useful as consistent focus on decision making and effective responses;
(e) an overall lack of follow-up limited the organizations capacity to evaluate the longer-term effects of interventions.

Willis et al. (2007) concluded with the observation that COMPSTAT is a more sophisticated version of reactive, traditional policing. The level of sophistication does not translate into a true value-add. Police receive conflicting messages about prioritization, and that interfered with their effectiveness. In some cases, police were frenetically reacting to an aggregate of crime spikes. The authors deduced that COMPSTAT may be more effective if there was a mechanism for careful, exploratory and deliberate review and more in-depth discussions of interventions, i.e., what worked, what did not work, and why.

Community oriented policing symbolizes a fundamental change in practice (Lumb, 1995; Cheurprakobkit, 2002). Given the dynamic and complicated nature of community-oriented policing, proper training is essential. Research designed to better understand the role of training on the implementation of community policing interventions was the focus of a study conducted by Cheurprakobkit (2002) obtained data from 198 respondents, 180 (92.3%) male and 15 (7.7%) female. Training on Community Oriented Policing Services was received by 134 (68%) of respondents; most received more than twenty hours of designated training.

Participants were surveyed to ascertain the attitudes about community policing and whether training influenced their attitudes. Of those surveyed, 88% of officers who received training agreed with the concept of community-oriented policing and felt COPS training was useful. Qualitative data provided insight into the remainder of respondents who had a less favorable attitude toward that approach to policing. A lack of manpower was the primary concern, followed by weak or inconsistent levels of commitment shown by administrators. The data has implications in adopting community-oriented policing approaches.

Community Program Review

Jurisdictions across the country have responded to the call to action toward progressive community policing. The community programs listed here are not an exhaustive list. What follows are some of the programs that have been cited in the literature as having promise or had some degree of a positive effect.

In Baltimore, Maryland, a nationally recognized community policing model was implemented and evaluated for effectiveness. CeaseFire, a Chicago-based violence prevention program, was utilized in the Baltimore market. The goal of Ceasefire was to engage the community in problem solving, particularly around violence (Hardin, 2016).

In Seattle, a micro-community policing plan was developed focusing on neighborhood safety. Micro-Community Policing plans have been designed to address the unique needs of each community/neighborhood. Data collected from the neighborhood-communities was used to garner a more complete picture of perceived and actual crime and public safety.

New York (state and city) have been at the helm of innovative program development. In the city of Newburgh, New York, City Manager Michael Ciaravino has assigned a substantial number of officers to foot patrols (ICMA, 2015). The New York Police Department (NYPD) designated 33% of officers' time, during their scheduled shifts for community building activities (Hardin, 2016). These activities ranged from youth programs to collaborative conflict resolution with neighborhood citizens. To better acquaint officers with the unique neighborhood cultures in New York City, a program called the Community Partner Program was established by the NYPD. That program matches officers with a community member who serves as a mentor-guide to increase exposure and familiarity in assigned neighborhoods (Bennet, 2015).

On March 15, 2016, the city of Ferguson, Missouri - a city personified as a hotbed of racial unrest - hosted open dialogue forums as part of Community Oriented Policing Services (COPS). Similarly, a community relations board was created in Cleveland, Ohio. This board has been charged with promoting positive cross-cultural communication between police and Cleveland citizens, most of whom are minorities (Hardin, 2016).

San Jose, California introduced a program called "Adopt A Cop" wherein officers received prayer and care by community members. Several youth mentoring programs were developed, including Youth Pride in Providence, Rhode Island, and Ambassadors in St. Paul, Minnesota. The "Challenges and Choices" Program was developed in Los Angeles. This innovative program offered police officers the opportunity to serve as teachers in the Los Angeles public schools.

An exemplary program that focuses on youth development in California is the Orange County Gang Reduction and Intervention Partnership (OC GRIP; Miller, n.d.). Since its inception, every year the program has arranged for roughly 2,000 students to attend a Los Angeles Angels Major League Baseball game; 250 officers attend games with the students. OC GRIP has collaborated with one of the largest entertainment gaming companies in an effort to introduce students to exciting career possibilities and stress the importance of education. OC GRIP has been shown to reduce school suspensions and expulsions, and to strengthen the relationship between law enforcement and the community. Further research is needed to formally evaluate the effectiveness of these programs and develop success indicators to measure progress (Calhoun, 2016).

Empirical Studies: Community Programs

A longitudinal study utilizing the Chicago Alternative Policing Strategy (CAPS) was conducted by Lombardo, Olson, and Staton (2010). That program, described as the largest community policing program in the United States, yielded promising results. Findings linked the CAPS program to an improvement in perceptions of police effectiveness and crime prevention. These findings illuminate the importance of building positive relationships between community members and officers. Analysis further showed evidence that the CAPS program led to a decline in drug and gang problems, and neighborhood depreciation, as well as a notably diminished level of dissatisfaction with the police.

An unexpected insight regarding the measurement of perceptions was extrapolated from the data at the conclusion of the CAPS study. When conflicting results were analyzed, a confounding factor was identified that may have skewed the data. Upon further analysis, the authors found an operational definition error as the confound. Specifically, respondents were not making a distinction between physical disorder and social disorder. As it turned out, perceptions were skewed negatively when physical disorder was addressed while social disorder was neglected.

Hybrid Outreach Workers (HOW) and Violence Interrupters are two distinct community - police programs. Both programs were evaluated in two U.S. cities: Baltimore and Chicago. Whitehall and colleagues (2014) found that both of these violence prevention programs produced greater qualitative success in Chicago, versus Baltimore. According to researchers, the most difficult challenge at the Baltimore site was how to most effectively intervene and mediate retaliation when there was a previous homicide or large amounts of money involved. Implications from this study provide insight into ways to collaborate with community members, professionals, and paraprofessionals in negotiating violence in urban areas (Whitehall et al., 2014).

Because youth have been noted to harbor negative attitudes toward the police, Goodrich, Anderson, and LaMotte (2014) designed a study to engender positive interactions between youth and police officers in a non-law enforcement setting. Qualitative data indicated that 98% of youth participants rated their experience as good or excellent. When surveyed at the conclusion of the study, all of the officers (100%) rated their experiences as good or excellent. The data provides support for importance of positive relationship building between police and community members, and in this case, young people. Additionally, interaction with police officers outside of the context of law enforcement can promote positive relationships between youth and police.

Youth-centered programming was also the focus of Leroux and McShane's (2017) study. They evaluated the effects of a policing program targeting 'at risk' youth. A total of 45 youth participated. Findings suggested that participation in the program was effective in reducing negative attitudes toward the police. Crime rate data was not found for these studies.

A community oriented policing strategy that assigned officers to a geographic locale was evaluated by Kane (2000) in the urban city of Philadelphia, Pennsylvania. This study suggested that permanent assignments of officers meaningfully altered police field behavior in a community policing context. Data was collected from officers serving in a Philadelphia public housing setting. A comparison of two groups was made: officers who were permanently assigned to public housing and the control group, who did not have a permanent assignment. The officers with permanent assignments demonstrated a significant increase in self-directed behavior. That is, the permanent assignment officers showed an increase in self-initiated field investigations when compared to the control group/s.

In a separate study, the Philadelphia Police Department instituted a randomized controlled trial policing strategy to determine effectiveness. They hypothesized that officers on foot patrol would have an effect on crime rates (Groff et al., 2013). Officers on foot patrol were assigned to violent crime 'hot spots' in the city. When compared to the control areas, crime in the foot patrol areas was reduced by 23%. Review of qualitative analysis showed that foot patrol officers in neighborhoods established order by negotiating rules and standards upon which residents and business owners could build (Groff et al., 2013).

Liou and Savage (1996) examined citizens' perceptions of crime before and after implementation of a community policing program. Overall, results of this study were favorable toward community-oriented policing. There was a 32% increase in perceived crime reduction. Over 85% of participants felt like crime was decreasing and neighborhoods had qualitatively improved. Thirty-one percent of respondents identified an improvement in effectiveness of police work. These findings were consistent across demographics and community groups in West Palm Beach, Florida. In summary, with the induction of community-oriented policing, citizens' fear of crime was reduced, police-community relationships were improved, and citizens reported favorable perceptions of police and their work.

There is conflicting evidence about whether there is a link between neighborhood or community policing and informal social control (Renauer, 2007). Informal social control represents a micro level social system in which neighbors or community members collectively set standards and informally intervene when undesirable behavior is displayed. The literature suggests that as community-police partnerships are strengthened, informal social control will increase.

Renauer (2007) surveyed eighty-one neighborhood leaders in Portland, Oregon. Results revealed an unexpected outcome: police attendance at community meetings is *negatively* correlated to informal social control. Further, police attendance was *not* shown to increase perceived police effectiveness. In the discussion of the results, Renauer (2007) explained that social cohesion and perceptions of a responsive government system were more strongly correlated to informal social control, than was police attendance at meetings. There were indications that police attendance at community meetings had the opposite effect of what scholars and researchers have suggested. In fact, frequent police presence at community meetings and having access to police officials did not equate to increased informal social control.

SCORE - "Second Chance OR Else" - is an unconventional program that was piloted and now being offered by the City of Mobile (Alabama) Police Department (https://www.mobilepd.org/second-chance/). Selected candidates, who most often reside in crime hot spots, are accepted in the program and offered an opportunity to defer or forego jail time provided successful completion of the program. Participants receive education and opportunities for rehabilitation and giving back to their communities (https://www.mobilepd.org/second-chance/). SCORE seeks to accomplish its goals by using a collaborative approach between community members and law enforcement officials to: a) reduce crime, b) increase public safety and c) build an alliance with the community (Dorton & Semien, 2016). Descriptive data provides evidence analyzing the success of the program in aligning with the mission and its practices. Most notably, there were measured improvements in neighborhoods (Dorton & Semien, 2016).

Evaluative Critique

Community Policing

Although community policing has been deemed a 'long awaited elixir' to an ailing law enforcement system (Palmiotto, 1995), taking a pragmatic approach to critically evaluating its efficacy and viability might offer a sobering perspective to inflated and potentially unrealistic expectations. There is debate about the effectiveness of community policing, but perhaps the results are impacted by a wide variation in program implementation. Because there is considerable variation across jurisdictions (Lawrence & McCarthy, n.d.), community policing has faced some structural and procedural problems. Undefined principal outcomes has led to inconsistent and confusing criteria for community oriented operational tasks (Renauer, 2007).

The implementation in police departments has been found to be 'irregular' and 'incomplete' (Pelfrey, 2004). Program initiatives such as foot patrol or police substations are a part of community policing, but in and of themselves do not constitute community policing (Scheider et al., 2009). An incomplete implementation has created obstacles for departments and researchers (Pelfrey, 2004), and has restricted the capacity for success.

Empirical evidence shows mixed results regarding the 'effectiveness' of community policing (Gill et al., 2014). With mixed results regarding community policing and its effect on crime, studies consistently show that efforts such as foot patrol, community meetings, and police-community interaction impacts residents' sense of safety. Opportunities for more meaningful connection, including outside of the law enforcement context, has implications for reducing crime and fear of crime (Gill et al., 2014). Critics suggest that community policing has been idealized by a set of powerful myths (Somerville, 2014). Some findings show weak measurable impact on crime statistics (Kerley & Benson, 2000).

The term "effectiveness" must be contextualized here. Effectiveness, as defined by much of the research, narrowly measures reported levels of crime. There are fundamental differences between science and policing, particularly in regard to what constitutes "effective" practice (Fyfe, 2013). Reliance on crime control as the primary outcome measure in evaluating community policing is limiting (Gill et al., 2014) and does not account for the broader qualitative goals of community policing such as community perceptions of fear, safety and trust. Therefore, limitations in study design preclude a complete evaluation of this model.

As a work in progress that is developing and evolving, community policing and its proponents solicit feedback and empirical evaluation to refine and improve its implementation (Wetzel, 2012). While community policing has been criticized for definitional abstraction and mixed empirical evidence measuring 'success,' the model shows promise in making meaningful changes in the reform movement. Community policing, in its ability to expand its framework, embraces collaboration and problem-solving with the community and other strategic partnerships.

RACE AND MARGINALIZED COMMUNITIES

The Race Card

It is difficult to author a chapter on progressive policing without acknowledging the social construct of race. Race is intertwined in much of the body of law enforcement literature be it implicitly or explicitly. Race, culture, and/or marginalized groups are mentioned either as a backdrop or positioned at the foreground of much of the literature on progressive policing, community-oriented policing, or law enforcement as a whole.

America is a striking amalgamation of cultures, races, ethnicities, religions, beliefs, sub-cultures, and economic striations. While American society boasts of a rich cultural heritage, this cornucopia is also encumbered with a painful past of racial injustice and inequality. Thus, in structuring the template of progressive policing, the role of race relations must be included - i.e., "pulling the race card."

Inequality in historically marginalized and disenfranchised groups has been well documented. Perhaps even more than 'race' as a general topic, racial inequity and disparities in law enforcement is germane to this discussion. What follows in this section is the examination of law enforcement at the intersection of race and marginalization.

Further analysis of the definition of *progressive* (see Introduction section) points to the role of race in the progressive policing movement as a pivotal issue. To be progressive is to make use of opportunities to change and improve the social climate by forward moving action. To link the concepts, progressive policing makes use of opportunities to improve the racial social climate by taking forward moving actions. Remember from our definition, gradual improvement is still an improvement, just as incremental steps are still progressive. By taking even one meaningful step toward addressing racial dynamics, America can parlay that step into a bigger win: cultivating a societal landscape that is conducive to enhanced social order and cohesion.

The police/community relationship is at the nucleus of community oriented policing. Relationship building and repairing - has become a top priority in the U.S. (Posick & Hatfield, 2017), especially in marginalized communities. Communities that most need police attention are the ones with higher crime rates. Building a bridge into these communities is a key step in any progressive movement.

The most pressing problems in these communities are crime, safety, social and physical disorder, and neighborhood decay (Chappell, 2008). Although the police are not charged with taking on community problems, they can play a critical role in developing a shared solution that is linked to crime and social disorder; for example, limiting criminal opportunities and collaborating to address underlying conditions (Scheider et al., 2009). Shared solutions that involve the cooperation of community members are consistent with the idea of informal social control (Renauer (2007).

The contemporary community policing movement was conceived out of public dissatisfaction (Scheider et al., 2009). Communities complained about the diminished effectiveness and efficiency of police (Scheider et al., 2009). A recent national poll found that confidence in police has dropped dramatically and is at its lowest in nearly 25 years (Posick & Hatfield, 2017). Too often, community members' perceptions are limited to or shaped by negative interactions with the police (Culbertson, 2000).

Harmful policing in the context of poor community relations renders law enforcement less effective, undermines community partnerships, and compromises the safety of officers (Harmon, 2012). When conflicts arise, they manifest as resistance on the street level between officers and citizens. Unchecked and uncorrected, suspicion and mistrust thwart efforts to problem solve (Lumb, 1995).

Racial minorities have arguably been the most vocal about mistrust of police. Where there is cultural or racial disparity, there is often a decline in trust and legitimacy (Hasisi, 2008). Racially disparate groups also tend to challenge the idea that law enforcement can be fair even when police voice the intent to improve or progress.

Whether there is a link between race and unfair practice continues to be up for debate. The body of literature is mixed or conflicting, and research is inconclusive as to whether racial minorities are specifically targeted in the use of force and other racially motivated behavior. There is abundant evidence that prejudice, racism, and discriminatory practices lurk below the surface - or at times in painfully plain sight - of the justice system (Lumb, 1995). Yet Miller (2015) refuted that argument, claiming that there is no evidence that police employ excessive force disproportionately against members of racial groups compared with other minority groups. Although the use of physical force is the exception, Miller (2015) stated that certain attitudes, personality types and experiences predispose some officers to be more aggressive or to use forceful coercion in a racial context. Split-second decisions require an officer to make a choice about the appropriate intervention based upon attitudes and other factors, reflecting a multi-layered process (Robin et al., 2011).

This issue is complicated by the intrinsic contradiction between providing service and imposing control (Lumb, 1995). Dissonance can be experienced by officers when they are tasked with clashing roles. The same officer who works to build relationships in the community is also tasked with restoring order, which may involve tactics such as the use of force.

Police and Racial Minorities

Minority communities express feelings of invalidation, making any attempt to resolve conflict divisive. Minority communities become intolerant of or in some cases hostile toward the police presence in their communities (Lumb, 1995). There is a growing list of highly publicized incidents where young black men have been injured or killed by those who claim (and perhaps believe) they were acting to maintain public safety and order (LePere-Schloop & Lumpkin, 2016).

Law enforcement is under fire following a torrent of incidents involving police officers and predominantly young black males. Some of these incidents have garnered extensive media attention, with accumulating evidence that people of color are being exposed to excessive force in confrontations with the police (Ruggs et al., 2016). These recent events are set against a backdrop of tense relations between minorities and law enforcement that dates back as far as Jim Crow. More recently, the Trayvon Martin case was a figurative match that ignited a firestorm.

On February 26, 2012, seventeen-year-old Trayvon Martin was involved in a physical altercation with George Zimmerman, culminating in Martin's death from a bullet fired by Zimmerman. George Zimmerman was reportedly the neighborhood watch coordinator for the gated Sanford, Florida community in which this incident occurred. Although Martin was unarmed at the time of the altercation, Zimmerman claimed self-defense and pointed to some relatively minor injuries. A national debate ensued around the issues of 'Stand Your Ground' and self-defense laws.

George Zimmerman was the former captain of the neighborhood watch. Although Zimmerman was not a sworn officer, the 'public' viewed him as representative of the police (LePere-Schloop & Lumpkin). In cases like this, where there is a blurred line of demarcation between sworn officers and volunteers or 'para-police,' public perception often reflects no difference. Sensationalized coverage is often based on perception or assumption rather than factual information (LePere-Schloop & Lumpkin, 2016).

Early coverage of this case portrayed racially motivated behavior by George Zimmerman, suggesting his actions against Trayvon Martin were based on racial profiling. The emphasis on race incited public outrage, which spurred protests around the country. It was only later clarified and publicized that Zimmerman was "Hispanic," although in the absence of information, his race was defaulted to white in the public domain.

Following nation-wide citizen protests arguing against racial profiling, George Zimmerman was charged with second-degree murder. A jury found him not guilty, and the US Department of Justice concluded that there was not enough evidence to convict Zimmerman of a hate crime. In many respects the trial of George Zimmerman was a 'litmus test' that would define 'fair outcomes' in the criminal justice system (Thompson, 2015).

The Trayvon Martin/George Zimmerman case was the first of a string of high profile incidents involving race as the predominant issue. Another occurred on August 9, 2014 in a suburb of St. Louis called Ferguson, Missouri. Michael Brown, an 18-year-old Black/African American male was fatally shot by a White/Caucasian officer named Wilson who claimed that Brown attempted to take control of his gun while Wilson was sitting in his police vehicle. Wilson described his pursuit of Brown as he fled on foot. Wilson fired his gun, firing a total of twelve bullets. Of the twelve shots, six apparently hit Michael Brown.

The public responded in protests throughout the country shouting the phrase "Don't Shoot". Again, there were vehement accusations of racially motivated behavior, and in this case, criticism of militarized police tactics as well. Officer Wilson was charged with a racially motivated crime, but on March 4, 2015, the Department of Justice concluded that Officer Wilson shot Brown in self-defense and they cleared him of civil rights violations.

The case of Laquan McDonald has also been cited as a case of racial profiling. On October 20, 2014, in Chicago, officers were dispatched in response to vehicle break-ins. Once on location, they encountered seventeen-year-old Laquan McDonald. McDonald was described as 'acting erratically' and holding a folding knife with a three-inch blade, walking briskly down the middle of a multi-lane road. Officer Van Dyke jumped out of the passenger side of his police vehicle and ordered McDonald to drop the knife. McDonald continued walking with his knife in hand and appeared to ignore Van Dyke's commands. Van Dyke opened fire with a total of sixteen shots. Officer Van Dyke's partner, who was driving at the time, quickly emerged to assist. The officer also aimed his firearm at McDonald, but as reports indicate, did not shoot because Van Dyke was in the line of fire. Initially, Van Dyke's actions were deemed justified. However, the police cam video released a year later showed the actual events, leading a jury to convict Officer Van Dyke of second-degree murder and 16 counts of aggravated battery with a firearm.

On November 23, 2014 in Cleveland, Ohio, another racially charged incident occurred. Police shot and killed a twelve-year-old African American male, Tamir Rice. Police were responding to a call about a "Black male" who was pulling out a gun and pointing it at people. According to reports, when officers asked the young man to show them his hands, it appeared to them that Rice was attempting to pull a gun out from the waist/torso area. The officers fired two shots, one of which struck Rice. He died the following day from the gunshot wounds. It was later discovered that the gun Rice was carrying was a "toy" gun, apparently not marked in any way to suggest to the police officer that it was a toy gun. Although the officers in this case were acquitted of charges, the family brought a lawsuit against the city of Cleveland and was awarded a $6 million settlement.

Another recent case fed the debate over the use of 'overly aggressive' and 'brutal' police tactics. In 2014, in the borough of Staten Island, NYPD officers attempted to arrest Eric Garner on suspicion of a misdemeanor. Garner was reported to have resisted arrest and was placed in a prone position restraint. Garner allegedly tried to alert officers that he was unable to breathe. The resultant death of Garner was reported by the NYC Medical Examiner's Office as a neck compression during the physical restraint, limiting the suspect's airway. The incident was filmed, igniting widespread criticism of police brutality.

A phenomenon that I've termed "cyclical hostility" occurred. This is a sequence seemingly unrelated events involving the same factors serving to intensify antagonism and hostility expressed and experienced by all involved parties. Culpability can be found on all fronts. All parties have responsibility for feeding the frenzy of reactive cycles of anger and hostility: groups of citizens pointing the finger of blame; sensationalized portrayals of victimization; citizen failure to take some responsibility for engaging in resistant behavior; overly-aggressive tactics by police toward citizens, and heightened fear/threat responses triggering disproportionately aggressive counter-tactics. The narrative is cyclically rehearsed and recapitulated, resulting in the 'demonization' of police by citizens (Lumb, 1995) and the criminalization of minorities and members of disenfranchised groups by law enforcement.

Retaliation crimes against police have exacerbated an already turbulent atmosphere between police and racial minorities. On July 7, 2016, an attack on Dallas police officers left five officers dead (Posick & Hatfield, 2017). This incident, as with countless others, was said to be racially motivated.

Another tragic case involving the New York Police Department underscores the devastating impact of amped-up race relations in America. This particular case was dubbed a 'payback' or retaliation crime, as sources reported that the assailant was avenging the deaths of Black males who had recently been killed by police. The gunman open-fired on two NYPD officers, Wenjian Liu and Rafael Ramos, at close range. The officers were on duty and were murdered while sitting in a clearly marked patrol car. The shooter, after killing the officers, shot and killed himself in a New York City subway station.

The loss of these officers' lives while serving their communities is unconscionable. Also distressing is the fact that both officers were easily identifiable as minority community members themselves. There is probably much more to this story than meets the eye, but from the available information there is room to infer that the gunman suffered from severe and/or chronic mental illness.

Cases like these are rife with stereotypical interpretation. Conjectures and biases abound in the interpretation of incidents; individuals become cast together in 'narratives about race' over which they have no control (Robin et al., 2011). The U.S. Department of Justice recognized a dire need to address 'tense' problematic racial relations between police and the African American community (Thompson & Kahn, 2016). A Department of Justice report articulated that theme subsequent to a civil lawsuit against the City of Portland (Oregon) police, concluding that the Portland police had demonstrated a pattern of excessive force, particularly against African-Americans and/or those with mental illness (Thompson & Kahn, 2016).

Collective Racialization

As these stories demonstrate, the 'race issue' in law enforcement is quite complex. To delve into all of the iterations of the debate goes far beyond the scope of this chapter. However, one other layer that lends to the discussion is the process through which race becomes deeply embedded into our societal consciousness and our institutions. Race is woven into the fabric of American institutions and systemic ideologies. Racialization is like fluoride in water; it is present even if undetectable. Race feeds into our conscious and unconscious constructs.

To illustrate this concept, the majority of people in authoritative positions in our legal system are White and from upper socio-economic classes. As a result, a White conservative upper-class worldview becomes the dominant view (Hodge & Matthews, 2011). This view is accepted without controversy, and it shapes the totality of law and order.

The media also un/consciously shapes societal constructs around race. Media has considerable power in configuring public perception. The media - through sensationalistic styles of broadcasting - can and does incite a discourse that is often misleading. Misperceptions are heightened by broadcasting or selecting stories that (mis)represent or overemphasize negative statistics about Blacks and Latinos, thus exaggerating fears about these groups (Sun, 2018). Consequently, public perception is more likely to reflect a generally accepted narrative that Blacks and Latinos are criminals. Conversely, the media often portrays a more humane aspect of Whites in news stories, and exaggerates White victimization (Sun, 2018). In both instances, these portrayals are not representative of actual data. Depicting certain racial groups as criminal suspects and Whites as victims provokes reactions that are prejudiced and biased (Mastro, et. al., 2009).

News reporting in the United States, even if not intentional, creates perceptual biases. The biases described here involve race, ethnicity, and culture. Both research and theory support that exposure to media contributes to perceptions about, and creates bias in attitudes, opinions, and behaviors regarding certain groups (Mastro, et. al., 2009). These biases influence judgments and behavior triggered by those judgments.

Clearly, we can infer that police officers' judgments are impacted by these factors as well. When officers are exposed to a barrage of media stories and professional experiences that confirm media-driven statistics, opinions about certain groups become embedded in their psychological structures. Moreover, their behavior reflects those attitudes and beliefs.

Perceptions drive behavior. When identifiable groups in a population are parsed as either negative or positive forces in society, then opinions and attitudes about them will unfold, triggering behavior consistent with these beliefs and attitudes. If law enforcement, and even policy makers act upon these biased perceptions, the results will continue to be damaging. Practices such as how suspects are treated (or mistreated), racial profiling, and creating policies that further criminalize certain groups will persist. These practices continue to widen the divide and systematize racial inequity and marginalization.

TRAINING IMPLICATIONS

There is a strong case for including training in the construction of progressive community policing. The research discussed in this chapter offers insight into training needs to reinforce community-oriented policing. The 'new era' of progressive policing mandates ongoing, quality training in the areas of cultural diversity, decision making, problem solving, communication, as well as crime prevention and defensive tactics (Chappell, 2008). If progressive community policing is committed to making changes in policing, then training must reflect and support those changes (Chappell, 2007).

Former President Barak Obama inaugurated the Task Force of 21st Century Policing that embodies training, retaining, and recruitment. The overall objectives of the Task Force center around: a) improving police - community relations, b) building credibility and trust in law enforcement, and, c) continued education and training from national to local law enforcement entities. The Task Force strives to accomplish its goals using a striated approach (Final Report of the President's Task Force on 21st Century Policing, 2015).

Hardin (2016) emphasized the importance of ongoing training and the need for changes in organizational culture. A top-down approach contributes to an organizational climate that values training and innovation (Final Report of the President's Task Force on 21st Century Policing, 2015). Agency-wide participation creates a culture to advance the mission and produce well-equipped team members. The Task Force further stressed the need for on-going training that begins at the academy and continues throughout the officer's career. Proper and thorough training for officers is one of the precepts in progressive policing (Jackson, 2015).

To be successful in the field of law enforcement, and to carry out the mission of progressive community policing, thorough cross-training at the intersections of law, policy, sociological constructs, emotional and social intelligence, and conflict management are required. Chappell (2008) added critical thinking, interpersonal skills, and communication to the list of training topics. An empathic approach to communication was recommended by Posick & Hatfield, (2017) who cited empathic communication as showing measurable improvements in outcomes.

One of the more critical areas of training is decision-making as in all areas of law enforcement (Hoffman, 2017). When an officer is trained in the intricate cognitive process of decision-making, liability for law enforcement agencies is minimized and policies are more closely adhered to (Hoffman, 2017). The job of a law enforcement officer is becoming increasingly exacting. Training in areas of cognition such as decision-making is essential if officers are to keep up with the pace of progressive policing.

Training must accurately reflect situations that officers are likely to encounter. Currently, officer training focuses primarily on technical and mechanical aspects while neglecting the skills officers are likely to use most frequently. On average, officers receive 60 hours of firearms training, 36 hours of emergency vehicle operations, 44 hours of self-defense training, and 12 hours of non-lethal weapons use (Harmon, 2012). While these are important, there is no substitute for a well-trained officer who has a strong knowledge and skill set to defuse tense or hostile situations (Schoenle, 2017). This requires a greater emphasis on cognitive skill building and social intelligence.

Training that supports the development of skills and knowledge around problem-solving and partnership development is a value-add that results in measurably enhanced performance (Scheider et al., 2009). Similarly, developing integrity in practice through training in ethics fulfills an officer's critical obligation. Currently, only eight hours each is devoted to ethics/integrity, and mediation/conflict management (Harmon, 2012).

A brief mention of technology also warrants discussion, because of the inextricable nature of technology and law enforcement in present day society. There is a need for training in this area. Technology and cyber-security is a bourgeoning branch of practice in law enforcement. For better or for worse, technology spans the gamut of utilitarianism, including the enabling of more sophisticated and elusive methods of criminal activity (McQuade, 2006). Law enforcement seeks to stay ahead of the curve by introducing training and expertise that gives them an advantage over technology crime threats (McQuade, 2006). McQuade (2006) offered guidance about 'perpetual innovation' and the danger of law enforcement agencies becoming inert while criminals become savvier in their use of technology. The goal here would be to educate, train, and equip officers and departments to anticipate, prevent, and hopefully disable crime threats (McQuade, 2006).

Cultural Competency Training

Social and political controversy surrounding police, racism, and historically disenfranchised groups has polarized the American landscape (Moon et al., 2018). Scholars advocate for moving toward a culture of inclusion and greater understanding between groups. There is a relative absence of training and assessment in the area of cultural competency (Moon et al., 2018).

When cultural competence is included in training programs, the focus needs to include both the external group dynamic and intra-personal dynamics. The latter is often ignored. The term 'intra-personal' describes how one's personal viewpoints and constructs direct an officer's attitudes and behavior.

Racial Constructs and Bias

Officers are under pressure to manage intense external circumstances while simultaneously mitigating internal factors and the effects of those factors (American

Psychological Association, 2002). Daily, officers need to make quick, important decisions. As a result, cognitive shortcuts are unavoidable and necessary.

Unpacking these cognitive shortcuts (heuristics) that our minds manufacture begs these questions: Why does the brain make these assumptions? From a cultural/racial lens, why does the brain naturally use these short-cuts by making assumptions about groups of people? Why does the brain need to classify groups of people negatively, for example as criminals? Moreover, why do we consistently and often automatically act on these assumptions, even if they are not necessarily based on true or accurate information?

Behavioral theory posits that behavior is an outward expression of what we think, experience, or to what we have been conditioned. Behavioral patterns emerge from beliefs and attitudes. Threading this theory into the race relations issue helps to clarify why people default to certain behaviors or judgments about certain groups, even if the assumptions are not entirely true. These judgments and behaviors are not easily changed, even with disconfirming evidence.

People unconsciously harbor associations and stereotypes regarding race, gender, or other personal characteristics. These biases influence decisions, behaviors, attitudes, and conceptions (Wirts, 2017). Moule (2009) found that people sometimes exhibit behaviors that are either engaging or disengaging toward or against others. Examples would be if an individual perceived someone's race or sexual orientation as favorable or unfavorable, that person may subtly or overtly engage or disengage based on their perception.

Azevedo and colleagues (2017) exposed more deeply embedded - and automatic - responses to racial stimuli. This critical research illuminates the predominance of bias in our racial constructs. The findings highlight automatic physical responses to racial stimuli that are consistent with theoretical research on bias. Analysis of the study revealed that negative unconscious information about Blacks in particular, can spark neurophysiological responses that correspond to threat signaling and startle reflexes (Azevedo et al., 2017). This phenomenon becomes evident in behaviors and responses that are triggered by unconscious attitudes and biases.

Implicit Bias

There is actually a term for this phenomenon called "unconscious bias" or "implicit bias." Unconscious/implicit bias is defined as "learned stereotypes that are automatic, unintentional, deeply ingrained, universal, and able to influence behavior" (wikipedia.com; p. 1; Greenwald & Banaji, 1995). Every human is prone to both implicit and explicit bias; it is not specific to police officers, or even White people. I want to emphasize that implicit or unconscious bias is outside of the realm of awareness, which means that often, biases are in our blind spots, and we may not realize that we are under such influences. Implicit bias can play out repeatedly, - unconsciously - and daily.

The power of implicit bias and the resulting into behavioral influences provides insights into how an officer might be more reactive when facing young men of color, for instance. In addition to cultural competence, conscious and implicit bias training is needed in officer training (Schoenle, 2017). The Task Force also advocated for training that recognizes and confronts implicit bias and cultural responsiveness (Final Report of the President's Task Force on 21st Century Policing, 2015).

Unpacking our own biases is indispensable to confronting perpetuated negative attitudes and progressing toward building a more cohesive society (Moule, 2009). Although bias is largely an internal construct - meaning that our biases lie within our own minds - developing awareness of others is another aspect of managing bias. Understanding ourselves in relation to cultural mores and communication styles of other groups can lend to more productive interactions. Lack of awareness about our own racial identity or the cultural norms, mores, and communication styles of other groups can lead to significant misinterpretation and counter-productive behavior.

Misidentification resulting from unchecked racial biases can have serious repercussions (Azevedo et al., 2017). Perhaps a fictional scenario will illustrate the ramifications of unchecked biases: An officer misidentifies a harmless object as a weapon in the hand of a young Black male. Implicit racial stereotypes are activated and the level of immediate threat is (unintentionally) inflated by the officer. The officer fires shots, wounding the suspect.

Azevedo and colleagues (2017) measured physiological responses - phasic activation of arterial baroreceptors - that are indicated in the process of neural changes with the onset of fearful stimuli. They observed that activation of racial prompts corresponded with the cardiovascular cycle. Physiological conditions were affected by racial stimuli under conditions of ambiguity; that is, cardiac activity increased with the presence of racial cues. This research has implications for the effects of implicit bias on automatic behavioral responses.

Feemster (2010) proposed a dimension to training that has received sparse attention in the literature: spirituality. Optimal training, according to Feemster (2010), includes a spectrum of dimensions such as psychological, emotional, social, and spiritual proficiency. Spirituality fosters professional meaningfulness and offers a buffer to psychological stressors that are inevitable in police work.

The cumulation of these topics can seem daunting. Adding anything to an already packed curriculum may be overwhelming. Yet with the evolution of policing, exploring creative solutions to incorporate these topics is justified. Notably, continuous professional development, education, and training is needed throughout the officer's career to keep up with current trends in the field. The aim is to develop well-rounded, well-equipped officers, providing continuous training and support for them throughout their careers.

Successful engineering of a culturally competent police force positions law enforcement agents to be more responsive to the needs of the community and larger society (Blakemore, Barlow, & Padgett, 1995). Development of cultural competence combined with integrity practices have been found to positively impact community relations and facilitate effective policing (Calhoun, 2016). Broaching the subject of race as a training topic is intricate and complex, requiring diplomacy and finesse on behalf of training providers, who are encouraged to engage the topic in meaningful, constructive, and non-punitive ways.

Critical analysis of bias and exploration of racial/cultural identity are actionable tools that are offered by cross cultural training. These tools can be used to engage solution-focused interventions that address the rampant problems in the U.S. around race, criminalization, and marginalization.

TRAINING MODELS

The goal of training and education is to acquire new skills and be able to establish their practical uses (Lumb, 1995). To accomplish this, Chappell (2008) recommends an interactive adult learning style of pedagogy as officers are more likely to benefit and retain information. Training that engages the individual on a personal level is more meaningful and offers a greater impact on trainees (Blakemore et al., 1995). Individuals are more likely to experience change when they are engaged on cognitive, emotional, and experiential levels (Lumb, 1995).

Designing educational and training curricula from this framework has implications on cultural competence and bias (Lumb, 1995). Research on racial bias can inform the development of curricula that positively affects cognitive, attitudinal, and practice outcomes (Ruggs et al., 2016). Training should aim to uncover bias and promote behavioral change (Blakemore et al., 1995).

The Task Force advises departments to bring different disciplines and backgrounds together to 'cross-fertilize' ideas, leading to better and more diverse solutions. Bringing outside entities to provide intervention and training for law enforcement agencies has shown to be beneficial. Although law enforcement tends to be insular, the fresh perspective of an outside agency can prevent stagnation and sequestration that results from staying within a bureaucratic silo.

Taking direction from the Task Force's report to bring adoption of this directive, a training and development provider that offers exceptional workshops is ReelTime Creative Learning Experiences. ReelTime emerged out of a need for innovative training for attorneys, but has implications throughout the legal and law enforcement fields. ReelTime has since expanded their programming as well as their target audiences. They offer a variety of relevant topics (including sexual harassment awareness and diversity and inclusion) that are informative and interactive. Their training programs are thought-provoking and engaging, with a fresh spin on some rather difficult issues. Their program on implicit bias is stellar and has received overwhelmingly positive feedback from participants.

The Task Force referenced "Training Innovation Hubs" which are 'brain centers' for new innovations in the field of law enforcement. Training Innovation Hubs are microcosms of an ideological police culture. Similar to the College of Policing in England, Training Innovation Hubs intend to advance evidence-based training and practices. Federal funding has been earmarked for further development of these hubs.

CONCLUSION

The field of law enforcement has responded to the need for reform through sustained efforts to develop progressive policing models and establish legitimacy. Federal funding has stimulated considerable innovation and research. This chapter submits evidence that community policing is a preferred model, as it captures the overall needs of the reform movement. While community policing is staged as a preferred model, critics argue that community oriented policing has not been shown to be consistently effective. Still, the benefits of this model evidence continued promise for its utilitarianism in the United States.

One of the central precepts for community policing is to engage community participation in problem-solving, setting priorities, and establishing law and order. As police officers interface with communities throughout the country, particularly in marginalized communities, the role of race becomes salient. This chapter considers the role of race and cultural competence in facilitating police-community relations in disenfranchised communities. Conclusively, recommendations for training designed to reinforce progressive community oriented policing are offered.

REFERENCES

Aldana, S. (2018, September 19). 5 Workplace wellness statistics every employer should know [Article]. *Wellsteps - Effective Employee Wellness Solutions*. Retrieved from https://www.wellsteps.com/blog/2018/01/06.

American Civil Liberties Union. (n.d.) *Reforming Police Practices* [Article]. Retrieved from https://www.aclu.org/issues/criminal-law-reform.

American Psychological Association. (2002). *Specialty guidelines for forensic psychology*. Washington, DC: Author. Retrieved from http://www.apa.org/ practice/ guidelines/forensic-psychology.aspx.

Azevedo, R. T., Garfinkel, S. N., Critchley, H. D. & Tsakiris, M. (2017). Cardiac afferent activity modulates the expression of racial stereotypes. *Nature Communications*, *8*, 13854. doi:http://dx.doi.org/10.1038/ncomms13854.

Bennet, S. (2015). Examining police, community relations [Blog post]. *The RAND Blog*. RAND Corporation. Retrieved from http://www.rand.org.

Blakemore, J. L., Barlow, D. & Padgett, D. L. (1995). From the classroom to the community: Introducing process in police diversity training. *Police Studies*, *18*(1), 71.

Bosman, J. & Apuzzo, M. (2014, Aug 16). The militarization of America's police. *International New York Times* Retrieved from http://nclive.org/cgi-bin/nclsm?url=http://search.proquest.com.

Calhoun, J. A. (2016). Building trust between police and the communities they serve. *National League of Cities*. Retrieved from https://citiesspeak.org/2016/11/20.

Campbell, E. (2016). Policing and its spatial imaginaries. *Journal of Theoretical & Philosophical Criminology*, *8*(2), 71-89.

Chappell, A. T. (2008). Police academy training: Comparing across curricula. *Policing*, *31*(1), 36-56. doi:http://dx.doi.org/10.1108/13639510810852567.

Chappell, A. T. (2007). Community policing: Is field training the missing link? *Policing*, *30*(3), 498-517. doi:http://dx.doi.org/10.1108/13639510710778868.

Cheurprakobkit, S. (2002). Community policing: Training, definitions and policy implications. *Policing*, *25*(4), 709-725. doi:http://dx.doi.org/10.1108/ 1363951021 0450640.

Comey, J. B. (2015, February 12). *Hard truths: Law enforcement and race*. Georgetown University: Washington D.C. Retrieved from https://www.fbi.gov/news/speeches.

Culbertson, H. M. (2000). A key step in police-community relations: Identify the divisive issues. *Public Relations Quarterly*, *45*(1), 13-17.

DeGarmo, M. J. (2012). The diffusion of innovation among United States policing jurisdictions: A cautionary tale for theorists and researchers. *International Journal of Criminal Justice Sciences*, *7*(1), 450-465.

den Heyer, G. (2011). New public management. *Policing*, *34*(3), 419-433. doi: http://dx.doi.org/10.1108/13639511111157492.

Dorton, H. E. & Semien, D. S. (2016). "Collaborative Investment" Instead of Community Policing: An examination of an innovative drug market intervention program in Southern Alabama. *Race, Gender & Class*, *23*(1), 99-107.

Feemster, Samuel L. J. D. & Div, M. (2010). Addressing the urgent need for multi-dimensional training in law enforcement. *Forensic Examiner*, *19*(3), 44-49, 124.

Final Report of the President's Task Force on 21st Century Policing (May 2015). Retrieved from http://www.cops.usdoj.gov/pdf/taskforce/ TaskForce_FinalReport.pdf Recommendation 5.9, page 58.

Frank, K., IV. Frank, J. & Liederbach, J. (2014). Understanding police use of force. *Policing*, *37*(3), 558-578. doi: http://dx.doi.org/10.1108/PIJPSM-08-2013-0079.

Fyfe, N. R. (2013). Complex transition and uncertain trajectories. *Journal of Workplace Learning*, *25*(6), 407-420. doi: http://dx.doi.org/10.1108/JWL-08-2012-0059.

Gamal, F. (2016). The racial politics of protection: A critical race examination of police militarization. *California Law Review*, *104*(4), 979.

Gill, C., Weisburd, D., Telep, C. W., Vitter, Z. & Bennett, T. (2014). Community-oriented policing to reduce crime, disorder and fear and increase satisfaction and legitimacy among citizens: A systematic review. *Journal of Experimental Criminology*, *10*(4), 399-428. doi:http://dx.doi.org/10.1007/s11292-014-9210-y.

Goodrich, S. A., Anderson, S. A. & LaMotte, V. (2014). Evaluation of a program designed to promote positive police and youth interactions. *Journal of Juvenile Justice*, *3*(2), 55-71.

Gove, T. G. (2011). Implicit Bias and Law Enforcement. *The Police Chief*. October 2011, (78), 44–56.

Greenwald, A. G. & Banaji, M. R. (1995). Implicit social cognition: Attitudes, self-esteem, and stereotypes. *Psychology Review*, *102*, 4-27.

Gregory, A. (2014). Rise of the warrior cop: The militarization of America's police forces. *The Independent Review*, *19*(2), 271-275.

Groff, E. R., Johnson, L., Ratcliffe, J. H. & Wood, J. (2013). Exploring the relationship between foot and car patrol in violent crime areas. *Policing*, *36*(1), 119-139. doi:http://dx.doi.org/10.1108/13639511311302506.

Hall, A. R. & Coyne, C. J. (2013). The militarization of U.S. domestic policing. *The Independent Review*, *17*(4), 485-504.

Hardin, R. S. (2016). The criticality of a community perspective. *Industrial and Organizational Psychology*, *9*(3), 561-564. doi:http://dx.doi.org/10.1017/iop.2016.55.

Harmon, R. A. (2012). The problem of policing. *Michigan Law Review*, *110*(5), 761-817.

Harmon, R. A. (2009). Promoting civil rights through practicing policing reform. *Stanford Law Review*, *62*(1), 1-68.

Hartley, T. A., Burchfiel, C. M., Fekedulegn, D., Andrew, M. E. & Violanti, J. M. (2011). Health disparities in police officers: Comparisons to the U.S. general population. *International Journal of Emergency Mental Health*, *13*(4), 211-220.

Hasisi, B. (2008). Police, politics, and culture in a deeply divided society. *Journal of Criminal Law & Criminology*, *98*(3), 1119-1145.

Helms, R. & Gutierrez, R. S. (2007). Federal subsidies and evidence of progressive change. *Police Quarterly*, *10*(1), 87-107. doi: http://dx.doi.org/10.1177/1098611106296480.

Holmes, A. (2014). Bridging the information gap: The department of justice's "pattern or practice" suits and community organizations. *Texas Law Review*, *92*(5), 1241-1276.

International City/County Management Association, ICMA (2015, February 27). *3 Ways to improve police/community relations*. Retrieved from https://icma.org/articles/article/.

Jackson, B. A. (2015). *Respect and legitimacy - a two way street: Strengthening trust between police and the public in an era of increasing transparency.* [Blog Post] RAND Corporation (PE-154). Retrieved from http://www.rand.org.

Kane, R. J. (2000). Permanent beat assignments in association with community policing: Assessing the impact on police officers' field activity. *Justice Quarterly: JQ, 17*(2), 259-280. doi:http://dx.doi.org/10.1080/07418820000096321.

Lawrence, S. & McCarthey, B. (n.d.). *What works in community policing.* Chief Justice Earl Warren Institute on Law & Social Policy at the UC Berkeley School of Law. Retrieved from https:// www.law.berkeley.edu/ files/ What_Works_in_Community_Policing.pdf.

LePere-Schloop, M. & Lumpkin, J. H. (2016). Learning from Trayvon: Lessons and implications for police organizations and leaders. *Journal of Public Management & Social Policy, 23*(1), 61-73.

Leroux, E. J. & McShane, K. (2017). Changing youth attitudes toward the police through community policing programming. *Journal of Community Psychology, 45*(6), 810-822. doi:http://dx.doi.org/10.1002/jcop.21894.

Liou, K. T. & Savage, E. G. (1996). Citizen perception of community policing impact. *Public Administration Quarterly, 20*(2), 163-179.

Lombardo, R. M., Olson, D. & Staton, M. (2010). The Chicago Alternative Policing Strategy. *Policing, 33*(4), 586-606. doi: http://dx.doi.org/10.1108/ 136395110 11085033.

Lumb, R. C. (1995). Policing culturally diverse groups: Continuing professional development programs for police. *Police Studies, 18*(1), 23.

Mentel, Z. (2012). *Racial reconciliation, Truth-telling, and Police legitimacy.* U.S. Department of Justice: Office of Community Oriented Policing Services. Retrieved from http://ric-zai-inc.com/Publications/cops- p241-pub.pdf.

Maguire, E. R. & Katz, C. M. (2002). Community policing, loose coupling, and sensemaking in American police agencies. *Justice Quarterly: JQ, 19*(3), 503-536. doi:http://dx.doi.org/10.1080/07418820200095331.

McQuade, S. (2006). Technology-enabled crime, policing and security. *Journal of Technology Studies, 32*(1), 32-42.

Miller, T. (n.d.) Police community relations [Blog post]. *Police Foundation - Advancing Policing Through Innovation and Science.* Retrieved from https://www.policefoundation.org.

Mitchell, R. J. & Lewis, S. (2017). Intention is not method, belief is not evidence, rank is not proof. *International Journal of Emergency Services, 6*(3), 188-199. doi: http://dx.doi.org/10.1108/IJES-04-2017-0018.

Moon, S. H., Psy, D., Morgan, T., Psy, D. & Sandage, S. J. PhD. (2018). The need for intercultural competence assessment and training among police officers. *Journal of*

Forensic Psychology Research and Practice, *18*(5), 337-351. doi:http://dx.doi.org/10.1080/24732850.2018.1510274.

Moule, J. (2009). Understanding unconscious bias and unintentional racism. *Phi Delta Kappan*, *90*(5), 321-326.

Palmiotto, M. J. & Donahue, M. E. (1995). Evaluating community policing: Problems and prospects. *Police Studies*, *18*(2), 33.

Posick, C. & Hatfield, H. (2017). Putting H.E.A.R.T. into policing: A 21st century model for effective and fair policing. *Policing*, *40*(1), 128-140. doi:http://dx.doi.org/10.1108/PIJPSM-07-2016-0113.

Renauer, B. C. (2007). Is neighborhood policing related to informal social control? *Policing*, *30*(1), 61-81. doi:http://dx.doi.org/10.1108/13639510710725622.

Robin, S. Engel., Rob, Tillyer, Charles, F. Klahm. IV. & James, Frank. (2011). From the Officer''s Perspective: A Multilevel Examination of Citizens' Demeanor during Traffic Stops, Justice Quarterly, DOI: 10.1080/07418825.2011.574643.

Ross, C. T., Winterhalder, B. & McElreath, R. (2018). Resolution of apparent paradoxes in the race-specific frequency of use-of-force by police. *Palgrave Communications*, *4*(1) doi:http://dx.doi.org/10.1057/s41599-018-0110-z.

Ruggs, E. N., Hebl, M. R., Rabelo, V. C., Weaver, K. B., Kovacs, J. & Kemp, A. S. (2016). Baltimore is burning: Can I-O psychologists help extinguish the flames? *Industrial and Organizational Psychology*, *9*(3), 525-547. doi: http://dx.doi.org/10.1017/iop.2016.5.

Ryan, B. J. (2013). Reasonable force: The emergence of global policing power. *Review of International Studies*, *39*(2), 435-457. doi: http://dx.doi.org/10.1017/ S026021051 2000137.

Scheider, M. C., Chapman, R. & Schapiro, A. (2009). Towards the unification of policing innovations under community policing. *Policing*, *32*(4), 694-718. doi: http://dx.doi.org/10.1108/13639510911000777.

Schneider, S. R. (1998). Overcoming barriers to communication between police and socially disadvantaged neighbourhoods: A critical theory of community policing. *Crime, Law and Social Change*, *30*(4), 347-377. doi: http://dx.doi.org/ 10.1023/A:1008382621747.

Schoenle, Gerald W. Jr. (2017). Progressive policing in the 21st century: A blueprint for change. *Campus Law Enforcement Journal*, *47*(3), 16-17, 19.

Shusta, R. M., Levine, D. R. & Olson, A. T. (2005). Multicultural law enforcement: Strategies for peacekeeping in a diverse society. In *Multicultural Law Enforcement*, 7th Edition. Hoboken, NJ: Pearson Higher Education Press. Retrieved from http://wps.pearsoncustom.com/wps/media/objects/4173/4273671/Ch01.pdf.

Simmons, K. C. (2008). The politics of policing: Ensuring stakeholder collaboration in the federal reform of local law enforcement agencies. *Journal of Criminal Law & Criminology*, *98*(2), 489-546.

Somerville, P. (2009). Understanding community policing. *Policing*, *32*(2), 261-277. doi:http://dx.doi.org/10.1108/13639510910958172.

Sun, E. (2018, August 29). *The dangerous racialization of crime in U.S. news media.* Center for American Progress. Retrieved from https://www.americanprogress.org/ issues/criminal-justice/news/2018/08/29/455313/ dangerous-racialization-crime-u-s-news-media/.

Sylvester, A. L. & Teboh, C. (2016). Police social work and community policing. *Cogent Social Sciences*, *2*(1) doi:http://dx.doi.org/10.1080/23311886.2016.1212636.

Thompson, M. K. (2015). Blackness as character evidence. *Michigan Journal of Race & Law*, *20*(2), 321-348.

Thompson, M. & Kahn, K. B. (2016). Mental health, race, and police contact: Intersections of risk and trust in the police. *Policing*, *39*(4), 807-819. doi:http:// dx.doi.org/10.1108/PIJPSM-02-2016-0015.

Tilley, N. & Laycock, G. (2018). Developing a knowledge base for crime prevention: Lessons learned from the British experience. *Crime Prevention and Community Safety*, *20*(4), 228-242. doi:http://dx.doi.org/10.1057/s41300-018-0053-8.

Violanti, J. M. & Aron, F. (1993). Sources of police stressors, job attitudes, and psychological distress. *Psychological Reports*, *72*, 899-904.

Wetzel, T. (2012). Community policing revisited. *Law & Order*, *60*(4), 6.

Whitehill, J. M., Webster, D. W., Frattaroli, S. & Parker, E. M. (2014). Interrupting violence: How the CeaseFire program prevents imminent gun violence through conflict mediation. *Journal of Urban Health*, *91*(1), 84-95. doi:http:// dx.doi.org/ 10.1007/s11524-013-9796-9.

Williams, J. & Larcher, R. (2018, June 14). Why a cop's ongoing education is a matter of job security: The more we know, the better informed (and thus defensible) our actions will be [Article]. *PoliceOne*. Retrieved from https://www.policeone.com/ police-products/ training/ books-training-materials/ articles/ 476407006-Why-a-cops-ongoing-education-is-a-matter-of-job-security/.

Willis, J. J., Mastrofski, S. D. & Weisburd, D. (2007). Making sense of COMPSTAT: A theory-based analysis of organizational change in three police departments. *Law & Society Review*, *41*(1), 147-188. doi: http://dx.doi.org/10.1111/j.1540-5893.2007. 00294.x.

Wirts, A. M. (2017). Discriminatory intent and implicit bias: Title VII liability for unwitting discrimination. Boston College. Law School. *Boston College Law Review*, *58*(2), 0_1, 809-856.

Worrall, J. L. & Zhao, J. (2003). The role of the COPS office in community policing. *Policing*, *26*(1), 64-87. doi: http://dx.doi.org/10.1108/13639510310460305.

Zhao, Jihong (Solomon), He, N. & Lovrich, N. P. (2003). Community policing: Did it change the basic functions of policing in the 1990s? A National Follow-up Study. *Justice Quarterly: JQ*, *20*(4), 697-724. doi: http://dx.doi.org/10.1080/07418820300095671.

In: A Closer Look at Criminal Justice
Editors: J. A. Cooper and K. G. Jachimowski
ISBN: 978-1-53615-782-6

Chapter 8

POLICE, FORCE, AND EXPLOITATION BY THE MEDIA

Lindsey N. Smathers [*] ***and Samantha L. Bennett***
Indiana University of Pennsylvania, Indiana, PA, US

ABSTRACT

This chapter describes how unbalanced media coverage of police use of force incidents impact perceptions of police. Aimed at increasing broadcast ratings, unbalanced media coverage of police 'use of force' incidents exploit decades old racial tensions, which decreases the legitimacy of police in minority communities. Understanding public opinion and what affects public opinion could assist law enforcement in improving their image with the citizens they protect. This chapter will review the importance of police legitimacy; the impact of media on public perceptions of police through two highly publicized events; and the strategies used by police to enhance their image and media presence.

INTRODUCTION

Today, police in the United States appear to be experiencing a 'legitimacy crisis' due to an increased number of highly publicized incidents of police use of lethal force against minorities. The 2014 shooting in Ferguson, Missouri, of Michael Brown, an unarmed black teenager, by a white officer, Darren Wilson, only furthered a nationwide hysteria and concern over law enforcement's policies and procedures. This incident along with other recent highly publicized events such as, Freddie Gray, Eric Gardner, and Antwon Rose further altered and disrupted police-citizen relations.

[*] Corresponding Author's Email: gvpr@iup.edu

To increase broadcast ratings, unbalanced media coverage of police 'use of force' incidents exploit decades old racial tensions, which decreases the legitimacy of the police in minority communities. These depictions opened the police to public scrutiny that led to a mistrust of law enforcement. This can have a crucial impact on society, since negative perceptions of the police may reduce citizens' willingness to cooperate with, or assist, police officers (Callanan & Rosenberger, 2011). Understanding public opinion and what affects public opinion could assist law enforcement in improving their image with the citizens they protect.

In this chapter, a discussion of police use of force and the importance of police legitimacy is presented. Next, the impact of media on public perceptions of police are explored through two highly publicized events of police use of force. Finally, a discussion of the strategies used by law enforcement to enhance their image and media presence will be described.

Police Use of Force

Police officers have a great deal of authority when it comes to exercising their power of discretion. This provides law enforcement officers with the ability to make quick decisions during any interaction they have with the public. These discretionary decisions are made by officers on a day to day basis, which can range from deciding to stop a vehicle or let them go; to issue a ticket or warning; and what degree of force is required if and/or when there is an incident.

The National Institute of Justice discussed the concept of use of force; however, pointed to the fact that there are no universal definitions to precisely spell out what is "use of force". Although no definition has been universally agreed upon, the one that is often used is defined as, "the amount of effort required by police to compel compliance by an unwilling subject" (International Association of Chiefs of Police, 2012). Similarly, police use of force can also be stated as "force which is necessary or reasonable to effect an arrest or to defend themselves or another from bodily harm while making an arrest. Deadly force is justified when the officer believes that such force is necessary to prevent death or serious bodily injury" (PA General Assembly, PA Crimes Code Section 508, 2017). An important note to these definitions is the ability of different jurisdictions, specifically a state or commonwealth, to determine what precisely is 'use of force'. Many ensure to use key terms such as "necessary", "reasonable", or "justified" with their definition.

The use of force ultimately comes down to the discretionary decision-making of the police officer, which has the potential, for human error in judgment. There are several critical issues that arise with police use of force: excessive use of force and lethal force. In circumstances of excessive use of force, the officer's personnel records are evaluated by a supervisory officer and show a pattern of behavior, in which instances of force are used at an abnormally high-rate overtime (National Institute of Justice, 2016). It is important to note, that 'excessive use of force' differs from the 'use of excessive force'. Incidents of use of excessive force is when the officer uses an unreasonable amount of force during a specific and isolated incident.

Finally, and most frequently discussed, is the use of lethal or deadly force, which is defined as "force that a law enforcement officer uses with the purpose of causing, or that the officer knows to create a substantial risk of causing, death, or serious bodily harm (Bureau of Justice Statistics, 2019). The officer in these situations should only employ lethal force, after justifiably eliminating all other lesser means of compliance, which is often referred to as the continuum of force. This prescribes the appropriate responses for differing incidents with lethal force as a last resort. However, real-life encounters may not provide the officers with sufficient time to systematically eliminate lesser means of apprehension and therefore, is not a legal requirement. Meaning, if the officer believes lethal force is 'necessary' to prevent serious bodily injury or death, the officer can immediately utilize lethal force without first attempting to use other lesser forms of force (e.g., baton, taser, etc.)

There is a plethora of research pertaining to police and use of force. One aspect of use of force is the frequency at which force is employed by police officers. In 2008, the Bureau of Justice Statistics released data on the frequency of police-citizen contact and reported that there approximately 40 million interactions annually. When observing the rate of occurrences of police threat of use of force, it was estimated to occur 1.9% (776,000) of the 40 million interactions between police and citizens. (International Association of Chiefs of Police/COPS Office Use of Force Symposium, 2012). These estimates would suggest the incidents of police use of force are not as widespread or common as the media would have one believe.

Despite the media's glamorization of police shootings, to date there are no known national numbers on the specific rate of incidents of police shootings in the United States (Lowrey, 2014). This is largely due to the lack of inconsistent measurement of 'use of force', and different reporting of rates of force among police departments. While national estimates continue to be difficult to obtain for police use of deadly force, many websites and news sources continue to keep track of their occurrences. Kindy, Fisher, Tate, and Jenkins (2015) discussed a database, in which the Washington Post created and updates to keep track of incidents of police use of deadly force annually in the U.S. These raw numbers assist researchers in understanding how often these incidents are occurring in the United States annually. For instance, this database reported that in 2015, 995 police incidents resulted in death, compared to 963 in 2016; and 987 in 2017 (Lawson, 2018). Similarly, the Police Foundation (2016) reported that there were approximately 67 million direct (face-to-face) incidents of police-citizen contact, which equates to roughly

1 million contacts per week. Of these reported contacts, deadly force was used in nearly 1 in every 67,000 or 0.0015%.

Police Legitimacy and Compliance

The image of police and their legitimacy is crucial to their role as law enforcement, since officers of the law rely heavily on legitimacy to manage the tasks of the job (Harris, 2009). In fact, Tyler (2006) has explained in several versions of his theory on police that legitimacy is crucial to compliance and cooperation with law enforcement. According to Tyler's (2001) theory of procedural justice, police legitimacy is determined primarily by the perceived fairness of the procedures conducted by law enforcement (Sunshine & Tyler, 2003; Tyler, 1990).

Legitimacy refers to the extent to which the public perceives police officers as trustworthy, honest, and able to protect and defend citizens against crime. In addition, perceptions of legitimacy are derived from an individual's evaluations of and reactions to the law (Tyler, 2011). This assessment then shapes their individual judgments about the justness and fairness of the procedures used by police officers (Slocum et al., 2016; Sunshine & Tyler, 2003; Tyler, 1990). Meaning, when citizens perceive law enforcement officers as trustworthy, fair, and legitimate, they are more likely to cooperate and comply with law enforcement (Tyler 2001; Tyler & Huo, 2002). Therefore, it is crucial for law enforcement's actions, decisions, and policies to be viewed as legitimate through what society would consider to be impartial, just, fair, and competent to gain compliance from the public (Tyler, 2006).

This model suggests that if police exercise their authority in a manner that is viewed as fair, trustworthy, and respectful, then citizens are more likely to hold favorable attitudes toward law enforcement (Tyler, 2001; Tyler, 1990). Specifically, when police exercise their authority that aligns with the public expectations of how police should act, society is much more likely to perceive law enforcement in a positive way (Sunshine & Tyler, 2003). Comparatively, when citizens hold negative perceptions of the police it reduces their willingness to cooperate with, or assist law enforcement (Callanan & Rosenberger, 2011). For instance, the 2016 CATO Institute study found that majority of the public view police in a favorable light, while the minority community did not share this opinion (Ekins, 2016). An explanation for this finding may be related to the disproportionate police-contact with citizens.

Generally, the majority live in more affluent areas where a patrol car or contact with an officer is a rare occurrence. While, minorities, who see and interact with police in their communities daily, hold a much lower opinion about law enforcement. Empirical research offers support for the procedural justice framework, citing that those individuals who perceive police officers' actions as procedurally fair, are far more likely to perceive them as a legitimate and trustworthy (Nix, Wolfe, Rojek, & Kaminski, 2015; Tyler & Huo, 2002; Sunshine & Tyler, 2003; Tyler, 2005). Public perceptions of police are a major component of police legitimacy and further cooperation with the law and those administering it.

HISTORICAL CONTEXT

Law enforcement and minority communities have had a long and tenuous relationship in the United States. Historical racial inequality and police bias toward minorities, prompted the first survey of public perceptions of law enforcement more than one hundred years ago (Du Bois, 1899). As the public grew aware of the corrupt practices of police departments, and criticism surrounding the procedures of law enforcement officers grew, citizens demanded reform.

In the 1960s and 1970s, civil rights protests and riots brought highly publicized conflict between law enforcement officers and American society, especially minority communities. As a result of increased pressure placed on federal, state, and local governments to reform police departments, President Johnson initiated a review designed to examine and alleviate the hostility between law enforcement officers and the community (Webb & Marshall, 1995). The Commission on Civil Disorders, also known as the Kerner Commission, conducted one of the earliest efforts to study public perceptions of law enforcement officers on a national level. The results of the Kerner Commission suggested that the public's perceptions and satisfaction of the police differed by race. Specifically, African Americans were more likely to be critical of and to have had negative encounters with law enforcement than their counterparts (Webb & Marshall, 1995; Campbell & Schuman, 1972).

Despite this effort to address the strained relationship that existed between law enforcement and the public, incidents of violence were still prevalent. Many of these issues stem from historical events within the United States such as slavery, Jim Crow laws, and the civil rights movements. This history of racial inequality, as well as, disproportionate policing of minority groups has continued to disrupt police-citizen relations. These issues significantly impacted public perceptions of police, specifically of minority communities. A discussion of this contentious relationship will be presented in the following section.

Public Attitudes of Police

According to Ekins (2016), the majority of Americans hold positive attitudes toward law enforcement. However, empirically and politically, race has been cited as the most important characteristic that shapes public opinion of police (Weitzer, 2002). For instance, a national survey of Americans' perceptions found that Whites (68%) hold more favorable views of police compared to African Americans (40%) (Ekins, 2016). In addition, African Americans (73%) were twice as likely to report police were too quick to use lethal force, compared to Whites (35%) and Hispanics (54%); and were more likely (56% of African Americans) to endorse the notion that police behaved too harshly.

In addition, when examining perceptions of police justness, 64% of Whites, 42% of Hispanics, and 31% of Africans Americas supported the notion that police officers treated citizens equally. When analyzing public perceptions of law enforcement competency (whether officers are competent at enforcing the law and are quick to respond to calls for service), 60% of Whites, 50% of Hispanics, and 40% of African Americans supported the notion that police officers were competent at their job (Ekins, 2016). This suggests that the race of individuals who interact with law enforcement officers have a strong impact on their perceptions of police. According to Cochran and Warren (2012), these perceptions are in part, a result of the disadvantages that racial and ethnic minorities experience within the criminal justice system and the treatment they may have experienced during their encounters with police.

Exposure to Media

Exposure to media, in all formats, has been a popular topic of study since the creation of television and Gerbner and Gross' (1976) cultivation theory. The premise of this theory relates to how television (the popular source of media at the time) is regularly consumed that creates a cultivation process of the major themes and messages being presented to the viewers (Gerbner, Gross, Morgan, & Signorielli, 1986). Today, the drastic increase of media in American society has prompted a need to identify how much individuals are exposed to mass media, and what images the audience cultivate.

The concept of "if it bleeds, it leads" has often been used as a description for how media present images to the public. Fridkin, Wintersieck, Courey, and Thompson (2017) found that there were three frames that media relied on: law and order, race, and police brutality. These frames become important to understanding how the audience will gather their information about crime and law enforcement, which then may alter their perceptions of reality. News networks rely on these frames because it increases broadcast ratings and promotes the ideology of the network itself. For instance, Beddingfield (2012) examined *The Wall Street Journal's* editorial pieces and found that the articles tended to promote a conservative agenda, while Senior (2009) found that *The New York Times* tended to frame its articles toward a more liberal agenda.

This is problematic because the article is then framed within the network's ideology, rather than reporting the facts of the case. This omission may reinforce inaccurate representations of social problems in the United States, which in turn, shape public attitudes. For example, articles that are framed within a conservative agenda may favor law and order crime, while articles with a more liberal agenda, may frame the article to highlight racial inequality and police brutality in the United States. Any bias from news media, especially without informing the audience of this bias nature, can impact their audiences' views and understanding of a matter. This becomes crucial when examining the messages of justice and amount of exposure to these depictions that everyday citizens receive from media.

The Impact of Media

Today, news media, as well as other platforms, have become more present in Americans lives, with the 24-hour, 7-day-a-week news cycle. It becomes important to acknowledge the significant influence the media has in our daily lives, since the majority of information citizens know and understand about the law and criminal justice system, is from their consumption of either print news or televised-broadcasting (Dowler, 2003).

Previous scholars have suggested that the media depicts both factual and fictional crime stories in a manner that selectively distort and manipulate public perception. These deliberate distortions are often slanted against the officer (i.e., white officer vs black suspect) and creates a false picture of crime that promotes society's stereotyping, bias, and prejudice of law enforcement and the criminal justice system. The purpose of these crime stories is to boost ratings, but the fallout causes more racial tension between the police and minority communities.

Studies that have examined the role of media in public perceptions of law enforcement have generally focused on citizen exposure to news media (Donovan & Klahm IV, 2015). Individuals who report having heard or read about incidents of police misconduct, also believe that police misconduct is more prevalent than those who report less news media exposure (Weitzer & Tuch, 2004). Similarly, other studies that specifically assessed exposure to local TV news have found that citizens, predominantly minorities, hold more negative perceptions toward law enforcement officers when highly publicized incidents of police misconduct are broadcasted (Weitzer, 2002). For instance, Weitzer (2002) examined the impact of several highly publicized events of perceived police misconduct in Los Angeles and New York City. He then observed the public's opinion by tracking their attitudes toward the police before and after each publicized incident. He found that that public opinion of police tended to significantly decrease after an incident of misconduct aired on the news. He also found that Blacks were more likely than Whites to support the notion that the police engage in frequent misconduct and viewed incidents of misconduct as being more serious and disturbing (Weitzer, 2002).

News coverage and crime television shows and movies have been examined for their impact on societal views of police. Dowler and Zawilski (2007) examined what impact these media depictions of police would have on viewers' opinions of police misconduct and discrimination. The results of the study suggested that heavy consumers of network news and minority viewers were more likely to hold the belief that police engaged in frequent misconduct. Specifically, minorities with heavy consumption of news were significantly more likely to believe that Whites were treated in a fairer and more just manner compared to the officers' behavior with minority suspects. These results suggest that media, especially televised news media, can alter and shape the audiences' perceptions of law enforcement and their legitimacy.

Sensationalized Media Events of Police Use of Force

The media's glamorization of racially motivated, police-citizen encounters has received a great deal of attention within the last several decades. The national broadcasting of past and live criminal events has sparked a great interest within the public and have become not only newsworthy but great ratings boosters and money makers. This section describes two highly-publicized incidents of police use of force reported in the media: Rodney King and Michael Brown.

Pre-Ferguson: The Beating of Rodney King

The March 1991 beating of Mr. Rodney King Jr. was a crucial moment in the United States' history for police and citizen relations. In the early hours on the third day of March in Los Angeles, the California Highway Police attempted to conduct a routine traffic stop. After the car refused to pull over, an 8-mile high speed chase ensued. Once the vehicle was subdued, Mr. Rodney King Jr. and his passengers were asked to remove themselves from the vehicle. While Mr. King remained in the car, his passengers were alleged to have been mishandled by the police. It was not until Mr. King left his car that the event would spiral further out of control. Mr. King waved his arms at the officers both those on the ground and the police helicopter above. He began reaching behind himself, which prompted the police to assume he had a weapon on his person. Following law enforcement protocol, the officers' attempted to arrest Mr. King by conducting a "swarm" tactic, to which four officers held down Mr. King as another officer handcuffed him.

The beating and use of brutal force by these officers occurred after the attempted arrest of King. The officers alleged that he resisted arrest and appeared to be high on the drug PCP, which is known to have a common side effect of a decreased or elimination of the sensation of pain. Therefore, the officers' argued that the use of added force was because King was difficult to apprehend due to his drug-induced state. Officers involved in the beating of King were found to have used their tasers, beaten him with their batons, and pushed, kicked, and punched Mr. King. Afterwards he was restrained, handcuffed, and awaited emergency medical attention for his injuries.

That night Mr. King, his passengers, and the police were not the only witnesses to the incident. Mr. George Holliday lived in an apartment across the street where the beating took place and recorded the entire incident. The quality of the picture in the video is distorted or blurry because of the distance to which the video was filmed. Despite the clarity, the video was sufficient enough for the media to broadcast it on every news network channel. The event shocked both Black and White Americans across the country. This also sparked conversations about whether the police involved should be convicted, which resulted in 66% of whites and 78% of blacks for their conviction (Sigelman, Welch, Bledsoe, & Combs, 1997). However, it is this video and the ultimate acquittal of all officers that drew in an immense amount of attention and sparked a debate about police use of force that would eventually incite the L.A. Riots.

This event marked one of the first and most crucial moments in history where media has played an important role in police and citizen relationships. The filming and distribution of this incident created one of the country's first times in which everyday citizens could watch an event involving the police from their own home. Sigelman, Welch, Bledsoe, and Combs' (1997) examined two major events surround the police and use of force, which included the Rodney King Jr. beating. They found that the news presenting these stories impacted the belief that African Americans were treated differently than Whites.

Ferguson: Michael Brown Shooting

In August of 2014, approximately 23 years after the Rodney King events, the police department in Ferguson, Missouri faced similar controversy. The incident began early in the morning after Mr. Brown, with a friend, was seen on a closed-circuit television recording him stealing at the Ferguson Market. After finishing his prior call, Officer Wilson of the Ferguson Police Department, began looking for the suspects that had evaded the other officers. In the early afternoon, Officer Wilson came across both Mr. Brown and his friend Dorian Johnson. Several eyewitnesses and various testimony have described the incident that transpired after this initial stop. After Officer Wilson stopped the two men, Mr. Brown approached the car where and struggle with the officer, in which Wilson's gun was fired twice in the vehicle. This wounded Mr. Brown in the right hand, and as Officer Wilson got out of the vehicle more shots were dispensed. The whole incident was only minutes long, but in the aftermath, Mr. Brown was left dead in the street. Police and other first responders came to the scene over the next few hours until Mr. Brown's body was released to the morgue around 4:00 pm.

Like the case of Rodney King Jr., the events that took place involving Mr. Brown created lasting implications. The issues involved in this shooting, specifically that of race, has remained a constant story even in today's news. In 2014, the Pew Research Center conducted a survey after the incident and the release of the video of Mr. Brown and his friend stealing from the convenience store. The poll examined what the participants thought about the shooting bringing up important racial issues in the country. The results revealed a significant difference in perception between races; 80% of African American respondents agreed that the shooting was unjustified while a much smaller percentage (37%) of whites agreed (Parker, 2014).

Following the media coverage of Mr. Brown and subsequent protests, the "hands up don't shoot" movement began to move across the nation. This movement was aimed at raising awareness and acting against police shootings of unarmed minorities. The campaign was based on the media's manipulation of news coverage of the incident, which stated that Mr. Brown put his hands up, despite no documented reports of Mr. Brown doing so. The media will often exclude the 'full details' of an incident by frequently reporting the more slanted and sensationalized circumstances of the event to increase their broadcast ratings. This selective reporting can subsequently agitate racial tension between law enforcement and minorities; further perpetuating minorities' unfavorable perceptions of police. Moreover, news networks often compete against other networks to release the latest info. This has led to a great deal of misinformation about the details of the case, which potentially was an immense factor in the quick judgment and perceptions of the incident. This all suggests that mass media has the potential to shape the public's perceptions of law enforcement and incidents of use of force.

POLICE AND POLICING THEIR IMAGE

Due to the increased availability and access to media technology and following the controversial media coverage of police-use of force incidents, police have begun to adopt a more proactive approach to media publicity. As discussed above, the increased exposure to stories of police and use of force has created what some may consider to be a public relations issue with the police and the public at large.

Today, the realm in which police organizations use for community outreach has shifted from in-person to online techniques. The use of social media has become a popular method for both an individual officer and the whole organization to "police" the image of law enforcement (Jewkes & Linnemann, 2018). This provides them with multiple platforms and formats, in which they can provide their own message to the public. For example, the use of the social media platform *Twitter* allows the agency to "tweet" a message within 280 characters, accompanied by links to websites, photos, and videos to their followers. Another popular social networking site among law enforcement is *Instagram*, which is a photo and video sharing platform that allows their followers to view, comment, and like posts shared by the department. As society continues to rely heavily on social media platforms for news and information, police departments may expect an increase in their use of social media outreach.

It is important to note that each department has their own strategies for using technology and operating their social media platforms. These techniques are not mutually exclusive, but rather a continuum of strategies designed to enhance law enforcement's image and media presence. These techniques include: (1) public awareness; (2) humor; (3) charity and achievements; and (4) transparency.

Public Awareness

A 2013 study of 600 law enforcement agencies found that 95% used social media to promote community relations and to solve and prevent crime (International Association of Chiefs of Police, 2014). It is not uncommon for police organizations to have specific individuals operating some form of social media on behalf of the department (i.e., Twitter, Facebook, Instagram). These media platforms allow simple and inexpensive avenues for police departments to share information (i.e., crime alerts/reports, local events and fundraisers, community policing initiatives, etc.) with the public in an unprecedented manner.

The Pennsylvania State Police Department often uses social networking to alert citizens of ongoing crimes or missing person alerts that they continue to update as the incident continues. The PA State Police have also used these outlets to raise awareness of local events, classes, and other community outreach initiatives within the community. Their #SavingPALives posts promote resources that are available in the community for those impacted by the opioid epidemic. This department has also used their social media to advertise National Coffee Day, in which they notified their followers of various locations that their officers were handing out free coffee and enjoying a cup with the communities they patrol.

Another example of law enforcement that utilizes social media platforms to raise public awareness is Lawrence Kansas Police. This department updates their citizens with #PublicSafety posts that notify the public of various topics such as inclement weather and local crime reports. This section demonstrates how the police, using media to show positive interactions with the public, are attempting to mitigate frequently seen negative contacts in the minority neighborhoods and viewed repeatedly on news coverage are trying to improve public attitudes.

Humor

The second technique that has been used by police departments is to use humor in their social media posts. These officers use social media to both make the public aware, yet they use humor to entertain and gain the attention and interest of the public. The Lawrence Kansas Police Department often uses humor to communicate on social media with their community. On several posts on Twitter, the Department makes jokes and mocks the number of incidents that occur when bars in their community close. In one specific post, they poll their citizens asking their believed likelihood that no bar fight will occur, to which they got the response of not likely. They have commented on ways to leave the bar without fighting, and they have commended them when there was a lack of bar fights. The use of humor on their social media page allows them to inform, discuss, and interact with individuals in their town, city, or state with some lightness or comical relief. Police officers' ability to use humor may assist in decreasing any citizen's perception of a harsh, separated, and authoritative police force.

Charity and Achievements

A third technique used by police departments is to show the police in a positive light by depicting them as both good within the community and successful at their job. The use of social media is primarily used to communicate positive images of officers with the public (Mawby, 2010). This section will briefly describe two ways that agencies present positive images: (1) "trophy shots" and (2) displays of philanthropy.

In many cases, these images included those that have messages of power, intelligence, and a prowess of the police department. These are usually offered to the audiences through images of police seizures and forfeitures, often referred to as "trophy shots". These images generally depict the officer(s) in front of large amounts of money, guns, illicit drugs, and other illegal materials that they were able to seize (Linnemann, 2017). These *achievements* by the officers can be viewed by the followers as their agency being successful, not only at keeping citizens safe but police force doing a great job.

Many agencies use this technique to show their followers the hard work of the officers within their department. The New York Police Department is known for posting on Twitter and Instagram photos of various seizures or forfeitures. One example comes from their Instagram page, which shows a display of a seizure of over 70 illegal weapons. In the image, there is a table filled with large illegal weapons, and behind this table is a display of the New York City Police Department plague, an NYPD flag, and an American flag.

Positive images do not just pertain to the abilities of the police department, but also show the good nature of those who make up the agency. Police departments are often displayed in a philanthropic manner in their social media posts. For instance, the New York Police Department is often shown with the babies they deliver, children or adults they have assisted in their work, but they are also shown going behind what is seemingly required for their job. One Instagram post from the department shows an officer who stopped her day to help an elderly man cross the busy streets of New York City. The purpose then of these images are to show the community that the police are not simply there to enforce the law and apprehend criminals, but they are there to "serve and protect" the greater community every day.

Transparency

A fourth technique in which police have used media or technology to increase their image, as well as their transparency, is the use of body-cameras. This strategy has become increasingly popular after highly publicized incidents of police shootings in the last ten years. In 2014, the Obama Administration funded an increase use of body-cameras by allocating 75 million dollars for 50,000 body worn cameras over a three-year time span (Jennings, Lynch, & Fidell, 2015). Similar to dashboard photographic equipment in patrol vehicles, these cameras are mounted on either an officer's eyeglasses or chest to record the interactions between police and the public.

These cameras allow for more accountability and transparency within police work (Coudert, Butin, & Le Métayer, 2015). The use of this equipment is widely supported by police officers because it improves officer behavior, decreases citizen complaints, and provides documented evidence of the police-citizen encounter (Jennings, Fridell, Lynch, 2014). Jennings, Lynch, and Fidell (2015) conducted research to examine the benefits of body-worn cameras within Orlando police, and found that with the use of body-worn cameras had a 65% reduction in serious external complaints and 53% fewer incidents involving resistance. Likewise, Farrar (2014) examined the use of body-worn cameras over a one-year period and found that there were 60% fewer incidents of officer use of force and 80% fewer citizen complaints between the year prior to camera implementation and the year following deployment (Farrar, 2014).

The proliferation of body-worn cameras by police agencies raise several concerns regarding privacy and cost of implementation. The use of body-worn cameras has raised concerns regarding the violation of citizens' right to privacy. All citizens have the right to privacy (underlined in the Fourth and Ninth Amendment), which many argue cannot be protected while they are being filmed by the police officer's body worn camera. Some states have enacted "two-party consent" legislation, which legally requires the officer to inform and obtain consent from the individual(s) to record and monitor the encounter (Miller & Toliver, 2014). This law can create barriers to implementing body-worn cameras and as a result, less transparency and accountability of police operations.

However, in some states police executives have worked with state legislatures to waive the consent requirement. For instance, in 2014 Pennsylvania enacted a law that waived the two-party consent mandate for law enforcement officers using body-worn cameras (PA Act 22, Title 18, Section 57).

Another concern surrounding the use of body-worn cameras is the cost of implementation. The price of officer-worn cameras generally ranges from approximately $120 to $2,000 for each device, with some agencies reporting between $800 and $1,200 (Miller & Toliver, 2014). Although most departments in the country are smaller and more likely with proper funding to obtain the small number of cameras needed; many larger departments struggle to receive appropriate funding (Police Executive Research Forum, 2018). Although the initial costs of implementation can be costly, many law enforcement agencies have stated that data storage is the most expensive. Moreover, these also create issues of how long the footage should be kept, who is the owner, who is granted access, and how to handle any requests for disclosure (Coudert, Butin, & Le Métayer, 2015).

It is also important to compare the annual average lawsuits costs to the annual cost of body-worn cameras. The Police Executive Research Forum (2018) released their data on three different locations and found the for two of the locations the annual costs were higher for the cameras than annual average lawsuit costs, while the one saw more benefit fiscally with their use of cameras. For the Phoenix department (10% of their force had cameras) their annual cost for the cameras was $1,009,050 compared to the average lawsuit cost of $1,306,349. Mesa (44% of their force had cameras) and Dallas (30% of their force had cameras) saw the opposite with $725,350 for cameras annually and $637,327 for lawsuits and $1,125,000 for cameras compared to $527,759 for lawsuits respectively (Police Executive Research Forum, 2018). The adoption and implementation of body-worn cameras by law enforcement agencies must continue to be diligent at balancing these concerns with the need for transparency of police work. This means making important and careful decisions about privacy considerations and cost.

Summary and Conclusion

This chapter has presented the reader with information on how media, specifically unbalanced media coverage, plays an important and crucial role in shaping public perceptions of police. The public has internalized these perceptions throughout generations of racial tension between police and minority communities. The media then reinforces these viewpoints through its depictions of police encounters with minority groups and incidents of police use of force.

Public attitudes are increasingly important as they have the potential to establish how society interacts and receives law enforcement and their practices. As Tyler (2006) discussed, an individual's willingness to comply with the law is impacted by their conceptualization and understanding of justice. Therefore, the consistent negative depictions by media may create a society who view police as illegitimate, thus increasing potential for non-compliance. Whereas, a more positive image can enhance the perception of a legitimate and just-police force, which in turn promotes citizen compliance.

The media portrayal of law enforcement has also impacted the daily practices of officers, as well as, overall community-outreach. Various media platforms have enabled an exponential increase of law enforcement agencies' media presence and use of technology with the goal of fostering positive images of police. This use of technology and the depictions presented by media offer scholars a plethora of opportunities to examine the impact of images on the relationship between law enforcement and society.

Moreover, there is a need for a standardized definition of police use of force, as well as, consistent tracking of these incidents to better estimate the frequency of these events. This will allow researchers and policymakers alike to better gauge the scope of police misuse of force. Furthermore, the media should take greater accountability to ensure unbiased and balanced coverage of police encounters and use of force. In summary, greater journalistic integrity coupled with transparent police practices, may have the ability to improve citizens', specifically minority groups, perceptions of legitimacy and confidence in law enforcement within the United States.

REFERENCES

Bureau of Justice Statistics. (2019). *Use of force.* Office of Justice Programs. Retrieved from https://www.bjs.gov/index.cfm?ty=tp&tid=84.

Callanan, V., & Rosenberger, J. (2011). Media and public perceptions of the police: Examining the impact of race and personal experience. *Policing & Society, 21*(2), 167-189.

Campbell, A., &Schuman, H. (1972). A comparison of Black and White attitudes and experiences in the city. In C. M. Haar (Ed.), *The End of Innocence: A Suburban Reader* (pp. 97-110), Glenview, IL: Scott, Foresman.

Coudert, F., Butin, D., & Le Métayer, D. (2015). Body-worn cameras for police accountability: Opportunities and risks. *Computer Law & Security Review*, *31*(6), 749-762.

Donovan, K. M., & Klahm IV, C. F. (2015). The role of entertainment media in perceptions of police use of force. *Criminal Justice and Behavior*, *42*(12), 1261-1281.

Dowler, K., & Zawilski, V. (2007). Public perceptions of police misconduct and discrimination: Examining the impact of media consumption. *Journal of Criminal Justice*, *35*(2), 193-203.

Ekins, E. E. (2016). *Policing in America: understanding public attitudes toward the police. Results from a national survey.* The CATO Institute. Retrieved from https://www.cato.org/survey-reports/policing-america.

Farrar, W. (2014). Operation candid camera: Rialto police department's body-worn camera experiment. *The Police Chief, 8*(1), 20-25.

Fridkin, K., Wintersieck, A., Courey, J., & Thompson, J. (2017). Race and police brutality: The importance of media framing. *International Journal of Communication, 11*, 21.

Gerbner, G., & Gross, L. (1976). Living with television: The violence profile. *Journal of Communication*, *26*(2), 172-199.

Gerbner, G., Gross, L., Morgan, M., & Signorielli, N. (1986). Living with television: The dynamics of the cultivation process. *Perspectives on Media Effects*, *1986*, 17-40.

International Association of Chiefs of Police. (2014). *The police chief: The professional voice of law enforcement: Technology and social media.* Retrieved from https:// www.theiacp.org/search-documents/social%20media/1/All/All?keywords_top=social%20media.

International Association of Chiefs of Police/COPS Office Use of Force Symposium. (2012). *Emerging use of force issues: Balancing public and officer safety.* U.S. Department of Justice.

Jefferis, E. S., Kaminski, R. J., Holmes, S., & Hanley, D. E. (1997). The effect of a videotaped arrest on public perceptions of police use. *Journal of Criminal Justice*, *25*(5), 381-395.

Jennings, W. G., Fridell, L. A., & Lynch, M. D. (2014). Cops and cameras: Officer perceptions of the use of body-worn cameras in law enforcement. *Journal of Criminal Justice*, *42*(6), 549-556.

Jennings, W. G., Lynch, M. D., & Fridell, L. A. (2015). Evaluating the impact of police officer body-worn cameras (BWCs) on response-to-resistance and serious external complaints: Evidence from the Orlando police department (OPD) experience utilizing a randomized controlled experiment. *Journal of Criminal Justice*, *43*(6), 480-486.

Jewkes, Y. & Linneman, T. W. (2018). *Media and Crime in the U.S.* Thousand Oaks: SAGE Publications Inc.

Lawson Jr, E. (2018). Police militarization and the use of lethal force. *Political Research Quarter,* 1-13.

Lowrey, W. (2014, September 08). How many police shootings a year? No one knows. *The Washington Post.* Retrieved from https://www.washingtonpost.com/news/post-nation/ wp/ 2014/ 09/ 08/ how-many-police-shootings-a-year-no-one-knows/ ?noredirect=on&utm_term=.bab6cd5979e7

Matsa, K. E. (2018). *Fewer Americans rely on TV news; What type they watch varies by who they are.* Pew Research Center. Retrieved from http://www.pewresearch.org/

fact-Tank/ 2018/ 01/ 05/ fewer-americans-rely-on-tv-news-what-type-they-watch-varies-by-who-they-are/

Mawby, R. C. (2010). Police corporate communications, crime reporting and the shaping of policing news. *Policing and Society*, *20*(1), 124-139.

Miller, L. & Toliver, J. (2014). *Implementing a Body-Worn Camera Program: Recommendations and Lessons Learned.* Police Executive Forum. Washington, DC: Office of Community Oriented Policing Services.

National Institute of Justice. (2016). *Police use of force.* Washington, DC. Retrieved from https://www.nij.gov/topics/law-enforcement/officer-safety/use-of-force/pages/welcome.aspx.

Nix, J., Wolfe, S. E., Rojek, J., & Kaminski, R. J. (2015). Trust in the police: The influence of procedural justice and perceived collective efficacy. *Crime & Delinquency*, *61*(4), 610-640.

Parker, K. (2014). Within the black community, young and old differ on police searches, discrimination. *Pew Research Center.* Retrieved from http://www.pewresearch.org/fact-tank/2014/08/27/within-the-black-community-young-and-old-differ-on-police-searches-discrimination/.

Police Foundation. (2016). *Use-of-force infographic.* Retrieved from https://www.policefoundation.org/general-resources/use-of-force-infographic/.

Sigelman, L., Welch, S., Bledsoe, T., & Combs, M. (1997). Police brutality and public perceptions of racial discrimination: A tale of two beatings. *Political Research Quarterly*, *50*(4), 777-791.

Slocum, L. A., Wiley, S., & Esbensen, F. A. (2016). The importance of being satisfied: A longitudinal exploration of police contact, procedural injustice, and subsequent delinquency. *Criminal Justice and Behavior*, *43*(1), 7-26.

Smykla, J. O., Crow, M. S., Crichlow, V. J., & Snyder, J. A. (2016). Police body-worn cameras: Perceptions of law enforcement leadership. *American Journal of Criminal Justice*, *41*(3), 424-443.

Sunshine, J., & Tyler, T. R. (2003). The role of procedural justice and legitimacy in shaping public support for policing. *Law & Society Review, 37*(3), 513-548.

Tyler T. R. (1990). *Why People Obey the Law: Procedural Justice, Legitimacy, and Compliance.* New Haven: Yale University Press.

Tyler, T. R. (2001). Public trust and confidence in legal authorities: What do majority and minority group members want from the law and legal institutions? *Behavioral Sciences & the Law, 19*(2), 215-235.

Tyler, T. R. (2011). Trust and legitimacy: Policing in the USA and Europe. *European Journal of Criminology*, *8*(4), 254-266.

Tyler, T. R. (2006). *Why People Obey the Law.* Princeton, NJ: Princeton University Press.

Webb, V. J., & Marshall, C. E. (1995). The relative importance of race and ethnicity on citizen attitudes toward the police. *American Journal of Police,* 14(2), 45-66.

Weitzer, R. (2002). Incidents of police misconduct and public opinion. *Journal of Criminal Justice, 30*(5), 397-408.

Weitzer, R., & Tuch, S. (2004). Race and perceptions of police misconduct. *Social Problems, 51,* 305-325.

Wolfe, S., & Nix, J. (2016). The alleged "Ferguson Effect" and police willingness to engage in community partnership. *Law & Human Behavior, 40*(1), 1-10.

In: A Closer Look at Criminal Justice
Editors: J. A. Cooper and K. G. Jachimowski

ISBN: 978-1-53615-782-6

Chapter 9

THE EFFECT OF CITIZENS' PERCEPTIONS OF POLICE LEGITIMACY ON VIOLENCE: REDEFINING THE FERGUSON EFFECT AS A LEGITIMACY PROBLEM

Liana Marmolejos*
Indiana University of Pennsylvania, Indiana, PA, US

ABSTRACT

In recent years, law enforcement officials and criminal justice researchers have voiced concerns that media scrutiny of police use of force, following high profile incidents would make police departments and their officers reluctant to engage in proactive policing strategies, leading to an increase in crime rates. Some have argued that the spike in homicide rates in some cities in 2015 was evidence of a "Ferguson effect". The typical argument has been that the increase in homicide rates was the result of decreased police activity. Few have examined perceived legitimacy of law enforcement as a possible explanation for the recent increase in homicide rates seen in some cities. This chapter expands on suggestions made by Rosenfeld (2016) regarding the possible impact of legitimacy perceptions on the homicide rate. The chapter will explore the research regarding the effects of declines in citizens' perceptions of police legitimacy on compliance, cooperation, and crime. In addition, the author will explain why perceptions of legitimacy should be considered as a possible explanation for the 2015 homicide increase. The findings of the literature synthesis provide preliminary support for Rosenfeld's (2016) legitimacy crisis hypothesis.

* Author's Email: lsm77791@gmail.com

Introduction

In 2015, the United States saw a sizable increase in homicide rates with estimates ranging from a roughly 11 to 17 percent increase from 2014 (Wheeler & Kovandzic, 2018). The recent increase in homicide is one of the most substantial increases in several years and has mostly been attributed to a few large cities such as St. Louis and Baltimore (Rosenfeld, 2016; Wheeler & Kovandzic, 2018). There have been several factors examined by researchers in attempts to explain the recent homicide spike, including drug markets, age cohorts, gang violence, and gun availability (Fagan & Richman, 2017; Rosenfeld, 2016). The explanation that has garnered the most attention is the Ferguson effect (Nix & Pickett, 2017; Nix & Wolfe, 2016; Pyrooz, Decker, Wolfe, and Shjarback, 2016; Rosenfeld, 2016; Shjarback, Pyrooz, Wolfe, & Decker, 2017; Wolfe & Nix, 2015). Law enforcement officials and criminal justice scholars hypothesized that media criticism of police following the shooting of Michael Brown in Ferguson, Missouri and other high-profile use of force incidents led to a decline in the use of proactive policing tactics, which allowed for the homicide rate to increase (Nix & Pickett, 2017; Nix & Wolfe, 2016; Pyrooz et al., 2016; Rosenfeld, 2016; Shjarback et al., 2017; Wolfe & Nix, 2015). Rosenfeld (2016) suggested that the events at Ferguson had created a "legitimacy crisis" in policing and considered legitimacy as a possible explanation for the 2015 homicide increase (p. 5).

This chapter expands on suggestions made by Rosenfeld (2016) regarding the possible impact of legitimacy perceptions on the homicide rate increase in 2015. The author will discuss the literature explaining how legitimacy perceptions are shaped by experiences and encounters with legal authorities, how legitimacy perceptions affect conformity to the law, (Tyler, 2001; Tyler, 2005; Tyler, Fagan, & Geller, 2014; Walters & Bolger, 2018), and how highly publicized use of force incidents can further strain relationships between police and disadvantaged communities, impacting crime rates in those communities (Desmond, Papachristos, & Kirk, 2016; Kane, 2005; Kochel, 2017). This chapter will conclude with a discussion of implications for future research and policy implications for enhancing police legitimacy and to increase compliance and cooperation with law enforcement (Fagan & Richman, 2017; Gill, Weisburd, Telep, Vitter, & Bennett, 2014; Kochel, 2017; Walters & Bolger, 2018).

Homicide Increase

Homicide Data

In 2015, the United States saw a sizable increase in homicides, raising concerns amongst scholars and criminal justice leaders alike that the increase was evidence of a

Ferguson effect on crime (Rosenfeld, 2016; Pyrooz et al., 2016). Several scholars have since examined the recent homicide increase and their studies revealed similar findings, but they each drew different conclusions. Pyrooz et al. (2016) examined crime data from 81 large city police departments and analyzed changes in monthly crime rates one year before and after the incidents at Ferguson in the summer of 2014. The authors' analysis revealed that there were no statistically significant differences in crime rates post Ferguson with the exception of robbery; however, the analysis did reveal notable homicide increases in several large cities post Ferguson, particularly those with a larger number of black residents, large police presence, and low socioeconomic status. Similarly, Rosenfeld (2016) found that ten cities with the greatest homicide increases had a larger number of black residents and higher levels of poverty. Furthermore, these ten cities "accounted for two-thirds of the total homicide increase between 2014 and 2015" (Rosenfeld, 2016, p. 8). Overall, Rosenfeld's analysis of crime data from 56 cities revealed a nearly 17 percent increase in homicide in 2015. Rosenfeld argued that the large increases in homicide in several cities warranted additional study. He noted that large percentage increases in homicides in the top 10 cities in 2015 were exceptional, and on "only 15 occasions since 1985" did the cities experience homicide increases larger than they did in 2015 (Rosenfeld, 2016, p. 10). Similarly, Wheeler and Kovandzic's (2018) analysis of UCR homicide data from 1960 to 2015 and part of 2016 found that homicide had increased nearly 11 percent in 2015 from 2014; this percentage increase was one of the "largest year-to-year percentage increases seen in homicide rates in decades" (p. 131). Not only did the homicide rate increase in 2015, but Wheeler and Kovandzic (2018) anticipated that the homicide rate would increase in 2016 based on their analysis of UCR half-year data. Fagan and Richman (2017) analyzed 2014 to 2016 crime data from the 30 largest cities in the United States and found that the homicide rate rose by roughly 13 percent in 22 of the 30 cities.

Despite the notable increases in homicide in 2015 and anticipated increase in 2016, scholars cautioned against drawing any conclusions that the homicide spikes were evidence of a trend. Wheeler and Kovandzic (2018) and Pyrooz et al. (2016) both noted that several large cities that experienced homicide increases in 2015 had high homicide rates before Ferguson. Using funnel charts and time-series fan charts, Wheeler and Kovandzic (2018) were able to compare different cities and evaluate homicide trends in certain cities overtime, allowing the authors to predict how many homicides each city would need to have to be considered an outlier. The authors concluded that the homicide increases observed in some cities in 2015 such as St. Louis and Baltimore were not unprecedented considering both cities had high homicide rates going back decades and the spikes in homicides observed in some cities did not exceed predicted rates. Fagan and Richman (2017) noted that the available data did not explain whether the 2015 homicide increase was the start of a new trend or simply a short-term spike. The authors warned that errors in predictions about violent youth crime in the 1990's led to broad legal policy changes that negatively impacted young offenders. Wheeler and Kovandzic (2018) noted that it is difficult to determine which factors affect increases or declines in homicide due to its volatility. The authors explained that reliance on percentage changes in homicide rates to determine trends was problematic due to issues such as identifying outliers. Overall, the data confirmed Pyrooz et al.'s (2016) conclusion that there was no evidence that the events at Ferguson had a widespread effect and that if Ferguson had any impact on homicide rates it was limited to specific cities; these cities had a larger number of black residents, large police presence, and low socioeconomic status.

Possible Factors Influencing Homicide Increases

Interestingly, the recent increases in homicide rates in some cities do not appear to be associated with the same factors that were influential in past homicide increases. One factor explored by both Fagan and Richman (2017) and Rosenfeld (2016) as a possible explanation for the 2015 homicide increase was the opioid epidemic. Fagan and Richman (2017) discussed homicide trends during the 1960's, 70's, and 80's and how spikes in homicide rates during these time periods were closely tied to illegal drug markets, specifically, heroin, cocaine, and crack-cocaine. Fagan and Richman (2017) and Rosenfeld (2016) noted that the opioid epidemic began years before the increase in homicides and that those most affected were whites in rural areas, not minorities in urban areas as was the case with the crack cocaine epidemic. Both Fagan and Richman (2017) and Rosenfeld (2016) expressed skepticism about a possible relationship between the recent spike in homicide in 2015 and the ongoing opioid epidemic. Fagan and Richman (2017) examined other explanations for the homicide increase in 2015, such as birth cohorts, gun availability, and gang violence. The authors found that these factors accounted for a rise in homicide in some cities, but not in others. The authors concluded that the factors associated with the "homicide spikes of the past fifty years are either not present today or perhaps less salient" (Fagan & Richman, 2017, p. 1272). Overall, Fagan and Richman's (2017) and Rosenfeld's (2016) findings suggested that the rise in homicides in 2015, subsequent to the events at Ferguson, appeared to be different than past homicide spikes.

The Ferguson Effect: De-Policing or Legitimacy Crisis

De-Policing and Crime

Some law enforcement officials and researchers have claimed that the shooting of Michael Brown and subsequent high-profile shootings of black men created a Ferguson effect (Nix & Pickett, 2017; Rosenfeld, 2016; Shjarback et al., 2017). Proponents of the Ferguson effect have argued that criticism of police officers by the media led to a decline in proactive policing tactics and subsequent increases in crime (Nix & Pickett, 2017; Nix & Wolfe, 2016; Pyrooz et al. 2016; Rosenfeld, 2016; Shjarback et al. 2017; Wolfe & Nix, 2015). Shjarback et al. (2017) examined Missouri police departments' traffic stops, searches, and arrests data from 2014 to 2015 to assess whether the events at Ferguson resulted in a decline in proactive policing. The authors found that Missouri police department officers did conduct significantly fewer traffic stops in 2015 than in 2014; however, there were no significant declines in search and arrest activity within the same period. Interestingly, the authors discovered that increases in the proportion of African-American residents in a patrol area resulted in statistically significant declines in traffic stops, searchers, and arrests. Shjarback et al. (2017) concluded that Ferguson appeared to have had a "racialized de-policing" effect (p. 48). The authors noted that changes in Missouri police officers stop, search, and arrest activity did not significantly impact officers' detection of contraband, nor did it significantly impact crime rates.

A similar study by Morgan and Pally (2016), examined Baltimore Police Department crime incident data from 2010 through 2015 and arrest data from 2013 through 2015 to test whether the protests in Ferguson, the death of Freddie Gray and subsequent riots, and the appointment of a new police commissioner impacted crime and police arrest behavior. The authors conducted an interrupted time series analysis controlling for seasonality and found mixed results for a Ferguson effect in Baltimore. An analysis of the Ferguson period revealed that crimes such as, homicide and robbery had declined, but shooting, carjacking, and arson had increased; however, during the Freddie Gray period, all crime incidents increased with the exception of larceny. Baltimore saw substantial percentage change increases in homicide, which increased by over 90 percent, and shootings which increased by roughly 140 percent. Morgan and Pally (2016) concluded that any evidence of a Ferguson effect on crime in Baltimore was mild and that the crime increases after the arrest and death of Freddie Gray appeared to reflect a "genuine Gray effect" rather than a Ferguson effect (p. 46).

While Morgan and Pally (2016) did not find strong support for a Ferguson effect on crime in Baltimore in 2015, they did find evidence of an effect on policing. The authors noted a 19 percent decline in arrests during the Ferguson period. Most of the decline in arrests were attributed to fewer arrests for less serious crimes such as disorderly conduct. Similar to the Ferguson period, after the Freddie Gray incident there were roughly 30 percent fewer arrests for less serious offenses such as police non-compliance; however, unlike the Ferguson period, arrests for violent offenses such as murder, robbery, and aggravated assault declined as well. During the Freddie Gray period there were roughly 30 percent fewer arrests for homicide and attempted homicide and roughly 45 percent fewer arrests for homicide and attempted homicide during the period of the riots. After the appointment of the new police commissioner, arrests increased for all offense categories with the exceptions of court non-compliance and prostitution. The authors concluded that the patterns of arrests during the different periods appeared to support the de-policing aspect of the Ferguson effect. The authors cautioned that other factors such as changes in police practice could have influenced changes in arrest patterns.

Citizens' Perceptions of Law Enforcement

In addition to findings that de-policing occurred in Baltimore City and Missouri, there was evidence that the events at Ferguson had a negative impact on both citizens' perceptions and officers' morale. A 2015 Gallup poll revealed Americans confidence in police had declined to the lowest level since 1993, following the Rodney King beating (Jones, 2015). Similarly, the Pew Research Center found that the public viewed recent high-profile incidents as part of a "broader problem between police and blacks" (Morin et al., 2017, p. 5). Both Jones (2015) and Graziano and Gauthier (2017) suggested that declines in the public's perceptions of police may be tied to media scrutiny of high-profiled police use of force incidents.

Researchers have found media to be a powerful tool in shaping public perceptions about police conduct (Graziano, Schuck, & Martin, 2010; Dowler & Zawilski, 2007; Miller & Davis, 2008). Graziano et al. (2010) conducted a study testing media effects on public perceptions of racial profiling. The researchers found that participants in the study were more likely to believe that a traffic stop incident was racially motivated after viewing a news segment about the incident. Dowler and Zawilski (2007) found that people who watched a lot of news programs were more likely to have negative views regarding police conduct, and the effect was greater for non-whites. Non-whites who regularly watched news programs were more likely to believe that police treated whites better (Dowler & Zawilski, 2007). Similarly, Miller and Davis' (2008) survey study on public perceptions of police misconduct revealed that people who reported high levels of news consumption were more likely to believe police engaged in misconduct. The authors explained that the negative attitudes held by news viewers regarding police behavior were likely due to the fact that news stories tended to focus on officers who had done something wrong.

In addition, studies by Graziano and Gauthier (2017) and Kochel (2017) found that media coverage of high-profile police use of force incidents and negative personal encounters with police can negatively impact citizens' perceptions of police legitimacy. Graziano and Gauthier (2017) surveyed nearly 1,200 residents of a mid-sized city in California to determine the effects of negative media portrayals of police and firsthand encounters with police on perceptions of police legitimacy. The authors found that respondents with greater exposure to media reports of police misconduct and unfair treatment of minorities had lower perceptions of police legitimacy. Additionally, the authors evaluated the impact of negative media coverage and prior police contact on respondents' perceptions of police legitimacy. The authors found that respondents who had more exposure to negative media portrayals of police and had reported a negative personal encounter with police had lower perceptions of police legitimacy.

Kochel (2017) used survey data from 390 residents residing in high-crime areas in St. Louis County to evaluate changes in perceptions of police before and after the shooting of Michael Brown in Ferguson, Missouri. The author noted that perceptions of trust, procedural justice, and police legitimacy all significantly declined following the shooting of Michael Brown and subsequent unrest in Ferguson, and that the effect was greater for African-American residents. The author noted that African-American respondents had greater declines in legitimacy perceptions of police, expressed greater support for the civil unrest and rioting that followed, and expressed higher levels of disapproval for how the police dealt with the protestors and rioters.

Kochel suggested that African-Americans in St. Louis County may have been more negatively impacted by the events at Ferguson because many of them had or knew someone who had a negative encounter with the police. One young black female respondent in Kochel's (2017) study stated that "the police have been bothering me my whole life" (p. 18), and another black female stated, "I and my family have been and are targeted by police" (p. 19). The author further explained that a highly publicized use of force incident involving a black suspect could prompt notable declines in perceptions of police among African-Americans because many African-Americans view such incidents as evidence that blacks are unfairly targeted by law enforcement.

Officer Morale

A national survey of close to 8,000 police officers by the Pew Research Center found that most officers believed that high-profile use of force incidents had further strained relationships between police and blacks, had made policing more difficult, and had reduced officers' willingness to engage in proactive policing tactics (Morin, Parker, Stepler, & Mercer, 2017). The survey uncovered racial differences in officers' perceptions with the majority of black officers expressing concern that high-profile use of force incidents were signs of an extensive problem between blacks and police. Over 60 percent of black officers surveyed viewed protests following use of force incidents as a tactic to ensure police accountability, but less than 30 percent of white officers shared this view according to the survey. In addition, less than 30 percent of black officers believed that the U.S. has done enough to guarantee blacks were treated equally (Morin et al., 2017).

Nix and Pickett (2017) surveyed police officers in a southeastern police department and found that media criticism of police following highly publicized use of force incidents resulted in officers being more concerned with being accused of misconduct. Also, officers were more likely to believe that crime had gotten worse, and that citizens' perceptions of police officers had declined. A study by Nix and Wolfe (2016) examined the effects of organizational justice on officers' sensitivity to media scrutiny. The authors found that organizational justice helped reduce the impact of media scrutiny on officers' levels of motivation, perceptions of danger, and perceptions of relationships between the police and the public. A similar study by Wolfe and Nix (2015) revealed a relationship between negative media coverage of police use of force incidents and police officers' willingness to work with members of their communities; however, increases in officers' perceptions of self-legitimacy and organizational justice diminished the impact of the Ferguson effect on willingness to work with the public.

Legitimacy Crisis

Both Rosenfeld (2016) and Fagan and Richman (2017) explored legitimacy perceptions and cynicism as possible explanations for the recent homicide spike. Rosenfeld (2016) and Fagan and Richman (2017) both suggested that tensions between the police and minority communities likely worsened due to high-profile use of force incidents, thereby increasing cynicism and decreasing perceptions of legitimacy. Some scholars have referred to the state of police-citizen relationships as a legitimacy crisis (Rosenfeld, 2016) and others have suggested that Ferguson and other highly publicized use of force incidents triggered declines in legitimacy perceptions; these declines in legitimacy could have potentially increased violence in disadvantaged minority communities (Kochel, 2017; Rosenfeld, 2016). Although studies examining the Ferguson effect often cite legitimacy issues as a possible factor that influenced the homicide increases in 2015, only a few studies have tested the impact of Ferguson and other high-profile incidents of police use of force on citizens legitimacy perceptions of police or law-abiding behavior (Desmond et al., 2016; Kane, 2005; Kochel, 2017). No study to date has examined the possible effects of declines in legitimacy perceptions on the homicide increase in 2015. The next section will further explore Rosenfeld's (2016) legitimacy crisis hypothesis by examining the effects of legitimacy perceptions on compliance, cooperation, and law-abiding behavior to explain how declines in police legitimacy in the wake of Ferguson may have provoked homicide increases in 2015.

POLICE LEGITIMACY, CITIZEN COOPERATION, AND CRIME

Legitimacy Theory

An extensive amount of literature has been dedicated to the concept of legitimacy, its impact on citizens' perceptions of legal authorities, and its effect on citizens' compliance and cooperation with legal authorities (Tyler, 2004; Tyler & Fagan, 2008; Tyler et al., 2014). Legitimacy theory has several interpretations. The first interpretation of legitimacy is that it is an "internal obligation to obey" both the law and the commands of legal authorities even when there is no incentive for doing so or the risk of punishment is low (Tyler, 2004, p. 87; Tyler et al., 2014). Tyler et al. (2014) noted that some scholars argued that authorities were inherently legitimate, and subordinates felt obliged to obey even when they did not agree with their commands. Another common interpretation of legitimacy is that it is something that legal authorities gain through interactions with subordinates by acting in ways that promote compliance with the laws they seek to enforce; therefore, legitimacy can be "corroded through negative interactions" (Tyler et al., 2014, p. 754). Authorities can ensure compliance through fear or achieve compliance by acting justly; the latter approach is tied to aspects of procedural justice (Papachristos, Meares, & Fagan, 2012; Tyler et al., 2014; Tyler & Jackson, 2014). Several studies have found that individuals assess their interactions and experiences with legal authorities by the manner in which authorities carry out their duties and by the perceived fairness of treatment, rather than the outcomes of the experience; these encounters shape legitimacy perceptions, which in turn influence compliance (Tyler, 2001; Tyler, 2004; Tyler, 2005; Tyler & Fagan, 2008; Tyler et al., 2014; Walters & Bolger, 2018). A second commonly discussed outcome of legitimacy is cooperation (Tyler, 2001; Tyler, 2005; Tyler & Jackson, 2014). Cooperation, similar to compliance, is said to be motivated by procedural justice; however, cooperation differs from compliance in that it is an active, rather than passive state (Tyler, 2001; Tyler, 2005; Tyler & Jackson, 2014). Citizens' not only adhere to the law, but participate in combating crime (Tyler & Jackson, 2014).

Compliance, Cooperation, and Law-Abiding Behavior

Walters and Bolger (2018) conducted a meta-analysis of 64 studies measuring the effects of procedural justice and legitimacy perceptions on law abiding attitudes and behaviors. The meta-analysis not only included several samples from the United States, but from around the world, which improved the generalizability of the results. The authors found a significant positive relationship between procedural justice and legitimacy perceptions, between legitimacy perceptions and conformity to the law, and between procedural justice and conformity to the law. When evaluating longitudinal studies, the authors found only the relationships between procedural justice and legitimacy perceptions, and between legitimacy perceptions and conformity to be statistically significant. The authors concluded that the findings of the meta-analysis suggested that procedural justice shaped legitimacy perceptions and legitimacy perceptions influenced conformity to the law.

In addition to Walter and Bolger's (2018) meta-analysis, Papachristos et al. (2012), Tyler et al. (2014), and Tyler and Jackson (2014) examined the effects of legitimacy perceptions on compliance. Papachristos et al.'s (2012) study was unique in that it evaluated how legitimacy perceptions affected compliance in an active group of violent offenders. The authors found that increases in legitimacy perceptions decreased the likelihood of respondents carrying a firearm. Papachristos et al. (2012) found that respondents' perceptions of police were influential in shaping their "belie[f] in the legitimacy of the law" (p. 436). Likewise, Tyler and Jackson (2014) found a positive correlation between legitimacy perceptions and law-abiding behavior for both minor and serious offenses. Tyler et al. (2014) conducted telephone surveys with over 1,200 New York City young male residents to analyze the effects of personal experiences with police stops on legitimacy perceptions, self-reported criminal behavior, and cooperation with law enforcement. The authors found that declines in legitimacy perceptions increased the likelihood that a respondent had committed a crime.

Tyler (2001), Tyler (2005), Tyler and Fagan (2008), and Tyler et al. (2014) found that procedural justice impacted perceptions of legitimacy and that legitimacy affected citizens' cooperation. Tyler (2001) evaluated several studies regarding citizens' trust in the police and courts to determine whether procedural justice was more important in shaping citizens' perceptions than outcomes and effectiveness. Two studies, one in Chicago and one in Oakland, California measured respondents' perceptions of police performance and service as well as aspects of procedural justice such as fairness of treatment. Tyler noted that the studies revealed quality of treatment and outcomes mattered, but that quality of treatment had a greater effect on respondents' perceptions of police performance and obligation to comply with the law. In addition, Tyler noted that the results were similar for both white and minority respondents which suggested that fairness of treatment was central to respondents' judgements of police.

Tyler (2005) analyzed the effects of citizens' trust on willingness to cooperate with police and whether procedural justice influenced citizens' trust. Using survey data from a racially and ethnically diverse sample of New Yorkers, the author found that trust influenced willingness to cooperate and that procedural justice influenced trust. The study revealed that there were some racial differences in citizens' assessments of trust in police. Tyler (2005) found that African-American respondents had the "lowest level of trust" (p. 332) in the NYPD and lowest "level of cooperation in fighting crime" (p. 333). Additionally, the author found that quality of treatment was a crucial component of trust for African-Americans.

Tyler and Fagan (2008) surveyed 830 New York City residents in 2002 and conducted a follow-up survey in 2004 to determine whether procedural justice shaped perceptions of police effectiveness and legitimacy, and if assessments of police effectiveness and legitimacy influenced compliance and cooperation. The authors found that fair treatment by the police improved legitimacy perceptions, reduced the likelihood that individuals would file a complaint, and made it more likely that they would accept the outcome of the police encounter. The authors concluded that police can maintain legitimacy even when they do not produce desired outcomes simply by using procedural justice.

Tyler et al. (2014) found that respondents who had repeated personal encounters with police viewed the police as less legitimate. Also, the authors found that the manner in which police stops were conducted affected legitimacy perceptions. Respondents who believed the stops were unfair or invasive had lower legitimacy perceptions, while respondents who believed that police acted in a procedurally fair manner had much higher perceptions of police legitimacy. The authors found that an increase in stops negatively impacted police legitimacy perceptions.

The Effects of Reduced Legitimacy Perceptions on Crime

Desmond et al. (2016) examined the number of police calls for service in Milwaukee, Wisconsin before and after a locally publicized excessive use of force incident. The authors found that calls to report crimes significantly declined after the media reported the use of force incident. The authors estimated that the highly publicized incident created a loss of over 22,000 calls to report crimes including violent crimes. Also, the authors found that other high-profile use of force incidents in Milwaukee and Queens, New York led to a decline in calls to report crimes in Milwaukee neighborhoods. Desmond et al. (2016) noted that black neighborhoods accounted for the majority of the decline in calls; this finding is concerning since the authors noted that "predominately black neighborhoods have higher call volumes" (p. 864). The authors found that the decline in crime reporting coincided with a spike in homicides in Milwaukee. The authors examined homicides in Milwaukee from 2004 through 2010 and noted that the six months following the local media's report about the excessive use of force incident "were the deadliest in the seven years observed in [the] study" (Desmond et al., 2016, p. 870). The authors concluded that highly publicized excessive use of force incidents could negatively impact perceptions of police and reduce cooperation, and this was especially true for black neighborhoods.

An earlier study by Kane (2005) examined the effects of police misconduct and responsiveness on violent crime rates in structurally disadvantaged communities in New York City. Using police misconduct and responsiveness as measures of reduced legitimacy, the author found that changes in these factors predicted changes in violent crime rates in high and extremely disadvantaged communities, but not in communities with low structural disadvantage. Similarly, Tyler et al. (2014) found that "low legitimacy double[d] the risk of involvement in recent past year criminal activity" in a sample of young men in New York City (p. 774). Kane concluded that police misconduct likely impacted violent crime in structurally disadvantaged neighborhoods because these areas were already afflicted with violence and residents in these areas lacked the resources that more socially organized communities had to hold legal authorities accountable. The author suggested that procedural justice may have a greater impact on crime in structurally disadvantaged communities. Overall, the literature provides support for Tyler et al.'s (2014) interpretation of legitimacy, in that legitimacy can be weakened through negative experiences with legal authorities and reduce cooperation and law-abiding behavior.

DISCUSSION

Findings for the Ferguson effect are mixed. Both Morgan and Pally (2016) and Shjarback et al. (2017) found that while Ferguson did appear to have some impact on police activity in terms of stop, search, and arrest behavior, there were no significant or notable changes in crime rates. The changes in police activity observed in both Morgan and Pally's and Shjarback et al.'s studies suggested that Ferguson had a "racialized de-policing effect" (Shjarback et al., 2017, p. 48). Shjarback et al. (2017) found that traffic stops, searches, and arrests declined in patrol areas with greater proportions of African-American residents. Shjarback et al.'s findings may help to explain the declines in arrest that Morgan and Pally (2016) observed in Baltimore after Ferguson. Morgan and Pally (2016) provided a demographic breakdown of Baltimore City's police districts which revealed that most of the districts had high percentages of black residents. The racial composition of the police districts in Baltimore may have influenced the declines in arrests after Ferguson similar to what Shjarback et al. (2017) observed in Missouri; however, Morgan and Pally (2016) did not assess whether race had any impact on arrest decisions.

Kochel (2017) observed noteworthy declines in perceptions of police after the events at Ferguson, particularly among African-Americans. The author found that perceptions of trust, procedural justice, and police legitimacy declined after Ferguson, but the effects were more pronounced for African-American respondents. Tyler (2005) found that perceived fairness of treatment was important in shaping individuals' perceptions of police legitimacy, but fairness of treatment was found to be more influential in shaping African-Americans' perceptions of police.

Desmond et al. (2016) and Kane (2005) examined how high-profile incidents of police misconduct impacted calls for service and crime rates. Both Desmond et al. (2016) and Kane (2005) found that police misconduct and excessive force incidents had a more negative impact on African-Americans and residents of structurally disadvantaged communities. Tyler (2005) and Tyler and Jackson (2014) found that procedural justice, trust, and legitimacy impacted cooperative behaviors such as reporting crime. Furthermore, Papachristos et al. (2012) and Tyler et al. (2014) found that negative legitimacy perceptions increased the likelihood that an individual would be criminally involved. Walter and Bolger's (2018) meta-analysis revealed that legitimacy was important in shaping law-abiding behavior. The declines in calls for service observed in Desmond et al.'s (2016) study and the increases in criminal behavior observed in Kane's (2005) study, following high profile incidents of police misconduct may be partially explained by declines in legitimacy perceptions. Unfortunately, Desmond et al. (2016) did not examine legitimacy perceptions as a possible explanation for the decline in calls, and Kane (2005) only indirectly tested legitimacy.

One theme that appears throughout the literature regarding the Ferguson effect, the 2015 homicide increase, and legitimacy perceptions is the issue of race (Kochel, 2017; Rosenfeld, 2016; Shjarback et al., 2017; Tyler, 2005). Rosenfeld (2016), Pyrooz et al. (2016), and Wheeler and Kovandzic (2018) found that the 2015 spike in the homicide rate was driven by a few large cities; these cities were predominantly black and low income. Interestingly, Fagan and Richman (2017) and Rosenfeld (2016) noted the factors that once explained homicides spikes in the past, did not appear to explain the current phenomena. Rosenfeld (2016) proposed that the events at Ferguson and other high-profile police use of force incidents may have provoked anger in black communities, leading to declines in legitimacy, and an increase in homicides. Overall, the literature provides preliminary support for Rosenfeld's (2016) hypothesis that the events at Ferguson created a legitimacy crisis, sparking violence in low-income, minority communities.

Implications of Findings

Future Research

Highly publicized incidents of police use of force can negatively impact perceptions of police, which can have serious consequences, such as decreases in crime reporting, involvement in criminal activity, and increases in violence (Desmond et al., 2016; Kane, 2005; Tyler et al., 2014). Both Desmond et al. (2016) and Kane (2005) found that publicized incidents of misconduct and excessive use of force had significant negative impacts on African-Americans and residents in socially disadvantaged neighborhoods. Desmond et al. (2016) and Kochel (2017) noted that high-profile use of force incidents may actuate declines in legitimacy and increase cynicism among African-Americans because many African-Americans may identify with the individual on the basis of race. Desmond et al.'s (2016) and Kochel's (2017) findings suggested that high-profile use of force incidents may indirectly impact African-Americans' legitimacy perceptions because African-Americans may have had negative experiences with law enforcement or already believe that they are subjected to unfair treatment. Tyler (2001), Tyler (2005), Tyler & Fagan (2008), and Tyler et al. (2014) found that people's perceptions of legitimacy were shaped by their experiences and encounters with legal authorities and if individuals perceived their experience as unfair or negative, they would have lower legitimacy perceptions. Future research should pay particular attention to how race and socioeconomic disadvantage moderate the effects of legitimacy on criminality.

In addition, researchers should test Rosenfeld's (2016) hypothesis that the events at Ferguson and high-profile police use of force incidents, reduced legitimacy perceptions of law enforcement in African-American neighborhoods and resulted in an increase in homicides in certain cities. These cities, as noted by Rosenfeld (2016) and Pyrooz et al. (2016), have a greater number of black residents and higher levels of poverty. Rosenfeld (2016) recommended surveying residents in the cities that experienced increases to determine whether perceptions of legitimacy were impacted by publicized use of force incidents, and if shifts in legitimacy perceptions influenced violent crime increases. Researchers could look to Tyler and Fagan (2008) and Tyler et al. (2014) for examples of how to measure cooperation and law-abiding behavior and should ask participants about their involvement in criminal activity before and after Ferguson. Rosenfeld (2016) also recommended that researchers analyze NCVS data to assess if there were increases in unreported crime among African-Americans. In addition, researchers could replicate Desmond et al.'s (2016) study in other cities and compare crime reporting before and after Ferguson and other publicized use of force incidents to assess whether there were changes in crime reporting and whether changes in reporting were correlated with changes in crime rates. Finally, researchers could replicate Morgan and Pally's (2016) study using a time series design to examine crime rates before and after publicized police use of force incidents in other cities with demographics similar to Baltimore.

Policy and Practice

Walters & Bolger's (2018) meta-analysis of procedural justice and legitimacy effects on conformity and Tyler's (2001), Tyler's (2005), Tyler & Fagan's (2008), and Tyler et al.'s (2014) findings, underline the importance of procedural justice in shaping legitimacy perceptions and how legitimacy perceptions can affect law abiding attitudes and behavior. Police leaders should consider these findings and ensure that officers are using procedural justice during their interactions with their communities. In addition, police leaders should use organizational justice in their departments since it can insulate officers from negativity and increase their willingness to work with the public (Nix and Pickett, 2017; Nix and Wolfe, 2016; Wolfe and Nix, 2015).

Another option police leaders should explore is community-oriented policing strategies. Gill et al. (2014) conducted a meta-analysis using 25 studies regarding community-oriented policing and measured its effect on several variables including crime, fear of crime, and police legitimacy. The results showed that community-oriented policing had positive effects on citizen satisfaction and police legitimacy. In addition, given the impact of negative media portrayals of police on public perceptions of legitimacy (Graziano & Gauthier, 2017; Kochel 2017), police leaders may consider utilizing media to improve public perceptions of and attitudes towards police. Nix and Pickett (2017) suggested that police departments could use different forms of media to establish open lines of communication with members of their community; for example, using social media. There is evidence to suggest that police departments can use media outlets to improve the public's attitudes and understanding about police conduct (Granziano et al., 2010). Dowler and Zawilski (2007) discovered that the effects of negative news coverage was greater for non-whites. Therefore, it may be beneficial for police departments to use media outlets to highlight positive police activities and to specifically target minority communities to reduce negative perceptions.

Lastly, policy makers and police leaders should reevaluate the use of certain proactive policing tactics such as discretionary stops and arrests. Shjarback et al. (2017) speculated that a decline in aggressive policing tactics in African-American communities may have improved police legitimacy because such tactics could be viewed as harassment. The authors noted that at least in Missouri, de-policing did not result in increased crime rates. Tyler et al. (2014) found that procedural justice and legitimacy perceptions were "increasingly negative with each additional stop reported" (p. 771) and that fewer stops predicted increases in perceptions of police effectiveness. Shjarback et al.'s (2017) and Tyler et al.'s (2014) findings suggest that police leaders can improve legitimacy simply by reducing the use of aggressive tactics and that doing so may not negatively impact crime rates.

CONCLUSION

The literature provides preliminary support for Rosenfeld's (2016) hypothesis that Ferguson created a legitimacy crisis in African-American communities with high poverty rates, which led to the homicide increases observed in several cities in 2015. However, as Pyrooz et al. (2016) noted, there was no evidence to support that Ferguson had a nationwide effect on crime. Morgan and Pally (2016) and Shjarback et al. (2017) found no evidence that either media coverage of Ferguson or de-policing increased crime rates in Baltimore City and Missouri. While Morgan and Pally (2016) did observe substantial increases in crime after the arrest and death of Freddie Gray, the authors' findings suggested that the effects of police use of force incidents may be localized. Kochel (2017) found that black residents in high crime neighborhoods in St. Louis County reported declines in legitimacy perceptions after the shooting of Michael Brown and subsequent unrest; however, the study provided no evidence that the declines had any effect on crime rates. Desmond et al. (2016) and Kane (2005) found that high-profile use of force incidents and police misconduct can affect crime rates, but neither of these studies surveyed residents to assess whether the events negatively impacted their perceptions of law enforcement, so the findings provide only circumstantial evidence of a legitimacy effect on crime.

In order to determine whether Rosenfeld's (2016) hypothesis has any merit, more empirical studies must be conducted to improve scholars' understanding of the factors that influenced the 2015 rise in homicide. Both Rosenfeld (2016) and Fagan and Richman (2017) noted that the 2015 homicide increase appeared to have been influenced by different factors than previous homicide increases. Declining legitimacy perceptions in the wake of Ferguson may prove to be an important factor that impacted the homicide increases experienced in several cities. Although no study to date has directly tested the effects of legitimacy perceptions on the homicide rise in 2015, there have been numerous studies about procedural justice and its importance in forming legitimacy perceptions. Police leaders should use the research evidence to encourage officers to use procedural justice in their interactions with the public. Although there is no direct evidence linking legitimacy perceptions to homicide increases in 2015, using procedural justice to improve citizens' legitimacy perceptions of police would be prudent given the current climate and claims by scholars of a legitimacy crisis in policing.

REFERENCES

Desmond, M., Papachristos, A. V., & Kirk, D. S. (2016). Police violence and citizen crime reporting in the Black community. *American Sociological Review*, *81*(5), 857-876.

Dowler, K., & Zawilski, V. (2007). Public perceptions of police misconduct and discrimination: Examining the impact of media consumption. *Journal of Criminal Justice*, *35*(2), 193-203.

Fagan, J., & Richman, D. (2017). Understanding recent spikes and longer trends in American murders. *Columbia Law Review*, *117*(5), 1235-1296.

Gill, C., Weisburd, D., Telep, C. W., Vitter, Z., & Bennett, T. (2014). Community-oriented policing to reduce crime, disorder and fear and increase satisfaction and legitimacy among citizens: a systemic review. *Journal of Experimental Criminology*, *10*(4), 399-428.

Graziano, L. M., & Gauthier, J. F. (2017). Media consumption and perceptions of police legitimacy. *Policing: An International Journal*, *41*(5), 593-607.

Graziano, L., Schuck, A., & Martin, C. (2010). Police misconduct, media coverage, and public perceptions of racial profiling: An experiment. *Justice Quarterly*, *27*(1), 52-76.

Jones, J. M. (2015, June 19). In U.S., confidence in police lowest in 22 years. *Gallup News.* Retrieved from http://www.gallup.com/poll/183704/confidence-police-lowest-years.aspx.

Kane, R. J. (2005). Comprised police legitimacy as a predictor of violent crime in structurally disadvantaged communities. *Criminology*, *43*(2), 469-498.

Kochel, T. R. (2019). Explaining racial differences in Ferguson's impact on local residents' trust and perceived legitimacy: Policy implications for police. *Criminal Justice Policy Review*, *30*(3), 374-405.

Miller, J., & Davis, R. C. (2008). Unpacking public attitudes to the police: contrasting perceptions of misconduct with traditional measures of satisfaction. *International Journal of Police Science & Management*, *10*(1), 9-22.

Morgan, S. L., & Pally, J. A. (2016). *Ferguson, Gray, and Davis: An analysis of recorded crime incidents and arrests in Baltimore City, March 2010 through December 2015.* Baltimore, MD: John Hopkins University. Retrieved from https://socweb.soc.jhu.edu/ faculty/morgan/papers/MorganPally2016.pdf.

Morin, R., Parker, K., Stepler, R., & Mercer, A. (2017, January 11). *Behind the badge: What police think about their jobs.* Pew Research Center. Retrieved from http://www.pewsocialtrends.org/2017/01/11/behind-the-badge/.

Nix, J., & Pickett, J. T. (2017). Third-person perceptions, hostile media effects, and policing: Developing a theoretical framework for assessing the Ferguson effect. *Journal of Criminal Justice*, *51*, 24-33.

Nix, J., & Wolfe, S. E. (2016). Sensitivity to the Ferguson Effect: The role of managerial organizational justice. *Journal of Criminal Justice*, *47*, 12-20.

Papachristos, A. V., Meares, T. L., & Fagan, J. (2012). Why Do Criminals Obey the Law? The Influence of Legitimacy and Social Networks on Active Gun Offenders. *Journal of Criminal Law & Criminology*, *102*(2), 397–440.

Pyrooz, D. C., Decker, S. H., Wolfe, S. E., & Shjarback, J. A. (2016). Was there a Ferguson Effect on crime rates in large U.S. cities? *Journal of Criminal Justice*, *46*, 1-8.

Rosenfeld, R. (2016). Documenting and explaining the 2015 homicide rise: Research directions. *National Institute of Justice*, NCJ 249895. Office of Justice Programs. Retrieved from https://www.ncjrs.gov/pdffiles1/nij/249895.pdf.

Shjarback, J. A., Pyrooz, D. C., Wolfe, S. E., & Decker, S. H. (2017). De-policing and crime in the wake of Ferguson: Radicalized changes in the quantity and quality of policing among Missouri police departments. *Journal of Criminal Justice*, *50*, 42-52.

Tyler, T. R. (2001). Public trust and confidence in legal authorities: What do majority and minority group members want from the law and legal institutions? *Behavioral Sciences and the Law*, *19*, 215-235.

Tyler, T. R. (2004). Enhancing police legitimacy. *The Annals of the American Academy of Political and Social Science*, *593*(1), 84-99.

Tyler, T. R. (2005). Policing in black and white: Ethnic group difference in trust and confidence in the police. *Police Quarterly*, *8*(3), 322-342.

Tyler, T. R., & Fagan, J. (2008). Legitimacy and Cooperation: Why do people help the police fight crime in their communities? *Ohio State Journal of Criminal Law*, *6*(1), 231-275.

Tyler, T. R., Fagan, J., & Geller, A. (2014). Street stops and police legitimacy: Teachable moments in young urban men's legal socialization. *Journal of Empirical Legal Studies*, *11*(4), 751-785.

Tyler, T. R., & Jackson, J. (2014). Popular legitimacy and the exercise of legal authority: Motivating compliance, cooperation, and engagement. *Psychology, Public Policy, and Law*, *20*(1), 78–95.

Walters, G. D., & Bolger, C. (2018). Procedural justice perceptions, legitimacy beliefs, and compliance with the law: A meta-analysis. *Journal of Experimental Criminology*, 1-32. doi: 10.1007/s11292-018-9338-2.

Wheeler, A. P., & Kovandzic, T. V. (2018). Monitoring volatile homicide trends across U.S. cities. *Homicide Studies*, *22*(2), 119-144.

Wolfe, S. E., & Nix, J. (2015). The alleged "Ferguson Effect" and police willingness to engage in community partnership. *Law and Human Behavior*, *40*, 1-10.

In: A Closer Look at Criminal Justice
Editors: J. A. Cooper and K. G. Jachimowski
ISBN: 978-1-53615-782-6

Chapter 10

MENTAL HEALTH AND CIT IN A PRISON SETTING

***Kayla G. Jachimowski*[1,*] *and Carley J. Smathers*[2]**
[1]Saint Vincent College, Latrobe, PA, US
[2]Indiana University of Pennsylvania, Indiana, PA, US

ABSTRACT

At most angles of the intersection between mental health and the criminal justice system there are inconsistencies, disagreements, and falsehoods that make it difficult for researchers to see the silver-lining. Depending on the literature being reviewed, studies report as few as 20%, or as high as 60% of the total prison population being diagnosed with a mental health disorder. One highlight of recent literature suggests there is some agreement between researchers and practitioners on the general lack of resources for correctional staff and inmates with mental health disorders. This book chapter examines interventions used in the correctional setting when encountering mental illness with a specific focus on the implementation of Crisis Intervention Teams (an adaptation of CIT originally developed for police).

Prison is quite literally a ghetto in the most classic sense of the word, a place where the U.S. government now puts not only the dangerous but also the inconvenient - people who are mentally ill, people who are addicts, people who are poor and uneducated and unskilled.

-Piper Kerman, *Orange is the New Black*

DEFINING MENTAL ILLNESS

Defining mental illness is a complicated task for researchers and practitioners alike because the definition shifts based on cultural, political, economic, and scientific factors

[*] Corresponding Author's Email: kayla.jachimowski@stvincent.edu

(Goldman & Grob, 2006; McNally, 2011; Varelius, 2009; Wakefield, 1992). Depending on the scope of the politician, researcher, public, or mentally disordered individual, the definition may be narrow, such as serious mental illness (SMI), or broader to include non-serious mental illness (nSMI), which continues to complicate the problem of determining a unified definition. Plus, to add another layer of complexity, the mental health field cannot agree on singular words either. For example, psychopathology, mental illness, abnormality, mental disorder can vary in definition but are used synonymously (Bergner & Bunford, 2017). Bergner and Bunford (2017) argue the lack of singular definition is because "... [research has] attempted to settle this question of the meaning of the concept 'mental disorder,' not on the basis of empirical evidence, but from our armchairs (p. 26)." Even the Diagnostic and Statistical Manual of Mental Disorders (DSM), a widely used and the most comprehensive collection of mental health diagnoses, fails to offer full definitions of psychiatric disorders (Wakefield, 1992). So, to be clear, we cannot seem to agree on why there is a lack of unified definitions, let alone a solution to having a more cohesive approach to understanding mental health disorders.

Take practitioners out of the picture for a moment, as researchers we push for the use of empirical evidence, citing the importance of using established or promising programs, and policies. And yet, when it comes to mental illness, there is even more disagreement among researchers than practitioners. Varelius (2009) discusses a multitude of different definitions used through the literature, for example, K. W. M. Fulford (1989, as cited in Varelius, 2009) defines mental disorder as an individual's incapacity to engage in their environment without a breakdown. More still, Gert and Culver (2004) define a mental disorder as a clinically significant behavioral or psychological pattern or display of symptoms which occur in an individual simultaneous to distress and disability with the potential of leading to death, pain, or the loss of freedom (as cited in Varelius, 2009).

Most frequently cited is the DSM and the 1999 mental health report from the U.S. Surgeon General. For the purposes of this chapter, we will use the DSM-5 definition when discussing mental health disorder. Recently, the DSM was revised (2013) and offers the following definition of mental illness:

> A mental disorder is a syndrome characterized by clinically significant disturbance in an individual's cognition, emotion regulation, or behavior that reflects a dysfunction in the psychological, biological, or developmental processes underlying mental functioning. Mental disorders are usually associated with significant distress or disability in social, occupational, or other important activities. An expectable or culturally approved response to a common stressor or loss, such as the death of a loved one, is not a mental disorder. Socially deviant behavior (e.g., political, religious, or sexual) and conflicts that are primarily between the individual and society are not mental disorders unless the deviance or conflict results from a dysfunction in the individual, as described above. (American Psychiatric Association, 2013, p. 20)

MENTAL HEALTH IN THE CRIMINAL JUSTICE SYSTEM

Deinstitutionalization and Criminalization

Over 61 years ago, the number of in-patients in psychiatric state hospitals peaked around 559,000 in 1955; however, in 2003 there were 47,000 inpatients (Davis, Fulginiti, Kriegel & Brekke, 2012). This dramatic decrease in patients residing in state hospitals can be attributed to multiple and somewhat simultaneous changes that occurred during the latter half of the 20th century. A review of deinstitutionalization is critical to understanding mental illness and crime, as this was a turning point for individuals with mental disorders (MHD) and the resources available to them. More so, it offers a historical foundation and explanation for the increased rate of police interactions with individuals with MHD, increased rates of sentencing, longer sentences for individuals with MHD, and challenges faced in correctional facilities.

Psychiatric deinstitutionalization refers to the emptying and closing of state mental hospitals; plus, the philosophy and the process of shifting mental health care to community-based facilities (Kim, 2014; Torrey, Kennard, Eslinger, Lamb, & Pavle, 2010). Prior to 1948, like many other aspects of society (juvenile justice, criminal justice), the solution to dealing with the poor, uneducated, mentally disordered, or minorities was to institutionalize them. In fact, at this time, almost half of the United States relied on in-patient treatment facilities, for rehabilitation, treatment, and interventions. However, in just a few years, the United States would hit the peak number of available psychiatric beds, at a time when a perfect storm was just on the horizon. Depending on the researcher, there are one to five different reasons for the beginning of the end for psychiatric hospitals. Though, it is fair to say it was likely a combination of things which all came to a head at the same time.

Shifting philosophies and the development of pharmacological intervention, helped establish outpatient facilities, where individuals could get treatment without having to be admitted into the hospital. In 1954 there were approximately 1,200 outpatient facilities and by 1959 there were more than 1,400 (Accordino, Porter, & Morse, 2001). Antipsychotic drugs, such as chlorpromazine, quickly became available during the mid-1950s (Kim, 2014); supporting the change from in-patient interventions to outpatient treatment. Not only were these drugs used as a community-based alternative to institutionalization, but research suggested that antipsychotic drugs were capable of curing a multitude of disparate diagnoses, such as depression and anxiety disorders (Kim, 2014; Rochefort, 1984). By 1956, over two million patients had been prescribed chlorpromazine, and the majority of states were prescribing some type of antipsychotic drug to their patients (Harcourt, 2011). Through the use of antipsychotic drugs, the need for physical restraints decreased and the use of tranquilizing drugs began creating an overall image of reform for the mental health field, mental institutions, and individuals with MHD.

In addition to drug therapy, the military began experimenting with different therapeutic treatments leading to major advancements in therapeutic psychology (Rochefort, 1990). Interestingly enough, the public shied away from discussing mental health, or specific diagnosis even among family members. It was not until military personnel came back from WWII that the public began to see mental health disorders could affect anyone. Support started to slowly poor in to 'get our strong, brave, boys better' (Kim, 2014). Thus began, the study of psychiatric patterns, effects, and causes, otherwise known as psychiatric epidemiology; a key factor in the groundbreaking research being conducted on mental illness (Rochefort, 1990; Davis et al., 2012). The emphasis and focus of psychological epidemiology combined with the increase in professionally trained mental health personnel led to alternatives to hospitalization and an increased use of diversion away from psychiatric hospitals.

Another factor which pushed people away from institutions was allegations of poor conditions. Patients not being cared for, dangerous and experimental psychiatric treatments and unexpected deaths without explanations, fueled by the public's growing interest in mental health care facilities. Ultimately, this resulted in civil liberty advocates demanding change. Advocates pushed for a reformation of in-patient care and facilities. One side of this coin was challenging two legal policies: procedural due process and minimum standards of care (Davis et al., 2012; Harcourt, 2011). Procedural due process focused mostly on the concept of involuntary commitment, when an individual was committed to a mental institution against their will. After civil liberty advocates succeeded in changing the process of involuntary commitment, there was dramatic effect on institutionalization, as this was the most common way to be committed to a state hospital (Harcourt, 2011).

Finally, the catalyst of reform came from the *Community Mental Health Centers (CMHC) Act of 1963* (Mechanic & Rochefort, 1990). Formed from the basis of the *Mental Health Study Act of 1955*, the CMHC Act of 1963 mandated state and local mental health facilities to increase the rate of treatment in community facilities (Lynum & Hill, 2015). During President John F. Kennedy's message to Congress, he outlined the shift to community health care and set a quantitative target to decrease the number of patients in state hospitals and asylums by 50% within 20 years (Davis et al., 2012; Harcourt, 2011; Mechanic & Rochefort, 1990). Concomitantly, these factors began changing the public's opinion about mental health, both in terms of treatment and those diagnosed with mental health problems.

With support from the public and the government, individuals who were incapacitated for mental illness were able to reintegrate themselves into society. Unfortunately, some families were unprepared emotionally, financially, or unwilling to provide support and treatment to these individuals; leaving them to fend for themselves.

And, community facilities were unable to accommodate the influx of individuals with mental health problems. Deinstitutionalization created a society that demanded community-based treatments for individuals with MHD without the means to adequately provide resources for all of these people (Lamb, 1984). Thus, individuals who were without treatment, support, and basic human resources found themselves on the streets and encountering the police. The criminalization of mental illness has become an unforeseen consequence of deinstitutionalization (Ringhoff, Rapp & Robst, 2012).

The criminalization of mental illness refers to individual behaviors that can be managed by transporting an individual to a psychiatric hospital but, due to lack of resources are managed by placing the individual into the criminal justice system through arrests (Fisher, Silver, & Wolff, 2006). The criminalization of mental illness in conjunction to the increasing number of individuals with MHD in correctional facilities became a societal issue during the early 1970s when the United States saw an increase in individuals with MHD who were incarcerated (Chaimowitz, 2011; Ringhoff et al., 2012). Deinstitutionalization promised to shift government funds from state psychiatric hospitals to the community to increase community-based treatment programs for individuals with MHD (Chaimowitz, 2011). Unfortunately, this is not what in fact happened; far less money was invested in the community, resulting in numerous individuals with MHD ending up in the criminal justice system instead of being diverted to psychiatric hospitals. Thus, mental illness became *de facto* criminalized.

In 1972, March Abramson was the first person to coin the phrase, *criminalization of mental illness*. Individuals with MHD often are subjected to arrest and prosecution in the criminal justice system for minor offenses (Perez, Leifman, & Estrada, 2003). During the initial interactions between individuals with mental disorders and the criminal justice system, there is usually a lack of diversion strategies, such as community support systems and rigorous criteria for civil commitment (Perez et al., 2003). Offenders who had MHD typically are labeled as criminal before being released back onto the streets, becoming part of the prison's revolving door. For individuals with MHD who are not arrested and incarcerated, there are a multitude of different locations where they may end up. Thus, rather than receiving needed services, offenders with MHD are placed behind bars where they merely can be "controlled." Two of the most common contributors to the disproportionate rate of arrests of individuals with MHD are substance abuse and homelessness (Compton, Thomas, Stinson, & Grant, 2007; Kessler, Chui, Demler, & Walters, 2005; Lamb; 1984; Robinson, Sareen, Cox, & Bolton, 2009; Slate, Bluffington-Vollum & Johnson, 2013; White, Chafetz, Collins-Bride, & Nickens, 2006).

Increased drug and alcohol use by individuals with a mental health diagnosis is commonly attributed to the idea of self-medicating (Robinson et al., 2009; Slate et al., 2013; Thornton et al., 2012). When community health care facilities lost funding, the ease of getting medications became more difficult and individuals with MHD sought other ways to medicate themselves (Moore & Elkavich, 2008; Slate et al., 2013). Another reason is individuals with co-occurring mental illness and substance abuse disorders report that, unlike psychiatric medications, the use of drugs gives the individual a pleasurable experience, allowing them to enjoy life (Slate et al., 2013; Thornton et al., 2012).

Homelessness is considered an intermediate factor when discussing the pathway to incarceration (White et al., 2006). According to Perez, Leifman, and Estrada (2003), when individuals with MHD do not receive adequate treatment or the appropriate resources it is likely they will enter the criminal justice system. In a study conducted by White et al. (2006), the majority of individuals diagnosed with a mental health disorder had been arrested prior to the survey. Additionally, 86 percent of individuals who reported being homeless in the past six months were arrested. Although in recent years, individuals who have a mental health diagnosis who have been arrested could be moved to a mental health court; it is likely they will be sent to a correctional facility where they are likely to be victimized and disproportionately punished.

Disparity in Police Contact

The nature of the criminalization of mental illness (though a debated topic) warrants the discussion of police officers and their interaction with individuals with MHD. Police officers act as a gatekeeper for individuals with mental health problems and the criminal justice system (Jennings & Hudak, 2005). As gatekeepers, the role police officers play in diverting or placing individuals with MHD into the criminal justice system is essential. However, more often than not, police departments lack the training, policies, and procedures to adequately manage the responsibility of being a gatekeeper in this capacity (Ruiz & Miller, 2004). It should be noted, though, police departments throughout the country are working hard to secure funding, training, and altering policies to better handle interactions when it comes to individuals with MHD. In recent years, the amount of disproportionate arrests and incarceration sentences of individuals with MHD has become a growing concern. According to Akins, Burkhardt, Lanfear, Amorim, and Stevens (2014), at most, individuals with MHD make up 5% of the population but are 7% - 10% of police contacts. Which is not the only problem police officers and individuals with MHD are facing.

One study found that nearly half of individuals with MHD surveyed had at least one repeated interaction with a police officer within 60 days of the initial encounter (Akins et al., 2014). And while diversion may be the top priority (in some cases) there are many times an officer will not be willing to divert. Especially, the moment a person becomes a danger to themselves or society; further complicating the police officer's role. Police have a difficult task of protecting individuals with MHD, while protecting the community at the same time. These two common-law doctrines clash during calls for service or interactions between police and individuals with MHD (Jennings & Hudack, 2005). According to Bittner (1967), while police officers recognize that interacting with individuals with MHD is a part of their job, they are not confident in making decisions regarding placement, and more importantly, they do not feel that it is their job to make these decisions.

Traditionally, the defined role of police officers in these situations is unclear and extends beyond the literal enforcement of the law. While police are charged most frequently with protecting the public, more recently, police have been considered "community problem-solvers" (Sellers, Sullivan, Veysey, & Shane, 2005). In the context of mental health calls for service, this newer mandate focuses officers on assisting individuals to gain access to the mental health system. However, in cases where there is little to no guidelines surrounding the handling of individuals with MHD, police officers' default to a public safety perspective, opposed to that of a peacekeeper (Ruiz & Miller, 2004). While there is a disagreement among researchers as to the percent of police/mental health interactions, there is agreement on the disproportionality of contact between the two groups.

Diversion Strategies

In a 1998 study conducted by Borum, Deane, Steadman and Morrissey, the researchers reported that police agencies began re-evaluating their role in the community and the increase in service calls. Furthermore, they report the three response programs that were being integrated into police departments for the turn of the century. These programs include: *police-based specialized police response*, which includes officers who have mental health training (i.e., Crisis Intervention Teams); *police-based specialized mental health response*, which include mental health professionals who are not sworn-officers but are employed by the police departments; and *mental-health-based specialized mental health response*, which includes a team response between mental health providers and police officers.

It is beyond the scope of this book chapter to discuss diversion strategies at length; however, it is important to highlight that CIT training appears to be the best practice for police interactions with individuals with MHD; and, consequently, a potentially useful strategy for correctional officers. To that end, it is important to discuss the other alternatives which have not been as successful. One such approach is the use of *mobile crisis teams (*MCT) or *mobile crisis units* (MCU); a dual partnership between CIT officers and mobile crisis dispatch programs (Murphy, 2012). Some studies suggest that MCT and MCU decrease the rate of arrests; however, the problem lies in the fact that there are so few studies which have been completed. Unlike CIT research, MCT research has not been able to discern the varying aspects which are contributing to the effectiveness of diversion (Lord & Bjerregaard, 2014).

The *Crisis Outreach and Support Team* (COAST) was developed in Albuquerque, New Mexico in 2005 and "... expanded the basic scope of a sworn CIT program and involved civilians acting as crisis outreach personnel (Rosenbaum, 2010, p. 176)." There are five "crisis specialists" in the civilian unit, they are employed by the Albuquerque Police Department (APD) and are supervised by an APD police sergeant. This team is responsible for providing crisis intervention, for individuals with a MHD, this includes but is not limited to: suicide intervention and stabilization, referrals, housing needs, and substance abuse (Rosenbaum, 2010). Overall, COAST was developed to decrease the rate of instances where officers were dispatched to a location to respond to these types of situations, thus freeing up the police. However, members of COAST were unable to provide services of psychiatric medicine or give long term care. COAST now employees an outreach psychiatrist to aid the COAST members as well as the police. While Rosenbaum (2010) reports that the "COAST plus psychiatrist model" is successful at "diverting nonviolent, non-criminal cases away from front-line officers," this article did not include any methodological evidence to support this claim (p. 180). However, this strategy has not been fully explored, or tested with methodological rigor.

PREVALENCE OF MENTAL HEALTH IN PRISONS

Inmates with MHD in Prison

Typically speaking, individuals with MHD fall into three categories when they are arrested, displaying symptoms of mental illness in public, those who commit petty crimes, and those who commit serious or violent crimes (Schug & Fradella, 2015). Individuals with MHD who commit serious of violent crimes pose the biggest challenges for policy makers and the criminal justice system. Without a doubt, these individuals are the ones who make headlines, skew public perception of the dangerousness of individuals with MHD, and need most of the resources once imprisoned; specifically care during incarceration and a strict, manageable program upon re-entry.

It is estimated that inmates with MHD comprise more than 20 percent of the state prison population, 50 percent of the local jail population (Blumstein, 2018). Prisons were not designed to house or rehabilitate these individuals and one of the biggest problems facing inmates with MHD is the scarcity of resources and programmatic options (Adams & Ferrandino, 2008). Research suggests there is a lack of suitable and effective treatment options for offenders and inmates with MHD, despite having a large population of individuals who suffer from one or more mental disorders in the United States. Due to correctional facilities becoming pseudo-mental health facilities it has put undue pressure on the entire correctional system. Officers who are ill-equipped to handle these inmates, create more challenges and potentially escalate situations. The inability to manage and treat these individuals leads to pervasive problems and concerns.

A lack of training among correctional staff increases the risk of victimization for these inmates. Inmates with MHD are more likely to display diminished rational thinking processes, this can often lead to increased inappropriate behavior. For example, offenders with MHD are more likely to commit a prison infraction, like disobeying a rule, unintentional aggression, opposition to general instruction, the inability to follow the rules, and violence, compared to inmates without a mental health diagnosis (Benton & Masciadrelli, 2013; Geiman, 2007). Ignorance, on the part of the correctional staff, leads to inappropriately handling the inmate (physically or verbally,) creating a hostile environment for everyone involved (Adams, & Ferrandino, 2008).

Unfortunately, inmates unable to conform to prison rules and norms, are placed in solitary confinement; this is especially true for inmates with MHD. Plus, there are few treatment alternatives for these individuals to use. Solitary confinement is all too often the "go-to" treatment for dealing with inmate who violate rules, especially when they engage in violence towards themselves or others. However, treatment should be the immediate reaction for inmates with MHD, and this does not always occur. According to Gater (2007), many inmates are unable to receive the treatment they need for their disorder while in the criminal justice system.

White, Chafez, Collins-Bride, & Nickens (2006) state that arrests and victimization of inmate with MHD are linked. Those with severe mental illness have high rates of interaction with law enforcement officers, arrests, and incarceration. This involvement with the justice system can exacerbate mental illness. Similarly, violent victimization has shown to be associated with mental illness and violence and causes a disruption in the individuals already chaotic life (Silver, Felson, & Vaneseltine, 2008; White et al., 2006). Exposure to, or a history of victimization often leads young offender to engage in "assaultive violence"; homicide and physical assault resulting from a dispute (Silver et al., 2008).

In addition to being more likely to experience victimization in the community, inmates with MHD also are more likely to be victimized once they are incarcerated (Jachimowski, 2018). This victimization often stems from a lack of understanding the disorder by other inmates. Blitz, Wolff, and Shi (2008) report found substantial differences between the occurrences of staff-on-inmate and inmate-on-inmate physical victimizations. Nearly fifty more, per 10,000, staff-on-inmate physical victimizations occur when the inmate had a MHD compared to when the inmate did not have a MHD. Indicating that the mental health of the inmate is likely contributing to increased occasions of physical interactions with staff. Similarly, inmates with a MHD are far more likely to be physically victimized by another inmate. Just over 100 more, per 10,000, physical victimizations occur if one of the inmates has a MHD, compared to if both do not have a MHD. Once again, indicating that the presence of one inmate with a MHD vastly increases the likelihood of being physically victimized by other inmates (Jachimowski, 2018).

While the research on the prevalence of violence and mental illness tends to find mixed results, there does appear to be some consistencies. Jachimowski (2018) report that some mental disorders were associated with violent offending. More so, Felson, Silver, and Remster (2012) claim that mental illness has the potential to lead to aggression and violence when it is coupled with delusional thinking. Other studies report that even though it is unlikely, individuals with mental disorders are more likely to engage in violent offending than those without a mental disorder (Flynn, Rodway, Appleby, & Shaw, 2014). Research on mental illness and violence have found many common risk factors. Some of these include age, race, socioeconomic status, physical and sexual abuse, substance abuse, gender, and stressful life events (Felson et al., 2012).

In addition to being more likely to have a longer sentence, and being victimized in prison, inmates with MHD are more likely to commit a prison infraction. For example, disobeying a rule when compared to inmates without a mental health diagnosis. Ignorance, on the part of the correctional staff, leads to inappropriately handling the inmate (physically or verbally,) creating a hostile environment for everyone involved (Adams & Ferrandino, 2008). Mental illness can diminish the rational thinking process of inmates causing them to exhibit inappropriate behaviors (Benton & Masciadrelli, 2013; Geiman, 2007). These behaviors include forms of unintentional aggression, opposition to general instruction, the inability to follow the rules, and violence.

The adaptation of CIT training, when it is implemented, is used in conjunction with other strategies to manage inmates who suffer from a mental health disorder. While outside of the scope of this chapter to discuss each of these strategies in more depth, we feel it is important to highlight the good, the bad, and the ugly when it comes to available options for correctional officers when responding to situations with inmates with a MHD. While some of these options have proven more successful than others, the key elements of CIT would suggest it should be used as a first approach before, or in combination with the following strategies.

Solitary Confinement

A frequent solution to rule-breaking in prisons is the use of solitary confinement. According to Haney (2009), solitary confinement is defined as the involuntary confinement of prisoners as punishment. The goal of solitary confinement is to segregate the individual from the mainstream population in attached housing units or freestanding facilities. These individuals can be confined for upwards of 23 hours a day, with extremely limited direct and indirect social interaction with other people.

To date, there exists a robust scientific literature displaying the negative consequences of utilizing solitary confinement. The essence of the experience of solitary confinement itself has been found to have profoundly negative effects on the inmates. Prisoners placed in solitary confinement are at greater risk of serious psychological harm (Haney, 2018), increased likelihood of self-harm and suicide (Kaba et al., 2014), and stress-related trauma (Haney, 2018). The absence of meaningful human contact combined with the oppressive nature of the setting results in an extremely harsh and dehumanizing experience. These conditions impair psychological functioning (Haney, 2018). The negative consequences are further exacerbated with long-term solitary confinement. Haney's (2018) results found prisoners reported twice the number of symptoms of stress-related trauma and isolation-related pathology in comparison to long-term general population inmates.

Beyond the substantial amount of literature displaying the negative effects solitary can have on inmates, there is a troubling finding that suggests inmates with MHD are more likely to have spent time in restrictive housing (Beck, 2015). Unfortunately, inmates who are unable to conform to the norms of prison, and are offered few treatment alternatives, and often find themselves locked in solitary confinement (Adams, & Ferrandino, 2008; Benton, & Masciadrelli, 2013; Pfeiffer, 2007). They are more likely to engage in disruptive and rule-breaking behaviors, such as refusing to come out of their cell, setting fires, destroying property, or engaging in self-mutilation (Arrigo & Bullock, 2008). Additionally, the likelihood of solitary confinement significantly increases when the staff predicts that the inmate is likely to engage in violence towards themselves or others. A trend emerges of the overuse of solitary confinement for these individuals due to these outburst, and then solitary confinement exacerbates the mental health concern, leading to more outbursts. Treatment should be the immediate reaction for inmates with MHD, and this does not always occur. According to Gater (2007), many inmates are unable to receive the treatment they need for their disorder while in the criminal justice system. Overall, there is an emerging consensus, based on the consequences, costs, and iatrogenic nature of solitary confinement, that the punishment's use needs to be banned or at least limited (Ahalt et al., 2017; Haney, 2018).

Mental Health Wings

Inmates with MHD are often placed into healthcare wings, commonly termed mental health wings (Needham-Bennett & Cumming, 1995). Mental health wings within prisons operate as the front-line for mental illness triaging. The wings are intended to provide care for complex individuals displaying considerable behavioral disturbances (Forrester, Chiu, Dove, & Parrot, 2010).

Most mental health wings are housed in self-contained accommodation units comprised of cells. In older prisons, these areas were called wings, today they are called housing blocks. Mental health wings often act as a limbo between the prison community and hospital placement. This status results in many occupants remaining "invisible" when trying to obtain the necessary treatment. However, these wings are still considered a better "alternative" placement than going unwell in the community (Needham-Bennett & Cumming, 1995).

It is not uncommon, for these individuals to wait months for transfers to hospital, referral to local services, assessment, and other decision-making processes (Needham-Bennett & Cumming, 1995). The wait for these prisoners can be very troubling. While in prison, many do not receive adequate services. Psychiatric professionals working in prisons are not nearly capable of producing equivalent treatment as patients in hospitals (Needham-Bennett & Cumming, 1995). The services offered within these wings consistently fall short of the expectations of those offered in hospitals and even the community, instead these services often reflect the needs of the prison in which they are located (Forrester et al., 2010).

Indeed, many of the faults associated with mental health wings can be attributed to resource cutbacks and staff shortages. The vast majority of prisons operate at near maximum capacity. Inconsistencies concerning prison intake and assessment often leave prisons with large numbers of new receptions and inadequate tools to meet the individual needs of the prisoners (Birmingham, 2003). Therefore, many prisons find it necessary to use whatever accommodation available which is often the use of health care centers, or wings. The placement of these offenders can reduce the time staff spend with them (Birmingham, 2003).

Psychological Treatments

There are a considerably large variety of psychological interventions within the prison system for treating inmates with MHD. These interventions include but are not limited to, cognitive behavioral therapy (CBT), interpersonal, dialectical behavioral (DBT), meditation-based, and group therapies. Unfortunately, evaluations of the effectiveness of these interventions have resulted in inconsistent findings (Fazel, Hayes, Bartellas, Clerici, and Trestman, 2016). CBT has been a consistently well reviewed and supported therapy for a variety of concerns, mental health included. Studies have found relatively strong support for its use within prisons. It appears to improve the psychological well-being of inmates with MHD and reduces psychopathological symptoms (Khodayarifard, Shokoohi-Yekta, & Hamot, 2010). In addition to CBT, other cognitive processing therapies have found successful results, particularly cognitive processing therapy treatment has found reductions in symptoms of anxiety, depression, intrusion, avoidance, and numbing (Ahrens & Rexford, 2016)

Other treatment interventions that have found some success are group therapies. Group therapy has been linked to significant reductions in levels of anxiety and depression for incarcerated youth (Biggam & Power, 2002). Group therapy has also found positive results for incarcerated women with histories of abuse, in particular the therapy demonstrated reductions in symptoms of post-traumatic stress disorder (Bradley & Follingstad, 2003). Dialectical Behavioral Therapy (DBT) is another psychological treatment, which has found results indicating significant reductions in aggression (Shelton, Sampl, Kesten, Zhang, & Trestman, 2009). However, not all the research has found supportive findings (see Wilson, 1990; Zlotnick, Johnson, & Najavits, 2009), resulting in a collection of evidence for these interventions that is mixed.

One final psychological treatment intervention to discuss was determined one of the top evidence areas of treating mental health in prisons, this treatment is called integrated dual disorders. Integrated dual disorders treatment targets issues of mental health and substance abuse at the same time. Both the substance abuse and mental health treatments are integrated together, as opposed to treating them separately (Morgan et al., 2012). A review of the research studying integrated therapy finds the treatment to be highly effective, particularly at reducing trauma symptoms and substance abuse (Torchalla, Nosen, Rostam, & Allen, 2012), and finds the treatment to produce better outcomes in comparison to segregated treatments (Sterling, Chi, & Hinman, 2011).

Pharmacologic Therapy

Collaborative psychopharmacology is one of the top evidenced areas of treating inmates with MHD to date. Few would argue against the effects that psychotropic medication produces for those with a MHD (Morgan et al., 2012). While the number of trials examining the impact of a variety of medications has been particularly low (Fazel et al., 2016), there has been several evaluations providing strong supportive evidence for reductions of a variety of mental health diagnoses. Several studies have found positive effects for treating ADHD with the use of osmotic-release oral system (OROS) methylphenidate. The evaluations found the treatments to significantly improve ADHD, reducing symptom severity and global functioning (Ginsberg & Lindefors, 2012), and even reducing risk for relapse to substance use (Konstenius et al., 2014). Research has also found adherence to medication is imperative for inmates with MHD, particular for Bipolar Disorder. Utilizing an implementation plan that pairs baseline adherence, appropriate time in treatment, and biweekly symptom severity increases the positive impact of the medication (Ehret et al., 2013). Overall, work with medication within prisons is limited. In particular future research needs to focus on researching the impact of commonly prescribed psychotropic medication in this setting (Fazel et al., 2016).

The Crisis Intervention Team Model

To improve police contact with individuals with MHD, the Crisis Intervention model was developed in 1988 (Compton, Broussard, Munetz, Oliva, & Watson, 2011). Crisis Intervention Teams (CIT) were developed as a police-based program intended to reduce violent encounters between individuals with MHD and the police. CIT is collaborative effort between law enforcement, advocates, and mental health communities. The main goal of CIT is to improve safety for the police officer, subject, and community. Safety can be achieved through the comprehensive mental health training on the part of the police officer, to reduce the use of force and increase referrals to mental health facilities (Compton et al., 2014). To accomplish appropriate diversion of individuals with mental health concerns, officers are trained to refer these individuals to mental health services, for this reason it is encouraged for police department and psychiatric emergency services partnerships to be formed.

The CIT model involves 40 hours of training for specialized officers, mental health professionals, family advocates, and consumer groups (Compton et al., 2011). The training develops skills to improve officer response to mental illness by improving identification and response to signs and symptoms of mental illness, improved de-escalation skills, appropriate dispositions, and knowledge of local resources and the law. Once training is complete, the police officer is a specialized first responder to dispatches involving individuals with mental health concerns (1). These trained specialist act as a liaison between the initial responder of a call and the mental health system. An advantage of attempting to adopt the CIT model to a correctional facility is the abundance of recent literature and support for the training.

The Albuquerque Police Department (APD) modeled their CIT after the creation of the Memphis CIT. In 1999, more than five out-of-state police departments graduated from the Albuquerque program, and at the time the CIT made-up one-fourth of the field patrol (Bowers & Pettit, 2001). Despite the age of the evaluation and the increased use of CIT in the modern police department, it is important to review one of the first CIT evaluations.

Overall Bower and Pettit (2001) report that there were impressive results after gathering three years' worth of data regarding the effectiveness of the Albuquerque program. In that time, the CIT responded to more than 3,200 calls and transported individuals with a mental health issue to a mental health facility in just under half of those calls. Additionally, just over one percent of the calls resulted in an injury to the civilian (Bower & Pettit, 2001).

A six-year longitudinal study was conducted between 1998 and 2004 in the Akron Police Department. During this time, there were more than 1.5 million calls for service, 10,000 of which were calls for service that was related to mental disturbances (Teller, Munetz, Gil, & Ritter, 2006). There were seven actions which an officer was likely to respond: transport to psychiatric services; transports to other treatment facilities; arrest and transport to jail; formal interaction where transport to jail was unnecessary; transportation to another location; no police interaction; and actions which were taken but are unknown (Teller et al., 2006).

After the implementation of the CIT, the rate in which citizens were arrested and taken to jail decreased slightly and officers who were on the CIT were more likely than non-CIT officers to have taken individuals with a MHD to jail (Teller et al., 2006). However, during mental health calls for service, CIT officers were more likely than non-CIT officers to transport an individual with a MHD to an emergency psychiatric facility but were less likely to transport them to another location (including other treatment facilities or a residence) (Teller et al., 2006).

Ritter, Teller, Marcussen, Munetz, & Teasdale (2011) conducted a study based on the characteristics of the officer dispatch team in Seattle, Washington (the Seattle Police Department,) to determine if there was a relationship between the dispatchers and the action officers would take once they arrived on scene. To this end, researchers gathered official records on the interactions between police officers once arriving on the scene, the coding process of the call, and the interaction between dispatch and the officers (Ritter et al., 2011). Ritter and colleagues (2011) analyzed 2,174 officer reports when the officer described responding to a call for service and interacted with a person perceived to have a MHD. Foregoing the level of training the responding officer possessed, the models' (likelihood of transportation) were different depending on whether the call was specific about a mental illness (more likely to be transported to a treatment facility) or the way in which the call was dispatched (Ritter et al., 2011). Their results indicate that there are unknown results when examining whether an individual assessment from a CIT (on-scene) is related to the dispatch code; and, consequently, whether the person was transported to jail or a treatment facility.

There also has been a more recent study on whether crisis intervention teams increase the linkage between police departments and mental health resources, and if CIT decreases the use of force between police and citizens (Watson et al., 2010). Unlike the other studies examined in this chapter, Watson sampled districts and personnel for comparison between the systems. In total, there were 333 officers invited to participate in the study. The results of Watson's (2010) study suggest that while controlling for district, training, and personal officer characteristics, individuals on the CIT were 18 percent more likely to direct citizens to some type of service than those without the training. However, being a CIT officer did not have a significant direct effect on referral to services. Instead, it largely depended on how the citizen interacted with the CIT officers, and whether the officer had a positive outlook on the available mental health resources (Watson et al., 2010). With regards to the use of force variable, there were no significant results for a decrease in use of force, regardless of the officers' training, but there was a difference among districts. Watson (2010) speculates that because of the increased levels of mental health resources and CIT in those two districts, the saturation of potential exposure to CIT training could be high and explain the difference between districts.

Despite the overwhelming positive results that CITs have received, in terms of effectiveness, it still is difficult to say whether they "work" definitively. One reason this is so difficult is because of the lack of empirical evidence that looks specifically at the effectiveness of multiple outcomes. More so, most studies have been conducted looking at the training or police perceptions of CIT, with few studies looking at a change in arrest rates. It is likely that as CIT continues to become popular there will be an increased rate of research evaluations. Before the discussion of adopting CIT as a correctional strategy, we have included a brief explanation of theoretical support for using CIT with inmates with MHD.

Theoretical Framework

Peplau's theory of interpersonal relations offer concepts which have since shaped the strategies nurses use to deliver treatment to patients who are facing a varying range of dilemmas (Peplau, 1997). The theory was introduced during the late 1940s and early 1950s, focusing on the interpersonal relationships developed between nursing staff and their clients. Peplau (1992) suggests that while her theory of interpersonal relations is useful among general nurse practitioners, the theory is the most effective in psychiatric nursing because individuals with MHD typically have a difficult time with communication and relatedness with other people (Thelander, 1997). Thelander (1997) describes his success using Peplau's theory of interpersonal relations in a psychiatric hospital across a multitude of diagnoses, including schizophrenia, major depression, and borderline personality disorders. These diagnoses usually are referred to as serious mental illnesses (SMI). While these individual's make-up a relatively small percentage of the general population, individuals with SMI make-up 25% to 33% of homeless individuals (Davis et al., 2012) and 16% of the jail and prison population.

Due to the success of using Peplau's theory of interpersonal relations in a clinic setting, we submit the focal aspects of the theory can be applied by correctional officers during interaction with inmates with MHD and crisis situations. Participant observation, as opposed to spectator observation, includes collecting information on the observer's behavior, the behavior of the observed, and noting the interaction which happens between the two individuals; this is one of the most important aspect of interpersonal relations (Peplau, 1992; 1997). Peplau (1992) goes on to explain the importance of taking in the person's verbal and nonverbal language and taking the time to collect as much information as possible. Following the initial observation, officers, using interpersonal relations, should be deliberate in their wording, as this step of the invention process is critical (Beeber, 2010). CIT correctional officers are chosen because of their superior communications skills, in which using the verbal inputs, deliberate wording of Peplau's theory of interpersonal relations can be incorporated during their interactions with inmate MHD.

Officers who can identify individuals who are in a crisis can begin using verbal language and nonverbal language, such as approaching in a non-aggressive manner, to build trust. Finally, it should be noted that the main implementation of this theory is in laboratory, hospital, or clinical settings because of the length of time needed to breach some of these concepts of the theory (Courey, Martsolf, Draucker, & Strickland, 2008; Thelander, 1997). While it may be difficult for correctional officers to establish the same intense change in behavior patterns, it is plausible that officers can use components of the theory to enhance CIT training. More importantly, the theory's overarching components are the facilitation of problem-solving skills, therapeutic interactions, and investing time and energy into the relationship. These components directly overlap with the goals, and approaches used by officers with CIT training (Bower & Pettit, 2001).

Crisis Intervention Team Model in Corrections

To date, adaptation of the CIT model into the correctional setting is relatively limited despite coming up infrequently in training manuals, program proposals, and academic journals since 2005. After being featured at the 1999 White House Conference on Mental Health, CIT was accepted and replicated nationwide; though it still took six years for the same model to adapt to correctional settings. The National Alliance on Mental Illness (NAMI) spearheaded a pilot study using the CIT model for correctional facilities in Maine (Cattabriga, Deprez, Kinner, Louie, & Lumb, 2007). Before the implementation of the CIT, NAMI conducted a pre-evaluation to determine the attitudes, approaches, and feelings of necessity towards the new program. Similar to studies conducted on police, correctional officers reported not feeling prepared to interact with inmates with MHD, previously having inadequate training and not having resources to de-escalate situations (Ruiz & Miller, 2004; Sellers et al., 2005). Following the pilot study, another attitudinal evaluation was given to the correctional officers. Again, like police officers, correctional officers reported feeling more comfortable handling situations when individuals with a MHD were involved, more understanding towards mental illness, and the ability to recognize maladaptive behaviors.

Before exploring the possibility of success for the CIT model being used in corrections, it is important to analyze the functionality of the program. To that end, there are a number of core elements that the NIC (2010) reports as playing a key role in CIT. Aside from the program itself, common core elements described by the NIC and other organizations which have implemented CIT, are helping officers to identify and understand psychiatric signs and symptoms; training officers to use de-escalation techniques; providing resources for correctional officers which can be easily accessed in case of a crisis; networking the officers with mental health service providers; and administer the initial training, as well as continuing training and consultation (Cattabriga et al., 2007; Dochetry, 2017; NIC, 2010). Generally, speaking most CIT models in a correctional setting have these core elements; however, some programs have more core elements or fewer elements than what we mentioned here.

Example of CIT Role Playing modified from the National Institute of Corrections program Crisis Intervention Teams: A Frontline Response to Mental Illness in Corrections [Lesson plans and participant's manual] (NIC, 2010).

Corrections Based Scenarios –

Scenario 1:

An inmate is in their cell, alone. Lunch was distributed and the officer comes to collect the tray from John, a 50-year-old, male inmate. The officer notices John did not touch his food, pacing the floor and mumbling about "the lights being too bright and angry."

Role Player: Inmate John

You have now missed breakfast and lunch for the second day in a row. You are very hungry but are worried that the food has been poisoned by the correctional officers, and the prison is trying to distract your thoughts about poison by forcing radio waves into your cell. You were diagnosed with schizophrenia in your early 20s and have been off your medication for a few weeks. The lights appear to be getting brighter every time you think about eating the food, as a way to remind you about the poison. You spot an unopened bag of chips on the officer's desk and want that because it is sealed.

Role Player: Officer

It is lunchtime as you go around to collect the inmate's trays. When you approach John's cell, you notice he has not eaten his lunch for the second day in a row. He is pacing around his cell talking about radio waves and the bright lights, noting that the lights are no brighter than normal. You begin talking to John to figure out why he is not eating his food.

An organization starts developing their CIT program by first identifying key community stakeholders including local families, and mental health service providers who would be interested in sharing their experiences, recommendations, role playing, and hands-on training (Cattabriga et al., 2007). By using these key stakeholders in the training, the program can focus on changing attitudes, behaviors, and responses correctional officers have toward inmates with MHD. Role playing is an essential component of the training; helping officers respond to inmates with a mental health disorder more appropriately. Essentially, reducing the danger, escalation, and tension seen in correctional facility crisis situations.

Another main element of the program is having officers who are interested in becoming certified in CIT training; however, there are two approaches to this element. A facility wide agenda to get as many officers as possible to take the training or asking for volunteers who want to participate in the training. Research suggests that police officers who volunteer for the CIT training had higher rates of perceiving the program as a success, were more comfortable with interactions when arriving to the scene, and a decreased rate of use of force; this is true for correctional officers, as well (Cattabriga et al., 2007).

One of the largest selling points of CIT are the benefits that follow the successful completion of the program. For one, creating a safer environment for the correctional staff as well as the inmates. Officers report being more comfortable interacting with offenders with MHD, and successfully de-escalating situations where force would have otherwise been used. Additionally, officers report their most frequent source of stress is the threat of violence by inmates and the strain of inmates with MHD can only exacerbate these feelings (Aufderheide, 2012). Secondly, although the data on the effectiveness of CIT in correctional facilities is limited, the studies which have been done suggest this is a promising strategy which should continue to be implemented throughout the country.

To date, there are two main studies which focus on the effectiveness of CIT (Cattabriga et al., 2007; Davidson, 2016), and a few pilot studies (Aufderheide, 2012; BetaGov, 2017; Canada, Watson, & O'Kelley, 2017); however, the local and small-scale studies are not adequately reported. The Memphis Crisis Intervention Team (CIT) training curriculum for police and correctional officers was evaluated. Utilizing a panel design, 179 police officers and 100 correctional officers were surveyed. The research design included a pre and post survey to examine the impact of the CIT training on the officers measuring for several objectives. The officer-level objectives that were targeted are: increased knowledge of mental illness, improved self-efficacy when responding to mental health crises, and enhance perceptions of verbal de-escalation abilities. A central goal of the research was to determine whether CIT training was similarly effective for both police and correctional officers. The results of the survey found training to effectively increase all of the objectives for both police and correctional officers; however, these results appeared to decline by the one-month follow-up. For each objective, the CIT training produce significant positive effects on the post intervention survey, with self-efficacy increasing by 16 percent, knowledge of mental illness by 10 percent and perceptions of verbal de-escalation by 6 percent (Davidson, 2016). The findings indicate that CIT training is effective for both police and correctional officer; however, it is imperative that models be tailored to better fit either group. Future research needs to explore this area to determine how the difference in job characteristics may inhibit or improve CIT training.

Pennsylvania's Department of Corrections instituted a pilot project to implement CIT training within two Residential Treatment Unit pods within SCI Greene. The design included CIT training for all staff in the intervention conditions. When compared to the control units who followed normal procedures, the intervention group trained in CIT had significant differences in informal resolutions and grievances. The intervention pods had a lower percentage of informally resolved misconducts and less grievances reported. This pilot examination found positive preliminary results which indicate that further implementation of CIT training would be beneficial. Further research, particularly with a randomized controlled trial design is warranted (BetaGov, 2017).

Another evaluation of CIT training implemented into the correctional setting evaluated the NAMI Maine expansion Crisis Intervention Team (CIT). The expansion CIT training program was developed to educate both police and correctional officers to properly recognize and respond to mental health problems. The expansion program builds upon the pilot project they completed in 2005. The expansion included seven counties, in which CIT training was initiated in a week-long session. To accomplish the goals set out by the project, NAMI made a point to provide ongoing support to the sites. To collect the data survey were employed as well as focus groups with correctional officer and stakeholder interviews. There were several outcomes measured, they can be sorted into three domains: implementation, officer perceptions, and CIT program outcomes. To measure the implementation, they utilized the interviews and incident forms. Likert scales were used to assess officers' perceptions on satisfaction and self-efficacy regarding training, these surveys were implemented at both a pre and post period, they also utilized the focus groups for officer perceptions pre-implementation. Finally, the program outcomes evaluated the officer behaviors, specifically seclusion/restraint incidents, and rates of injury among CIT documented.

The Maine projected produced compelling results. After intervention, officers felt more self-confidence when encountering those displaying signs of mental illness, recognizing signs and symptoms, and de-escalating situations. The officers also felt better prepared to handle people with MHD during a crisis. Job satisfaction due to administrative support increased post CIT training, as well as having the skills and knowledge to resolve crises. De-escalation practices increased drastically, with 54.9 percent of the CIT incidents reported using verbal de-escalation, compared to only 25.3 percent reporting use of force (restrains or chemical agents). Overall, the main findings are supportive of the impact of CIT training in both law enforcement and corrections. The main areas CIT appeared to benefit the most were broadening understanding of MHD, higher degree of comfort in interactions with people displaying signs of MHD, increased self confidence in their abilities, and increased referral to a provider or service from CIT incidents (Cattabriga et al., 2007).

As mentioned throughout this chapter, there are challenges to implementing CIT in a correctional setting. For example, getting correctional officers and leadership to buy into the program. Any training or effective program comes from top-down communications indicating that leadership is devoted and feels there is importance in learning more about, and how to interact with, individuals with MHD (Aufderheide, 2012). However, there are many incentives which are provided to leadership in correctional facilities to try CIT training; including offering the training for free, or at a reduced cost (PA DOC, 2013). Training was also well received by administration when NAMI and training organizations were supportive, easy to get ahold of, and willing to answer questions.

There may still be push back from the correctional staff if mandated to participate. Though, it should be mentioned, even when officers did not volunteer for the training there is a belief by researchers, and program stakeholders that the training is valuable to all officers regardless of temperaments, interest levels, and backgrounds (Cattabriga et al., 2007). Additionally, Davison (2016) reports specific CIT program may be even more beneficial and well received by catering specifically to the unique challenges faced by correctional officers when responding to inmates experiencing mental health crises. The logistics of training an entire correctional staff also presents a problem, which supports the approach of asking for volunteers. Given the 40 hours of training necessary to cover the CIT curriculum, to have all staff members participate in a large facility means a lot of flexible hours, adequate staff to supervise inmates at all times, and completion of all authorization paperwork.

The last significant challenge faced by correctional facilities is finding the balance and appropriate adaptation between the policing CIT models and correctional CIT models. The key elements remain the same between both programs, increased understanding, de-escalation techniques, risk for injury, and collaboration between officers and mental health resources (Canada, Watson, & O'Kelley, 2017). However, being in the correctional setting presents an interesting dynamic to which police officers are not subjective. For example, police officers work in the public sphere, meaning resources, if available, are more readily available. Imagine a police officer arrives to a scene and calls a crisis resource who can come to the scene and assist to de-escalate the situation. The same resource would be difficult to access in a correctional setting due to the safety regulations coming into the prison.

Additionally, though this difference is twofold, correctional officers have more regular and continued contact with inmates with MHDs. To be sure, correctional officers should not replace mental health care workers, namely counselors, psychiatrists, or psychologists; however, this is the situation in which they find themselves. One downside to CIT for police officers is the lack of familiarity and consistent interaction, unless there is a dispatch system which links specific CIT officers to specific cases. Correctional officers' benefit from being able to create relationships and trust with inmates who have a MHD. Nevertheless, the consistent interaction with these inmates, and the pressure of acting as a liaison for the mental health system can be a daunting task, especially when there is a lack of adequate training (Canada, Watson, & O'Kelley, 2017).

DISCUSSION

Largely due to the deinstitutionalization of mental health services in hospitals, and the increasing criminalization of mental illness, the United States correctional system continues to be solution to deal with individuals with MHD. Throughout history, our prison system has been altogether under resourced and unprepared to handle the intense rehabilitation process. Recent programs and policies aimed to decrease the rate of inmates with MHD having varying levels of success and effectiveness. With some strategies, such as solitary confinement, potentially causing further harm to a prisoner's mental health. While other interventions, such as psychological and pharmacological treatments, can reduce symptoms of various mental health diagnoses. A promising step towards creating a safer environment and reducing the need for unsuccessful strategies (see solitary confinement) is to implement CIT in a correctional setting. With this training, staff will be better equipped to recognize and respond to inmates with MHD or those displaying signs of mental illness.

CIT literature continues to grow as more police departments across the United States are looking for solutions to help those suffering from MHD and keeping officers safe when responding to calls for service. CIT training for officers was a clear first step to help divert individuals with MHD away from incarceration and into appropriate treatment. What is interesting though, is the lack of focus on using CIT in a correctional setting; despite the "idea" showing up sporadically over the last 14 years. Based on the limited but successful research findings, there is clear a constellation of benefits from implementing CIT training for correctional officers. As the pilot studies demonstrate, it is clear that challenges still exist when implementing CIT in corrections. Continued use of positive pharmacological and integrated treatment for inmates with MHD, as well as CIT training for prison staff could produce an evolving standard of approaching treatment for mental health in prisons.

It should be mentioned that even the most successful program(s) during incarceration will ultimately be unsuccessful if the criminal justice system fails to rehabilitate offenders and reduce recidivism rates. This means a successful follow-up and strict program during re-entry for inmates with MHD. Additionally, while in prison, rehabilitation and reform is necessary for successful prison programs to flourish. Though it is important to emphasize the need for continued diversion strategies for individuals with MHD. Mental health courts and CIT for law enforcement are promising approaches that need further implementation and evaluation. Any long-term solution to reform treatment of individuals with MHD will require an approach targeting all aspects of the criminal justice system. Without the follow through and successful diversion strategies, it is likely individuals with MHD will continue to be dumped into local jails and prisons; in which case, we can only hope to do a better job the next time.

REFERENCES

Accordino, M. P., Porter, D. F. & Morse, T. (2001). Deinstitutionalization of persons with severe mental illness: Context and consequences. *Journal of Rehabilitation*, *67*(2), 16-21.

Adams, K. & Ferrandino, J. (2008). Managing mentally ill inmates in prisons. *Criminal Justice and Behavior*, *35*, 913-927.

Ahalt, C., Haney, C., Rios, S., Fox, M. P., Farabee, D. & Williams, B. (2017). Reducing the use and impact of solitary confinement in corrections. *International Journal of Prisoner Health*, *13*(1), 41-48.

Ahrens, J. & Rexford, L. (2002). Cognitive processing therapy for incarcerated adolescents with PTSD. *Journal of Aggression, Maltreatment & Trauma*, *6*(1), 201-216.

Akins, S., Burkhardt, B., Lanfear, C., Amorim, M. & Stevens, K. (2014). *Law enforcement response to people with mental illnesses in Benton County*. Retrieved from http://www.co.benton.or.us/da/wcjc/documents.php Google Scholar.

American Psychiatric Association. (2013). *Diagnostic and statistical manual of mental disorders* (5th ed.). Arlington, VA: American Psychiatric Publishing.

Arrigo, B. A. & Bullock, J. L. (2008). The psychological effects of solitary confinement on prisoners in supermax units: Reviewing what we know and recommending what should change. *International Journal of Offender Therapy and Comparative Criminology*, *52*(6), 622-640.

Aufderheide, D. (2012). Crisis intervention teams: Improving outcomes for inmates with mental illness. *Correct Care*, *26*, 10-12.

Beeber, L. (2010). Letter to the editor. *Journal of the American Psychiatric Nurses Association*, *16*(4), 1.

Benton, D. & Masciadrelli, B. P. (2013). Legitimacy of correction as a mental health care provider: Perspectives from U.S. and European systems. *Journal of the Institute of Justice and International Studies*, *13*, 1–15.

Bergner, R. M. & Bunford, N. (2017). Mental disorder is a disability concept, not a behavioral one. *Philosophy, Psychiatry, & Psychology*, *24*(1), 25-40.

BetaGov. (2017). *Crisis intervention training (CIT).* The Marron Institute of Urban Management. New York University: New York, NY. Retrieved from https://marroninstitute.nyu.edu/uploads/content/CIT_Snapshot_.pdf.

Biggam, F. H. & Power, K. G. (2002). A controlled, problem-solving, group-based intervention with vulnerable incarcerated young offenders. *International Journal of Offender Therapy and Comparative Criminology*, *46*(6), 678-698.

Birmingham, L. (2003). The mental health of prisoners. *Advances in Psychiatric Treatment*, *9*(3), 191-199.

Bittner, E. (1967). Police discretion in emergency apprehension of mentally ill persons. *Social Problems*, *14*(3), 278-292.

Blitz, C. L., Wolff, N. & Shi, J. (2008). Physical victimization in prison: The role of mental illness. *International Journal of Law and Psychiatry*, *31*(5), 385-393.

Blumstein, A. (2018). Science and technology and the President's Crime Commission: Past and future. *Criminology & Public Policy*, *17*(2), 271-282.

Borum, R., Deane, M. W., Steadman, H. J. & Morrissey, J. (1998). Police perspectives on responding to mentally ill people in crisis: Perceptions of program effectiveness. *Mental Health Law & Policy Faculty Publications*, *16*, 393-405.

Bower, D. L. & Pettit, G. W. (2001). Albuquerque Police Department's crisis intervention team: A report card. *FBI Law Enforcement Bulletin*, *70*(2), 1-6.

Bradley, R. G. & Follingstad, D. R. (2003). Group therapy for incarcerated women who experienced interpersonal violence: A pilot study. *Journal of Traumatic Stress*, *16*(4), 337-340.

Cattabriga, G., Deprez, R., Kinner, A., Louie, M. & Lumb, R. (2007). Crisis Intervention Team (CIT) training for correctional officers. *The Center for Health Policy, Planning, and Research*.

Canada, K. E., Watson, A. & O'Kelley, S. (2017, August). Utilizing CIT in prison: Impact, barriers, and achievements. *Presented at the CIT International*, Ft. Lauderdale, FL.

Chaimowitz, G. (2011). The criminalization of people with mental illness. *The Canadian Journal of Psychiatry*, *57*(2), 1-6.

Compton, W. M., Thomas, Y. F., Stinson, F. S. & Grant, B. F. (2007). Prevalence, correlates, disability, and comorbidity of dsm-iv drug abuse and dependence in the United States. *Archives of General Psychiatry*, *64*(5), 566-576.

Compton, M. T., Broussard, B., Munetz, M. R., Oliva, J. R. & Watson, A. C. (2011). *The Crisis Intervention Team (CIT) Model of collaboration between law enforcement and mental health*. Nova Science Publishers.

Compton, M. T., Bakeman, R., Broussard, B., Hankerson-Dyson, D., Husbands, L., Krishan, S. & Watson, A. C. (2014). The police-based crisis intervention team (CIT) model: I. Effects on officers' knowledge, attitudes, and skills. *Psychiatric Services*, *65*(4), 517-522.

Compton, M. T., Bakeman, R., Broussard, B., Hankerson-Dyson, D., Husbands, L., Krishan, S. & Watson, A. C. (2014). The police-based crisis intervention team (CIT) model: II. Effects on level of force and resolution, referral, and arrest. *Psychiatric Services*, *65*(4), 523-529.

Courey, T. J., Martsolf, D. S., Brauker, C. D. & Strickland, K. B. (2008). Hildegard peplau's theory and the health care encounters of survivors of sexual violence. *Journal of the American Psychiatric Nurse Association*, *14*, (2), 136-143.

Davidson, M. L. (2016). A Criminal Justice System–Wide Response to Mental Illness: Evaluating the Effectiveness of the Memphis Crisis Intervention Team Training Curriculum Among Law Enforcement and Correctional Officers. *Criminal Justice Policy Review*, *27*(1), 46-75.

Davis, L., Fulginiti, A. Kriegal, L. & Brekke, J. (2012). Deinstitutionalization? Where have all people gone? *Curr Psychiatry Rep*, *14*, 259-269. doi:10.1007/s11920-012-0271-1

Docherty, J. P. (2017). *Creating new hope for mental illness and the criminal justice system*. National Alliance on Mental Illness. Retrieved from https://www.nami.org/ Blogs/ NAMI-Blog/ October-2017/ Creating-New-Hope-for-Mental-Illness-and-the-Crimi.

Ehret, M. J., Shelton, D., Barta, W., Trestman, R., Maruca, A., Kamath, J. & Golay, L. (2013). Medication adherence among female inmates with bipolar disorder: Results from a randomized controlled trial. *Psychological Services*, *10*(1), 106.

Fazel, S., Hayes, A. J., Bartellas, K., Clerici, M. & Trestman, R. (2016). Mental health of prisoners: prevalence, adverse outcomes, and interventions. *The Lancet Psychiatry*, *3*(9), 871-881.

Felson, R. B., Silver, E. & Remster, B. (2012). Mental disorder and offending in prison. *Criminal Justice and Behavior*, *39*(2), 125-143.

Fisher, W. H., Silver, E. & Wolff, N. (2006). Beyond criminalization: Toward a criminologically informed framework for mental health policy and services research. *Administration and Policy in Mental Health and Mental Health Services Research*, *33*, 544-557. doi:10.1007/s10488-006-0072-0.

Flynn, S., Rodway, C. & Appleby, L. (2013). Serious violence by people with mental illness. *National Clinical Survey*, *29*(8), 1438-1458.

Forrester, A., Chiu, K., Dove, S. & Parrott, J. (2010). Prison health-care wings: Psychiatry's forgotten frontier? *Criminal Behaviour and Mental Health*, *20*(1), 51-61.

Gater, L. (2007). Trends in treating mentally ill inmates. *Corrections Forum*, *16*, 13–19.

Geiman, D. (2007). Managing inmates with mental health disorders. *Corrections Today*, *69*, 22–23.

Gert, Bernard. & Culver, Charles M. (2004). Defining mental disorder. In Jennifer Radden (ed.), *The Philosophy of Psychiatry: A Companion*. Oxford: Oxford University Press.

Ginsberg, Y. & Lindefors, N. (2012). Methylphenidate treatment of adult male prison inmates with attention-deficit hyperactivity disorder: randomised double-blind placebo-controlled trial with open-label extension. *The British Journal of Psychiatry*, *200*(1), 68-73.

Goldman, H. H. & Grob, G. N. (2006). Defining 'mental illness' in mental health policy. *Health Affairs*, *25*(3), 737-749. doi:10.1377/hlthaff.25.3.737.

Haney, C. (2009). The social psychology of isolation: Why solitary confinement is psychologically harmful. *Prison Service Journal*, *181*(1), 12-20.

Haney, C. (2018). Restricting the use of solitary confinement. *Annual Review of Criminology*, *1*, 285-310.

Harcourt, B. E. (2011). Reducing mass incarceration: Lessons from the deinstitutionalization of mental hospitals in the 1960s. *University of Chicago Public Law and Legal Theory Working Paper*, *335*, 1-32.

Jachimowski, K. G. (2018). The relationship between mentally disordered inmates, victimization, and violence. *Journal of Offender Rehabilitation*, *57*(1), 47-65. doi:10.1080/10509674.2017.1416438.

Jennings, W. G. & Hudak, E. J. (2005). Police responses to persons with mental illness. In R. G. Dunham & G. P. Alpert (Eds.), *Critical Issues in Policing: Contemporary Readings* (5th ed., pp. 115-128). Long Grove, IL: Waveland.

Kaba, F., Lewis, A., Glowa-Kollisch, S., Hadler, J., Lee, D., Alper, H. & Venters, H. (2014). Solitary confinement and risk of self-harm among jail inmates. *American Journal of Public Health*, *104*(3), 442-447.

Kessler, R. C., Chui, W. T., Demler, O. & Walters, E. E. (2005). Prevalence, severity, and comorbidity of 12-month dsm-iv disorders in the national comorbidity survey replication. *Arch Gen Psychiatry*, *62*, 617-627.

Khodayarifard, M., Shokoohi-Yekta, M. & Hamot, G. E. (2010). Effects of individual and group cognitive-behavioral therapy for male prisoners in Iran. *International Journal of Offender Therapy and Comparative Criminology*, *54*(5), 743-755.

Kim, D. (2014). Psychiatric deinstitutionalization and prison population growth: A critical literature review and its implications. *Criminal Justice Policy Review*, *27*(1), 3-21. doi: 10.1177/0887403414547043.

Konstenius, M., Jayaram-Lindström, N., Guterstam, J., Beck, O., Philips, B. & Franck, J. (2014). Methylphenidate for attention deficit hyperactivity disorder and drug relapse in criminal offenders with substance dependence: a 24-week randomized placebo-controlled trial. *Addiction*, *109*(3), 440-449.

Lamb, H. R. (1984). Deinstitutionalization and the homeless mentally ill. *Hospital and Community Psychiatry*, *35*(9), 899-907.

Lord, V. B. & Bjerregaard, B. (2014). Helping persons with mental illness: Partnerships between police and mobile crisis units. *Victims and Offenders*, *9*, 455-474. doi:10.1080/15564886.2013.878263.

Lynum, K. S. & Hill, A. M. (2015). Psychiatric services: A platform for mtm. *Journal of Pharmacy Practice*, *28*(1), 13-20. doi: 10.1177/0897190014562352.

McNally, R. J. (2012). *What is mental illness?* Harvard University Press: Cambridge, MA.

Mechanic, D. & Rochefort, D. A. (1990). Deinstitutionalization: An appraisal of reform. *Annu Rev Social*, *16*, 301-327.

Moore, L. D. & Elkavich, A. (2008). Who's using and who's doing time: Incarceration, the war on drugs, and public health. *American Journal of Public Health*, *98*(5), 782-786.

Morgan, R. D., Flora, D. B., Kroner, D. G., Mills, J. F., Varghese, F. & Steffan, J. S. (2012). Treating offenders with mental illness: A research synthesis. *Law and Human Behavior*, *36*(1), 37.

Murphy, K. (2012). Crisis intervention teams and mobile crisis management. *North Carolina Medical Journal*, *73*(3), 200.

Needham-Bennett, H. & Cumming, I. (1995). Waiting for a disaster to happen. *BMJ: British Medical Journal*, *311*(7003), 516.

National Institute of Corrections (NIC). (2010). Crisis intervention teams: A frontline response to mental illness in corrections [Lesson plans and participant's manual]. *National Institute of Corrections (NIC)*. Washington, DC. Accession Number: 024797.

Peplau, H. E. (1992). Interpersonal relations: A theoretical framework for application in nursing practice. *Nursing Science Quarterly*, *5*(1), 13-18.

Peplau, H. E. (1997). Peplau's theory of interpersonal relations. *Nursing Science Quarterly*, *10*(4), 162-167.

Perez, A., Leifman, S. & Estrada, A. (2003). Reversing the criminalization of mental illness. *Crime & Delinquency*, *49*(1), 62-78. doi: 10.1177/0011128702239236.

Pfeiffer, M. B. (2007). Mentally ill inmates face a cruel system. *Corrections Forum*, *16*, 60–62.

Ringhoff, D., Rapp, L. & Robst, J. (2012). The criminalization hypothesis: Practice and policy implications for persons with serious mental illness in the criminal justice system. *Best Practices in Mental Health*, *8*(2), 1-19.

Ritter, C., Teller, J. L., Marcussen, K., Munetz, M. R. & Teasdale, B. (2011). Crisis intervention team officer dispatch, assessment, and disposition: Interactions with individuals with severe mental illness. *Int J Law Psychiatry*, *34*(1), 30-38.

Robinson, J., Sareen, J., Cox, B. J. & Bolton, J. (2009). Self-medication of anxiety disorders with alcohol and drugs: Results from a nationally representative sample. *Journal of Anxiety Disorders*, *23*, 38-45. doi:10.1016/j.janxdis.2008.03.013.

Rochefort, D. A. (1984). Origins of the "third psychiatric revolution": The community mental health centers act of 1963. *Journal of Health Politics, Policy and Law*, *9*(1), 1-29.

Rosenbaum, N. (2010). Street-level psychiatry – A psychiatrist's role with the Albuquerque police department's crisis outreach and support team. *Journal of Police Crisis Negotiations*, *10*, 175-181.

Ruiz, J. & Miller, C. (2004). An exploratory study of Pennsylvania police officers' perceptions of dangerousness and their ability to manage persons with mental illness. *Police Quarterly*, *7*(3), 359-371. doi:10.1177/1098611103258957.

Sellers, C. L., Sullivan, C. J., Veysey, B. M. & Shane, J. M. (2005). Responding to persons with mental illnesses: Police perspectives on specialized and traditional practices. *Behavioral Sciences and the Law*, *23*, 647-657. doi:10.1002/bsi.633.

Shelton, D., Sampl, S., Kesten, K. L., Zhang, W. & Trestman, R. L. (2009). Treatment of impulsive aggression in correctional settings. *Behavioral Sciences & the Law*, *27*(5), 787-800.

Silver, E., Felson, R. B. & Vaneselstine, M. (2008). The relationship between mental health problems and violence among criminal offenders. *Criminal Justice & Behavior*, *35*(4), 405-426.

Slate, R. N., Buffington-Vollum, J. K. & Johnson, W. W. (2013). *The Criminalization of Mental Illness: Crisis and Opportunity for the Justice System* (2nd ed.). Durham, NC: Academic University Press.

Sterling, S., Chi, F. & Hinman, A. (2011). Integrating care for people with co-occurring alcohol and other drug, medical, and mental health conditions. *Alcohol Research & Health*, *33*(4), 338.

Teller, J. L. S., Munetz, M. R., Gil, K. M. & Ritter, C. (006). Crisis intervention team training for police officers responding to mental disturbance calls. *Psychiatric Services*, *57*(2), 232-237.

Thelander, B. L. (1997). The psychotherapy of hildegard peplau in the treatment of people with serious mental illness. *Perspectives in Psychiatric Care*, *33*, (3), 24-32.

Thornton, L. K., Baker, A. L., Lewin, T. J., Kay-Lambkin, F. J., Kavanagh, D., Richmond, R., Kelly, B. & Johnson, M. P. (2012). Reasons for substance use among people with mental disorders. *Addictive Behaviors*, *37*, 427-434. doi:10.1016.j. addbeh.2011.11.039.

Torchalla, I., Nosen, L., Rostam, H. & Allen, P. (2012). Integrated treatment programs for individuals with concurrent substance use disorders and trauma experiences: A systematic review and meta-analysis. *Journal of Substance Abuse Treatment*, *42*(1), 65-77.

Torrey, E. F., Kennard, A. D., Eslinger, D., Lamb, R. & Pavle, J. (2010). *More Mentally Ill Persons Are in Jail and Prisons than Hospitals: A Survey of the States.* Treatment Advocacy Center and National Sheriffs Association.

Varelius, J. (2009). Defining mental disorder in terms of our goals for demarcating mental disorder. *Philosophy, Psychiatry, & Psychology*, *16*(1), 32-52.

Wakefield, J. C. (1992). Disorder as harmful dysfunction: A conceptual critique of DSM-III-R's definition of mental disorder. *Psychological Review*, *99*(2), 232-247.

Watson, A. C., Ottati, V., Morabito, M., Draine, J., Kerr, A. N. & Angell, B. (2010). Outcomes of police contacts with persons with mental illness: The impact of CIT. *Adm Policy Ment Health*, *37*, 302-317.

White, M. C., Chafetz, L., Collins-Bride, G. & Nickens, J. (2006). History of arrest, incarceration and victimization in community-based severely mentally ill. *Journal of Community Health*, *31*, 123–135.

Wilson, G. L. (1990). Psychotherapy with depressed incarcerated felons: A comparative evaluation of treatments. *Psychological Reports*, *67*(3), 1027-1041.

Zlotnick, C., Johnson, J. & Najavits, L. M. (2009). Randomized controlled pilot study of cognitive-behavioral therapy in a sample of incarcerated women with substance use disorder and PTSD. *Behavior Therapy*, *40*(4), 325-336.

In: A Closer Look at Criminal Justice
Editors: J. A. Cooper and K. G. Jachimowski
ISBN: 978-1-53615-782-6

Chapter 11

AGING INMATES: THE GRAYING OF AMERICA'S PRISONS

Selye Lee*
The Department of Criminology, Sociology, and Geography
Arkansas State University, Jonesboro, AR, US

ABSTRACT

In the past three decades, prisons in the United States have experienced rapidly growing numbers of inmates, including elderly inmates. As the number of aging inmates increases, so do facilities and financial expenses to the federal and state prison. This substantial upsurge raises questions regarding the causes and the impact of such a change. Inmates over the age of 55 present unique challenges to the extent they experience age-related adaptions to prison life and special needs. This chapter reviews the causes of the growth in the elderly inmates and focuses on appropriate strategy toward the issues of the aging inmates: decreasing the prison population, saving costs, and retaining public safety. This chapter also offers a perspective for evaluating current and prospective correctional system responses and suggest policies that might benefit the correctional systems as well as the communities.

INTRODUCTION

The prison population in the United States has increased six-fold in the past three decades. Incarcerated inmates over the age of 55 has dramatically grown in high numbers within the country (Williams, Lindquist, Sudore, Strupp, Willmott, & Walter, 2006). As the number of elderly inmates increases, so do facilities and financial expenses to the

* Author's E-mail: serina131@gmail.com.

Federal Bureau of Prisons (FBOP) and the state Department of Corrections (DOC) (Rikard & Rosenberg, 2007). In correctional systems, aging in place for this older population is a rising concern.

Inmates age 55 and older are the fastest rising population in correctional institutions throughout the United States, in part due to the crime control model during the 1980s and 1990s. Mandatory minimums, the increased use of life sentences, and truth-in-sentencing laws have led to a substantial increase in the inmate population (Chiu, 2010). As increasingly stringent policies have led to longer prison sentences, correctional institutions are home to an increasing number of older inmates. Today, correctional systems in the United States are finding the need to make accommodations for the special needs posed by the elderly inmates.

This article seeks to accomplish three goals: 1) to highlight the challenges that aging presents for correctional facilities and elderly prisoners, 2) to discuss how this aging inmates and their unique needs and issues will continue to grow in the United States, and 3) to offer appropriate strategies toward the issues of the aging inmates: decreasing the prison population, saving costs, and retaining public safety. In addition, this article provides details and critiques about the reasons that the current policies have not resulted in the desired impact. Finally, it offers potential alternatives to such policies which would be viable in practice.

Context and Importance of the Problem: The Growth of an Aging Inmate Population

In 1900, the number of people 65 or older were only four percent in the United States. By 2000, the older population grew approximately 13 percent of the overall population (Hooyman & Kiyak, 1999). Due to advances in technology and medical science, life expectancy largely increased from 47 to 78 years over the same period. The number of Americans aged 65 or older will double because baby boomers, who were born between 1946 and 1964, will reshape America's older population (Hooyman & Kiyak, 1999; Rikard & Rosenberg, 2007). By the time all the baby boomers (approximately 88 million) will have turned 65, about one in five adults will be in that age group in the United States.

Unfortunately, rapid increases in life expectancy have not bypassed inmate populations. A number of factors contribute to the growth of the aging inmate population, however the incarceration rate and the elderly inmate population they comprise will increase dramatically (Cole & Gertz, 2013; Rikard & Rosenberg, 2007).

During the past 30 years, as mentioned in the introduction, the population of elderly inmates has been rapidly increasing in the United States (Cole & Gertz, 2013; Moraff, 2013; Pew Charitable Trusts, 2013). According to a report from Human Rights Watch released in 2012, between 1995 and 2010, the number of people 55 or older – the official threshold age – grew to 63 percent of the overall population (Moraff, 2013). In 2015, the Federal Bureau of Prisons data also revealed that the numbers of the older inmate population (50 and older) are growing at a fast rate (cf. Office of the Inspector General, 2016). For instance, the number of inmate population age 65 to 69 grew 41% of the overall population; inmate population age 70 to 74 grew 51%; inmate population age 75 to 79 grew 43%; and inmate population age 80 and over grew 76%. Some studies have estimated that older inmate population will be increasing 21% to 33% in the United State by 2020 (Cole & Gertz, 2013).

More specifically, in many states, the number of older inmates has been growing dramatically. In California, for example, the population of elderly prisoners, which represented 4% of the population in 1994, will represent an increase of more than 200% by 2020 (Cole & Gertz, 2013). In Virginia, the elderly inmate population grew approximately six-fold, from 715 to 4,678, from 1990 through 2008 (Chiu, 2010; Sieff, 2010). One of the states with the fastest increasing rates of older inmates was North Carolina (Price, 2006). The number of older prisoners who are 50 and older increased by 61% to 3,490, while the general inmate population grew by 16%, from 2001 to 2005 (Chiu, 2010; Price, 2006).

In recent year, scholars and practitioners have turned their attention to this significant increase in the portions of aging inmates. As mentioned above, the number of older inmates is growing much faster than the younger inmate population, raising concerns about the social and economic implications of a greater portions of prisoners age 55 and older in state and federal prison. Elderly inmates cost much more to house than do the general inmate as a result of increased medical needs. Due to the increasing number of elderly inmates, state, federal, and private correctional facilities face substantial financial burden (Cole & Gertz, 2013; Rikard & Rosenberg, 2007).

Discussion of the issues with older inmate must begin with a review of the changes in correctional policy and sentencing in the 21st century and how these changes impact the older inmate population and the criminal justice system in general.

The Crime Control Model in Criminal Justice

Until the mid-1970s, rehabilitation was the primary goal of correctional policy and sentencing in the United States. Many inmates were encouraged to resolve psychological issues and to develop work-related skills through different rehabilitative programs. Prisoners received court sentences that they could "prescribe a cure" through treatment in the correctional system (Cole & Gertz, 2013; Griset, 1991). After the socially turbulent 1960s, however, corrections and sentencing practices moved toward a crime-control model that focused on punishment as the main function of the prison system in the United

States. During the 1980s and 1990s, this crime-control model of criminal justice became prevalent (Cole & Gertz, 2013).

The changes in correctional policy and sentencing practices can be characterized by the emphasis on mainly four goals. The four primary goals of corrections and sentencing include deterrence, retribution, incapacitation, and rehabilitation. First, deterrence is based on the belief that prisoners are discouraged from committing criminal behaviors due to a rational calculation on the cost of punishment. There are two different types of deterrence: general and specific deterrence. General deterrence focuses on the impact of the threat of legal punishment on the public at large by making examples of specific deviants. On the other hand, specific deterrence focuses on the impact of the legal punishment on those being charged with a crime to discourage future criminal behavior. Second, retribution refers to just deserts; people who commit crimes deserves to be punished. Incapacitation deprives people of the opportunity to break the law because they are physically detained in prison and isolated from the society. Lastly, rehabilitation emphasizes the change of prisoners' criminogenic thinking and behavior by offering rehabilitative treatments, so they do not continue to break the law. Though correctional policy and sentencing practices often address these goals in practice, as mentioned, the primary goal has changed considerably during the past three decades. As the goals of sentencing have been changing from rehabilitation toward incapacitation, the number of people who are under correctional supervision has dramatically increased.

The Sentencing Reform Act of 1984, part of the Comprehensive Crime Control Act of 1984, offers evidence of the shift from the change of correctional policy and sentencing practices from rehabilitation toward incapacitation (King & Mauer, 2001; Rausch, 1996). The Sentencing Reform Act abolished federal parole and created the United States Sentencing Commission. Judicial discretion in sentencing was virtually eliminated; thus, prosecutors or judges were not able to consider such factors as perceived risk to the community, health conditions, or age. The Sentencing Reform Act implemented maximum terms of imprisonment and specific terms of incarceration for specific federal offenses such as drug offenses.

By the 1990s, about 13 states had passed sentencing reform acts (Flynn, Flanagan, Greenwood, & Krisberg, 1995; Mackenzie, 2001). The Federal Violent Crime Control and Law Enforcement Act was enacted in 1994. The act allocated approximately $9.7 billion for expending prison systems and $6 billion for crime prevention programs, including those to counteract violence against women. This shift in the dominant rationale for sentencing keeps more criminals detained for longer terms of incarceration, contributing to rapid growth in the proportion of aging inmates (Auerhahn, 2002).

Numerous factors have contributed to the dramatic growth of the aging inmates. However, studies suggest that the explosion of the aging inmates (approximately 675,000 arrests of older inmates every year) is a consequence of the aforementioned crime control model during the 1980s and 1990s (Williams et al., 2006). This repercussion of the policy has led to a considerable number of aging inmates in the United States. Because of policies in states with longer sentencing, including mandatory minimums, the increased use of life sentences, and truth-in-sentencing laws, the aging inmate population has increased and will constantly grow (Chiu, 2010).

Three-strikes laws, passed in the 1920s and 1930s and were adopted by many states and the federal government in the 1990s, mandate longer terms of confinement for habitual offenders deemed to pose a threat to the community (Tonry, 2009). According to the Sentencing Project, for example, California's three-strikes law played a role in increasing the aging of the California prison system (King & Mauer, 2001, p. 4).

In 1994, California enacted its Three Strikes Sentencing Law. With this law, an increase of approximately 50,000 prisoners were incarcerated in prison by 2001 (King & Mauer, 2001, p. 3). The third conviction did not need to be serious or violent crime to receive a life sentence with the California's three-strikes law. About 60 percent of the third-strike offenders had been convicted of non-serious and non-violent offenses three years after the three-strikes law was implemented (Males & Macallair, 1999). Although one of the main goals of the California's three-strikes would reduce levels of serious and violent crime, little research shows that the laws have had any positive impact (Zimring, Hawkins, & Kamin, 2003). Some empirical evidence shows that the laws actually increased some crime rates and led the increased of the aging inmate population (Males & Macallair, 1999).

In addition to the three-strikes law, recent research points out the increased use of life-without-parole (LWOP) statues or life sentences as the major contributor to the rapid growth of the aging inmate population (Nellis & King, 2009). Many states started using LWOP since the early 1970s and the use of LWOP considerably increased (Nellis & King, 2009). The number of the prisoners who received the life sentences grew by more than 100 percent from 1992 to 2008. Importantly, as more offenders are sentenced to life in prison without the possibility of parole, more inmates reach old age in prison.

Research also point to the adoption of "truth-in-sentencing" laws as leading to the growth of aging inmates. In 1994 states began adopting "truth-in-sentencing" laws which requires prisoners to serve at least 85% of their sentence prior to being eligible for parole (Violent Crime Control, 1994, Travis, Western & Redburn, 2014). Many states enacted the laws after the Violent Crime Control and Law Enforcement Act of 1994 provided federal grants to states that implemented "truth-in-sentencing" policies (Violent Crime Control, 1994). Importantly, the federal system and many states eliminated eligibility for release on parole as the adoption of "truth-in-sentencing" laws and determinate sentencing systems (Curtin, 2007). As judicial and parole board discretion was limited in the federal system and many states, prisoners remained behinds bars for longer terms of their sentence (Cole & Gertz, 2013). The challenge of the elderly inmate population thus results from different trends: the shift of the philosophy of criminal justice system, the explosion of the prison population throughout the country, and the current growth of the aging inmate population.

A Gerontological Perspective

Defining Age (Who is "Old" or "Elderly")

Gerontology becomes more significant in criminal justice policies with increasing American prison population ages (Cole & Gertz, 2013). Many scholars and policy makers have been attempting to identify the older inmates. The first way of defining age is a chronological age which is common for people. One of the advantages to such a definition is that it allows us to allocate individuals to life stages including teenager, adulthood, and elderly. However, this way of defining age is considered as a deficient measure of life stage. Health does decline with age; however, a chronological age may not be the best measure of prisoners' health and their needs (Rikard & Rosenberg, 2007). With this definition, resources focused to inmates of a specific age who do not necessarily need them are more likely to receive than other inmates who do.

Another method of age-grading is based on biological or physiological indicators. One's age can be categorized based on physiological indicators such as chronic health issues, bone density, cardiovascular fitness, or neuromuscular response and biological characters. The third age-grading approach is functional age based on personal hygiene or job characteristics which are often associated with physiological aging (Cole & Gertz, 2013; Rikard & Rosenberg, 2007). The age-grading method is based on one's capability to deal with necessary tasks such as job or personal hygiene.

Even though policy makers and scholars have been attempting to classify the older inmates, there is no national consensus about defining who is "old" or "elderly" (Chiu, 2010). For example, the National Institute of Corrections uses a chronological age of 50 as its threshold for "elderly" inmates (Price, 2006). However, The U.S. Census Bureau defines "old" inmate population as those 65 and older (Chiu, 2010; Jaye Anno, Camelia, James, & Ronald, 2004).

According to Anthorny and their colleague's research in 2008, 27 states have definition of "older prisoner". More specifically, more than half of the states including Ohio (15 states, 56%) used 50 years, five states including Alabama (18%) used 55 +, four states including Oklahoma (15%) used 60 +, two states (7%) used 65 +, and one state (4%) used 70 years as a threshold (Anthorny, Greta, & Greta., 2008). In regards of defining age, states need to consider combining the threshold of age.

The Challenge: Increasing Cost for the "Special Needs" Population

With the number of older prisoners increasing, so does costs for the 'special needs' inmate population. The advances in medical science and technology have led to significant impact in the elderly inmate population. Nevertheless, older inmates tend to have issues of alcohol and drug abuse and lack of medical care (Cole & Gertz, 2013; Williams et al., 2001).

Elderly inmates have poorer health conditions, such as increased risk of diseases, psychological disorders, and gross functional disabilities compared to younger inmates (Cole &Gertz, 2013; Williams et al., 2006; Chiu, 2010). During their incarceration, older inmates often suffer from chronic illnesses (Cole & Gertz, 2013). Adequate medical services and equipment needed to offer medical care for the elderly prisoners include physician availability, laboratory, 24-hour nursing coverage, x-ray, rehabilitative physical care resources, and pharmacy (Rosefield, 1993).

Due to their special needs, the cost of maintaining the elderly inmates are about two to three times greater than younger inmates (Cole & Gertz, 2013; Price, 2006; Rikard & Rosenberg, 2007; Johnson & Beiser, 2013). In fact, the cost of the elderly offenders' health care has grown considerably at both the federal and state levels. The report by the Federal Bureau of Prisons (FBOP) revealed that the average cost was $24,538 for an aging inmate to incarcerate while the average cost was $22,676 for the younger inmate in 2013. The FBOP also differentiated it from the medical needs, including the cost of medication, for elderly prisoners. They found that the range between the highest and the lowest percentages of elderly prisoners are between $10,114 and $1,916 (The Federal Bureau of Prisons, 2016). In North Carolina (cf. Price, 2006), the health costs such as dental, medical and mental health for an inmate age 50 or older was about $7,159, which was about more than four times the spending compared to that on younger prisoners, while that cost was $1,919 for an inmate who was under age 50 in fiscal year 2004 to 2005 (Price, 2006). In Georgia, one of the ten largest prison systems in the United States, the health care costs for an inmate who was age over 65 was about $8,500 while the cost was $950 for younger inmates according to the Aging-inmate Population Project (Katrina, 2013). They reported that inmate medical care cost is approximately $3 billion a year in the country (Katrina, 2013).

Policy makers and scholars anticipate that the number of older inmate population will be continuously rising (Cole & Gertz, 2013). The increasing numbers of the aging inmate population, the growing costs of health care for the aging inmate indicates that a feasible alternative to the issue is needed for cost savings (Cole & Gertz, 2013).

Statistically Lower Recidivism

With developmental perspectives on crime, 'age' is one of the most reliable predictors in crime and criminality, especially recidivism (Strupp, 2010). It has been shown that the rate of delinquent or criminal behavior peaks at the early age of adolescence, especially 17 years old, and decreases over age (Vold, Bernard, & Snipes, 2002).

The elder offenders have less likelihood of committing crimes when they are released than offenders who are younger (Cole & Gertz, 2013; Rikard & Rosenberg, 2007; Johnson & Beiser, 2013). According to the U.S. Department of Justice Bureau of Justice Statistics (BJS), the recidivism rate was lower for offenders age 50 and older while that of younger offenders under age 30 was over 70% in the country in 2014 (U.S. Department of Justice, 2016). In addition, some studies found that the recidivism rate among the offenders age 50 and older was only 9.5 percent while that of the younger offenders who are under 21 was 35.5 percent (Chiu, 2010). This study shows that released older inmates have statistically low possibility of risk to the public safety. The research conducted by U.S. Department of Justice also found that, within three years of their release, 58 (15%) were re-arrested for new criminal acts among 381 older inmates. In addition, they also reported that re-arrest for new crimes of older inmates decreased with age within their sample (cf. Office of the Inspector General, 2016).

Many states have enacted policies of compassionate or geriatric release as a way to reduce the cost to maintain them since elder inmates are less likely a risk to the community than younger inmates (Cole & Gertz, 2013; Chiu, 2010).

For instance, in 2008 and 2009, a number of states such as North Carolina and Washington enacted geriatric policy which permits inmates to be released and complete their sentences in the community (Chiu, 2010). In 2015, 46 states out of 50 states plus Washington, DC and a Federal Law had a compassionate or geriatric release laws. Yet, four states including Illinois, South Carolina, South Dakota, and Utah do not have any public records of compassionate or geriatric-related release policies (Maschi, Kalmanofsky, Westcott, & Pappacena, 2015). As follows, many state policy-makers intend to allow the release of the aging inmates who have a low possibility to risk to the community (Cole & Gertz, 2013).

However, these policies have not realized a substantial release of older prisoners (Chiu, 2010). For example, although the elderly prisoners have a lower rate of re-arrest for new crimes once released and less likely involved in misconduct while incarcerated, the Federal Bureau of Prisons policies restricts the number of elderly prisoners who can be eligible for early release (The Federal Bureau of Prisons, 2016). Some states such as Maryland and Oklahoma have not released any elder prisoner under geriatric release provisions (Chiu, 2010). In addition, Colorado released three prisoners per year from 2001 to 2008 (Williams et al., 2006; Chown, 2005).

CRITIQUE OF POLICY OPTIONS

Regarding the issues of the aging inmates, there are mainly two interest areas for policy makers and scholars: "release and reintegration" and "prison facility design and management" (Cole & Gertz, 2013; Drummond, 1999; Duckett, Fox, Harsha, & Vish, 2001; Goetting, 1983; Holeman, 1998; Ornduff, 1996; Yates & Gillespie, 2000; Rikard & Rosenberg, 2007). Some states, such as Louisiana, have made it easier for inmates who are older and non-violent offenders to be released early, while others have created prison facility design such as separate housing accommodations (Mikle & Park, 2013). Yet, there is no consensus between release and management of the older inmates (Aday, 2003; Coalition, 1998; Drummond, 1999; Duckett et al., 2001; Goetting, 1983; Ornduff, 1996; Yates & Gillespie, 2000). Perhaps, releasing the older inmates before the end of their sentence would be the most controversial issue related to the aging inmate (Cole & Gertz, 2013; Goetting, 1983; Ornduff, 1996; Rikard & Rosenberg, 2007).

Releasing the older inmate occurs when they have a "terminal disease" or "the record of the incarcerated behavior" (Cole & Gertz, 2013; Rikard & Rosenberg, 2007). Such approaches vary across states and include medical releases also known as "compassionate" release and discretionary parole (Cole & Gertz, 2013; Chiu, 2010). Some states such as Kansas, Maine, and the District of Columbia have medical release which specifically targets the aging prisoners (Rikard & Rosenberg, 2007). Other states have enacted parole or medical release for the elderly prisoners while adding age-specific criteria. In New York, Georgia, Ohio, Oklahoma, Oregon, and Texas, medical parole can be revoked, and the aging inmates need to return to prison if the inmate's medical condition improves (Russell, 1994; Rikard & Rosenberg, 2007). In addition, others have extended statutes that consider both medical and geriatric release (Cole & Gertz, 2013; Chiu, 2010).

For geriatric release, inmates must meet the eligibility requirements including age, health condition, or possibility of risk to public safety (recidivism) (Chiu, 2010). States often preclude some inmates who commit serious offenses such as violent or sexual offense regardless of their health condition. Such requirements also vary across states. Some states, such as Louisiana which has the lowest threshold age of eligibility, 45, include eligible inmates broadly (Chiu, 2010). On the other hand, other states such as Maryland define eligibility narrowly; even if Maryland precludes specific physical conditions, inmates must be 65 and have served at least 15 years of their sentence (Chiu, 2010). To be released, prisoners must meet eligibility requirements including physical conditions such as terminal disease. Most states define the eligible age at 60 or 65 for the early release (cf. Chiu, 2010).

States including Washington, Texas, Missouri, and Oregon do not set thresholds for age. Yet, inmates must meet the eligibility criteria such as physical debilitation (Chiu, 2010). For example, Washington allows medical parole for inmates who have a grave medical condition which is expected to need long-term and costly health care due to their age, or if they are expected to be physically debilitated at the time of release (Chiu, 2010; Jaye Anno et al., 2004).

In regard to geriatric release policies, there is a gap between intent and impact. State policymakers intend to authorize the release of the older prisoner who has a low possibility to threaten public safety (Chiu, 2010). Yet, geriatric release provisions have not enacted in practice effectively. For example, some states such as Maryland or Oklahoma never released an elderly inmate under geriatric release provisions in 2009 (Chiu, 2010). Colorado released three inmates and Oregon released only two inmates per year from 2001 to 2008 (Chiu, 2010). Why do the geriatric release policies have low impact on the older prisoners in many states? There should be more factors, but two main issues would be related to the disparity: eligibility requirements issues and the process of application.

Considering eligibility requirements, first, the eligible population may be defined narrowly under geriatric release provisions. In the inmate population, for example, violent offenders or sex offenders and prisoners with life sentence often are excluded under the geriatric release procedures (Chiu, 2010). This practice is rational in some goal of criminal justice, retribution or incarceration (Cole & Gertz, 2013). This may outweigh the cost-effectiveness or consideration of the possibility that the older inmate has a low risk to public safety (Cole & Gertz, 2013).

However, the result is that geriatric release statutes or procedure may be only applied to a small portion of people (Chiu, 2010). Since the number of violent offenders or sex offenders increases in prison and they are excluded from the eligible population, it will be much harder to save cost and reduce the inmate population by releasing the elderly inmate. In 2006, North Carolina inmates 50 and older were more likely to have been incarcerated for violent or sex offense, including sexual assault or habitual felonies; the majority of inmates were serving maximum sentences of 10 years or more (Price, 2006).

As such, only a small number of older inmates, who have a terminal disease or serious health condition, are out of the jails under the restricted requirement of geriatric release. For example, in Washington State, only 22 inmates who were physically debilitated due to their age, were released within five years under the geriatric release statute (Chiu, 2010). However, in 2009, the statutes were changed by including those who are "expected" to be physically waning (Chiu, 2010). As a modification of the eligible population under the geriatric release statute, the Washington State can reduce the expense of medical cares for the older inmates by releasing some prisoners before they will be physically in poor health. By releasing 44 inmates age 55 and older, Washington State estimated that they can save money up to $1.5 million between 2009 and 2011 (Chiu, 2010).

Procedural issues also may cause confusion or delays which may restrict the release of inmates (Chiu, 2010). It would be time-consuming and complex for some inmates to be released. Those who look for geriatric release deal with some application procedures such as clarifying the eligible population, reviewing the appropriate information by the parole board or procuring medical care in the community. Such procedures may discourage some inmates. For instance, Alabama enacted the medical furlough programs for which geriatric inmates age 55 or older are eligible except when they committed sexual offense or murder. Yet, even after several changes of the process, only three prisoners were released in 2009 under the geriatric policy since the procedures were lengthy and complex (Chiu, 2010).

A growing number of states have increased early release programs including compassionate release programs and medical furloughs to diminish prison populations. However, relatively few researches have been performed on the issue of older releases or their medical care post-release from correctional institutions (Cartwright, 2016).

PRISON FACILITY DESIGN AND MANAGEMENT

The other area of general interest for both scholars and policymakers is a key inquiry of whether elderly inmates should be consolidated into or segregated from the general prison population (Cole & Gertz, 2013; Drummond, 1999; Duckett, Fox, Harsha, and Vish, 2001; Goetting, 1983; Holeman, 1998; Ornduff, 1996; Yates & Gillespie, 2000; Rikard & Rosenberg, 2007). However, there is no agreement on policy regarding segregation from or consolidation of the elderly inmates into the correctional facility (Cole & Gertz, 2013). The study by the National Institute of Corrections revealed that 23 states provide specified services and programs for the aging inmate (U.S. Department of Justice, 1997). Among these states, about 15 states have separate facilities for elderly inmates for their medical services (U.S. Department of Justice, 1997). Furthermore, there is no agreement among researchers on whether elderly prisoners should be segregated or consolidated into the general inmate population (Adams, 1995; Aday, 1994a, 1994b, 2003; Cole & Gertz, 2013; Duckett et al., 2001; Goetting, 1983, 1984a, 1985; Holeman, 1998; Johnson, 1988; Merianos et al., 1997; Neeley et al., 1997; Ornduff, 1996; Rikard & Rosenberg, 2007; Rosefield, 1993; Wiegand & Burger, 1979; Yates & Gillespie, 2000).

Scholars have considered the issue of whether the prison environment would be improved by having elderly inmates or worsen as making them potential victims for younger prisoners. Some scholars believe that the presence of aging inmates can actually produce a calming effect on the younger inmate population (Adams, 1995; Aday, 1994b, 2003; Morton, 1992; Ornduff, 1996; Yates & Gillespie, 2000). Moreover, correctional administrators support consolidation since it allows the elderly prisoners to engage in rehabilitative programs such as educational or vocational program. (Adams, 1995; Aday, 1994b; Goetting, 1983; Morton, 1992; Ornduff, 1996; Yates & Gillespie, 2000). On the other hand, some researchers support the segregation of aging inmates from the general prison population. Segregation can offer aging inmates the opportunity to build self-esteem and self-respect and reduce feelings of despair and loneliness by maintaining networks with their age groups and building friendships in prison (Adams, 1995; Aday, 1994b, 2003; Goetting, 1984b; Morton, 1992; Ornduff, 1996; Yates & Gillespie, 2000). In addition, segregation can prevent aging inmates from being victimized by younger inmates (Adams, 1995; Aday, 1994b, 2003; Ornduff, 1996; Yates & Gillespie, 2000). Age-based segregation provides an "elder-friendly" physical environment and focuses on aging inmates' physical limitations and safety needs (Adams, 1995; Aday, 1994b, 2003; Bouplon, 1999; Duckett et al., 2001; Neeley et al., 1997; Rosefield, 1993; Wiegand & Burger, 1979).

CONCLUSION

The need to reduce costs of federal and state correctional departments without threatening public safety offers federal and states prisons with an opportunity to initiate or enhance geriatric release policies. The challenge is to create current policies more efficient and to identify new approaches to dealing with an aging population that is continuously expected to increase.

State corrections systems in the United Sates face considerable challenges with the aging inmate population. Regarding the issues with the elderly inmates, there are five policy recommendations. A majority of prisons in states are over capacity in service; the problem is that the budgets to operate it have been diminished in a weakened economy. In addition, it is getting harder to decide about who is "the elderly" inmate and how they can be released.

Policy Recommendations

First, states should examine thoroughly the procedure of the application to identify potential problems and obstacles related to the geriatric release. States also should recognize whether the process of the application is complex or confusing; thus, it takes much time for reviewing the cases. States should review the procedure in other states which one have more feasible criteria and have implemented them successfully; so, each state can save money effectively (Price, 2006).

Second, states should develop reliable instruments for assessing eligible population who have low possibility to threaten the public safety since it is an important and inevitable concern related to early release of inmates (Chiu, 2010). With the assessment instruments, especially states should identify the eligible older inmates with low risk of recidivism.

Third, under the geriatric release policy, states should identify whether the eligible requirements are too narrow; thus, it restricts prisoners to be qualified. More specifically, states should not limit to inmates who have terminal disease or serious health issues. States should identify the older inmates who are not yet infirm but are *expected* to be severely debilitated when they are released; it will allow the inmates to complete the last of their sentence in their own residence (Chiu, 2010). States should consider developing a pilot program to make sure the policy is effective. Yet, by doing so, the economic burden of the incapacitated inmates would shift to their family or community services (Cole & Gertz, 2013). In addition, due to the length of incarceration, some have lost contacts from their families (thus, no home to stay) while some older inmates have the support of family when they are released. Considering this issue, states should consider the additional healthcare service and housing at the state level. More importantly, stages need to be developed and executed with supervision and reentry program in an effective way (Cole & Gertz, 2013). The programs should consider the older inmates' special need such as medical, housing, employment, and social needs by collaborating with the stakeholders including policymakers, correctional administrators, probation and parole staff, health and social care providers, scholars related to the special needs (Chiu, 2010).

Fourth, policy makers and scholars have been attempting to classify the older inmates. However, there is no national consensus about defining who is "old" or "elderly" (Chiu, 2010). States should define "age" of the elderly inmate with a lower age. Doing so would make more aging inmates eligible for geriatric release as well as saving cost. In addition, states also should consider combining the cut-off of a lower age regarding geriatric special needs and risk.

Lastly, states should monitor each state geriatric release policies, and report it annually. For instance, Washington, Alabama and New Mexico require the reporting the information including applications, grants and the procedure to the legislature annually (Chiu, 2010). Doing so will be beneficial to states to assess and develop their mechanism over time.

REFERENCES

Abner, C. (2006). Graying prisons: States face challenges of an aging inmate population. *State News*, *49*(10), 8-12.

Adams, J. E. (1995). The incarceration of the older inmate. *Nova Law Review*, *19*(2), 455-475.

Aday, R. H. (1994a). Aging in prison: A case study of new elderly offenders. *International Journal of Offender Therapy and Comparative Criminology*, *38*(1), 79-91.

Aday, R. H. (1994b). Golden years behind bars. *Federal Probation*, *58*(2), 1-19.

Aday, R. H. (2003). *Aging prisoners: Crisis in American corrections*. Penn State Press.

Anthorny, A. & Greta, L. (2008). A national survey of older prisoner health, mental health and programming. *Correction Today, 70.4.*

Auerhahn, K. (2002). Selective incapacitation, three strikes, and the problem of aging prison populations: Using simulation modeling to see the future. *Criminology, 1*, 353-388.

Jaye Anno, B., Camelia, G., James, E. L. & Ronald, S. (2004). *Correctional Health Care: Addressing the Needs of Elderly, Chronically Ill, and Terminally Ill Inmates* (Washington, DC: U.S. Department of Justice, National Institute of Corrections, 2004).

Bouplon, R. A. (1999). *1999 Annual Report*. Tallahassee, FL: Florida Corrections Commission.

Carole Keeton Strayhorn. (2000). "Public Safety and Corrections," in *Recommendations of the Texas Comptroller*. (Texas: Comptroller of Public Accounts, 2000).

Cole, G. G. & Gertz, M. G. (2013). *The Criminal Justice System: Politics and Policies* (10th ed.) Belmon, CA: Wadsworth.

Chiu. (2010). *It's about Time: Aging Prisoners, Increasing Costs, and Geriatric Release*. Vera Institute of Justice.

Chown, Bill. (2005). *The Aging of the Oklahoma Prison Population: Implications for Health Care Costs*. Oklahoma Criminal Justice Resource Center, July 2005.

Curtin, T. (2007). The Continuing Problem of America's Aging Prison Population and the Search for a Cost-Effective and Socially Acceptable Means of Addressing It. *Elder LJ*, *15*, 473.

Drummond, T. (1999). US: Cellblock Senior. *Times Magazine (US)*, p. 60.

Duckett, N., Fox, T. A., Harsha, T. C. & Vish, J. (2001). *Issues in Maryland sentencing—The aging Maryland prison population*. College Park, MD: Maryland State Commission on Criminal Sentencing Policy.

Flynn, E. E., Flanagan, T., Greenwood, P. & Krisberg, P. (1995). Three-strikes legislation: Prevalence and definition. *Critical Criminal Justice Issues (National Institute of Justice Report 158837*, pp. 122-133). Washington DC: National Institute for Justice.

Goetting, A. (1983). The elderly in prison issues and perspectives. *Journal of Research in Crime and Delinquency, 20*, 291-309.

Goetting, A. (1984a). The elderly in prison: A profile. *Criminal Justice Review*, *9*(2), 14-24.

Goetting, A. (1984b). Prison program and facilities for elderly inmates. In E. S. Newman, D. J. Newman, & M. L. Gewirtz (Eds.), *Elderly Criminals,* (pp. 169-176). Cambridge, MA: Oelgeschlager, Gunn, & Hain.

Goetting, A. (1985). Racism, sexism, and ageism in the prison community. *Federal Probation*, *44*(3), 10-22.

Griset, P. (1991). *Determinate Sentencing: The Promise and the Reality of Retributive Justice*. Albany, NY: State University of New York Press.

Holeman, B. (1998). Nursing homes behind bars: The elderly in prison. *Coalition for Federal Sentencing Reform*, *2*, 1-4.

Hooyman, N. & Kiyak, H. A. (1999). *Social Gerontology: A Multidisciplinary Approach*, (5th ed., Vol. *520*). Needham Heights, MA: Allyn & Bacon.

Johnson, E. H. (1988). Care for elderly inmates: Conflicting concerns and purposes in prisons. In B. McCarthy & R. Langworthy (Eds.), *Older Offenders: Perspectives in Criminology and Criminal Justice*, (pp. 157-163). New York: Praeger.

Johnson & Beiser. (2013, July 11). Aging prisoners' costs put systems nationwide in a bind. *USA Today*, Retrieved from http://www.usatoday.com/story/news/nation/2013/07/10/cost-care-aging-prisoners/2479285/.

Katrina, D. (2013). The aging-inmate population project. Georgia department of correction.

King, R. S. & Mauer, M. (2001). *Aging behind Bars: "Three Strikes" Seven Years Later*. Washington, DC: The Sentencing Project.

Mackenzie, D. L. (2001). *Sentencing and Corrections in the 21st Century: Setting the Stage for the Future* (NCJ report 189089). Washington, DC: U.S. Department of Justice, Office of Justice Programs, National Institute of Justice.

Males, M. & Macallair, D. (1999). Striking out: The failure of California's three strikes and you're out law. *Stan. L. & Pol'y Rev.*, *11*, 65.

Maschi, T., Kalmanofsky, A., Westcott, K. & Pappacena, L. (2015). *An analysis of United States compassionate and geriatric release laws: Towards a rights-based response for diverse elders and their families and communities*. New York, NY: Be the Evidence Press, Fordham University. Available at www.betheevidence.org.

Merianos, D. E., Marquart, J. W., Damphouse, K. & Hebert, J. L. (1997). From the outside in: Using public health data to make inferences about older inmates. *Crime and Delinquency*, *43*, 298-313.

Mikle, J. & Park, A. (2013, March 31). States face a potential fiscal time bomb as their prison populations steadily grow older. *USA Today*. Retrieved from http://www.usatoday.com/ story/ news/ nation/ 2013/ 03/ 31/ health-care-costs-for-older-inmates-skyrocket/2038633/.

Moraff, C. (2013, August 21). It's time to let grandpa out of jail. *Philadelphia News and Opinion*, Retrieved from http://www.phillymag.com/news/2013/08/21/time-grandpa-jail/.

Neeley, C. L., Addison, L. & Craig-Moreland, D. (1997). Addressing the needs of elderly offenders. *Corrections Today*, *59*(5), 120-123.

Nellis, A. & King, R. S. (2009). *No Exit: The Expanding Use of life Sentences in America*, (p. 3). Washington, DC: Sentencing Project.

Orndduff, J. S. (1996). Releasing the elderly inmate: A solution to prison overcrowding. *Elder Law Journal*, *4*, 20.

Pew Charitable Trusts. (2013). *Managing Prison Health Care Spending*. Washington, D.C.: Author.

Price, C. A. (2006). *Aging inmate population study.* Addendum Report. (North Carolina: Department of Corrections Division of Prisons, 2007).

Rausch, S. P. (1996). Foreword: Current issues in prison management. *Criminal Justice Review*, *21*, 1-19.

Rikard, R. V. & Rosenberg, E. (2007). Aging inmates: A convergence of trends in the American criminal justice system. *Journal of Correctional Health Care*, *13*(3), 150-162.

Rosefield, H. A. (1993). The older inmate:" Where do we go from here?" *Journal of Prison & Jail Health.*

Sieff, K. (2010, September 8). Virginia's prison system struggles to handle the surge in elderly inmates. *The Washington Post*, Retrieved from http://www. washingtonpost.com/wp-dyn/content/article/2010/09/07/AR2010090706514.html.

Strupp, H. (2010). *California's Older Prisoner Crisis: Facts and Figures.* San Francisco: Legal Services for Prisoners with Children.

Tonry, M. (2009). Explanations of American punishment policies: A national history. *Punishment & Society*, *11*(3), 377-394.

Travis, J., Western, B. & Redburn, F. S. (2014). *The Growth of Incarceration in the United States: Exploring Causes and Consequences*. Washington, DC: The National Academies Press.

U. S. Department of Justice, National Institute of Corrections. (1997). *Prison Medical Care: Special Needs Populations and Cost Control*. Longmont, CO: Author.

U. S. Department of Justice. Office of the Inspector General. (2016, February). *The Impact of an Aging Inmate Population on the Federal Bureau of Prisons*, Retrieved from https://oig.justice.gov/reports/2015/e1505.pdf.

Violent Crime Control and Law Enforcement Act of 1994. (1994). HR 3355. Washington, DC: United States Department of Justice.

Vold, G. B., Bernard, T. J. & Snipes, J. B. (2002). *Theoretical criminology* (5th ed.). New York: Oxford University Press.

Wheeler, M., Connelly, M., & Wheeler, B. (1995). Aging of prison populations: Directions for Oklahoma. *Journal of the Oklahoma Criminal Justice Research Consortium, 2*, 72-79.

Wiegand, N. D., & Burger, J. C. (1979). The elderly offender and parole. *The Prison Journal*, *59*(2), 48-57.

Williams, B. A., Lindquist, K., Sudore, R. L., Strupp, H. M., Willmott, D. J. & Walter, L. C. (2006). Being old and doing time: functional impairment and adverse experiences of geriatric female prisoners. *Journal of the American Geriatrics Society*, *54*(4), 702-707.

Yates, J. & Gillespie, W. (2000). The elderly and prison policy. *Journal of Aging & Social Policy*, *11*(2-3), 167-175.

Zimring, F. E., Hawkins, G. & Kamin, S. (2003). *Punishment and Democracy: Three Strikes and You're Out in California*. Oxford University Press on Demand.

In: A Closer Look at Criminal Justice
Editors: J. A. Cooper and K. G. Jachimowski
ISBN: 978-1-53615-782-6

Chapter 12

Juvenile Justice in the United States and Germany: A Comparative Perspective

Sarah Kuehn [*] ***and Kerry Edwards***
Slippery Rock University of Pennsylvania, Slippery Rock, PA, US

Abstract

This chapter reviews the history and current developments in the juvenile justice system ranging from processing minor delinquents to the most recent Supreme Court decisions regarding serious juvenile offenders in the United States. The chapter also offers a comparative perspective, detailing Germany's juvenile justice system and its response to juvenile offenders. This comparison reveals common trends in juvenile justice and suggests that each of the two countries could learn from the other's perspectives, strategies, and difficulties in responding to juvenile offending.

Introduction

While most adult systems are surprisingly similar in general terms (e.g., what constitutes a criminal offense and that the sentence should fit the severity of a crime), juvenile systems display significant differences among countries. For instance, status offenses such as breaking curfew or truancy exist in some (e.g., the United States (U.S.) but not in others (e.g., Canada and Germany) (Doob & Tonry, 2004). Further, the age of criminal responsibility varies widely from country to country and, in the U.S., from state to state (Doob & Tonry, 2004). Despite these differences, western democracies agree

[*] Corresponding Author's Email: sarah.kuehn@sru.edu

that, in relation to adult offenders, juveniles should be treated differently, are less culpable, and are more receptive to rehabilitation efforts (Doob & Tonry, 2004).

Rather than being captured by the traditional, binary distinction of welfare and justice systems, most (Juvenile Justice System) JJSs reflect complex constellations and competing rationales, which fall somewhere between "a 'pure' welfare model" and "a 'pure' criminal law or punishment model" (Doob & Tonry, 2004, p. 2; Dünkel, 2014; Muncie, 2008). When examining different jurisdictions, and even countries, it is important to note that comparisons should not be limited to formal laws and policies. Rather, it is important to look at structures and practices, in other words the implementation of these laws when examining legal responses to juvenile offending (Doob and Tonry, 2004). This chapter has accomplished that by reviewing the history and current developments in juvenile justice and providing a comparative perspective of juvenile justice in the US and Germany. This comparison allows for the examination of what the two countries can learn from each other when responding to juvenile crime. In particular, this chapter examines the age of criminal responsibility and application of the juvenile law as well as juveniles' entry into the juvenile justice system, sanctions, and treatment.

Juvenile Justice in the United States

Throughout U.S. history, the perception of children's responsibilities and culpability has undergone several philosophic and legal iterations. These shifts in perspective were prompted by societal forces and conditions, such as those associated with strain from changes in population density, family structure, and industrialization. From the 17th to very early 19th century, children were perceived as miniature adults; only the very young, seven years old or younger, were exempt from adult responsibilities, in general, and from adult sanctions in response to breaking laws (OJJDP, 1999). As industrialization led to rapid and significant societal changes, such as extraordinary urban population growth and poverty, the plight of children increased, including lawbreaking, and perceived "threats to the social order" became starkly visible (Fox, 1996, p. 29). Throughout much of the 19th century, the Child Savers Movement promoted a paternalistic approach towards children who had unmet needs through the family and/or were engaged in unruly behavior or lawbreaking (Pemberton, 1894). The movement led to placing needy children in boarding houses (Pemberton, 1894) and placing unruly or lawbreaking youth in reformatories intended to "prepare them to live healthy and productive lives as they mature into adulthood" (Monell, 2017, para. 1). The trend towards paternalistic reforming and special treatment of "dependent, neglected and delinquent children" (Hurley, 1907, p. 20) was codified, "using a *parens patriae* (state as parent or guardian) role" through the Illinois Juvenile Court Act of 1899 (Hinton, Sims, Adams, & West, 2007, p. 468); instead of focusing on proportionate sentences matching the seriousness of the offense, this act focused on juvenile's rehabilitative needs and the best interest of the child (Hinton et al., 2007).

The Illinois *Juvenile Court Act* of 1899 also prompted the formation of the juvenile court for youth (males under 17 years of age and females under 18 years of age, and continued jurisdiction until the age of 21 for both) in Cook County, Illinois. The Act provided several specific rules and tools: probation, parole, no jail confinement for children under 12 years of age, and separate facilities of confinement from adults (Hurley, 1907). By 1925, the "juvenile court movement" had prompted legislation supporting such courts in all but one state and the development of the courts in all cities with populations over 100,000 (Lenroot & Lundberg, 1925, p. 1).

The juvenile courts were tasked with determining the delinquent child's "fitness for rehabilitation and de-emphasized the adjudication of the offense itself" (Fox, 1996, p. 29). To accomplish this, the courts utilized personal involvement, informally building rapport to assess and influence the child, and professional services to aid in rehabilitation, such as social workers and psychologists (Fox, 1996). This personal and informal approach survived intact, although not without some challenges even prior to the establishment of juvenile courts, until the 1960s, when two landmark Supreme Court decisions altered the landscape of the JJS. Both *Kent v. United States* (1966) and *In re Gault* (1967) imposed due process rights upon the JJS that changed the relationships in the juvenile courtroom to more closely resemble the adversarial adult court system. Thus, although seeking the best interest of the child remains an espoused value in many of the U.S. states' JJS (Sickmund & Puzzanchera, 2014, p. 88), the addition of significant due process rights, formerly only afforded adults, shifted the juvenile system to a more mixed-model of both welfare and justice elements.

In 1974, the federal *Juvenile Justice and Delinquency Prevention* (JJDP) *Act* was passed to "prevent delinquency and improve the juvenile justice system" (OJJDP, n.d. a, para. 1). The legislation established the Office of Juvenile Justice and Delinquency Prevention (OJJDP) designed to assist the states and municipalities in this effort, and created several rules, including the following: the deinstitutionalization of youth who have only violated laws that are illegal due to the youth's age (status offenders); sight and sound separation from adults in detention/ confinement settings; no detention/ confinement in adult jails/facilities except in very few circumstances (1980 amendment); and, a mandate to address disproportionate minority contact throughout the JJS (1988 amendment) (OJJDP, n.d. a).

Over a period of approximately 25 years after the JJDP Act was enacted, an increase in crime, including violent crime among juveniles, gave rise to public fear; the term *super-predator* arose (Dilulio, 1995)[1] and augmented a *get tough on crime* stance that further pushed the perspective of juvenile justice towards the adult justice model. Lengthier juvenile incarcerations became more common, as did trying juveniles in adult courts. Although the OJJDP remained committed to the vision of juvenile justice uniquely different from the adult system, citizens, state legislators, and some practitioners believed that the practices in place were not working and were demanding more punitive responses to juvenile offending (Torbet, 1998). In fact, most states made juvenile transfers to adult court easier and introduced mandatory minimum custody sentences (Howell, Feld, Mears, Farrington, Loeber, & Petechuck, 2013; Liles & Moak, 2014; Muncie, 2008). It seemed the approach towards delinquent youth had gone full circle, returning to the perspectives of the 17th and 18th centuries. Although unintentional, this pathway provided a key turning point for juvenile justice efforts.

During an ad-hoc OJJDP conference in 1996 to address the pressing issues within the system, participants promoted a newer approach to justice that would balance offender competencies (skills and resiliency) and accountability with restorative justice (the collective effort at rehabilitation involving the offender, the victim, and the community), *Balanced and Restorative Justice* (BARJ). The Attorney General's Office identified several areas for the OJJDP and federal partners to pursue, including information gathering and evaluation, providing training and technical assistance, arranging funding for programs, leadership and facilitation of prevention, and prosecuting the most violent and serious offenders. Additionally, practitioners advocated numerous strategies and programs, such as collaboration across agencies and governmental levels in areas of police, education, mental health, community service, restitution, supervision, and families (Torbet, 1998). Since the conference in 1996, OJJDP has implemented many of the federal objectives, indicated in the myriad of online services, including funding opportunities at the state, local, and community levels, informational sites, research and statistical information, training, and evidence-based program models (see ojjdp.gov).

The current state of the U.S. JJS is quite different than any other justice era. OJJDP's role in shaping juvenile justice and the BARJ approach to juvenile offending appear to be at the center of the current state of the U.S. JJS. Diversion programs and specialty courts are utilized in many jurisdictions as well (see National Association of Youth Courts, n.d.). Additionally, relatively recent constitutional challenges at the Supreme Court of the United States level have reined in the most extreme punitive sentence options for juveniles, e.g., the death penalty and mandatory life without parole (Merlo & Benekos, 2017). These constitutional limitations apply at both the federal and state levels. Although juveniles may be prosecuted at both the federal and state levels, federal prosecutions are rare, as juveniles arrested by federal law enforcement or arrested for

[1] John Dilulio, who has been credited as coining the term *super-predator*, has since expressed his regret over his role in stoking fear that led to the significant increase in the punitive treatment of juvenile offenders (Becker, 2001).

federal offenses usually are transferred to the appropriate state system for prosecution. As of December 2015, only 26 juveniles were in federal custody, and, even still, those persons were housed in state or local facilities on behalf of the federal authorities until the juveniles reach 18 years of age and will then be transferred to the adult federal bureau of prisons facilities (Schwartzapfel, 2016).

Juvenile Justice in Germany

Germany is a federal republic, which consists of 16 states. While states do have some autonomy, for example in terms of education and culture, they are subject to the Federal (juvenile) criminal law (Dünkel, 2006). The German JJS, like its counterparts in Europe and North America, was created in the 19th century with the recognition that children had different needs and required special protections from the adult world, including the criminal justice system (CJS). The youth court movement in Germany leaned on its sister movement - the child-saving movement in the U.S. - stressing rehabilitation, separation from adult offenders, and individualized and professional services for juvenile delinquents (Albrecht, 2014). Similar to the U.S., the creation of the JJS was linked to modernization, industrialization, and urbanization (Albrecht, 2014). In 1908, some courts introduced "special court chambers that specialised [in] issues concerning young delinquents" (Dünkel, 2006, p. 226) and separate prisons for juvenile offenders followed shortly after (Doob & Tonry, 2004). The German *Juvenile Justice Act* (JJA) (*Jugendgerichtsgesetz*) was implemented in 1923 and established the age of juvenile court jurisdiction as ages 14-17, who committed a criminal offense as described under the general criminal law for adults (Dünkel, 2006).

One year prior to the creation of the JJA, Germany introduced the Youth Welfare Law (*Jugendwohlfahrtsgesetz*) in 1922. Both laws assume that it is the state's responsibility to take over if parents have failed or do not have the resources to provide proper care and education to the child. While both systems work in tandem, the JJA is applicable if there is a "suspicion and indictment of a criminal offense". In contrast, the admission to the Youth Welfare Law "requires establishing the need for care and education of a child or a juvenile" with no minimum age requirement (Albrecht, 2014, p. 445).

Germany uses a mixed model of juvenile justice, which combines educational and rehabilitative measures (e.g., mediation or social training courses) [welfare model] and legal safeguards and procedures [justice model] for juvenile offenders. The underlying principle is *Erziehung* (education and care) and rehabilitation with an emphasis on minimal intervention and diversion (Dünkel, 2006). Further, juvenile's prosocial development should be promoted (Albrecht, 2014). The German JJS is a specialized jurisdiction, which requires that juvenile justice personnel, such as judges and prosecutors, undergo specialized training on juvenile criminology and education (see §§37, 38 JJA). They are life-tenured civil servants hired by the Ministry of Justice (Brownsberger, 2018). Some of the basic principles of juvenile justice are (1) priority of diversion and minimum intervention; (2) mediation and restorative justice; and (3) educational and community sanctions. As mentioned above, the JJS employs a dualistic approach. The first track is the Juvenile Welfare Act (JWA) (*Sozialgesetzbuch* VIII) for "Children in Care" ranging from 0-18 years of age (up to, in some cases, the age of 27), which is based on the *parens patriae* doctrine.[2] The second track is the JJA for juveniles (14-17 years old) and eligible young adults (18-20 years old), who have committed an offense defined by the general Criminal Law for adults (*Strafgesetzbuch*). Juveniles under the age of 14 have no criminal responsibility and, thus, cannot be prosecuted. Instead, they are dealt with through welfare agencies and social services, which are established at the local community level and must be accredited by the regional youth welfare departments. Further, there is no completely separate juvenile offending law (e.g., there are no status offenses as there are in the U.S.). Rather, the JJA is based on the adult criminal law with specific provisions in terms of sanctions and procedural rules for educational measures, sanctions, and juvenile court proceedings (e.g., juvenile trials are not open to the public) (Dünkel, 2006). Many of the states' juvenile justice systems are being criticized for denying juvenile offenders due process and for promoting second class justice. This, however, only applies to the German JJS to a minor extent as, otherwise, rules and procedures are very similar to the adult system and deviations are based on educational means (Dünkel, 2006).

Germany's juvenile justice policies have been relatively stable, except for the three years under the Nazi regime when Germany changed its approach to its juvenile offender population. Similar to the 1980s and 1990s' fear of *super-predators* in the U.S. (Merlo & Benekos, 2017), in the late 1930s, criminal justice personnel and Nazi party officials were alerted by what they perceived as an increase in serious juvenile crime. They came up with a "new criminal type of the *Jugendlicher Schwerverbrecher* [which] was essentially a juvenile version of the so-called dangerous habitual criminal" (Waite, 2014, p. 263). Consequently, in 1939, they introduced a law for the Protection against Juvenile Serious Offenders, which allowed juvenile offenders to be tried as adults and receive harsher sentences, including the death penalty if they were over the age of 16 (Waite, 2014). Further, in 1943, the age of criminal responsibility was lowered to 12 years of age and juveniles of any age could be transferred to adult court if "they possessed adult maturity," they were "*charakterlich abartige Schwerverbrecher*" (i.e., if they had the character of dangerous habitual criminal), or if an adult punishment was deemed appropriate because of a "healthy popular feeling (gesundes Volksempfinden)" (Waite, 2014, p. 264). However, this more punitive approach only lasted three years, and after

[2] The JWA states that juveniles and young adults have the right to support and education and to being protected in their personal development by the child and youth welfare agencies (sec. 1).

World War II, "as part of the general cleansing of fascist ideology from the legal system", the law was reversed to its original version (Albrecht, 2004, p. 446). In 1953, legislators introduced probation sentences in lieu of (suspended) prison sentences (Albrecht, 2014). Further, in 1990, among other changes, several amendments abolished indeterminate sentences, expanded opportunities for diversion and victim-offender mediations, and restricted pre-trial detention (Albrecht, 2014). While there have not been any more recent major legislative amendments to the JJA, German juvenile justice has adopted significant changes by juvenile justice personnel such as social workers, prosecutors, and judges creating and implementing innovative programs, for example introducing new community sentences, social training courses, and other divisionary measures in the 1980s ("*reform through practice,*" Dünkel, 2006, p. 228; Dünkel, 2014).

Interestingly, in the 1960s and 1970s, Germany became somewhat close to completely abolishing its JJS and treating all juvenile delinquents under the Welfare system. The Ministry for Youth, Family and Health introduced a draft juvenile law, which would reserve punitive sanctions for juveniles over the age of 16 and impose welfare measures to younger juvenile delinquents. However, this proposal never succeeded, in part due to strong opposition from criminal justice professionals (Albrecht, 2014).

Age of Criminal Responsibility and Application of the Juvenile Law

US System of Juvenile Jurisdiction

The U.S. Federal Government and the individual U.S. states both have separate jurisdiction over juvenile offenders. While, generally, federal jurisdiction covers all offenses that would be a federal crime for adults, federal prosecution of juveniles does not take place unless one of three conditions are present: a state cannot or will not assert jurisdiction; a state is unable to provide adequate programs and services to the juvenile; or, the offense involves violence, firearms, or is drug related; additionally, under any one or more of these conditions, the federal prosecution must assert that there is "substantial federal interest" (U.S. DOJ, n.d. a, 9-8.110). The individual states and territories have independent jurisdiction. These state-level jurisdictions control both the processing of juvenile status offenses and juvenile offenses that would be deemed criminal if committed by an adult. The individual state jurisdictions have much autonomy, with the exception of a few areas, of which the Federal Government also is subject: due process rights afforded to juveniles, including the rights to representation by counsel, notice of the charges, confront witnesses, and not incriminate oneself (see *In re Gault, 1967*); the death penalty is not an option for an offense that was committed by a juvenile before the age of 18 (see *Roper v. Simmons, 2005*); and, life imprisonment without parole cannot be imposed mandatorily (see *Miller v. Alabama, 2012*). Still, there is much variation among the jurisdictions – states and the Federal Government –on numerous matters concerning juvenile offenders, including assessment of culpability as it pertains to age and processing young offenders as juveniles or adults.

In 1938, the U.S. Federal Government enacted the *Federal Juvenile Delinquency Act*, its equivalent to the Illinois *Juvenile Court Act* of 1899. The federal law required the separation of juveniles from adults in facilities and limited to 21 years of age the period of which a juvenile's sentence could extend into adulthood, but it did not affect the age of culpability standard that had long been adhered to under common law. The common law standard classified persons under 7 years old as not guilty (or not culpable) of any felony or capital crime because such persons "could not entertain criminal intent," persons 7 years old to 13 years old as presumed not culpable, but provided that this classification could be rebutted, and persons 14 years old and older as prima facie culpable as are adults (U.S. DOJ, n.d. b, CRM 116). Surprisingly, although the purported intent of the subsequent 1974 *Federal Juvenile Justice and Delinquency Prevention Act* was to prevent unnecessary stigma of youth, prevent juveniles' exposure to adult offenders, and enhance prevention and rehabilitation, among other noteworthy endeavors, the act did not substantially raise the age of culpability; in Federal District Court, a juvenile offender who "is at least fifteen years of age and the government alleges that the juvenile committed certain enumerated transferrable offenses (e.g., violent crimes or controlled substance violations)" may be prosecuted as an adult if a prosecutor motions for such a transfer and is successful (U.S. DOJ, n.d. b, CRM 117). Thus, there are three options for the federal processing of a juvenile offender: referral to state jurisdiction, prosecution as a juvenile, or transfer for prosecution as an adult if at least 15 years old and under certain offense criteria (U.S. DOJ, n.d. b, CRM 117) including a provision for mandatory transfer for certain offenses committed at age 16 or older (U.S. DOJ, n.d. b, CRM 140). The factors considered in the determination of whether to transfer the juvenile to adult court are age and social background, offense, prior delinquency record, intellectual development and psychological maturity, past treatment received and response, and availability of treatment programs (U.S. DOJ, n.d. b, CRM 131). Additionally, through several iterations of the federal juvenile code, there are a few circumstances, such as the imposing of revocations and commission of new crimes during the same time period that a juvenile already is under juvenile supervision or detention, under which a person again found delinquent can remain under juvenile supervision or detention for periods extending further into adulthood (age 26 for serious offenses, and age 24 for less serious offenses) (Legal Information Institute, n.d.).

These statutory and policy drivers of the federal processing of juvenile offenders turned towards a more deterrent-based and punitive strategy beginning in the late 1980s and 1990s in response to a surge in crime and perceptions of youth violence:

> "A close look at the nation's young people discloses something that is very alarming. Since 1985, we have seen an increase in the level of youth violence that is simply staggering, particularly for youth age fourteen to seventeen [...] This surge in youth violence is particularly frightening [...] Unmistakably, the current rise of youth violence presages the next generation of even more tragic crime and violence unless we do something now. We must reach out and hold our young people accountable when they do wrong. We must love them enough not to give up on them but to work with them to let them know that there will be fair, firm, certain punishment when they hurt others." (Janet Reno, United States Attorney General, Remarks at Landon Lecture Series on Public Issues, Kansas State University (October 24, 1995); U.S. DOJ, n.d. b, CRM 101, para. 2).

Despite Reno's call for punishment, the numbers of juveniles processed federally are very low, relative to the numbers processed at the state-level; this is primarily due to restrictive legislation that requires the federal justice system most often relinquish jurisdictions to states. Additionally, although the number of juveniles tried as adults in the federal system are typically extremely low (for instance, only 11 juveniles were incarcerated as of September 2018 following federal adult convictions (U.S. BOP, 2018), the proportion of juvenile offenders processed in the federal system who were prosecuted as adults is much higher than that at the state level. Still, the impact at the state level is much higher just by sheer numbers. Beginning in the 1980s and 1990s, individual states, using the same approach as advocated by Janet Reno, turned more towards deterrent-based punitive efforts in attempt to lower the juvenile offense rates.

The states differ, however, sometimes from the federal processes and from each other, in their methods of determining whether a juvenile is processed as a juvenile or as an adult. Most of the states have a set minimum age that a juvenile must meet to be eligible for adult processing, although the criteria of offense and offender history in combination with age vary. In 1992, the minimum age was not specified in 14 states, meaning that there was no lower age limit for trying a juvenile in adult court, given certain other circumstances; of those states that specified an age, the frequent mode was age 14 (18 states); 12 states had minimums of 15 or 16 years of age (Sickmund, 1994). In 2004, three more states had no lower age limit, bringing that total to 17 states, and, while the mode remained age 14 (19 states), no states had higher than age 14 as an absolute minimum threshold (OJJDP, 2006). In 2016, the mode changed to no minimum age (18 states), but two states moved their threshold up to age 15 (OJJDP, 2018a). Since 1992, the minimum age for adult prosecution of juveniles has decreased, and with the exception of two states raising their minimum age from 14 years old to 15 years old, there has been no significant change between 2004 and 2016, regardless of the decreased rate of crime since the mid-1990s; in fact, since 1992, the violent crime rate (2014) has dropped 50.4 percent, and the property crime rate (2014) has dropped 47 percent (FBI, 2017).

Germany

The Juvenile Justice Act (JJA) (*Jugendgerichtsgesetz*) is applicable for juveniles (14-17 years of age) and can be applicable for young adults (18-20 years of age), who have committed an offense defined by the general Criminal Law. Juveniles under the age of 14 cannot be held culpable of committing a criminal offense; the justice system never gets involved (even if it is a serious crime). Instead, the social Juvenile Welfare Act (JWA) (*Sozialgesetzbuch*) for "Children in Need of Care" is applicable. Juvenile welfare agencies can act on demand of parents; however, the Family Court can impose exceptional measures, including placements and close residential care. These juvenile welfare agencies, community welfare agencies (Jugendämter), and the youth services in youth court proceedings (Jugendgerichtshilfe (JGH)), work in cooperation with juvenile justice agencies. Thereby, in these types of cases, the agencies serve dual purposes: first, they fulfill purely welfare-orientated tasks (such as family aid, protection of children in need of care according to the JWA); second, they provide the prosecutors in juvenile court personal and family background information (similar to a pre-sentence report in the U.S.) for the trial to assist the judge in finding an appropriate sanction. They also are partly responsible for the implementation of educational measures (mediation, social training, etc.). The personnel of the JGH are social workers or teachers with university-level training in pedagogy (Dünkel, 2018).

Juveniles (ages 14 to under 18) have *relative criminal responsibility*. The JJA is applicable if the juvenile "according to his/her physical and psychological development is able to recognize the wrongdoing the criminal act according to his/her cognitive discernment" (§ 3 JJA). Young adults (age 18 to under 21) have *absolute criminal responsibility*. However, they can be dealt with in juvenile court under juvenile law *or* the general Criminal Law for adults (*Strafgesetzbuch*). Even if the young adult is prosecuted under the general Criminal Law, the procedures are the same as for juveniles. To determine if young adults should be treated as juveniles or adults the court makes the following determination: if a global examination of the offender's personality and his/her social environment indicates that at the time of committing the crime, the young adult and his/her moral and psychological development was like a juvenile (e.g., lack of autonomous judgment and ability to plan future life; living in the moment; risk seeking) *or* the motives and circumstances of the offense are those typical of a juvenile crime (e.g., spontaneous, careless, anger-motivated, impulsive behavior), then the individual will be treated as a juvenile (§105 (I) No. 1 and 2 JJA). Thereby, the court looks at each juvenile and his/her personal development individually rather than relying on rigid classifications (Dünkel, 2018).

ENTRY INTO JUVENILE JUSTICE SYSTEM AND JUVENILE SANCTIONS AND TREATMENT

Juvenile Justice Processes and Dispositions in the United States

Changes in the volume of U.S. juvenile court cases spanning the last three decades have reflected the changes in the overall crime rate, significantly rising from the mid-1980s, peaking in the mid-to-late-1990s, and declining thereafter; and, in 2013 the number of juvenile cases was close to the number in 1984 (approximately 1,058,500; see Furdella & Puzzanchera, 2015). Juveniles arrive to the JJS via multiple referral "sources, including law enforcement agencies, social service agencies, schools, parents, probation officers, and victims" (Hockenberry & Puzzanchera, 2015, p. 29) [for a juvenile case flow diagram see OJJDP (n.d. b)]. Following a referral, the case is routed to an intake process, usually conducted by a juvenile probation officer (JPO); the JPO assesses the case and the juvenile, including performing a risk and needs assessment, and determines how the case will be handled (Lindner, 2008).

Of the juveniles who are initially referred to the JJS, excluding those who are automatically placed into the adult system due to statutory waiver, etc., less than 1 percent are subsequently bound-over to adult court—e.g., approximately 4,000 of the 1,058,500 (.3%) juvenile offenders in 2013 (Furdella & Puzzanchera, 2015). In some jurisdictions, and depending on the waiver processes, a JPO is tasked with providing an in-depth assessment and recommendation to the court regarding the amenability of a juvenile facing transfer to an adult venue. The majority of juveniles, however, are not charged as adults, but instead are processed as juveniles for both delinquent acts and status offenses. Following the JPO's intake procedure, the juvenile may be processed informally, such as counseled and released, placed in a diversion program, directed to services, or made party to informal probation supervision; conversely, the case may be handled formally through court hearing[s], during which the JPO's intake report and recommendation also are taken into consideration (Lindner, 2008). The possible outcomes of the formal processing - a petition to the court, similar to bringing charges in an adult court (to which 55% [582,800] of juvenile cases were subject in 2013; Furdella & Puzzanchera, 2015) - are numerous possible lengths of probation supervision with a variety of conditions which may include out-of-home placement and/or rehabilitative programs, various lengths of placement at a juvenile secure correctional facility, or dismissal (Furdella & Puzzanchera, 2015). In certain cases, the JPO will complete an additional pre-disposition report for the court prior to the disposition hearing. Via these types of procedures, in 2013, combining both formal and informal processing, approximately 7.5 percent of juveniles were placed in a secure correctional facility, 29.5 percent received probation, 20.4 percent received other sanction, and 32 percent of the cases were dismissed (see Furdella & Puzzanchera, 2015). Formal processing alone illustrates a slightly different distribution, but still shows a focus on rehabilitation within the community setting.

Some communities may even use probation as a way of informally monitoring at-risk youth and preventing their progression into more serious problem behavior. With such varied uses, there is no doubt that probation touches large numbers of juveniles. For example, "probation was ordered in 49 percent of the 601,700 delinquency cases that received a juvenile court sanction in 2015, compared with 11 percent that received placement in an out-of-home facility" (OJJDP, n.d. c, para. 1).

While there is a distinct and most significant difference between probation supervision and the conditions of residing in a secure correctional facility, both situations may use similar treatment programming. Programs that have garnered support include restorative justice techniques, motivational interviewing, cognitive skills building, strengths-based rehabilitation techniques, such as resilience building and protective factors (Barton & Butts, 2008), wrap-around services, functional family therapy (FFT), and multi-systemic therapy (MST) (Underwood, von Dresner, & Phillips, 2006). Each situation, however, does have its own unique elements. Conditions of probation may include adherence to a curfew, community service, restitution, and counseling, among other requirements (OJJDP, 2003). Secure correctional facilities oftentimes have additional programs pertinent to their unique conditions, such as group therapy and reentry programs (Indiana Division of Youth Services, n.d.).

There is no shortage of program models. For example, Indiana identifies 20 rehabilitative juvenile programs operating under the Indiana Division of Youth Services (Indiana Division of Youth Services, n.d.); Underwood et al. (2006) identify 7 "best-evidence" treatment programs; OJJDP's Model Programs Guide identifies over 54 effective programs for juveniles in several different areas: prevention; detention, confinement, and supervision; courts; and, offending (OJJDP, n.d. d). But, how often are the best and effective programs operated and how many juveniles participate in these services?

If the use of specialty problem solving courts (PSC) is indicative of utilization patterns for other programs as well, there may be underutilization of effective programs. In 2012, there were approximately 3052 PSCs in the U.S. (Strong, Rantala, & Kyckelhahn, 2016). Of these PSCs, 244 were "youth specialty" PSCs, which remarkably reported that 100 percent of the participants completed the program, compared to 57 percent of PSC completions overall (Strong et al., 2016). If completion is a pathway to effectiveness, it would seem that youth specialty PSCs are encouraging. Of these courts, however, approximately half (53%) admitted less than 50 participants during 2012; this is similar to the limited use in the overall PSC system, although not as severe, wherein 72 percent of all PSCs, including all adult PSC courts and juvenile PSCs that specialize in drugs, mental health, etc., admitted fewer than 50 participants during the same year (Strong et al., 2016).

It may be that certain types and foci of programs are used more than others. Restorative justice principles, for instance, are historically and partially represented among JJS sanctions, such as restitution and community service, which are widely used. However, to what extent is the comprehensive approach applied? As mentioned above, in the 1990s, OJJDP initiated the BARJ Project. The BARJ approach, initially inspired by Maloney, Romig, and Armstrong's *balanced approach* work, which integrated the offender, victim, and the community in holding the juvenile accountable while restoring the victim and rehabilitating the juvenile to be a productive community member (1988), has now expanded across the U.S. Only 10 states do not identify BARJ approaches in their state statutes or codes (Pavelka, 2016). The BARJ approach includes practices such as "victim offender mediation, community conferencing circles, neighborhood accountability boards and reparative boards" (Pavelka, 2016, p. 5).

It is apparent that the pattern of disposition types has shifted in the last 20 years towards rehabilitation and restorative justice for less serious offenders. Although the shift is philosophically significant, the number of juvenile participants in the most effective programming may be relatively low, perhaps, simply a problem of underutilization. Pavelka (2016) explains,

> "[…] the degree to which the policy and legislation is explicitly or implicitly applied varies. Further, few mandates and structure are inclusive to support systematic implementation with adequate and necessary funding mandates which are necessary for reasonable returns in pursuit of policy goals and successful practices" (p.13).

SERIOUS JUVENILE OFFENDERS IN THE U.S.

In terms of more serious offenders, as mentioned above, states and the federal government have different methods of determining whether a juvenile is processed as a juvenile or as an adult. All the methods by which this is conducted include meeting various criteria, such as the offender's age, type of offense, and offending history. The four general methods are as follows: *Judicial Waiver* —whereby the prosecutor petitions the court to waive (forego) jurisdiction, thus forwarding the case to adult criminal court or whereby a certain combination of factors have been statutorily pre-defined to classify the offender as culpable by adult standards, and, after the court verifies the criteria, the case then is automatically forwarded to adult criminal court; *Prosecutorial Discretion* or *Concurrent Jurisdiction* - whereby a prosecutor, without judicial approval, is permitted to decide whether the juvenile is processed as a juvenile or an adult; *Statutory Exclusion* - through which statutes have identified criteria that automatically place a juvenile offender's case in the adult criminal court; and, *Presumptive Waiver* - which is similar to Statutory Exclusion, except that the juvenile has the opportunity to convince the juvenile court that he or she is amenable to treatment, and, thus, should be processed as a juvenile

(Griffin, Addie, Adams, & Firestine, 2011; Griffin, Torbet, & Szymanski, 1998). While only happening in less than one percent of all cases, it still affects thousands of juveniles who are transferred to adult court (Furdella & Puzzanchera, 2015; Griffin et al., 2011)

Germany's Emphasis on Diversion

In Germany, juvenile prosecutors are the gatekeepers. They conduct pre-trial investigations and can call experts to further inquire about a case (Rap & Weijers, 2014). Police officers do not have a lot of discretion and are subject to the so-called *legality principle*: all cases must be brought up to the prosecutor who decides whether or not to file charges (Dünkel, 2006; Matthews, Schiraldi, & Chester, 2018; Rap & Weijers, 2014). As mentioned above, the emphasis on diversion and the principle of minimum intervention are some of the main principles of the German JJS. In fact, approximately 70 percent of juvenile cases are dealt with by diversionary measures, compared to 40 percent in the early 1980s (Dünkel, 2014). These principles are applied even to more serious and repeat offenders. There are four types of diversion:

> (1) Diversion without any sanction: there is no intervention for non-serious (petty) offenses if the youth has no educational needs. This is the most common response. (2) The second level is diversion with educational interventions of others. For instance, if the prosecutor believes that parents or schools have sufficiently intervened, s/he can dismiss the case. The law specifically mentions successful reparation by the offender to the victim for this level of diversion. (3) For the third level (diversion with an intervention), the juvenile prosecutor can recommend educational measures or minor obligations to the judge. Examples of these measures or obligations include warnings, community service, mediation or victim offender reconciliation, participation in a training course for traffic offenders, payment of compensation or reparation, an apology to the victim, community service (usually between 10 and 40 hours) or paying a fine to a nonprofit organization. If the juvenile successfully fulfills these obligations, the juvenile prosecutor in cooperation with the juvenile judge dismisses the case (Dünkel, 2006). A fourth type of diversion can happen *after* charges have been filed. This is the case if the juvenile, for instance, went through a victim offender mediation while awaiting trial and, when it comes to the court proceedings, the judge deems further sanctions unnecessary.

If cases are not dismissed or diverted after charges have been filed, juvenile courts have a wide range of more formal sanctions at their disposal. All of these formal sanctions are based on the principle of minimum intervention. They range from educational measures (for instance, community service, participation in a victim offender mediation, vocational training, or social training course, which is a group program that aims to improve social competence), and disciplinary measures (for instance, formal cautioning by a judge, paying a fine, completing community service, or short-term detention up to four weeks or during weekends and spare time in a special unit separated from the youth prison) to youth imprisonment, including suspended youth prison sentences (if less than two years) and unconditional youth prison sentences. The minimum prison sentence is six months, which "is based on the belief that treatment and education of a juvenile offender are efficient only if a minimum of secure confinement is available (Albrecht, 2004, p. 473). The maximum youth prison sentence is generally five years. In cases where the adult prison sentence would be more than 10 years, the youth sentence may not exceed ten years (Albrecht, 2004). If the sentence is suspended, which happens in more than two thirds of the cases, probationary services become involved (Dünkel, 2006). Similar to juvenile probation in the U.S., probation and other disciplinary measures can contain court orders, which are meant to educate the juvenile offender and prevent at risk situations. For example, the juvenile can be ordered to not associate with certain persons or frequent certain places. Generally, Germany's emphasis on diversion and informal sanctions has been shown to be very successful as an effective response to most juvenile offending, as indicated by the relatively low recidivism rates (Dünkel, 2006).

Germany's Approach to More Serious Offenders

In the German JJS, adult transfers do not exist; juvenile cases are never waived to adult court, including the most serious cases. If young adults are treated under the general criminal law for adults, there are limitations in terms of possible sanctions. Approximately, two thirds of young adults are sentenced under the juvenile law (Dünkel, 2006). Most importantly, juvenile imprisonment also is based on the *principle of last resort,* i.e., it can only be used if other educational or disciplinary measures do not seem appropriate. Further, it should only "be imposed either as a consequence of the necessity to educate the juvenile offender and to respond to negative habits indicated by the offense committed" (Albrecht, 2004, p. 474). Germany's youth prisons are based on a rehabilitative ideal. Therefore, a therapeutic approach (including social workers and psychologists) is key. In terms of imprisonment length, 14–17 year-olds can receive a maximum sentence of 5 years. For the most serious crimes, for which adults could be sentenced to more than 10 years, young adults' (ages18-20) maximum length of imprisonment would be 10 years. Youth are only eligible for these maximum sentences if they show "dangerous tendencies" which render community sanctions inappropriate or because of their "gravity of guilt" concerning the most serious crimes such as murder and aggravated robbery (§ 17(2) JJA). While there is some variation between states, approximately two thirds of young adults are sentenced according to the JJA, including the most serious offenses such as homicide and rape (Dünkel, 2014; Schiraldi, 2018).

Discussion

Both countries, the U.S. and Germany, use mixed models of juvenile justice, which recognize the difference between juvenile and adult offenders and promote individualized sentences, separate facilities, legal protections, and an emphasis on rehabilitation and treatment. In contrast to "pure" justice models, Dünkel (2014) suggests that there is now a "differentiated picture of a 'new complexity'," which includes both more punitive [more so in the U.S. than in Germany] juvenile justice policies and reform efforts of juvenile prosecutors, courts, social workers, and juvenile welfare agencies which resist penal populism and increased punitiveness to juvenile offenders (p. 69).

Despite the commonalities, there are some distinct differences between the two countries. In fact, it is generally found that the U.S. incarceration rate significantly exceeds other countries (McCarthy et al., 2016). Interestingly, when looking at what types of offenders are behind bars in the U.S., it does not only seem to be the most violent offenders. In fact, almost two thirds of incarcerated juveniles are incarcerated for non-person offenses such as property, public order, and drug crimes, including probation violations and status offenses (McCarthy et al., 2016).[3] Further, while only in a minority of cases, juveniles continue to be transferred to adult court (Furdella & Puzzanchera, 2015). This more punitive approach to juvenile offenders gained momentum in the 1980 and 1990s when "getting tough" approaches to juvenile crime became popular and nearly every state expanded its transfer laws by broadening the eligibility for transfers, authorizing prosecutors (and not judges) to decide on possible transfers, or replacing individual discretion with automatic and categorical mechanisms (Griffin et al., 2011; Howell et al., 2013).

These punitive approaches to juvenile offending seem to apply more often to minority groups, and the JJS has guided much of the concern over the racial disparity among juveniles involved in the system. In 2002, the OJJDP was tasked with overseeing state's efforts to reduce disproportionate minority contact (DMC) in the JJS (Soler & Garry, 2009). Even though crime rates and the numbers of juveniles processed in the JJS have decreased, racial disparities remain stable (Rovner, 2014). In fact, minority youth continue to be over-represented at all stages of the JJS (Howell et al., 2013; Merlo & Benekos, 2017). In 2017, for instance, 15 percent of youths under 18 years of age were Black (OJJDP, 2018b), yet, of the cases in juvenile courts in 2016, 35.5 percent were Black (Sickmund, Sladky, & Kang, 2018). Specifically, they are more likely to be arrested, referred to court, and detained by the police than their white counterparts. This especially applies for drug offenses, even though Black and white offenders have similar rates of self-reported drug use (Howell et al., 2013; Rovner, 2014). Minority youth, and

[3] Note, however, that most of these charges were plea-bargained and do not account for what the judge may have based the sentence on (e.g., offense gravity score or the prior record score).

especially Black youth, also are more likely to be waived to adult court (Merlo & Benekos, 2017). Some suggest that this over-representation and harsher treatment can be explained by legal factors such as prior record and seriousness of the offense. More specifically it is argued that minority youth's *differential offending,* due to their complex risk profile, causes their greater involvement in the CJS (OJJPD, 2014, p. 3). In this regard, the National Research council stated that the

> "totality of these risk factors is such that minority youth are born into and raised in severely compromised familial, community, and educational environments that set the stage for a range of adverse behaviors and outcomes, including problems in school, relationships, and engaging in prosocial behavior" (2009, p. 224 in OJJDP, 2014, p. 3).

In fact, some research indicates that minority youth do commit more and more violent crimes. However, these types of offenses only reflect a minority of all juvenile arrests (approximately, 5 percent) (Rovner, 2014).

In contrast, another theoretical perspective suggests that racial disparities are caused by *differential treatment* and not by legal or extralegal factors (e.g., socioeconomic status or level of education) (OJJDP, 2014, p. 3). This framework argues that differential and more punitive treatment of minority youth starts early on and continues throughout the different stages of the CJS (OJJPD, 2014).

Both frameworks have been criticized for their respective shortcomings and there is some consensus that its DMC is not caused by one or the other. Rather, it is a multitude of factors and their interactions that contribute to the over-representation of minority youth in the CJS. The following quote by the National Research Council (2013) summarizes this consensus well:

> "We know that racial/ethnic disparities are not reducible to either differential offending or differential selection. Many other factors affect disproportionality of minority youth in the juvenile justice system, including the troubling entrenched patterns of poverty, segregation, gaps in educational achievement, and residential instability. DMC exists in the broader context of a 'racialized society' in which many public policies, institutional practices, and cultural representations operate to produce and maintain racial inequities." (p. 239 in OJJDP, 2014, p. 4)

The OJJDP has attempted to address the problem through extensive analysis, planning, and development culminating in its Disproportionate Minority Technical Assistance Manual, which covers numerous points of contact, e.g., school discipline, police activity, probation officer discretion, etc. The fourth version of the manual (2009) prescribes a 5-phase model for ongoing reduction efforts, which includes identification, assessment/diagnosis, intervention, evaluation, and monitoring, "to ensure equal and fair treatment for every youth in the juvenile justice system, regardless of race and ethnicity" (OJJDP, 2009, p. 4).

Despite these efforts, the disparate treatment of minority offenders in the criminal justice system remains a problem. As indicated in the above manual, the causes of the over-representation actually begin much earlier when minority youth are disproportionally disciplined and/or suspended for minor infractions as early as kindergarten. This difference in processing continues into school, where research has found that they are three times more likely to be expelled or suspended from school than white students (Merlo & Benekos, 2017). While factors other than race certainly play a role in these expulsions and suspensions (e.g., prior history of disruptive behavior, prior offense, lack of parent involvement, etc.), some researchers further suggest that minority youth "appear[ed] to be referred to the office for infractions that are both less serious and more subjective in their interpretations than white students" (Skiba, Michael, Nardo & Peterson, 2000, p. 13).

The role of schooling conditions and schooling discipline, such as zero-tolerance policies and the disparate application of suspensions and expulsions, in the creation of delinquency is commonly referred to as the "school-to-prison pipeline:"

> "[This is described as the] disturbing national trend wherein children are funneled out of public schools and into the juvenile and criminal justice systems. Many of these children have learning disabilities or histories of poverty, abuse, or neglect, and would benefit from additional educational and counseling services. Instead, they are isolated, punished, and pushed out" (ACLU, n.d, para 1.).

The question becomes as to why OJJDP's efforts to reduce DMC have not been successful, indicated by the continued disparate treatment of minority youths, starting as early as kindergarten and then peaking in the JJS. While some jurisdictions have successfully reduced DMC, more needs to be done. Rovner (2017) suggests that states should establish coordinating bodies, which oversee initiatives to reduce DMC. Further, he recommends data that identifies at which decisions points in the JJS disparate treatment exists should be collected and the implementation of DMC policies that attempt to reduce it be evaluated.

Fortunately, more positive developments are reflected in another area—recent U.S. Supreme Court decisions, which have recognized developmental and neuroscience research about juveniles and emphasized a more individualized and rehabilitative approach to more serious juvenile offenders. Particularly, the Supreme Court decided in *Roper v. Simmons* (2005) that it is it is unconstitutional to impose the death penalty for crimes committed while under the age of 18; *Graham v. Florida* (2010) ruled that the Constitution prohibits the imposition of a life sentence without parole on a juvenile who did not commit homicide. In *Miller v. Alabama (2012),* the court decided that a mandatory life sentence without parole for a juvenile is cruel and unusual punishment, even when the crime is homicide; and, finally, in *Montgomery v. Louisiana (2016)* it was decided that the previous *Miller* decision applied retroactively. These more recent

Supreme Court decisions acknowledge, to some extent, neurological research which shows that the part of juvenile brain that regulates impulse control and reasoning continues to develop well into the 20s and that young adults are more similar to children and juveniles than older adults in terms of their psychosocial development (Howell et al., 2013; Matthews et al., 2018; Pruin & Dünkel, 2015; Schiraldi, Western, & Bradner, 2015). While juveniles reach cognitive maturity (i.e., the ability to distinguish right from wrong) at age 15 or 16, their "psychosocial maturity of judgment, risk assessment, and self control" emerges much later (Howell et al., 2013, p. 18). This research has evoked calls to raise the jurisdiction of juvenile court to at least 21-year-olds and, even, to 24 or 25-year-olds with "gradually diminishing protections" for these young adults (Schiraldi et al., 2015, p. 3), which would be more comparable to the German approach to young adults.

Furthermore, there have been more recent and long-standing efforts of significantly reducing juvenile incarceration rates, moving towards deinstitutionalization, and focusing on community-based alternatives (see "Reduce, Reform, Replace, and Reinvest" examples in different states; McCarthy et al., 2016). Similarly, Merlo and Benekos (2010), who reviewed emergent policies in juvenile justice, suggest there appears to be a re-commitment to emphasize treatment and rehabilitation while holding juvenile offenders accountable. They suggest, "a softening in punitive attitude", which was "initiated by declining crime rates, fiscal constraints, new research on adolescent brain development and evidence of effective interventions" (p. 20 and 21).

It remains to be seen how juvenile justice policy will evolve in the U.S. This becomes especially interesting because of the inconsistencies between states and even between jurisdictions in the U.S. While some states have proposed some progressive changes, there has not been a systemic reform in any state (Matthews et al., 2018). In this regard, Howell et al. (2013) summarize the current system as "a bewildering and inconsistent array of juvenile and adult justice system responses "with many inconsistent processing and sentencing decisions in terms of whether or not juvenile offenders receive treatment" (p. 6). It is paramount to end the overreaction to juvenile crime and continue to push towards rehabilitation, individualized treatment, and evidenced based practice while, at the same time, holding juvenile offenders accountable for their actions.

In Germany, more recent trends show that the juvenile justice system has held on to its approach based on minimal intervention, mediation, educational measures, and imprisonment as the last resort. In fact, there has been a considerable increase in the use of diversions and educational measures, a decrease in short-term (up to 4 weeks) and long(er)-term youth imprisonment, despite the pressure from the media and politicians, which fueled debates about getting tough on youth crime (Dünkel, 2018). There seems to be a more lenient approach, focusing even more on newer community sanctions, such as mediation, social training courses, and community service. However, like the disproportionate minority contact in the U.S., young migrants and members of ethnic minorities are over-represented in the German JJS, including arrest and detention (Muncie, 2008). For instance, in Berlin, non-citizens immigrants reflect 60% of the young adults in prison, while recent citizens constituted another 20%, compared to the general population, in which native Germans reflect 70% and the other two categories are 15% (Brownsberger, 2018). Muncie (2008) suggests that "[t]his raises the question of a fundamental racialization of youth justice in Western Europe" (p. 112). Furthermore, also similar to the U.S., political calls demanding to increase the punitiveness of the juvenile justice system (e.g., lowering the age of juvenile court jurisdiction from 14 to 12 and eliminating or at least diminishing the possibility of treating young adults as juveniles) consistently emerge (Ostendorf, 2010). Improving the situation of juvenile minority groups, including their socio-economic status, educational opportunities, and differential treatment in the JJS should be a paramount policy concern in both countries.

This comparison reveals several themes for the two countries to consider in their attempts to improve the efficacy of their respective JJS. Germany's system appears to offer several elements which are significantly underutilized or missing in the U.S. system: treatment that regularly includes individual counseling and social work assistance, retaining full jurisdiction over offenders who are under 18-years-old, and the strong consideration of neurological development issues that cross the seemingly arbitrary line between childhood and adulthood and, thus, perhaps strengthens efforts to rehabilitate relatively young persons over the age of 18 who are still in a developmental stage. Similarly, the U.S. offers two elements which may benefit Germany: the use of widely accessible justice organizations, such as OJJDP, U.S. DOJ, etc., that collect, analyze, and share data, as well as disseminate best practices throughout the systems across the country; and a cautionary tale of unintended consequences from punitive policy inspired by a populist fear of crime.

Conclusion

When looking at these two countries it becomes clear that neither has developed a thorough best approach to respond to juvenile offending. Both systems use complex mixed models of juvenile justice, including both welfare and justice elements. While more recent in the U.S., both countries display promising reforms based on rehabilitation and evidenced-based practices especially for more serious offenders. Juvenile crime rates have been stable in both countries and there is a general consensus about what works best with juvenile offenders. It is likely that both countries will face significant challenges in maintaining their existing strengths and further honing their juvenile justice systems. Germany is facing a populist movement that may exert pressure to forgo Germany's commitment to rehabilitation over punishment. The U.S. is facing a deep-seated, 30-year-old fear of juveniles; if policy-makers are compelled to embrace rehabilitation, any change will have to be designed in a manner that is palatable to citizens who are fearful of the most brutal offenders being released into the community at the age of 21, yet, not rehabilitated; to retain jurisdiction over youth in order to rehabilitate, the U.S. juvenile justice system may have to forge new ground by not only asserting full jurisdiction over those under the age of 18, but also asserting continued and lengthy jurisdiction over the most serious offenders to expire only after rehabilitation has been achieved—a condition that would likely face significant challenges as well.

REFERENCES

ACLU (n.d). *School-to-Prison Pipeline*. Retrieved November 3, 2018 from https://www.aclu.org/issues/juvenile-justice/school-prison-pipeline.

Albrecht, H. (2004). Youth Justice in Germany. *Crime and Justice, 31*, 443-493 doi:10.1086/655346.

Barton, W. H., & Butts, J. A. (2008). *Building on Strength: Positive Youth Development in Juvenile Justice Programs*. Chicago, IL: Chapin Hall Center for Children.

Becker, E. (2001, February 9). As ex-theorist on young 'superpredators,' Bush aide has regrets. *The New York Times*. Retrieved from: https://www.nytimes.com/2001/02/09/us/as-ex-theorist-on-young-superpredators-bush-aide-has-regrets.html.

Brownsberger, W. (2018). *Young Adults in the German Criminal Justice* System. Retrieved from: https://willbrownsberger.com/young-adults-in-the-german-criminal-justice-system/

Decker, S. H., & Marteache, N. (2018). *International Handbook of Juvenile Justice*. Cham: Springer International Publishing.

Dilulio, J. (1995, November 27). The coming of the super-predators. *The Weekly Standard*. Retrieved from https://www.weeklystandard.com/john-j-dilulio-jr/the-coming-of-the-super-predators.

Doob, A. N., & Tonry, M. (2004). Varieties of Youth Justice. *Crime and Justice, 31*, 1-20. doi:10.1086/655333.

Dünkel, F. (2006). Juvenile Justice in Germany: Between Welfare and Justice. In J. Junger-Tas & S.H. Decker (Eds.), *International Handbook of Juvenile Justice* (pp. 225-262). Berlin, New York, Springer.

Dünkel, F. (2014). Juvenile Justice Systems in Europe – Reform Developments between Justice, Welfare and 'New Punitiveness'. *Kriminologijos Studijos, 1*. doi:10.15388/crimlithuan.2014.0.3676.

Dünkel, F. (2018). *Juvenile Justice, Sentencing and Youth Imprisonment in Germany*. Power Point Presentation. Retrieved from: https://webcache.googleusercontent.com/search?q=cache:Dlj-YSqtnX4J; https:// willbrownsberger.com/ wp-content/ uploads/

2018/ 04/ German- Juvenile- Justice- and- Youth- Impris32018-Final. pptx+ &cd= 2&hl=en&ct=clnk&gl=us&client=safari.

FBI (2017). State-by-State and National Crime Estimates by Year(s). *Uniform Crime Reporting Statistics, Estimated Crime: State Level.* Retrieved October 22, 2018 from http://www.ucrdatatool.gov/Search/Crime/State/RunCrimeStatebyState.cfm.

Fox, S. J. (1996). The Early History of the Court. *The Future of Children, 6*(3), 29-39. doi:10.2307/1602591.

Furdella, J., & Puzzanchera, C. (2015). Delinquency Cases in Juvenile Court, 2013 (NCJ 248899). *Juvenile Offenders and Victims, National Report Series.* Retrieved from http://www.ncjj.org/pdf/248899.pdf.

Gonzales, S. (2016). Kids in Prison: Germany Has a Different Approach, Better Results. *WNYC News.* Retrieved from: https://www.wnyc.org/story/being-kid-adult-prison-here-vs-other-countries/

Griffin, P., Addie, S., Adams, B., & Firestine, K. (2011). *Trying and Sentencing Juveniles as Adults: An Analysis of State Transfer Laws and Reporting*. Office of Juvenile Justice and Delinquency Prevention. Retrieved from http://www.ncjj.org/pdf/Transfer_232434.pdf.

Griffin, P., Torbet, P., & Szymanski, L. (1998). *Trying Juveniles as Adults in Criminal Court: An Analysis of State Transfer Provisions* (NCJ 172836). Washington, DC: U.S. Government Printing Office.

Hinton, W. J., Sims, P. L., Adams, M. A., & West, C. (2007). Juvenile Justice: A System Divided. *Criminal Justice Policy Review, 18*(4), 466-483. doi:10.1177/0887403407304578.

Hockenberry, S., & Puzzanchera, C. (2015). *Juvenile Court Statistics 2013.* Pittsburgh, PA: National Center for Juvenile Justice. Retrieved from http://www.ncjj.org/pdf/jcsreports/jcs2013.pdf.

Howell, J. C., Feld, B. C., Mears, D. P., Farrington, D. P., Loeber, R., & Petechuk, D. (2013). *Bulletin 5: Young Offenders and an Effective Response in the Juvenile and Adult Justice Systems: What Happens, What Should Happen, and What We Need to Know (Study Group on the Transitions between Juvenile Delinquency and Adult Crime) (*Grant Number 2008-IJ-CX-K402). Report Submitted to the U.S. Department of Justice. Retrieved from: https://www.ncjrs.gov/pdffiles1/nij/grants/242935.pdf.

Hurley, T. D. (1907) History of the Illinois juvenile court law. *Juvenile Court Record (Chicago Visitation and Aid Society), 8*(7, August), pp. 18 – 25. Retrieved from https://books.google.com.

Indiana Division of Youth Services (n.d.). *Juvenile Treatment Interventions.* Retrieved from https://www.in.gov/idoc/dys/2374.htm.

Junger-Tas, J., & Decker, S.H. (Eds.) (2006). *International Handbook of Juvenile Justice.* Berlin, New York, Springer.

Legal Information Institute (n.d.). *18 U.S. Code § 5037 – Dispositional Hearing*. Retrieved from https://www.law.cornell.edu/uscode/text/18/5037.

Lenroot, K. F., & Lundberg, E. O. (1925). *Juvenile Courts at Work* (United States Children's Bureau, Publication No. 141). Washington, DC: Government Printing Office. Retrieved from https://archive.org/details/juvenilecourtsat00unit/page/n1.

Liles, A., & Moak, S. C. (2014). Changing Juvenile Justice Policy in Response to the US Supreme Court: Implementing Miller v. Alabama. *Youth Justice, 15*(1), 76-92. doi:10.1177/1473225414529201.

Lindner, C. (2008). Probation Intake: Gatekeeper to the Family Court. *Federal Probation, 72*(1). Retrieved from http://www.uscourts.gov/sites/default/files/fed_probation_june_2008.pdf.

Matthews, S., Schiraldi, V., & Chester, L. (2018). Youth Justice in Europe: Experience of Germany, the Netherlands, and Croatia in Providing Developmentally Appropriate Responses to Emerging Adults in the Criminal Justice System. *Justice Evaluation Journal, 1*(1), 59-81. doi:10.1080/24751979.2018.1478443.

McCarthy, P., Schiraldi, V., & Shark, M. (2016). *The Future of Youth Justice: A Community-Based Alternative to the Youth Prion Model*. No 2. Available at: https://www.hks.harvard.edu/sites/default/files/centers/wiener/programs/pcj/files/ntcc_the_future_of_youth_justice.pdf.

Merlo, A. V., & Benekos, P. J. (2010). Is Punitive Juvenile Justice Policy Declining in the United States? A Critique of Emergent Initiatives. *Youth Justice, 10*(1), 3-24. https://doi.org/10.1177/1473225409356740.

Merlo, A. V., & Benekos, P. J. (2017). *Reaffirming Juvenile Justice: From Gault to Montgomery*. London: Routledge.

Monell, J. S. (2017). Juvenile reformatories [Abstract]. In K. R. Kerley, H. Copes, S. De Li, J. Lane, & S. F. Sharp (Eds.), *The Encyclopedia of Corrections*. Hoboken, NJ: Wiley-Blackwell. https://doi.org/10.1002/9781118845387.wbeoc069.

Muncie, J. (2008). The Punitive Turn in Juvenile Justice: Cultures of Control and Rights Compliance in Western Europe and the USA. *Youth Justice, 8*(2), 107-121. doi:10.1177/1473225408091372.

National Association of Youth Courts (n.d.). *Youth Courts Coast-to-Coast*. Retrieved from https://www.youthcourt.net/index.php/youth-courts-in-usa/youth-court-websites- by-state.

OJJDP (n.d. a). *Legislation/JDDP Act*. Retrieved from https://www.ojjdp.gov/about/legislation.html.

OJJDP (n.d. b). Case Flow Diagram. *Statistical Briefing Book: Juvenile Justice System Structure & Process*. Retrieved from https://www.ojjdp.gov/ojstatbb/structure_process/case.html).

OJJDP (n.d. c). Overview. *Statistical Briefing Book: Juveniles on Probation*. Retrieved from https://www.ojjdp.gov/ojstatbb/probation/overview.html.

OJJDP (n.d. d). *Model Programs Guide*. Retrieved from https://www.ojjdp.gov/mpg/.

OJJDP (1999). *Juvenile justice: A Century of Change* (NCJ 178995). Retrieved from https://www.ncjrs.gov/pdffiles1/ojjdp/178995.pdf.

OJJDP (2003). Probation as a Court Disposition. *Statistical Briefing Book: Juveniles on Probation*. Retrieved from https://www.ojjdp.gov/ojstatbb/probation/qa07101.asp?qaDate=20030811.

OJJDP (2006). Judicial Waiver Offense and Minimum Age Criteria, 2004. *Statistical Briefing Book: Juvenile Justice System Structure & Process*. Retrieved from https://www.ojjdp.gov/ojstatbb/structure_process/qa04110.asp?maplink=link1&qaDate=2004&text=yes.

OJJDP (2009). *Disproportionate Minority Contact Technical Assistance Manual*. Washington, D.C.: OJJDP. Retrieved from https://www.ncjrs.gov/html/ojjdp/dmc_ta_manual/dmcfull.pdf.

OJJDP (2014). *Disproportionate Minority Contact. Literature Review. A Product of the Model Program Guide*. Retrieved from: https://www.ojjdp.gov/mpg/litreviews/Disproportionate_Minority_Contact.pdf.

OJJDP (2018a). Judicial Waiver Offense and Minimum Age Criteria, 2016. In *Statistical Briefing Book: Juvenile Justice System Structure & Process*. Retrieved from https://www.ojjdp.gov/ojstatbb/structure_process/qa04110.asp?qaDate=2016&text=yes&maplink=link1.

OJJDP (2018b). Juvenile Population. *Statistical Briefing Book: Juvenile Population Characteristics*. Retrieved from https://www.ojjdp.gov/ojstatbb/population/qa01104.asp?qaDate=2017.

Ostendorf, H. (2010). Verschärfungen im Jugendstrafrecht- wider die kriminologische Vernunft [Making Juvenile Justice More Punitive- Contrary to Emperical Evidence]. *Humboldt Forum Recht*, 5/2010, 68ff. Retrieved from https://www. humboldt-forum-recht.de/media/Druckansicht/pdf/2010-05.pdf.

Pavelka, S. (2016). Restorative Justice in the States: An Analysis of Statutory Legislation and Policy. *Justice Policy Journal*, *2*(13), 1-23.

Pemberton, C. H. (1894). Boarding System for Neglected Children [Presentation at the *Twenty-first Annual Session of the National Conference of Charities and Correction*, May, 1894]. Retrieved from https://socialwelfare.library.vcu.edu/programs/child-welfarechild-labor/boarding-system-neglected-children-1894/

Pruin, I., & Dünkel, F. (2015). *Better in Europe? European Responses to Young Adult Offending. Full Report*. Retrieved from https://www.t2a.org.uk/wp-content/uploads/2015/02/T2A_Better-in-Europe_Report-_online.pdf.

Rap, S., & Weijers, I. (2014). *The Effective Youth Court: Juvenile Justice Procedures in Europe*. The Hague: Eleven International Publishing.

Rovner, J. (2014). *Disproportionate Minority Contact in the Juvenile Justice System*. Washington, DC: The Sentencing Project. Retrieved from https://www.sentencing

project.org/ wp-content/ uploads/ 2015/ 11/ Disproportionate-Minority-Contact-in-the-Juvenile-Justice-System.pdf.

Schiraldi, V. (2018). *In Germany, It's Hard to Find a Young Adult in Prison.* Retrieved from https:// thecrimereport.org/ 2018/ 04/ 10/ in-germany-its-hard-to-find-a-young-adult-in-prison/

Schiraldi, V., Western, B., & Bradner, K. (2015). *Community-Based Responses to Justice-Involved Young Adults* (New Thinking in Community Corrections Bulletin). Laurel, MD: U.S. Department of Justice, Office of Justice Programs, National Institute of Justice. Retrieved from https://purl.fdlp.gov/GPO/gpo83079.

Sickmund, M. (1994). *Update on Statistics: How Juveniles Get to Criminal Court* (NCJ 150309). Washington, DC: U.S. Government Printing Office. Retrieved from https://www.ncjrs.gov/pdffiles/juvcr.pdf.

Sickmund, M., & Puzzanchera, C. (Eds.). (2014). *Juvenile Offenders and Victims: 2014 National Report.* Pittsburgh, PA: National Center for Juvenile Justice.

Sickmund, M., Sladky, A., & Kang, W. (2018). *Easy Access to Juvenile Court Statistics: 1985-2016.* Retrieved from https://www.ojjdp.gov/ojstatbb/ezajcs/

Skiba, R. J., Michael, R.S., & Nardo, A.B., & Peterson, R.L. (2000). *The Color of Discipline: Sources of Racial and Gender Disproportionality in School Punishment.* Policy Research Report # SRS1. Retrieved from http://www.indiana.edu/~equity/docs/ColorOfDiscipline.pdf.

Soler, M., & Garry, L. M. (2009). Reducing Disproportionate Minority Contact: Preparation at the Local Level. *PsycEXTRA Dataset.* doi:10.1037/e623992009-001

Strong, S. M., Rantala, R. R., & Kyckelhahn, T. (2016). Census of Problem-Solving Courts, 2012 (NCJ 249803). *BJS Bulletin.* Retrieved from https://www.bjs.gov/index.cfm?ty=pbdetail&iid=5744.

Torbet, P. M. (1998). Track II: Getting Tough on Juvenile Crime: A Paradigm Shift for Juvenile Justice. In *Juvenile Justice*, *4*(1). Retrieved from https://www.ojjdp.gov/conference/track2.html.

Underwood, L. A., von Dresner, K. S., & Phillips, A. L. (2006). Community Treatment Programs for Juveniles: A Best-evidence Summary. *International Journal of Behavior Consultation and Therapy*, *2*(2), 286 – 304.

U.S. BOP (2018) *Statistics: Inmate Age.* Retrieved from https://www.bop.gov/about/statistics/statistics_inmate_age.jsp.

U.S. DOJ (n.d. a). Title 9: Criminal—9-8.000 - Juveniles. *Justice Manual*, 9-8.110. Retrieved from https://www.justice.gov/jm/jm-9-8000-juveniles.

U.S. DOJ (n.d. b). Criminal Resource Manual – CRM 1-499. *Justice Manual: Criminal Resource Manual,* CRM 101 – 140. Retrieved from https://www.justice.gov/jm/criminal-resource-manual-101-199.

Waite, R. G. (2014). Serious Juvenile Crime in Nazi Germany. *Crime and Criminal Justice in Modern Germany,* 247-269. doi: 10.2307/j.ctt9qct7p.13.

Cases

Graham v. Florida, 560 U.S.__ (2010).
Kent v. United States (1966).
In re Gault, 387 U.S. 1 (1967).
Miller v. Alabama, 567 U.S. __ (2012).

Montgomery v. Louisiana, 577 U.S. __ (2016).
Roper v. Simmons, 543 U.S. 551 (2005).

In: A Closer Look at Criminal Justice
Editors: J. A. Cooper and K. G. Jachimowski
ISBN: 978-1-53615-782-6

Chapter 13

THE U.S. MARIJUANA NEUTRAL STATE

Shavonne Arthurs*
Seton Hill University, Greensburg, PA, US

ABSTRACT

It's official: an industrialized country has just given recreational marijuana use the green light. Before you plan your first party, Canada was this forward-thinking country. Canada is set to garner approximately $3-5 billion in annual sales once the market is fully moving (Williams, 2018). Experts are estimating a market value of $22 billion by 2021, which is more net value than Canadian beer, wine, and spirit sales together. There are continued plans for international expansion and partnerships with large corporations, with strong management teams at the helm. Where does the United States land is this growing market? Still at the start line, taking the tortoise route of "slow and steady" will hopefully win the race. There are marked signs of hope, with the Drug Enforcement Agency (2018) requesting a large (452%) increase in requested marijuana production for "medical, scientific, research, industrial, and export needs for the year and for the establishment of reserve stocks". Even with this hope, the U.S. marijuana industry is unlikely to see drastic change due to political ties and social unsteadiness in views of general drug use and addiction. This chapter will muddle through the trenches of the tug-of-war marijuana legalization battle in the United States with speculation on what the future will potentially hold (and not hold) for our "buddy" cannabis.

Pot. Weed. Reefer. Mary Jane. Bud. Marijuana has many namesakes and is working on gaining acceptance into homes across the United States. Debates on the medical benefits of marijuana have been on the books for decades. More recently, the conversation has shifted to recreational legalization. While social support is visible, the federal government does not necessarily outwardly oppose, but is a bit hands off on the

---

* Author's Email: sarthurs@setonhill.edu

subject. Why is the United States lagging at the start line with an action that the population wants in majority support? While there is still a race to be had, as Uruguay and Canada are the only two countries to legalize marijuana so far, the United States does not have clear goals set. Even as states continue to push both medicinal and recreational legalization, the issue remains federally stagnant. Positive social support has teetered the scales in the "yes" direction but has yet to strongly influence the federal legalization process. With the wave of support, what exactly is the legislative hold up? This chapter digs into the variety of issues surrounding state and federal legalization movements, as well as the potential roadblocks of the near future.

It is important to outline the issues with marijuana starting from the first legislation that inhibited its use. The Marijuana Tax Act of 1937 imposed a heavy tax on hemp and cannabis products at all levels. Farmers would be taxed for cultivating hemp plants, physicians would be charged for writing out prescriptions, and pharmacists would be charged for selling those prescriptions. The taxing of hemp and cannabis was so great that it did not take long before people were discouraged from buying the product all together. It only took about four years after the act was initiated for cannabis to be removed from all pharmacies and a stigma has stuck around since.

The political and social ties to marijuana were visible then. Author Johann Hari discusses these points in the book *Chasing the Scream.* The large push in the negative viewpoints surrounding marijuana stem back to a man named Harry Anslinger. He initially headed the Department of Prohibition, which ended pretty poorly by being repealed by 1933. Anslinger got out in the nick of time when prohibition was beginning the downward trend in 1930 and was appointed the first commissioner of the Bureau of Narcotics (today it is known as the Drug Enforcement Agency or DEA). At the time, the bureau was only regulating cocaine and heroin that had been outlawed since 1914. That, and the failing of prohibition made Anslinger act in a way that has socially stuck since. He was initially recorded saying cannabis was no big threat to society during his prohibition days. Later, with a failed prohibition department linked to him and minimal drug issues to cover (dealing with cocaine and heroin) in his new position, Anslinger need "something" to essentially maintain viability in his new role. Anslinger had a major hand in the 1937 act and created a social warfare on cannabis to protect his career.

As often seen today, media hype can cause moral and social panics. Anslinger used this to his advantage and rode the coat tails of a small number of stories published on cannabis in the 1920s. These stories highlighted violent rage, manic episodes, and various psychoses related to marijuana use. In particular, Anslinger cited a story about a man named Victor Licata who used an ax to hack up his family while apparently high on marijuana. He planted the seed into social minds with this story and then added water to make it grow to great proportions. What is most ironic is that Licata's story was proven false: There was no proof he ever used marijuana and he had a long history of mental illness. Of course, Anslinger did not bother to investigate the story at the time. Along with this story, Anslinger was able to find one scientist to agree with the manic claims of marijuana. He latched onto these two items, which was all it took to create a social panic around the drug, even though the American Medical Association (AMA) strongly opposed the 1937 act and the alleged manic issues around marijuana.

The social panic around marijuana use developed quickly upon Anslinger's claims. A series of films were released surrounding the time frame of the 1937 act. *Reefer Madness* (1936), *Marihuana* (1937), *Assassin of Youth* (1937), and *Devil's Harvest* (1942) are just a few examples. The films displayed youth lashing out with manic episodes, partying, and even murdering people, while high on marijuana. Partially due to these films, marijuana socially became known as a gateway drug, an association that has yet to be shed. Anslinger also added a racial component to the fold, which was highly influential at the time. He claimed that marijuana use was largely tied to Blacks and Latinos. He also argued that jazz music (tied to those racial backgrounds) was nothing more than satanic rituals created around marijuana use.

Additionally, Anslinger got the backing of major timber and newspaper investors like William Randolph Hearst, Andrew Mellon, and the DuPont family. Hemp was a threat to these investors because it was a low-cost alternative to paper. An increase in hemp products would obviously kill their bottom line, decreasing profit. To add another ironic point, it was later determined that hemp lacked the qualities needed to produce strong enough paper-like products to use for newspapers, anyway.

Anslinger tapped into social fears at the time, which sadly had not much to do with the actual drug itself. He was able to create and entire social rhetoric around the drug and deflect the attention off the actual product. He created a medical, media, and organizational (financial) backing around criminalizing marijuana mostly for job security. If Anslinger could see the aftermath of this work, he might even be surprised at the withstanding power it has had culturally. By 1970, the Marijuana Tax Act was repealed, but replaced by the Controlled Substances Act, which placed marijuana as a Schedule I drug. It was lumped in the same category as LSD, cocaine, and heroin and was believed to have no accepted medical benefits, a high potential of abuse, and a lack of safety in use (Bradford and Bradford, 2016). This movement was created around the "war on drugs". Moving to current day, marijuana still sits in line with these drugs as Schedule I, even after many medical suggestions to lower its level.

California was the first to make attempts to shed the negative social imagery tied to marijuana. In conjunction with the Compassionate Use Act of 1996, the state became the first to legalize medical marijuana for use as treatment for chronic illnesses. Soon after, Oregon, Washington, Alaska, Maine, and Washington, D.C. medically legalized marijuana in the late 1990s. Moving into the early 2000s, Nevada, Montana, Rhode Island, Hawaii, Vermont, and New Mexico passed medicinal laws, as well. Currently, thirty-three states and Washington, D.C. have at least medical forms of legalization. Within those states, ten plus Washington, D.C. have legalized recreational use (Alaska,

California, Colorado, Maine, Massachusetts, Michigan, Nevada, Oregon, Vermont, Washington). It started with a push in 2012 with Colorado and Washington being the first to recreationally legalize.

So, what caused the social change of heart? Something must have happened from the heavy penalizing trends into the 1970s to the major legalization measures of the 1900s to current. Interestingly enough, it was not due to any strong medical testing of the drug. Due to the schedule classification, funding has been significantly restrictive for marijuana research. The change instead came from social pushes and state initiatives. Through experimentation, the baby boomer generation realized that marijuana was getting a bad rap. Lobbyists in favor of the drug also pushed reports that demonstrated successful medicinal treatments for a variety of ailments. Those two things coupled together began the marijuana upswing. The drug officially appealed to both sides of the political spectrum, as those with illnesses (and closely related) could see the benefits.

Moving to current day, there seems to be political support around marijuana, as President Trump has spoken in favor for medicinal treatments and urges state control of the issue. There are still a few detractors, though. For example, former U.S. Attorney General Jeff Sessions has largely spoken against legalization and believes marijuana should stay classified as a Schedule I drug, still relating it to being a gateway drug. There is social support for legalization, as well. To put things in perspective, in 1969 (directly prior to Schedule I classification), only 12% of Americans were pro federal legalization. By 2014, over half of Americans favored federal legalization, and it has been on a steady rise since with 64% in favor currently (Geiger-Oneto & Simkins, 2018; McCarthy, 2017). There is a higher level of support for users in comparison to non-users, but the non-users have important weight in the movement. Non-users are looking towards the greater good. Socially, the community benefits are visible. There are both health and financial benefits to legalization that are beginning to trend. In fact, it has been demonstrated that 94% of Americans support medical marijuana legalization (Hutzler, 2018). President Trump has followed that support, approving a measure that inhibits the Department of Justice from prosecuting medical marijuana businesses in states where legalized.

Thanks to states like Colorado and Washington, Americans are able to witness the outcomes of legalization. Since recreational use has been around for a few years, various things like criminal activity, health concerns, and financial issues can be analyzed. Overall, results are extremely mixed and scattered on a variety of subjects. A study by Aydelotte and colleagues (2017) found that changes in motor vehicle crash fatality rates for Colorado and Washington were not statistically different from similar states without recreational legalization. However, they did find an increase in out of state visitors to Colorado regarding emergency room visits related to the drug (Kim, Hall, Genco, VanDyke, Barker, & Monte, 2016). Regarding use itself, some studies have shown higher marijuana use in states that have legalized, but others have shown no significant changes in relation to state policy changes (Cerda, Wall, Keyes, Galea, & Hasin, 2012; Cohn,

Johnson, Rose, Rath, & Villanti, 2017; Harper, Strumpf, & Kaufman, 2012; Khatapoush & Hollfors, 2004; Wall, Poh, Cerda, Keyes, Galea, & Hasin, 2011). Most of the negative impact found in research has been centered on youth poly drug use. Concurrent use of marijuana and alcohol and/or tobacco use shows greater risk for psychological and health-related problems (Cohn, Johnson, Ehlke, & Villanti, 2016; Fairman, 2015; Wang et al., 2014). Regular and daily use in young people has been linked to negative health (both mental and physical) and social outcomes, as well (Arria et al., 2012; Volkow, Baler, Compton, & Weiss, 2014). Also, poison call centers among 9-17 year olds have increased and hospitalizations around 18-25 year olds tripled, reaching 8.1% currently. Additionally, there have been studies to counteract this point, demonstrating marijuana rates among adolescents and young adults remained steady around pre and post legalization with no significant health impacts (Vigil, Van Dyke, Hall, Contreras, Ghosh, & Wolk, 2018). Regarding criminal activity, research has found no significant difference in crime rates of non-legal to decriminalized/legal marijuana states (Maier, Mannes, & Koppenhofer, 2017). There is also no difference in the degree of legalization (measuring from decriminalization only to fully recreational legalization). The research found that property and violent crime actually appears to be lower in states with decriminalization and medical legalization, although not significantly lower. Overall, research has demonstrated an over exaggeration of previous issues, largely stemming from the "reefer madness" of olden day (Rauch, 2018).

In summary, there were major marijuana issues created through social and political propaganda that were eventually sleuthed out by a large generation to be false, which caused an uptick of legalization of a variety of levels that research has yet to show any significant impact one way or another. Seems pretty positive, right? The general movement has been in that direction. There is still much hesitation to move on federal legalization, though. It was mentioned earlier that President Trump has no issue with legalization, but wants it left to the states. Why exactly? It is potentially linked to those initial Anslinger motivations. There are social and political ties preventing movement. The federal lag causes significant issues in the state regulations, as well. The lack of proper regulations has caused what bit of social negativity is left. Until there is movement on the federal side, it looks as though states are going to have this legalization approval conundrum indefinitely.

It was mentioned earlier that 64% of people approve of recreational legalization. The number is a bit different when broken down by political affiliation. Specifically, republicans are still strongly divided on the subject, with 45% in favor and 51% opposed (Hartig & Geiger, 2018). From the same poll, approximately 69% of Democrats are in favor of recreational legalization. With strong republican ties at the federal level currently, it makes sense that feet are dragging in having a legalization discussion. It is next to impossible to talk about political movements without the necessary social backing. Also, it can be political career suicide to turn on one's affiliated party. So, there could be an indefinite amount of time spent shuffling feet around the issue unless political tides change. If the political landscape stays stationary, it is likely that mid-western and southern states will stay staunchly opposed, as those states have been the most difficult to infiltrate with any type of legalization. Ironically, the federal criminalization is having huge negative effects on state legalization and regulation. These effects are what detractors hold on to as reasons to not push federal legalization forward. It looks like the United States will be moving in circles without an end in sight.

State legalization without federal legalization has put the cart before the horse, so to speak. States began legalization without having regulating bodies in place. Many mistakes have been made and issues have occurred, which have caused "oops" moments on a variety of fronts including taxing, sales, and other regulations. First, upon recreational legalization, what limits should be placed on use and buying power? Since there are no national standards, states have had to develop their own, which causes a lack of uniformity. Colorado created the Amendment 64 Task Force in 2013 to address the issue. They recommended potency limits to not exceed 10 milligrams of tetrahydrocannabinol (THC) per serving size and 200 milligrams of THC per package. At the buying level, laws widely vary. For example, Montana allows 1 ounce and 4 plants per person, while Oregon allows 24 ounces and 24 plants per person (Bradford & Bradford, 2016; Chu, 2014; O'Keefe, 2013). Various regulations at the buyer level likely at least have a small influence on the research outcomes, especially related to health concerns. These issues could potentially be tied to the sheer amount of allotted consumption, but it is difficult to research with tourism and variation in buying powers.

Second, in relation to health concerns, there are no standardized practices for advertising and marketing like with other legalized drugs like alcohol and tobacco (Hammond, 2011). Colorado, Washington, and Oregon passed legislation that required THC warning labels to be placed on products, but addiction risks and dependence issues do not have uniformed product placement. The issues mentioned regarding youth and poly drug use could potentially be curbed a bit with adequate warning placement. Again, states generally look to states for regulations in this area. Upon legalization, states failed to realize they would have to create these types of entities on their own.

Third, there are issues in how to handle employees that use marijuana outside of the workspace with federal regulations still in place. A strong example of the issue is visible in the Christina Barbuto case (Bednar, 2018). Barbuto was fired from her job at Advantage Sales and Marketing after her first day on the job. She was diagnosed with Crohn's disease and was taking marijuana to manage it. She disclosed the information to her employers, who ensured her there would not be an issue, as the drug was medically legal in Massachusetts. She was drug tested and terminated after her first day of employment for testing positive for marijuana consumption. She sued her employer and the case went to the Massachusetts Supreme Court. There, they ruled in favor of Barbuto, citing that forbidding the use of medicinal marijuana outside of work (as long as there is no impairment on the job) was constituted as disability discrimination. A similar case occurred later in Massachusetts where a man was denied access to a homeless shelter over medical marijuana usage. Again, the Massachusetts Supreme Court sided with homeless man, citing disability discrimination. Recreational legalization will likely open up various case law, similar to what has developed on the medicinal side. Can employers fire based on recreational use? Likely, yes. Is there potential for invasion of privacy arguments? Maybe. Only time will tell. Without federal legality to look towards, there will not be uniformity on the legal front. The situations in Massachusetts could happen the exact same way in Colorado, but be ruled in a completely different manner. Issues like that could cause for argument within 14th Amendment rights, but constitutionality at the federal level cannot be argued while marijuana use is federally illegal.

Fourth, there are a slew of issues on the business side of marijuana cultivation and sales. First, just as there are no federal regulations around advertising and marketing, there are also no trademarks on marijuana products at the federal level. States are regulating trademarks internally, which does not allow for any uniformity across states. For example, rapper and entrepreneur Snoop Dogg has created a brand of edibles called Dogg Treats in Colorado. Another entrepreneur in Washington, D.C. could come up with edibles in the same regard with no legal repercussions. If federal legalization would come into play, it could become a dog race (pun intended) to which gains trademark ownership first. Then comes the issue of rebranding for many companies, potentially. Company information is not shared from state to state, so it is impossible to know how many crossover names are being used.

Another huge issue for businesses is in the banking side. Marijuana businesses cannot use most banks because it is considered money laundering at the federal level. Because of the inability to use major banks, marijuana businesses are unable to use the everyday features of ATMs, credit cards, and depositing. Since the larger banks are not willing to take risks on the marijuana industry, it is becoming a private industry with private financers. This also makes marijuana businesses largely cash in hand industry. Large amounts of cash are kept within businesses and many purchase armored vehicles to transport the large sums to the private banking industries. This likely causes added risks for marijuana businesses. This makes the industry more susceptible to employee skimming, as well as burglaries and robberies. Heightened criminal risks were likely not considered when first entering the business.

Also, there are huge financial burdens for those in the marijuana business. First, they are heavily taxed. The federal government created tax code 280E specifically for those who illegally traffick Schedule I and II drugs (Bednar, 2018). Yes, it is bizarre that the Internal Revenue Service (IRS) would like their share of illegal enterprises, but the federal government still wants their money even if what you are doing is illegal. The taxation code actually arose from a cocaine dealer who wrote off expenses for his armored cars and security. Under the 280E tax code, those engaging in illegal trafficking are not allowed the normal deductions of law-abiding businesses. So, all the overheads (paying employees, cost to service, standard bills, etc.) are unable to be written off as a tax deduction. Essentially, anything beyond the cost of goods sold is taxable for marijuana businesses. Also, it seems as though many cannabis businesses have faced "random" audits and have been taxed additional fees based on technicalities and obscured legal codes. For example, big targets of audits have been misfiling's of Form 8300, which is used to report cash deposits of over $10,000. The federal targeting on these businesses may shed a negative light socially on the industry. Outwardly, it may seem like tax evasion to lay people. In reality, it is more confusion in filing and biases in action of the federal government.

Another significant cost to the industry is regarding production and manufacturing. With legalization, much of the concentration has been on storefronts with the retail side of the industry. Minimal thought focuses on the intricacies in actually growing and manufacturing the crop. There are obviously land and areas that are more suitable to grow crops, just like any other type of agricultural product. Additionally, traditional methods of producing marijuana are highly inefficient (Caulkins & Kilmer, 2016). The federal regulations force higher costs in production because of inconsistencies in labor practices. To put things in perspective, high quality marijuana plants, prior to recreational legalization, cost was between $3,000 to $6,000 per pound (National Drug Intelligence Center, 2007). With the recreational legalization movement, costs have fallen to 50% that average, around $1,500-$3,000 per pound (Caulkins et al., 2015). If there is a movement to federal legalization, economists estimate the cost could be approximately $0.25-$0.50 per pound (equating to $113-$225 per pound). Federal legalization would obviously help with product costs. Additionally, national brands and marketing campaigns could be developed. This could influence more revenue development and support for a variety of industries and entertainment.

Tied into the costs to manufacturers is the cost to users. With state legalization, the national market has still grown, especially in terms of daily usage (Davenport & Caulkins, 2016). Medicinal and recreational users tend to differ. Specific to recreational use, marijuana users are economically "downscale" and resemble cigarette users. The daily users are equivalent to pack a day smokers and a large amount have annual incomes of approximately $20,000. Also, about half of these users have a high school diploma or less. Even with the low-income aspects, the marijuana networks are professionalizing, with fewer users looking to social entities for attainment. The sales are also small in weight, but not in price, which is likely related to the high cost of manufacturing and selling. There are potential hints that the market may be causing issues within low socioeconomic status and addiction style issues, but the area has not been researched to date.

Speaking of research, this is another area that takes a major hit due to federal roadblocks. On the criminal side, there are no tests to determine if someone is impaired from marijuana specifically. States are currently relying on the instrumentation in place for alcohol impairment, and are "lucky" in the sense that there is a lot of polydrug use between marijuana and alcohol. Funding is necessary to produce research and potential equipment, which will never happen without federal legalization. Federal grants are extremely limited. As mentioned at the start of the chapter, the DEA (2018) is requesting a large push in marijuana production for medical and scientific research, but results of this venture would not be seen for a few years. Current research has only happened with private money, which is subject to influence and biases. It is important to have federal weight in this area to eliminate those directly invested in the industry to also be involved in the research.

With all the issues listed above, it is important to end the state legalization conversation on a high note. Financially, states have reaped major benefits from the marijuana industry. Vermont has the potential to raise \$20-\$75 million in tax revenue, equating out to approximately \$330-\$750 for regular users (Caulkins & Kilmer, 2016). Colorado had approximately \$266.5 million in tax revenue for 2018, which much money was spent on improving state schools (Hutzler, 2018). Overall, in 2017, the legal marijuana market was at approximately \$10 billion in sales. There is a projected amount of \$11 billion for 2018 and \$21 billion by the year 2021. The assistance the tax money provides to a variety of social entities has likely assisted with the overall social acceptance of marijuana use. With the high numbers at the state levels, it could significantly impact social costs at the federal level, as well.

Now, circling back to the initial question, why has the federal government drug its feet in recreational legalization? States have successfully legalized, research has demonstrated no real significant changes in health concerns and criminality. Youth usage could be curbed with management on the marketing and advertising side, which would come with federal legalization. Much of the complications in the industry itself are due to the illegal nature of the drug at the federal level. There is a major amount of tax revenue that has done social good in areas of legalization. So, why are we still balking at federal legalization?

There is no clear answer to the question. A large chunk of the slowdown likely has to do with political affiliation mentioned previously. With republicans still teetering on the opposition side, federal legalization may be dependent on the political party in charge. Also, in citing state approval as a movement to federal legalization, many mid-western and southern states are largely disapproving of legalization. More liberal ideologies are needed in these areas for legalization to take place.

Also, moving back to the issues of opposition between state and federal levels, if research and grant funding continues to be halted, there will never be concrete answers about the benefits or detriments of marijuana usage. The federal government (at least for the moment) seems comfortable imposing the burden on individual states rather than taking a chunk of cost itself. Since the federal level is taking a back seat in its own country, maybe the plans are to take back seat at the international level, as well. With Canada just legalizing at the end of 2018, maybe the United States plans on taking notes and valuable points from the neighboring country without having to spend significant funds on research in it. Uruguay was the first country to legalize recreational marijuana use in 2017 and has shown much success. There has not been increases in addiction or side effects in using the drug. The issue lies within the international market and a fear of repercussions from other international industry. Additionally, the market in Uruguay seems to have political ties, as well. A shift in the Ministry of Public Health has caused legalization to spin in opposing directions (from priority in legalization to legalization relating to medical harms) (Gonzales, 2017). Uruguay seems to be leaning on Canada's legalization for further movement in the positive direction. Is there potential that the United States is seeing where the chips fall with Uruguay and Canada on the international market? Maybe.

Federal legalization will likely remain on the same terms for years to come due to the lax approach and party affiliation lines. Political affiliations are strongly divided for a variety of social movements at the moment, which makes it highly unlikely for the movement of federal legalization to be able to jump party lines and have republicans jump in support of the movement. An interesting twist of events may happen towards the next major election, though. Younger generations, particularly millennial voters, are becoming powerful. While poll voting is still low overall, the young voting population rose significantly in the Clinton/Trump presidential run. Young voters are particularly more liberalized in thoughts, as well. This is demonstrated by the previous election in 2016. Within the millennial group, voters were in staunch support of Clinton over Trump by an 18-point margin (Hutzler, 2018). On top of this, millennials have a more liberalized view of marijuana use, as well. In fact, around 80% of millennials believe marijuana is safer than alcohol. If the trend continues into the next election, there could be at least a stronger conversation about federal legalization. Currently, there is still a steady decline in Republican Party numbers, with representation as 25% republican, 34% democrat, and 39% independent (Gallup, n.d.). To note, it will be important to key in on the independent party group, as they currently hold the strongest group affiliation. It is unclear where the group stands on socialized issues, as many take a variety of standpoints. Also, it is important to think of the independents as the swing voters. It is important for politicians to obtain a high number of independent voters to swing an election in one's favor. The non-clarity of views regarding federal marijuana legalization within this group may cause federal politicians to sit on the issue indefinitely in fear of losing that middle ground support.

Federal recreational marijuana is a longstanding issue that has an unforeseen future. At best, it seems states are reaping major benefits from a variety of legalization standpoints, a key one being financial assets that assist with many socialized programs and funding. On the flipside, clarity within the potential harms of use will stay foggy without more willingness to open research grants and funding. Another concern is with issues on the political front. Not only are party lines generally divided on the marijuana issue in ties to political affiliation, the federal government is currently having a difficult time cooperating at all, demonstrated by the January 2019 governmental shutdown. Is it possible they may consider wiping over five decades of marijuana legislation upon reconvening? Sure, but not likely. It will likely take a party change in presidency, as well as someone willing to spearhead a movement with no concern for maintaining the majority of swing voters, a true weed crusader in the midst of a clouded climate (pun intended).

REFERENCES

Arria, A. M., Garnier-Dykstra, L. M., Book, E. T., Caldeira, K. M., Vincent, K. B., Baron, R. A., & O'Grady, K. E. (2013). Drug use patterns in young adulthood and post-college employment. *Drug and Alcohol Dependence, 127*(1), 23-30.

Aydelotte, J. D., Brown, L. H., Luftman, K. M., Mardock, A. L., Teixeira, P. G. R., Coopwood, B., & Brown, C. V. R. (2017). Crash fatality rates after recreational marijuana legalization in Washington and Colorado. *American Journal of Public Health, 107*(8), 1329-1331.

Barry, R. A. & Glantz, S. A. (2018). Marijuana regulatory frameworks in four US states: An analysis against a public health standard. *American Journal of Public Health, 108*(7), 914-923.

Bednar, J. (2018, October). Hazy picture: Legalized marijuana poses legal uncertainties. *Business West.*

Bradford, A. C. & Bradford, W. D. (2018). Factors driving the diffusion of medical marijuana legalization in the United States. *Drugs: Education, Prevention & Policy, 24*(1), 75-84.

Carnevale, J. T., Kagan, R., Murphy, P. J., & Esrick, J. (2017). A practical framework for regulating for-profit recreational marijuana in US States: Lessons from Colorado and Washington. *International Journal of Drug Policy, 42*, 71-85.

Caulkins, J. P. & Kilmer, B. (2016). Considering marijuana legalization carefully: Insights for other jurisdictions from analysis for Vermont. *Addiction, 111*, 2082-2089.

Caulkins, J. P., Kilmer, B., Kleiman, M. A., MacCoun, R. J., Midgette, G., Oglesby, P., ..., Reuter, P. H. (2015). *Considering marijuana legalization: Insights for Vermont and other jurisdictions*. Santa Monica, CA: Rand Corporation.

Cerda, M., Wall, M., Keyes, K. M., Galea, S., & Hasin. D. (2012). Medical marijuana laws in 50 states: Investigating the relationship between state legalization of medical marijuana and marijuana use, abuse and dependence. *Drug and Alcohol Dependence, 120*(1-3), 22-27.

Chu, Y.- W. L. (2014). The effects of medical marijuana laws on illegal marijuana use. *Journal of Health Economics, 38*, 43-61.

Cohn, A., Johnson, A., Ehlke, S., & Villanti, A. C. (2016). Characterizing substance use and mental health profiles of cigar, blunt, and non-blunt marijuana users from the National Survey of Drug Use and Health. *Drug and Alcohol Dependence, 160*, 105-111.

Cohn, A. M., Johnson, A. L., Rose, S. W., Rath, J. M., & Villanti, A. C. (2017). Support for marijuana legalization and predictors of intentions to use marijuana more often in response to legalization among U.S. young adults. *Substance Use & Misuse, 52*(2), 203-213.

Davenport, S. S. & Caulkins, J. P. (2016). Evolution of the United States marijuana market in the decade of liberalization before full legalization. *Journal of Drug Issues, 46*(4), 411-427.

Fairman, B. J. (2015). Cannabis problem experiences among users of the tobacco-cannabis combination known as blunts. *Drug and Alcohol Dependence, 150*, 77-84.

Gallup. (n.d.). *Party Affliation*. Retrieved from https://news.gallup.com/poll/15370/party-affiliation.aspx

Geiger-Oneto, S. & Simkins, T. (2018). A social identity perspective on the legalization of marijuana in the United States: The relative importance of status insecurity and group membership. *Journal of Macromarketing, 38*(2), 206-217.

Gonzales, E. (2018, October). Uruguay loses momentum in the marijuana legalization stakes. *El Pais*. Retrieved from https://elpais.com/elpais/2018/10/16/inenglish/1539687522_144922.html

Hall, W. & Weier, M. (2015). Assessing the public health impacts of legalizing recreational cannabis use in the USA. *Clinical Pharmacology & Therapeutics, 97*(6), 607-615.

Hammond, D. (2011). Health warning messages on tobacco products: A review. *Tobacco Control, 20*(5), 327-337.

Hari, J. (2015). *Chasing the Scream: The First and Last Days of the War on Drugs*. London, England: Bloomsbury Publishing.

Harper, S., Strumpf, E. C., & Kaufman, J. S. (2012). Do medical marijuana laws increase marijuana use? Replication study and extension. *Annals of Epidemiology, 22*(3), 207-212.

Hartig, H. & Geiger, A. (2018, October). About six-in-ten Americans support marijuana legalization. *Pew Research Center*. Washington, D.C.

Hutzler, A. (2018, August). What are republicans smoking? *Newsweek Global, 171*(6).

Kim, H. S., Hall, K. E., Genco, E. K., VanDyke, M., Barker, E., & Monte, A. A. (2016). Marijuana tourism and emergency department visits in Colorado. *New England Journal of Medicine, 374*, 797-798.

Khatapoush, S. & Hallfors, D. (2004). "Sending the wrong message": Did medical marijuana legalization in California change attitudes about and use of marijuana? *Journal of Drug Issues, 34*, 751-770.

Maier, S. L., Mannes, S., & Koppenhofer, E. L. (2017). The implications of marijuana decriminalization and legalization on crime in the United States. *Contemporary Drug Problems, 44*(2), 125-146.

McCarthy, J. (2017, October). Record high support for legalizing marijuana use in U.S. *Gallup News*. Retrieved from http://news.gallop.com/poll/221018/record-high-support-legalizing-marijuana.aspx.

National Drug Intelligence Center. (2007). *National Illicit Drug Prices: US Department of Justice*. Product no. 2007-L0424-002. Washington, DC.

O'Keefe, K. (2013). State medical marijuana implementation and federal policy. *Journal of Health Care Law & Policy, 16*, 39-58.

Rauch, J. (2018, December). Legalizing marijuana and gay marriage seemed impossible but losing taught libertarians how to win. *Reason*, 36-41.

Schnabel, L. & Sevell, E. (2017). Should Mary and Jane be legal? Americans' attitudes toward marijuana and same-sex marriage legalization, 1988-2014. *Public Opinion, 81*(1), 157-172.

Substance Abuse and Mental Health Services Administration. (2018). *Results from the 2017 National Survey on Drug Use and Health: Summary of national findings* (HHS Publication No. SMA 18-5068, NSDUH, Series H-53). Rockville, MD: Center for Behavioral Health Statistics and Quality, Substance Abuse and Mental Health Services Administration.

Vigil, D. I., Van Dyke, M., Hall, K. E., Contreras, A. E., Ghosh, T. S., & Wolk, L. (2018). Marijuana use and related health care encounters in Colorado before and after retail legalization. *International Journal of Mental Health and Addiction, 16*, 806-812.

Volkow, N. D., Baler, R. D., Compton, W. M., & Weiss, S. R. (2014). Adverse health effects of marijuana use. *New England Journal of Medicine, 370*(23), 2219-2227.

Wall, M. M., Poh, E., Cerda, M., Keyes, K. M., Galea, S., & Hasin, D. S. (2011). Adolescent marijuana use from 2002 to 2008: Higher in states with medical marijuana laws, cause still unclear. *Annals of Epidemiology, 21*(9), 714-716.

Wang, G. S., Roosevelt, G., Le Lait, M. C., Martinez, E. M., Bucher-Bartelson, B., Bronstein, A. C., & Heard, K. (2014). Association of unintentional pediatric exposures with decriminalization of marijuana in the United States. *Annals of Emergency Medicine, 63*(6), 684-689.

Williams, S. (2018, June). This Canadian medical marijuana giant just filed for an IPO in the U.S. *The Motley Fool*. Retrieved from https://www.fool.com/investing/2018/06/27/this-canadian-medical-marijuana-giant-just-filed-f.aspx

About the Editors

Jonathon A. Cooper, PhD
Associate Professor
Indiana University of Pennsylvania, Indiana, Pennsylvania, US

Jonathon A. Cooper earned his doctorate in criminology and criminal justice from Arizona State University. He is currently on faculty at Indiana University of Pennsylvania in the Department of Criminology and Criminal Justice. Cooper is committed not only to the theoretical understanding of modern criminal justice organizations, but to his students: his teaching philosophy begins and ends with "students are neither nuisances nor currency: they are what we are here for."

Kayla G. Jachimowski, PhD
Assistant Professor
Saint Vincent College, Latrobe, Pennsylvania, US

Kayla G. Jachimowski, PhD is an Assistant Professor of Criminology, Law, & Society at Saint Vincent College in Latrobe, PA. Her primary areas of research include the intersection of mental health and the criminal justice, and statistical methodology in criminology research.

LIST OF CONTRIBUTORS

Shavonne Arthurs, PhD is the Program Coordinator and Assistant Professor of Criminal Justice at Seton Hill University. Shavonne completed her PhD at Indiana University of Pennsylvania. Her research interests lie in the areas of drug and alcohol abuse and social deviance.

Samantha L. Bennett, **MA** is a doctoral candidate and teaching associate at Indiana University of Pennsylvania. Ms. Bennett's research interests include juvenile justice, delinquency, and policing. She has taught courses on crime and delinquency prevention and criminal courts.

Edward L. Bowman, PhD is an associate professor of criminal justice in the Department of Criminal Justice, Lock Haven University, Pennsylvania. His current research focus is on offender reentry in rural communities.

David R. Champion, PhD is a Professor in the Criminology and Criminal Justice department at Slippery Rock University in Pennsylvania. His academic interests include Integral Criminology, criminal behavior, and criminal justice ethics.

Sarah E. Daly, **PhD** is an Assistant Professor of Criminology, Law, & Society at Saint Vincent College in Latrobe, Pennsylvania. Her primary areas of research include mass violence, school violence, and issues of gender and crime. She also teaches courses in The Criminology of Race, Research Methods, and Policy Analysis. Prior to her academic career, she worked as a Spanish teacher and school counselor in New Jersey.

Kerry L. Edwards, PhD is an Assistant Professor at Slippery Rock University of Pennsylvania's Department of Criminology & Criminal Justice. Her research interest in the juvenile justice system stems from her prior experience as a juvenile probation officer.

Katherine Ely, PhD, is an associate professor of criminal justice in the Department of Criminal Justice, Lock Haven University, Pennsylvania. Her research and teaching interests currently focus on offender reentry, women and crime, and criminal justice research methods.

Blair Hillegass, MA is currently a master's student at Indiana University of Pennsylvania studying criminology. She received a Bachelor of Science in Middle Level Education with a specialization in Mathematics at Indiana University of Pennsylvania.

Kayla G. Jachimowski, PhD is an Assistant Professor of Criminology, Law, & Society at Saint Vincent College in Latrobe, PA. Her primary areas of research include the intersection of mental health and the criminal justice, and statistical methodology in criminology research.

Eric Kocian, PhD has a true passion for the field of criminology, law, and society and continually makes efforts to expand his knowledge and teaching abilities in all areas of the discipline. He is an assistant professor of criminology, law, and society at Saint Vincent College. In 2000, Kocian graduated from the University of Pittsburgh at Greensburg as a dual major in psychology and administration of justice. He earned a master's degree in criminology in 2002 and a PhD in 2010 from the Indiana University of Pennsylvania. Kocian is a prior service United States Marine Corps Reservist and was trained by the Federal Bureau of Investigation in 2012. He recently completed the Drug Enforcement Administration and Federal Bureau of Investigation Citizen Academies. Kocian continues to research the opioid epidemic and has briefed various local, state, and federal agencies and departments on his findings.

Sarah Kuehn, PhD earned her Jura Diplom (J.D. equivalent) at the Freie Universität Berlin, Germany. She then received her MA and PhD in Criminology at Simon Fraser University, BC, Canada. She is an Associate Professor of Criminology and Criminal Justice at Slippery Rock University of Pennsylvania. Her current research interests are program evaluations, public perceptions of offenders, and (comparative) juvenile justice.

Selye Lee, PhD is an Assistant Professor at the Department of Criminology, Sociology, and Geography at Arkansas State University. She holds a PhD in Criminology from Indiana University of Pennsylvania. Her research interests lie in policing and the community, the developmental and life-course features of criminal behavior, juvenile delinquency, special prison population, and comparative justice.

Liana Marmolejos, MA completed her MA in Criminology at Indiana University of Pennsylvania. Her research interests are focused on police legitimacy, police in the media, public perceptions of police, and evidence-based policing.

Daniel Scott, PhD is an Assistant Professor of Criminology and Criminal Justice at the University of West Florida. His research interests are in youth and gang violence, juvenile justice, gang involvement, policies and programs, theory, and mixed methods. His current research examines youth correctional violence, juvenile court practices, and gang member identification methods. His work has appeared in various journals including *Deviant Behavior, Journal of Ethnicity and Criminal Justice*, and the *Journal of Criminological Research, Policy, and Practice*.

Carley J. Smathers, MA is a doctoral candidate in the department of Criminology and Criminal Justice at Indiana University of Pennsylvania. Her primary research includes juvenile justice and delinquency with a focus on the influence of digital media.

Lindsey N. Smathers, MA is a doctoral candidate and teaching associate at Indiana University of Pennsylvania. Ms. Smathers' research focuses on media, crime, and policing. She has taught courses on the subjects of media and crime, as well as law, society, and social control

London S. Smith is an undergraduate student in the Criminology, Law, & Society at Saint Vincent College in Latrobe, Pennsylvania. She has interned with the Baltimore City Prosecutor's Office, and she served as the Youth Director of the NAACP Chapter in Maryland. After graduation, she plans to attend law school with a focus on civil rights and racial equality.

Andrea Weathersby, PhD received her PhD in psychology from Washington State University. She completed a psychology internship residency at the University of Florida. She currently has a private practice in which she provides psychotherapy, consultation, as well as professional development and training. She has a wealth of experience with interdisciplinary teams in fields such as health care, law, and education.

INDEX

A

B

C

D

E

F

G

H

I

N

O

P

Q

R

T

U

V

W

Y

Z

Related Nova Publications

Crime and Criminal Behavior

Editor: Analise Klein

Series: Criminal Justice, Law Enforcement and Corrections

Book Description: In this book, Chapter One begins with a discussion on the use of dogs in the courtroom. Chapter Two explores the research on the criminal narratives of general offending populations, and introduces new insight into Mentally Disordered Offenders (MDOs), and the impact various mental disorders may have on the structure of criminal narratives.

Softcover ISBN: 978-1-63485-566-2
Retail Price: $95